D1209801

Cognitive and Affective Responses to Advertising

Cognitive and Affective Responses to Advertising

Edited by
Patricia Cafferata
Young & Rubicam, Chicago

Alice M. Tybout
Northwestern University

659.1
C676

Lexington Books
D.C. Heath and Company/Lexington, Massachusetts/Toronto

Alverno College
Library Media Center
Milwaukee, Wisconsin

Library of Congress Cataloging-in-Publication Data

Cognitive and affective responses to advertising/edited by Patricia Cafferata, Alice Tybout.
p. cm.
Edited compilation of papers presented at the Fourth Annual Advertising and Consumer Psychology Conference, held in Chicago, Ill., July 11-12, 1985, sponsored by Division 23 of the American Psychological Association, the Marketing Science Institute, and Needham Harper Worldwide.
Includes index.
ISBN 0-669-14830-X (alk. paper)
1. Advertising—Psychological aspects—Congresses. 2. Consumer behavior—Congresses. I. Cafferata, Patricia. II. Tybout, Alice. III. American Psychological Association, Division of Consumer Psychology. IV. Marketing Science Institute. V. Needham Harper Worldwide. VI. Conference on Advertising and Consumer Psychology (4th : 1985 : Chicago, Ill.)
HF5823.C554 1989
659.1'01'9—dc19 88-16884

Copyright © 1989 by Lexington Books

All rights reserved. No part of this publication may be reproduced or transmitted in any form or by any means, electronic or mechanical, including photocopy, recording, or any information storage or retrieval system, without permission in writing from the publisher.

Published simultaneously in Canada
Printed in the United States of America
International Standard Book Number: 0-669-14830-X
Library of Congress Catalog Card Number 88-16884

The paper used in this publication meets the minimum requirements of American National Standard for Information Sciences—Permanence of Paper for Printed Library Materials, ANSI Z39.48-1984. ∞™

92 8 7 6 5 4 3

Contents

Preface

The fourth annual Advertising and Consumer Psychology Conference was held July 11–12, 1985. The purpose of this conference, jointly sponsored by Division 23 of the American Psychological Association, the Marketing Science Institute, and Needham Harper Worldwide, was to bring academic and industry researchers together to present and discuss ideas, theories, and approaches regarding consumers' responses to advertising. This book is an edited compilation of the papers presented at this conference, with some additional specially solicited chapters to provide an overview of the conference materials.

The conference was cochaired by Pat Cafferata, president and chief executive officer of Young & Rubicam Chicago, and Alice Tybout, professor of marketing in the J.L. Kellogg Graduate School of Management, Northwestern University. The differing backgrounds of the editors helped bring together the two research perspectives, academic and advertising industry, in both the conference itself and this book.

Pat Cafferata has twenty years of experience in advertising. At the time of this conference, she was research director at Needham Harper Worldwide, Chicago. She is an active participant in the American Marketing Association, the Advertising Research Foundation, and the Association for Consumer Research.

Alice Tybout represents the more theoretical perspective of the academician. Her teaching and research interests focus on consumer information processing and advertising issues. Her published work includes articles in the *Journal of Consumer Research,* the *Journal of Marketing Research,* the *Journal of Marketing* and the *Journal of Personality and Social Psychology.* Also, she is editor of *Advances in Consumer Research,* vol. 10.

Acknowledgments

This conference and proceedings would not have been possible without the help of many institutions and individuals.

Special thanks go to Bill Wells for his helpful advice and to Needham Harper Worldwide, which hosted the conference and provided funding. Additional support was provided by the Marketing Science Institute and Young & Rubicam Chicago. Thanks also are due to the J.L. Kellogg Graduate School of Management, Northwestern University, for donating facilities, services, and overall assistance throughout the editing process.

Our sincere appreciation goes to the authors who so graciously contributed their time and knowledge to the conference and to the preparation of their chapters. Among these authors are three noted psychologists (John Cacioppo, Alice Isen, and Richard Petty) who developed solicited chapters providing an overview of current thinking regarding cognition and affect.

Two people deserve special mention for making this conference and its proceedings a reality. Susan Claybough, administrative supervisor of Needham Harper Worldwide, provided all the logistical support and organization for planning and running the conference. Danna Givot, marketing research consultant, was our editorial assistant and shepherded the editing process to completion.

Acknowledgments

[illegible]

1
Introduction

Alice Tybout

Advertisers and consumer psychologists share a concern with understanding how consumers process information to form attitudes and to make purchase decisions. Despite this common goal, they approach such understanding from somewhat different perspectives and motivations.

The advertiser or practitioner, faced with client accountability, deadlines, and bottom-line-based incentives, is often concerned with what works (in the sense of what performs well on measures of ad effectiveness) and what features seem to characterize ads that do work. Theories are developed inductively on the basis of observing actual performance of a large number of ads over time. These theories may be used to shape an agency's overall approach to advertising and to create new ads.

The consumer psychologist, or academic, is removed from client pressures and often is motivated to think more abstractly. Such individuals are free to puzzle over why or how something works. Broad theories are postulated, and deductions from these theories are tested. Theories that receive support are used to make specific predictions about how advertisements will impact consumer attitudes and behavior.

The goal of this book is to present chapters by practitioners and by academicians so that their convergent and divergent perspectives are understood. Readers will see that although the language of advertisers and consumer psychologists sometimes differs, there is considerable agreement about the key factors underlying consumers' responses to persuasive communications.

The major theme emerging from the chapters in this book is that persuasive communications such as advertisements may include both cognitive and affective components and that these components engender distinct but interrelated responses in consumers. The term *cognitive* is broadly used to refer to aspects of communications that are descriptive of product features and are intended to provoke a conscious, thoughtful response. By contrast, the term *affective* is used to describe cues that convey more psychological benefits associated with owning and using products. Such cues stimulate emotions, moods, or feelings that may not be under the conscious control of the individual.

Although the authors of the chapters use the terms *cognitive* and *affective* in a manner consistent with this broad distinction, they also draw on additional terminology that is not always employed or employed in the same manner by other authors. Thus, to appreciate fully the common and diverging views expressed in the chapters, readers must focus more on shared concepts or constructs than on shared terminology.

This book begins by focusing on advertising stimuli and examining how they are classified, both by the people who create ads and by academicians. Bill Wells of DDB Needham Worldwide begins part I with "Lectures and Dramas" (chapter 2). He advances the proposition that advertisements have two components, lecture and drama, and that emphasis may be placed on either or both. Lecture is defined as a direct but arm's-length address from the spokesperson to the consumer. It is straightforward discussion of product or service benefits and typically draws an explicit conclusion. By contrast, drama is indirect in the sense that the actors speak not to the audience but to each other while the audience "eavesdrops." Like a good movie or play, an effective advertising drama draws in the audience, providing a vicarious experience of the feelings associated with the product or service and leading to self-generated (rather than explicitly stated) inferences about the benefits provided.

The distinction Wells makes between lectures and dramas is reinforced in chapter 3 by John Coulson of Communications Workshop, Inc. As the chapter title, "An Investigation of Mood Commercials," suggests, mood advertisements are examined by contrasting them with more rational appeals. Rational advertising, like lectures, focuses on direct communication of product benefits, whereas mood advertising shares with dramas a greater emphasis on positive emotions or feelings linked to the product or service. Coulson documents variation in commercials along a thinking-feeling continuum and explores how commercials varying on this dimension perform on measures of advertising effectiveness.

The consensus emerging from the Wells and Coulson chapters is that, at the most basic level, advertisements can be classified in terms of the extent to which they attempt to influence consumers through conscious, logical cognitive reasoning or the degree to which they evoke more automatic, emotional affective processing. This practitioner view serves as a starting point for academicians' effort to develop taxonomies for classifying advertisements.

In chapter 4 ("The Multidimensionality of Persuasive Communications: Theoretical and Empirical Foundations"), academicians Connie Pechmann and David Stewart acknowledge the rational versus emotional distinction but suggest that it is preferable to represent the rational and emotional components of advertisements in a multidimensional space rather than on a continuum ranging from rational to emotional. Such an approach allows for the combination of lecture and drama, which Wells notes is sometimes employed. Accordingly, on the basis of theoretical frameworks in the psychology literature, Pechmann and Stewart offer an advertising classification scheme having two orthogonal dimensions, one addressing the type of cognitive processing stimulated and the other assessing the extent to which emotional benefits are conveyed. This classification scheme is used to categorize actual advertisements and to draw theoretical and practical implications.

The general agreement that advertisements stimulate cognitive and affective responses implies that an understanding of the theoretical processes underlying such responses would be worthwhile. An overview of such processes is presented in the chapters in part II, authored by prominent psychologists well known for their theoretical and empirical work addressing cognition and affect.

In chapter 5 ("The Elaboration Likelihood Model of Persuasion: The Role of Affect and Affect-Laden Information Processing in Attitude Change"), John Cacioppo and Richard Petty present their Elaboration Likelihood Model (ELM), based on the premise that responses to communications are a function of the extent to which they stimulate cognitive elaboration. Elaboration, in turn, is viewed as a product of individuals' motivation and ability to process the information. When individuals are motivated and have the ability to process the communication, the substance of the central message in the communication is expected to guide response. This is known as the central route to persuasion. By contrast, when individuals lack either the motivation or the ability to process fully the communication, response may be guided by heuristics or cues peripheral to the central message (for example, the credibility of the source or the number of arguments in the message).

The ELM has been widely used to account for the effect of cognitive variables on response to communications. Of particular interest here is the discussion of how this same conceptual model also can account for the ways in which affective cues may influence response to communications. Three ways in which affect can operate are discussed. An affective response to a communication may itself serve as a central argument and thereby influence persuasion when substantial elaboration is stimulated. Alternatively, affect may serve as a more peripheral cue and may determine persuasion when little detailed thought is prompted. Finally, affect may influence response indirectly by guiding the direction and amount of elaboration and thereby determining whether response will be via the central or peripheral route.

The fact that the ELM can account for both cognitive and affective responses is desirable from the standpoint of achieving a parsimonious explanation of advertising effects. Moreover, it implicitly addresses a controversial issue: whether cognitive and affective responses are the product of a common process or are functionally independent. The view reflected by Cacioppo and Petty is that of a predominantly common process. This view is shared by the authors of other chapters in this book (the merits of a common process versus functional independence view are explicitly considered in chapter 11).

Chapter 6, by Alice Isen, "Some Ways in Which Affect Influences Cognitive Processes: Implications for Advertising and Consumer Behavior," complements the more abstract, conceptually driven treatment of affect in chapter 5 by focusing on specific empirical effects of affect and discussing their theoretical implications. Three categories of effects are considered in detail: the impact of affect on memory, the asymmetry of the influence of positive and negative affect on memory and behavior, and the influence of positive affect on cognitive organization. The central theme emerging from this chapter is that the effects of affect are best accounted for not by a strict automatic process of association (in the sense that all objects or ideas and affects that are experienced simultaneously or contiguously become memorially linked) but rather by a combination of automatic and interpretive processes wherein the meaning of the affect and the object jointly determine memory, recall, and thinking. Such a process would seem consistent with the central route to persuasion that Cacioppo and Petty proposed. Isen's conceptualization has a number of important implications for effective use of affect in advertisements.

The theoretical frameworks provided by Cacioppo and Petty and by Isen differ somewhat in their detail but are largely compatible. They share a common process orientation and an acknowledgment that the meaning of affect often plays a critical role in whether it will influence response.

With this general foundation and overview of the psychology literature in hand, we focus on more specific theoretical issues and empirical studies. Part III contains four chapters exploring issues predominantly related to cognitive processing. Part IV presents seven chapters examining issues that emphasize special aspects of affective processing.

All four chapters of part III pursue the notion of cognitive elaboration introduced by Cacioppo and Petty in chapter 5. Thomas Srull's "Advertising and Product Evaluation: The Relation between Consumer Memory and Judgment" (chapter 7) begins this part. Srull focuses on a critical dimension of elaboration; the direction that elaboration takes. In a series of three experiments using print ads, Srull examines the effects of three different goals on the relationship between recall and judgment: processing to comprehend the ad, processing to remember the ad, and processing to form an evaluation of the product.

Several interesting findings emerge. Recall and judgment are found to be most strongly related when individuals process with the intent of comprehending the information. Recall and judgment are also significantly related when individuals are instructed to remember the information. By contrast, when individuals have a goal of forming an evaluation of the product, recall and judgment are not highly correlated. Moreover, evidence is found to suggest that recall and judgment are stored independently in memory. These findings are argued to have important implications for advertisers who may fail to consider the processing goals of the target audience or may rely on recall measures to assess the effectiveness of advertisements.

Chapter 8, "Strategies for Designing Persuasive Messages: Deductions from the Resource Matching Hypothesis," authored by Punam Anand and Brian Sternthal, once again focuses on cognitive elaboration. However, in contrast to Srull's examination of the direction of elaboration, these authors concentrate on the extent of elaboration. Specifically, they take an applied focus and use the extent of elaboration as a basis for discussing how a variety of message characteristics affects persuasion.

Anand and Sternthal suggest that message features determine the elaboration or resources required for processing, whereas the processor's motivation and ability determine the resources available to perform the task. Persuasion is argued to be at a maximum when the resources required match those available. Accordingly this notion is labeled the *resource matching hypothesis.* The chapter focuses on using the resource matching hypothesis to outline strategies for bringing the resources required and those available into harmony. To this end, the effects of a wide range of message variables are discussed: the linguistic structure of a message, source credibility, message complexity, message congruity, personal relevance of the message, message repetition, music, and pictures. In addition, the chapter contributes to the literature reviewed by summarizing and interpreting a number of recent studies conducted in marketing contexts.

In "Advertising Art: Cognitive Mechanisms and Research Issues" (chapter 9), Fairfid Caudle, like Anand and Sternthal, focuses on how features of advertisements may affect cognitive elaboration and thereby guide persuasion. Attention here, however, centers on an aspect of advertisements not previously explored: advertising visuals that borrow from the world of noncommercial art. Caudle describes how many advertisements employ artistic styles used in paintings and sometimes incorporate well-known paintings themselves into ads. She then discusses three ways in which art in advertisements may affect processing. The use of art or artistic style may help the advertiser associate the product with rare, prized objects and give it high status, thereby enhancing the product image. Alternatively art may be used to create incongruities (for example, a well-known painting may be altered to incorporate the advertised product, or a surrealistic style may be employed in the visuals created), which have been found to prompt the processor to increase the cognitive resources devoted to the task (an observation also made by Anand and Sternthal in chapter 8). Finally, art can be used to convey metaphorical symbolism. This increases the resources required to appreciate fully the advertiser's message, and, as Anand and Sternthal note, increasing the resources required may have benefits when high levels of ad repetition might otherwise induce wearout and a decline in persuasion.

The analysis in chapter 10, "Gender Differences in Information Processing: A Selectivity Interpretation," by Joan Meyers-Levy, adds to the understanding of cognitive processing by examining gender, an individual difference important to many advertisers. Based on a detailed review of differences between males and females in their strategies for processing information, Meyers-Levy advances the selectivity hypothesis, which suggests that males often do not process all of the information available but instead use heuristic devices to simplify the task and facilitate rapid judgments. Females are viewed as taking a more comprehensive approach in which they attempt to assimilate all the available information but in so doing sometimes take longer to make judgments. Neither males' or females' approach is seen as inherently superior; instead each approach may be adaptive under certain conditions. More important, these different styles have distinct implications for how advertisements should be structured to communicate effectively with male or female targets. These implications are discussed in detail at the end of the chapter.

In part IV, the emphasis shifts to theoretical, methodological, and application issues related to affect. The part begins with chapter 11, "Nature of Effect of Affect on Judgment: Theoretical and Methodological Issues" by Guliz Ger, which directly addresses the question of whether cognitive and affective responses are the products of two functionally independent systems or whether both types of responses can be accounted for by a common process.

According to the functional independence view, affective and cognitive systems are represented differently, and affective states may be independent of cognitions. The alternative, common process view assumes that the two systems are intertwined and interact; affect can cue related cognitions, and cognitions can be recalled along with associated affect. The specific common process view examined is an associate network model of memory in which activation spreads from one concept to other adjacent concepts, decreasing in strength as it moves further away from the initially activated concept. On the basis of a literature review and two experiments she conducted, Ger concludes that the common process view provides the most parsimonious account of affect effects. This conclusion is consistent with the views of Cacioppo and Petty and Isen.

In chapter 12, "Emotional Advertising Appeals," Bobby J. Calder and Charles L. Gruder examine empirically how affect may operate in the associative network model Ger describes. Their two experiments demonstrate that emotional states induced independent of a product's benefits affect product evaluations only when the emotion and the product features are linked cognitively or semantically in an associative network. This finding reinforces Isen's conclusion that interpretive processes mediate affective effects. Moreover, Calder and Gruder interpret their findings as evidence for a common process model and state that "there is actually no such thing as a pure emotional appeal."

The issue of the process underlying affective response is further explored in chapter 13. David Aaker and Douglas Stayman focus on a specific emotion often used in advertising and pose the question, "What Mediates the Emotional Response to Advertising? The Case of Warmth." They discuss the characteristics of the audience, the context, and the commercial that tend to make warmth responses more intense. On the basis of their review of the literature, as well as their own qualitative research, they suggest that intense warmth responses will be more likely to occur among females, individuals who are emotional, and individuals who are involved in the subject matter of an ad and can identify with the characters or experience shown. Warmth responses will be stronger when the situation presents few distractions, employs low exposure to the ad, and prior commercials do not induce a warmth response. Finally, the advertising execution must stimulate cognitive empathy and be believable if an intense warmth response is to occur. These conclusions offer guidelines for creating the dramas or mood commercials discussed in part I. Aaker and Stayman's conclusions also converge with Meyers-Levy's contention that women more than men emphasize and incorporate the views of others into their own judgments.

Chapters 14 and 15 shift from issues addressing theoretical processes underlying affective responses to more methodological concerns that arise when attempting to study affective responses. A key dimension on which affective responses differ from cognitive responses is the amount of conscious attention or resources that each requires. Affective responses are assumed to be more spontaneous and less subject to conscious control than are cognitive ones. As the previous chapters establish, this need not mean that affective responses are produced by a separate system or that the semantic meaning or interpretation of affect plays no role in response. It simply implies that the connections to affective concepts are strong and therefore require little conscious effort to activate. As both Thorson and Friestad (chapter 14) and Allen and Madden (chapter 15) note, this distinction has implications for the measurement of affecive responses.

In "The Effects of Emotion on Episodic Memory for Television Commercials," Esther Thorson and Marian Friestad suggest that emotional or affective appeals may influence a type of memory, episodic memory, which is neglected by some measures of advertising effectiveness. In contrast to semantic memory (the abstract concept type of memory typically implied in earlier chapters describing associative network models), episodic memory involves information that is stored in a temporal or spatial fashion (for example, memory for how events typically unfold when eating at a restaurant or memory for the appearance of a house one lived in as a child). Whereas cued recall measures stimulate the type of search necessary to access semantic memory, more open-ended, uncued recall measures are needed to access storage in episodic memory. The authors suggest that the advantage of emotional commercials may go undetected in ad effectiveness studies if procedures favoring search of semantic rather than episodic memory are employed. On this basis, they call for greater attention to the development and use of measures that access episodic memory of advertisements.

In chapter 15, "Gauging and Explaining Advertising Effects: Emergent Concerns Regarding Construct and Ecological Validity," Chris Allen and Thomas Madden echo Thorson and Friestad's sentiment that affective responses cannot be captured adequately using techniques developed for measuring cognitive effects. These authors report a series of five experiments examining affective experiences and evaluative responses to advertising and find evidence to support their view that different measures are required to tap these different reactions. In addition, they present and test a procedure designed to assess the more spontaneous and ephemeral experience characteristic of affective responses. This procedure entails showing subjects an ad and then asking them to list four adjectives in response to it. This open-ended procedure is demonstrated to produce different (and presumably more affect-oriented) responses from structured self-report approaches. In order to measure affective responses accurately, the authors emphasize the need to avoid encouraging cognitive elaboration that would not occur naturally and spontaneously.

"The Role of Emotion in Advertising Revisited: Testing a Typology of Emotional Responses" (chapter 16), by Morris Holbrook and Richard Westwood, also addresses methodological issues but from a somewhat different perspective. In this chapter, the authors describe and test Plutchik's typology of emotional responses. Plutchik's typology offers eight categories of emotional response, which are organized around pairs of polar opposites: accept-disgust, fear-anger, joy-sadness, and anticipation-surprise. After analyzing individuals' judgments of the ability of fifty-four advertisements to evoke various emotions, Holbrook and Westwood conclude that Plutchik's typology may be appropriately applied in advertising settings. In addition, two key dimensions are found to underlie individuals' emotional response: negative-positive and serious-light. The finding of a negative-positive dimension is consistent with Isen's discussion of negative and positive affect, though it would seem to imply a symmetry of response not reliably observed, at least in psychology research. The serious-light dimension also is interesting because it may relate to Pechmann and Stewart's (chapter 4) dimension of the type of cognitive processing, which could be construed to encompass concepts such as the number and strength of linkages made to the emotion (as with associative network models in the previous section).

The final chapter in part IV bridges the theoretical, methodological and practical concerns associated with advertising affect. In "An Investigation of the Relationship between the MECCAs Model and Advertising Affect," Thomas Reynolds and Minakshi Trivedi illustrate a laddering procedure for linking specific means, such as products, to fundamental ends or values sought by consumers. This procedure involves matching components of the advertising strategy with the different levels of abstraction that characterize consumer information processing. An analysis of three commercials in terms of the MECCAs model revealed that the ad most conforming to the model was also most closely associated with affect at the critical leverage point level.

The final chapter of the book moves from the ivory tower of academic research back to the people on the firing line of everyday decision making. The chapter reports on a group discussion with advertising practitioners in which key ideas emanating from the book were presented and reactions were obtained. Thus, the book comes full circle. It begins with theoretical concepts born of experience in designing advertising. This knowledge is abstracted, and the reasons for the effects observed are explored from a theory testing perspective. Finally, the knowledge gained is returned to the uncontrolled real world to see if it can help guide decision making. This process is, as it should be, never ending. The book simply provides a snapshot at a point in time.

Part I
Classifying Advertising Stimuli

2
Lectures and Dramas

William D. Wells

One good way to think about television commercials is to imagine that each commercial is made of two basic ingredients: lecture and drama. In this context ''lecture'' means direct address. The speaker speaks outward from the television to the audience. The audience receives the message at a distance. ''Drama'' refers to indirect address. In a drama, the characters speak to each other, not to the audience. In fact they usually behave as though the audience were not even there. When a drama works, the audience is drawn in. Members of the audience become close-in observers of, and sometimes vicarious participants in, events unfolding on the stage. Lectures are directed at the audience; dramas are overheard. This distinction is important because lectures and dramas work in fundamentally different ways. They have different strengths and different weaknesses, and they use different mechanisms to persuade.

Definitions and Examples

In its most basic form, a television commercial lecture is like a platform speech. The speaker speaks directly to the audience, projecting information outward from behind the television screen. The speaker displays the product, talks about its features, and shows what it can do. In a lecture, the speaker presents evidence (broadly speaking) and uses argument and exhortation to persuade.

Sometimes the presenter is in costume on location—a kitchen, a living room, or an office, to name just a few. Costumes and locations add interest and texture, and possibly even a little credibility to what the speaker has to say. Sometimes presenters disappear, and illustrations—like a platform speaker's slides—fill the frame. Sometimes presenters do not appear at all. They lecture voice-over while viewers look at pictures of the lecture's main ideas. Sometimes two or three speakers succeed each other. Sometimes the lecture is not spoken but sung. The distinguishing mark of a television commercial lecture is that the message is projected through the frame to the audience, wherever each individual member of the audience may be. The basic model is that of an oration in which evidence is presented and arguments are made.

By contrast, the format here called "drama" is like a movie or a play. Characters in dramas address each other, not the audience. Members of the audience "go into" the television set to watch the happenings on the stage. This use of the term "drama" is not intended to imply profoundly emotional response. Some television commercial dramas are comic sketches; some are cartoons; some are conversations about household products or proprietary medicines. The distinguishing mark of a drama is that the viewer is an eavesdropper. The viewer is transported into an imaginary setting to observe events enacted in the play.

In a great many television commercials, lecture and drama are combined. One common combination begins as a drama. The drama is interrupted by a short lecture. The drama then resumes and is played through to its end. In another common combination, the commercial is almost all drama; a tiny lecture, like the moral of a story, is added as a tag. In still another common combination, the commercial is mostly lecture, but the lecture is illustrated with minidramas that amplify and personify the information stream.

The distinguishing mark of a lecture-drama is that the viewer must alternate between two different states of mind. In the lecture mode, the viewer is the object of a message projected outward from the screen. In the drama mode, the viewer changes his or her mental location to watch something occurring yonder, on the drama side of the frame. Ideally the lecture-drama combination delivers the best of both communication forms. But some lecture-drama combinations turn out to be a lot less effective than the sum of their separate parts.

How Lectures and Dramas Work

Over the centuries, lecturers and dramatists have learned how lectures and dramas work. Much (but not all) of that knowledge is transferable to lectures and dramas in commercials on television.

Some lectures work by virtue of imputed expertise. In a classroom, for example, students accept lectures because the teacher knows the subject being taught. "The professor is an expert; he or she must be right." Advertisers also invoke authority of one or another kind. Chuck Yeager, a former test pilot, appeared in advertisements for Delco auto parts. An actor who once played the role of "Marcus Welby, M.D." discussed health benefits of Sanka decaffeinated coffee. And Meredith Baxter-Birney personified the benefits of using L'Oreal. Compared with unknown presenters, such "authorities" are more likely to be heeded, and they almost always get some measure of respect. At the very least, they personify what the advertiser wants to say about the brand.

Lectures present facts intended to be believed. The presenter displays the product, demonstrates it, and talks about the benefits it can provide. Even when viewers are suspicious, they sometimes give the product the benefit of the doubt. In consumer language, "They said it was good, so I thought I'd give it a try." But many lectures meet a tougher fate. Faced with a lecture coming at them through the television screen, viewers occupy their minds with other matters, discount part or all of the evidence, derogate the source, or counterargue every point. In a great many cases, those responses dilute or even cancel the ideas the message was intended to convey.

So, lectures present argument and evidence, broadly defined. Members of the audience process that information at arm's length and use the outcome to help them think about how to behave.

Dramas exert influence in an entirely different way. Like fairy tales, movies, novels, parables, and myths, television commercial dramas are stories about how the world works. Viewers learn from dramas by inferring lessons from them and by applying those lessons to the circumstances they encounter in the conduct of their lives. The key word here is *infer.* Dramas do not depend upon direct address; they present object lessons. Viewers learn from dramas by observation and inference, just as they learn from stories they hear and from other things that happen to them every day.

To have this tutorial effect, a television commercial drama must get at least a passing realism grade. If a drama is "phony," "hokey," or too contrived, the viewer will revert from audience to critic and think dark thoughts about costumes, casting, dialogues, and sets. When that happens—when the drama does not ring true—the viewer will pull out of the drama, and the advertiser's inference will not be made.

Given at least minimal involvement and given that the intended inference does in fact get made, a television commercial drama can be very powerful indeed. The source of that power is the viewer's independent mind. When a drama rings true, the viewer migrates into the drama, draws conclusions from it, and applies those conclusions to the management of life. From the viewer's point of view, conclusions drawn from dramas are "mine," while conclusions urged in lectures are "ideas that other people are trying to impose on me."

Television commercial dramas have a second important strength. When a viewer migrates into an involving drama, he or she experiences some of the feelings associated with buying or using the advertised brand. After experiencing those feelings, the viewer may buy or use the product in order to reexperience more of the same.

This is not to say that television commercial lectures are incapable of generating emotional response. With vivid language and evocative effects, skillful presenters can and do arouse anticipation for the products they purvey. But by their very nature, lectures are secondhand abstractions, one step removed from life. Dramas can deliver a firsthand taste, a true sample, of the emotional reward the product can provide.

In summary, television commercial dramas have two extremely potent traits. First, because conclusions drawn from dramas are viewer made, they bypass defenses erected against ideas forced in from outside. Second, because dramas draw their viewers into the action, they provide free samples of the emotional rewards associated with the advertiser's brand. Such samples cannot be delivered as vividly in any other way.

In spite of those two formidable advantages, drama is not the dominant commercial type. Lectures have their own advantages, which can be strong enough to make lecture the better choice. One obvious advantage is that lectures generally cost less to produce. In some cases, that asset by itself dictates the choice. A second advantage is that lectures are more compact. A lecture can deliver a dozen copy points in fifteen seconds. A drama takes much longer to translate all that information into the sequences of a play. As commercials become shorter and shorter, lectures may be more and more frequently employed. A third and most important advantage is that a lecture can get right to the point. A lecture can be perfectly explicit; a drama must rely on the viewer to make the inference the advertiser needs. Sometimes viewers make that inference, but sometimes they do not. Thus, because lectures are relatively inexpensive, highly compact, and can be explicit as to the advertiser's point, more lectures than dramas find their way to the commercial screen.

Effective Lectures

Great public speakers have learned how to use lectures to persuade. Many of those lessons transfer to lectures in commercials on television. Surprisingly, some of the most obvious lessons are commonly violated.

For example, *credibility is key.* One way lectures work is by virtue of the presenter's expertise. Thus, many advertisers employ presenters who add credibility to their words. But some advertisers employ celebrities who have no connection with the lecture's main ideas. When that happens, the audience may attend to the celebrity but not to the product being sold. Another threat to credibility is the presenter who grabs attention in irrelevant, outlandish ways. Like the celebrity who distracts, the bizarre presenter diverts attention from the major purpose of the ad. The most extreme example of mismatch between lecture and presenter is the household product lecture delivered by an actress cast as a homemaker, who is required to deliver lines that make her IQ seem less than 9.

A second truism is that *the lecture should appreciate the viewer.* Expert speakers flatter their audiences. In sharp contrast, a surprising number of television commercial lectures hold the user of the product up to scorn. Product users are sensitive to insult, and they retaliate as best they can.

Third, *the illustrations should illustrate the lecture.* No accomplished speaker would dream of showing slides that take the audience away from the text. In a surprising number of cases, though, the pictures that accompany a television commercial lecture are irrelevant or out of phase.

Fourth, *the illustrations should not overwhelm the message.* When television commercial lectures are illustrated with vignettes, the illustrations can be so involving that viewers remember the illustrations but forget the advertiser's point. When that happens, the purpose of the advertisement has not been served.

These observations seem quite obvious. Indeed they are in the context of a platform speech. The value of dividing commercials into lecture and drama is that this dichotomy makes such hazards more evident than they otherwise would be.

Effective Dramas

Television commercial dramas teach object lessons about how products add to the quality of life. Under certain circumstances, they also provide true samples of the emotional rewards associated with the advertiser's brand. Both of those objectives require that the drama pass the viewer's realism test. This does not mean that a television commercial drama must be realistic, true, or believable in any literal sense. It does mean that the drama must live up to the viewer's standards for what seems right. Even when the drama is outright fantasy, the situations in the fantasy must follow the rules that would govern those situations if those situations did exist, and the characters in the fantasy must behave as such characters would behave if there were characters of that kind. That quality, often called verisimilitude, is never easy to create. It is especially difficult in dramas that represent real life. If a viewer knows exactly what to expect, even minor deviations are likely to make the drama seem contrived. The most common example of this violation is the drama in which characters lecture each other on the virtues of an advertiser's brand. Although such lectures may be noticed and remembered, they always lose the benefit of seeming to have been overheard.

A second requirement for commercial drama is that the drama must be about the brand. Great theatrical dramas elicit countless associations with myriad aspects of their viewers' lives. Every member of the audience may draw something different from them, and repeat viewers may get something different time after time. In sharp contrast, the best television commercials can be interpreted in just one way. They deliver singular messages, and they focus those messages on the superiority of one specific brand. The last thing an advertiser wants is the multiplicity of meanings that makes great dramas great.

Writers of television commercial dramas have two demanding tasks: they must make their dramas rich enough to engage the viewer, and they must make their dramas unequivocal enough to elicit a unanimous conclusion as to the superiority of a single brand. Those two objectives interfere with each other. Dramas that meet them both are hard to find.

Lecture-Dramas

When lectures and dramas are combined, the rules that govern both forms come into play: credibility is key; the message should appreciate, not demean, the viewer; the illustrations must illustrate the lecture; the illustrations must not overwhelm the lecture; the commercial must be about the brand. In addition, the lecture must interrupt the drama without destroying it, and the writer must find a way to introduce a lecture without provoking the very counter-arguments that a pure drama would avoid.

The last two requirements are exceptionally demanding because, in a lecture-drama, the viewer must alternate between two different states of mind. In the lecture mode, the viewer is the object of a message projected outward from the television screen. In the drama mode, the viewer reverses direction and enters the action on the stage. We do not know much about how those reversals work—how best to accomplish them, what factors impede them, or even how long they take. That lack of knowledge makes the lecture-drama an especially fertile field for increasing our understanding of how advertising communicates and persuades.

Research Implications

The burden of this discussion has been that what is known about lecture and drama outside of television can make useful contributions to our understanding of how advertising works. The distinction between lecture and drama also has some implications for how we conduct advertising research.

Differences between lectures and dramas can help us think about whether and how to test unfinished ads. If the commercial is a lecture, the advertiser needs to know whether the lecture will be understood and whether it will improve the viewer's attitude toward the brand. In many cases those two questions can be addressed with simple expositions of the lecture's main ideas. But when the commercial is to be a drama, a crude execution may miss the point. It may foreclose informed prediction as to whether the drama will ring true, and it may omit the very detail from which essential inferences might be made. The same caveats apply to lecture-dramas. A storyboard, for example, might permit useful conclusions about the lecture part but not include enough detail to give the drama a fair test. In that case, the lecture's contribution would receive undue attention, and the drama's contribution would be in danger of being overlooked. A storyboard seems particularly inadequate for portraying that hazardous transition from lecture mode to drama mode and back. That is a difficult and important reversal. We do not know much about how to make it work, and a storyboard does not seem to be much help.

The distinction between lecture and drama sheds some light on whether and how to evaluate the believability of an ad. Most lectures present evidence and argument, rhetoric and fact. It therefore makes sense to ask respondents whether they believe what a lecture said. But when the commercial is a drama, believability becomes much harder to define. It might mean verisimilitude, agreement with something someone in the drama said, that the viewer agrees with what he or she thinks the drama was intended to imply about the brand. When *believability* can have so many meanings, we cannot assume that every respondent will interpret a believability question in the same way.

The lecture-drama dichotomy extends to advertising in media other than television. Radio is the closest case. Many radio commercials are delivered by announcers who present information as if they were voice-over on television. Other radio commercials are dramas reminiscent of old-time network shows. Most magazine and newspaper advertisements can be thought of as visual lectures, with text and illustrations moving outward to the reader from the page. A few—very few—magazine and newspaper advertisements are visual dramas. Readers ''enter'' the picture, draw inferences, and apply those inferences to their lives.

Research procedures that prove useful in studies of television commercial lectures should prove useful in studies of lectures on the radio or in newspapers or magazines. Techniques that work for television commercial dramas should be adaptable to radio or print dramas even though the medium is not the same.

The lecture-drama dichotomy may be helpful in comparisons among media. Electronic media tilt toward drama; print media tilt toward lecture. That fact suggests media contrast, which heretofore has not been made.

Finally, the distinction between lecture and drama implies that some questions relevant to lectures might not be as relevant to dramas, and vice-versa. About lectures researchers might ask, Did the presenter add to or subtract from the advertiser's message? Were the words of the lecture clearly understood? Did the illustrations illustrate the lecture? Were the illustrations so interesting or so humorous that they overwhelmed the message the advertiser needed to convey? Those questions could be asked to dramas, but they would not quite fit because their meaning would not be quite the same.

About dramas, researchers might ask, Did the drama draw the viewer in? Was the intended inference strongly made? Did the drama generate a sample of the emotional reward to be obtained by buying or using the advertiser's brand? Those questions, critical to dramas, do not apply to lectures in the same way.

Most lecture questions are quite familiar, and a great many of them fit well-known research techniques. But drama questions seem a little strange.

Researchers have not thought much about them, and standard research methods seem embarrassingly naive in this context.

The distinction between lectures and dramas offers challenges and opportunities. To researchers, it offers a challenge to develop measurements that are as sensitive to the power of drama as current measurements are to the power of lecture. Most current measurements are lecture measurements—understandably so in view of the thousands of lectures researchers have given and received. But who can doubt the power of drama? Who can doubt that people learn from role models and behavioral examples set before them every day?

To advertisers the distinction between lecture and drama offers the challenge to shake off the handicaps imposed by lecture-based research. Advertising does convey information, and lectures do that very well. But that is not all advertising does. It invokes inferences and previews feelings the product can provide. Advertisers who do not take notice of those effects are ignoring more than half of what their investment in advertising could add to their brands.

To researchers the distinction between lecture and drama offers an opportunity to explore a whole new territory. We know a lot about lectures, but our understanding of dramas, and of lecture-dramas, is woefully incomplete. Finally, and possibly most important to advertisers, the distinction between lecture and drama offers an opportunity to outflank competitors who bind themselves to information narrowly defined. Logic does not always work. When logic fails, imaginative advertisers shift to overdrive.

Bill Bernbach once said, "The real giants have always been poets, men who jumped from the facts into the realm of imagination and ideas." When rhetoric is not enough, the real giants jump from concept to percept, from argument to narrative, from talking about the brand to showing how the brand enhances life. Successful poetry conveys its meaning to the inner chambers of the viewer's mind. The same message, now an argument, may find "no admittance" posted at the gate.

3
An Investigation of Mood Commercials

John S. Coulson

Advertising has been classified in many ways: hard sell, humorous, image, documentary, stand-up announcer, celebrity, personality, slice-of-life, and a variety of others. Over the years one type of advertising has persisted under many names: emotional, high feel, soft sell, and mood. It is usually indirect and involving, a piece of advertising well liked for its own sake. Presumably the liking for the advertising rubs off on the product. The old salesman's adage that he should first sell himself before he sells his product carries the same rationale as does mood advertising.

Mood advertising lies at one end of a continuum. Extreme examples of mood advertising are found in such product classes as perfume, cosmetics, alcoholic beverages, and other categories in which there is little or nothing to be said about the product. Rational advertising typically conveys facts about the product that are expected to make the recipient of the advertising want to buy the product. Extreme examples of rational commercials come to mind in drugs, business equipment, and household products where news and product differences give the advertisers something specific to say about the products. At the same time, examples of mood advertising and of rational advertising are found in almost every product class. Most advertising is a combination of rational and emotional appeals.

Generally research findings for mood commercials are quite different from those for rational commercials. For example, recall scores for rational advertising are typically higher than those for mood advertising. Foote, Cone and Belding published a study showing that although a mood commercial does not perform well on a Burke-type recall study, it does quite well on a Starch-type recognition study.

Most agency people are well aware that mood commercials do not score well on recall tests; however, one could not be certain whether the low scores resulted because the commercial was a mood commercial or perhaps a rational commercial deficient in its capacity to be recalled. The issue was decided largely on the basis of judgment and argument.

Recently a scale was added to the Verbal Response Profile (VRP) battery of scales that allows a commercial to be defined from the viewer's point of view as either a mood or a rational commercial. Leila Green of Leo Burnett Company was the author of the scale. The statement to which the respondents react is: "The commercial makes me 'feel' rather than 'think.'" The investigation of mood commercials in this chapter uses this consumer definition of a mood commercial in contrast to a rational commercial.

The Analysis

Purpose

The purpose of this analysis is to investigate consumer-designated mood commercials and to compare them to consumer-designated rational commercials. This exploration is intended to (1) establish these commercial types as distinct and (2) use VRP and motivation scales to identify similarities and differences between mood and rational commercials.

Method

The VRP was developed by Mary Jane Schlinger during the 1960s while she was working at the Leo Burnett Company and has been included in many publications. It is a series of six-point agreement scales covering many statements. The six points are:

1. I strongly disagree with the statement.
2. I disagree with the statement.
3. I somewhat disagree with the statement.
4. I somewhat agree with the statement.
5. I agree with the statement.
6. I strongly agree with the statement.

This analysis of mood commercials uses results from the most recent 247 animatic, photomatic, and commercial studies conducted at Communications Workshop, Inc. using a modified VRP system. Each of the studies consisted of a minimum sample of 40 viewers. The 247 commercials were arrayed on the basis of answers to the statement: "The commercial makes me 'feel' rather than 'think.'"

Figure 3–1 shows the mean of answers to this statement. This array roughly follows the bell-shaped curve; there is a sharp fall-off of cases above 4.0 and below 3.0. All of the cases above 4.0 were designated as mood commercials and those below 3.0 were designated as rational commercials. Thus, the number of commercials in the three types are: 24 commercials below 3.0 designated as rational commercials; 200 from 3.0 to 4.0 in the middle range; and 23 over 4.0 designated as mood commercials.

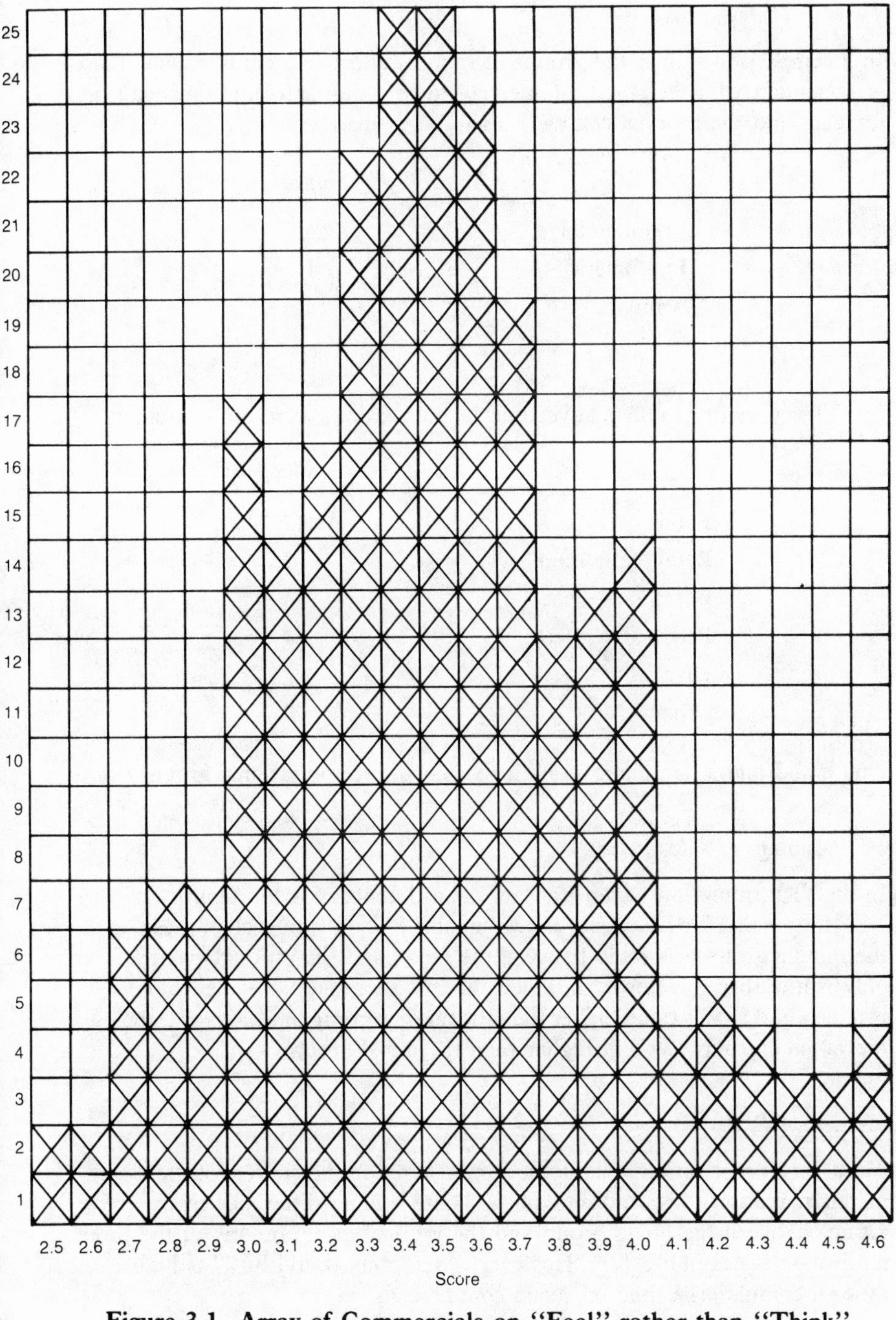

Figure 3-1. Array of Commercials on "Feel" rather than "Think"

Types of Commercials

In a comparison of just the groups of rational and mood commercials, there was a tendency for the mood commercials to be photomatics and finished commercials and the rational commercials to be animatics:

	Mood	*Rational*
Commercial	7	5
Photomatic	6	1
Animatic	10	18
Total	23	24

The types of products advertised in both groups were quite similar:

	Mood	*Rational*
Food	14	12
Retail/restaurant	3	2
Business service	2	4
Personal service	0	4
Drug	1	2
Other	3	0

One brand had an animatic in both the mood and the rational groups.

VRP Ratings of Advertising

In the VRP ratings on factor groupings, a difference of 0.3 is significant. The VRP factors and subfactors are shown in table 3–1. In almost all of these cases, the middle group was rated between the mood and the rational groups. The only real outlier was news, in which the middle group contained more new products and so was rated higher than the rational group in news; nevertheless, the rational group was still higher than the mood group.

Motivation Scales

Three direct motivation scales were administered to the viewers of these commercials, photomatics, and animatics. There was no difference in the mean ratings between the mood group and the rational group on any of the three motivation scales (table 3–2). However, ''definitely would buy'' is higher on rational commercials than on mood commercials.

Table 3–1
VRP Ratings of Advertising

	Mood	*Middle*	*Rational*
Relevant News			
News	3.2[a]	3.9	3.5[a]
Relevance of news	4.1	4.3	4.2
Brand acceptance			
Brand reputation	4.5	4.8	4.7
Brand reinforcement	4.5	4.5	4.4
Brand differentiation	3.5[a]	3.8	4.0[a]
Brand motivation	4.4	4.5	4.3
Believability			
Commercial brand congruence	4.6	4.7	4.5
Realism	4.3	4.3	4.2
Negative-commercial evaluation	2.1[a]	2.3	2.5[a]
Confusion	2.3	2.3	2.3
Stimulation			
Attention/enjoyment	4.2[a]	3.8	3.3[a]
Intrusiveness	2.6[a]	3.0	3.3[a]
Distinctiveness			
Unusual	3.7[a]	3.4	3.3[a]
Unfamiliar	4.4	4.7	4.5
Not worn out	4.8[a]	4.7	4.5[a]
Empathy/identification	3.7[a]	3.3	3.1[a]
Positive mood	4.5[a]	4.0	3.5[a]

[a]Indicates a significant difference.

Table 3–2
Intent-to-Buy Scales

	Mood	*Middle*	*Rational*
Definitely would buy	34%	44%	40%
Probably would buy	38	37	36
Might or might not buy	22	15	18
Probably would not buy	4	3	5
Definitely would not buy	2	1	1
Total	100%	100%	100%
Mean intent-to-buy rating	4.1	4.2	4.0
Mean interest-in-buying rating	3.5	3.5	3.5
Mean intent-to-mention rating	3.5	3.6	3.3
Range of mean ratings of intent to buy			
Highest	4.8	4.8	4.6
Lowest	3.4	3.2	3.5

Conclusions

The following conclusions can be drawn from this analysis:

1. A mood commercial is a distinctively different type of commercial from a rational commercial.
2. This difference can be defined by consumers on the basis of their answers to the VRP scale: "The commercial makes me 'feel' rather than 'think.' "
3. Both types of commercials are used by the same product classes and by a variety of products.
4. Rational commercials carry more news than do mood commercials. The old adage of creative people—"If you don't have anything to say, sing it"—appears to have a basis in fact.
5. There is no difference in the overall motivation scales of rational commercials and mood commercials; there are high- and low-scoring commercials in both groups. However, "definitely-would-buy" is higher for the rational group than for the mood group, indicating that possibly there would be a greater immediate response to a rational commercial than to a mood commercial.
6. Mood commercials rate higher than rational commercials on being attention getting/enjoyable, on being received less negatively, on being unusual and less worn out, and on evoking greater empathy/identification. On the other hand, mood commercials carry less news, do not differentiate the brand as sharply, and are less intrusive than rational commercials.
7. There is no difference in the believability of these two commercial types, nor are they different in being clear or in being familiar.

The mean ratings in all of the VRP scales are shown in appendix 3A.

Appendix 3A: Commercial Evaluation Scales

	Mood	*Middle*	*Rational*
Relevant news			
News			
I learned something from the commercial I didn't know before	3.3	4.0	4.0
The commercial gave me a new idea	3.4	3.8	3.5
The commercial told about product that is new to me	3.1	3.7	3.2
Total	3.2	3.9	3.5

	Mood	*Middle*	*Rational*
Relevance of news			
During the commercial I thought how the product might satisfy me	4.2	4.6	4.2
The commercial showed me the product had certain advantages	4.1	4.5	4.4
Important for me	3.8	4.2	4.2
Ad didn't have anything to do with me or my needs (invert)	4.5	4.8	4.6
Commercial told me about product I'd like to try	4.4	4.7	4.5
Reminded me I'm dissatisfied looking for something better	2.9	3.1	2.9
Would be interested in more information about product	4.2	4.4	4.2
As I watched, I thought, "Who cares"? (invert)	4.6	4.5	4.3
Total	4.1	4.3	4.2
Brand acceptance			
Good brand			
I know advertised brand is dependable, reliable	4.7	4.9	4.8
Good brand; wouldn't hesitate recommending it to others	4.3	4.6	4.5
Total	4.5	4.8	4.7
Brand reinforcement			
Thought of reasons would not buy product (invert)	5.0	4.8	4.8
Commercial strengthened my favorable views about brand	4.0	4.2	4.1
Commercial made me feel product is right for me	4.0	4.3	4.1
Commercial described characteristics undesirable to me (invert)	4.8	4.7	4.6
Total	4.5	4.5	4.4
Brand differentiation			
No real difference between product shown and competitors (invert)	3.8	4.2	4.1
Showed me a real difference between that brand and competition	3.1	3.4	3.8
Total	3.5	3.8	4.0

	Mood	Middle	Rational
Brand motivation			
I will definitely buy brand in commercial	4.3	4.4	4.3
Made me think might try brand—see if as good as they say	4.5	4.6	4.2
Total	4.4	4.5	4.3
Believability of commercial			
Commercial-brand congruence			
What they said about product was dishonest (invert)	5.1	5.0	4.9
Don't see how product has much to do with what shown in commercial (invert)	4.5	4.9	4.9
Didn't demonstrate claims they were making about product (invert)	4.3	4.5	4.0
Commercial made exaggerated (untrue) claims (invert)	4.9	4.9	4.8
Commercial gives me confidence in the product. I can trust it	4.0	4.1	4.1
Total	4.6	4.7	4.5
Realism			
Unrealistic ad; farfetched (invert)	4.7	4.7	4.6
Found myself disagreeing with some things in commercial (invert)	4.6	4.5	4.4
Commercial was very realistic—true to life	3.8	3.7	3.6
Total	4.3	4.3	4.2
Negative commercial evaluation			
Commercial irritated me—annoying	1.8	2.1	2.4
In poor taste	1.7	1.9	2.2
Silly	2.3	2.5	2.6
Commercial insults my intelligence	2.2	2.4	2.6
Commercial talked down to me	2.2	2.4	2.6
Total	2.1	2.3	2.5
Confusion			
So busy watching screen, didn't listen to the talk	2.9	2.6	2.5
Required effort to follow commercial	2.3	2.4	2.5
Too complex, wasn't sure what was going on	1.9	1.9	2.0
Total	2.3	2.3	2.3

	Mood	*Middle*	*Rational*
Stimulation			
Attention/enjoyment			
Dull and boring (invert)	4.9	4.6	4.2
Commercial was lots of fun to watch and listen to	4.3	3.9	3.2
Characters capture attention	4.5	3.9	3.7
Enthusiasm is catching—picks you up	4.2	3.9	3.3
Thought it was clever, entertaining	4.4	3.9	3.4
Amusing	3.9	3.7	3.1
Playful	3.8	3.6	2.9
Exciting	3.5	3.2	2.7
Music in commercial very good	4.4	4.0	3.6
Not just selling the product—entertaining me, I appreciate that	4.3	3.7	3.1
Total	4.2	3.8	3.3
Intrusiveness			
Soothing (invert)	2.4	3.0	3.4
Tender (invert)	2.9	3.8	4.2
Dreamy (invert)	3.5	4.3	4.7
There was some conflict in commercial	2.1	2.1	2.2
It was a pushy commercial	1.9	2.1	2.2
Total	2.6	3.0	3.3
Distinctiveness			
Unusual			
Unusual commercial; I'm not sure I've seen another like it	3.3	3.1	3.0
This commercial is different from the commercials of its competitors	4.0	3.7	3.6
A unique commercial	3.7	3.4	3.2
Commercial stands out from other commercials	3.8	3.5	3.3
Total	3.7	3.4	3.3
Unfamiliar			
Have seen before (invert)	4.7	5.0	4.9
The commercial was familiar (invert)	4.1	4.3	4.2
Total	4.4	4.7	4.5

	Mood	*Middle*	*Rational*
Worn out			
I've seen this commercial so many times; I'm tired of it (invert)	5.2	5.2	5.0
Commercial has been done so many times—same old thing (invert)	4.4	4.2	4.0
Total	4.8	4.7	4.5
Empathy/identification			
Felt I was right there in commercial experiencing same thing	3.7	3.4	3.1
Felt commercial was acting out what I feel like at times	3.5	3.3	3.1
Liked commercial because it was personal and intimate	3.7	3.2	3.0
That's my ideal—the kind of life the commercial showed	3.5	3.1	2.7
I was involved in the commercial	4.0	3.8	3.5
Total	3.7	3.3	3.1
Positive mood			
I like the mood of the commercial	4.7	4.3	4.0
The commercial made me "feel" rather than "think"	4.3	3.5	2.8
The tone of the commercial is appropriate	4.4	4.3	3.8
Total	4.5	4.0	3.5

Note: "Invert" indicates that mean given was subtracted from 7 so means can be averaged to determine the total factor.

4

The Multidimensionality of Persuasive Communications: Theoretical and Empirical Foundations

Cornelia (Connie) Pechmann
David W. Stewart

Traditionally it has been assumed that advertisers must choose between two qualitatively different types of commercial appeals: rational or emotional. This assumption has its roots in the work of Copeland (1924), who argued that an individual who buys a product will have either a rational or an emotional reason for doing so. As a result, firms must decide whether advertising dollars are more appropriately spent on emotional ads to promote emotional purchases or on rational ads to promote rational purchases.

Advertisers and advertising researchers who believe that rational and emotional advertising are two mutually exclusive options have expended considerable effort trying to determine which type of appeal is more effective (Plummer and Hecker 1984; Sentis 1984; Agres and Bernstein 1984; Golden and Johnson 1983; Ray and Batra 1983; Zielske 1982). It has become increasingly evident, however, that advertisers also have a third option: to use mixed commercials that contain both rational and emotional elements. Many copywriters explicitly advocate this alternative strategy. For example, according to Sterling Getchell, a prominent advertising copywriter, the most effective ads are those that contain both an emotional hook and a logical justification for purchasing the advertised brand (Runyon and Stewart 1987). The emotional hook is necessary because consumers generally buy for emotional or psychosocial reasons. The logical justification is equally important because consumers need to be able to attribute their purchase decisions to objective, functional characteristics of the brand.

There is now substantial empirical evidence that most broadcast ads are mixed (Stewart and Furse 1986; Stout and Leckenby 1984; Choi and Thorson 1983). Even researchers interested in determining the relative persuasiveness of purely rational versus purely emotional ads have been unable to identify ads that represent pure types. (For a conflicting view, see chapter 3 in this book.)

Instead, ads that were initially classified as rational were later found to elicit affective responses (Stout and Leckenby 1984; Golden and Johnson 1983). Similarly, so-called emotional ads often contained explicit verbal information (that is, statements) about functional or objective product benefits (Agres and Bernstein 1984; Ray and Batra 1983; Kisielius 1982; Rossiter and Percy 1980).

Since virtually all ads are composed of heterogeneous stimuli, it is probably overly simplistic to classify an ad as being either rational or emotional. The objective of this chapter is to propose a more useful system for classifying ads. We will demonstrate that in order to meaningfully categorize and evaluate a commercial, the stimuli it contains and the mediating or proximal responses it evokes must be portrayed along two dimensions: a systematic-heuristic dimension and an emotional (or, more generally, an experiential) benefits dimension. That is, an ad should be classified along a continuum ranging from appeals designed to facilitate systematic processing to largely heuristic appeals, based on the type of cognitive processing it evokes. Furthermore, an ad should be classified along a continuum ranging from primarily emotional or experiential benefit appeals to appeals that do not portray such benefits, based on the extent to which it elicits a vicarious experience of the brand's experiential or emotional benefits. Finally, an ad should be categorized using a two-stage process, first based on the stimuli it contains and then based on the proximal (or mediating) responses it evokes. If the ad's stimuli do not produce the expected response, the ad must be reclassified. For example, if an ad that is believed to use a heuristic appeal (because it contains a heuristic cue) is not processed heuristically, it must be reclassified.

This multidimensional stimulus- and response-based categorization of advertising differs from the traditional (rational-emotional) classification scheme in four ways:

1. According to the traditional approach, the antithesis of high systematic processing is high affective processing. In contrast, according to the proposed multidimensional classification scheme, the antithesis of high systematic processing is low systematic (heuristic) processing. Thus only the latter approach can correctly classify heuristic appeals since they evoke moderately low to very low systematic processing and do not necessarily elicit affective processing. This multidimensional view is consistent with recent work on attitude change (Chaiken and Stangor 1987; chapter 5), which appears to have arrived at a similar conclusion independent of the work that has been done in advertising.
2. In one-dimensional space, even a heterogeneous ad must be classified as rational, emotional, or some undefined mixture. In contrast, in multidimensional space, such an ad can be appropriately classified because it can be positioned both along the cognitive processing dimension and the

emotional benefits or experiential dimension. For example, an ad that evokes systematic processing (that is, has a logical justification) and that also portrays an experiential benefit (that is, has an emotional "hook") can be accurately labeled as having both types of appeals.

3. The classification system suggested in this chapter differentiates the use of *emotional benefit appeals* from the use of *emotion as a heuristic cue.* This distinction suggests that emotion-laden stimuli may operate in two very different ways.
4. The traditional approach to classifying ads has been stimulus based. The proposed classification scheme is both stimulus based and response based.

The advantage of stimulus-based operational definitions is that managers have direct control only over the stimuli contained in their advertisements; they cannot control viewers' reactions. Therefore managers will benefit most from research that evaluates alternative types of advertising stimuli rather than the various ways in which consumers respond to ads.

However, there is a problem with classifying ads solely on the basis of their stimulus components: although virtually every ad contains a heterogeneous set of stimuli, viewers may respond to only some of these stimulus elements. If the environment is distracting or viewers are unmotivated, they are more likely to respond to heuristic cues or to a portrayal of the brand's emotional benefits and to be oblivious to detailed arguments. If the environment is not distracting and viewers are motivated, they are more likely to follow a detailed argument about a brand's objective attributes and benefits and to ignore a heuristic cue or an emotional benefit claim. (See chapter 5.) As a result, although an ad can be tentatively classified on the basis of its salient stimulus elements, these classifications should later be verified by determining whether viewers' proximal responses to the ad conformed to its stimulus-based classification. The researcher must determine how systematically the information in the ad was processed and whether viewers vicariously experienced the brand's emotional benefits.

The examination of proximal responses evoked by stimuli represents an important check on the validity of causal statements. It is important to verify that stimuli produce a distal response via the hypothesized process (proximal responses). For example, Middlestadt and Fishbein (1987) reported an instance in which an orange juice ad composed entirely of visuals and music and containing no words created beliefs about the "naturalness" of the orange juice. Attitude change (a distal response) in such a case may just as readily be attributed to this change in beliefs (one proximal response) as to an affective response evoked by the music or visuals (another proximal response). This strongly suggests the need for manipulation checks, a practice standard among social psychologists doing persuasion research although less common among advertising researchers.

The next section of this chapter provides a theoretical rational for the proposed multidimensional classification scheme and describes the scheme in greater detail. Subsequently, empirical support for the classification scheme will be presented. Finally, conclusions and recommendations will be made.

Multidimensionality: Theoretical Perspectives

A Theoretical Rationale for the Proposed Classification Scheme

Social psychologists and advertising researchers engaged in persuasion research employ three different theoretical and empirical paradigms (Petty, Cacioppo, and Schumann 1983; Chaiken 1985, 1980; Peterson, Hoyer, and Wilson 1987). It has been empirically demonstrated that persuasion can occur via a systematic, a heuristic, or an affective processor route. Research grounded in the systematic paradigm explores how people are persuaded by detailed information about the merits of a particular issue. Studies generated by the heuristic paradigm attempt to explain how people are persuaded by a message's heuristic cues (the speaker's expertise, for instance). Finally, research stemming from the affective paradigm seeks to understand how an emotionally charged message can be persuasive.

In actuality, there are more than three different theories of persuasion; at least seven distinct theories have received empirical support. However, of these theories, three posit systematic routes to persuasion, two describe heuristic processes, and two predict that persuasion will be mediated by an emotional response—so effectively there are only three general classes of theories or paradigms, not seven.

The three general theories of how people are influenced by ads and other forms of persuasive communication are equally viable; there is no one correct explanation or perspective. The three paradigms complement each other rather than compete because each deals with a different type of persuasive message. In other words, there is a need for at least three different theories of persuasion because there are at least three qualitatively different types of persuasive appeals that vary along two dimensions.

First, it has been demonstrated empirically that there is a systematic-heuristic dimension. At the one extreme are the systematic appeals presenting logical and detailed arguments in favor of particular points of view. At the other extreme are the heuristic appeals suggesting that decisions should be based on more limited information in order to maximize efficiency at the possible cost of accuracy.

Second, it has been established that there is an affective dimension. At one extreme are emotional appeals that persuade their audiences by eliciting certain emotional reactions. At the other extreme are appeals that do not have an impact on their audiences' emotional states.

Thus persuasive messages are viewed as multidimensional. The most relevant dimensions along which appeals may differ are related to the levels of cognitive processing and emotional arousal that are evoked. Herein lies the theoretical rationale for classifying ads along both a systematic-heuristic dimension and an affective-nonaffective dimension.

Some social psychologists have argued that the systematic, heuristic, and affective routes to persuasion are all qualitatively different (Chaiken 1980, 1985); others contend that there are only two routes to persuasion—the central route (via systematic processing) and the peripheral route (via heuristic processing)—and that affective responses may or may not be elicited in either case (see chapter 5). However, these apparent differences of opinion are primarily semantic, not substantive.

Description of the Proposed Classification Scheme

Operational definitions of systematic (rational), heuristic, and emotional commercials can be derived from the theories of persuasion in which each is grounded. These definitions are provided in tables 4-1 and 4-2, which contain descriptions of the advertising stimuli comprising each type of commercial. In addition, these tables specify how viewers are expected to respond to each type

Table 4-1
Three Prevailing Paradigms in Persuasion Research

Paradigm	*Type of Message (Ad)*	*Predicted Immediate (Proximal) Responses*	*Predicted Delayed (Distal) Responses*
Systematic	Ads provide brand-relevant information	Conscious awareness, comprehension, evaluation, and acceptance of brand-relevant information	Brand purchases mediated by more favorable beliefs and attitudes
Heuristic	Ads provide heuristics, cues, problem frames, or choice rules (which suggest how to respond but are otherwise without justification); affect-laden stimuli may also be present	Use of heuristic, with or without conscious awareness, which precludes more systematic processing; an emotional reaction to the ad itself may also be evoked	Brand purchases mediated solely by the choice heuristic, not necessarily by more favorable beliefs
Affective	Ads contain stimuli capable of eliciting an emotional response	Emotional responses associated with the advertised brand, with or without conscious awareness	Brand purchases mediated by emotional responses (more favorable attitudes) but not necessarily by more favorable beliefs

Table 4–2
The Seven Theories of Advertising

Theories	*Type of Message (Ad)*	*Predicted Immediate (Proximal) Responses*	*Predicted Delayed (Distal) Responses*
Systematic			
Learning theories (Fishbein 1963; McGuire 1972; Fishbein and Ajzen 1975)	Ad claims the brand has a desirable attribute and may present arguments to support this claim	Conscious awareness, comprehension, evaluation, and acceptance of this information	A stronger belief that the brand has this attribute and (perhaps) a more positive evaluation of this attribute produces a more favorable brand attitude and behaviors
Cognitive response theories (Petty 1981; Olson, Toy, and Dover 1982)	Petty: Ad claims the brand has a desirable attribute Olson et al.: None specified; information about desirable brand attributes may be provided, inferred, or remembered	Petty: Conscious awareness, comprehension, and cognitive responding that reflects acceptance of this information Olson et al.: The generation of idiosyncratic cognitive responses about desirable brand attributes	A stronger belief that the brand has this attribute, which produces a more favorable brand attitude and behaviors
Dissonance theory (Festinger 1957; Ray 1982)	Ad claims the brand has and/or a competitor does not have a desirable attribute; and/or the brand does not have—and/or a competitor has—an undesirable attribute	Conscious awareness, comprehension, evaluation, and acceptance of this information	Modified beliefs about an attribute of the brand and/or of a competitor produce a relatively more favorable brand attitude and behaviors, thereby reducing dissonance
Heuristic			
Heuristic processing (Chaiken 1980)	Ad provides a heuristic cue and perhaps makes a favorable claim that may be unsubstantiated ("puffery"). The cue may be emotion laden or neutral	Exclusive reliance on the heuristic cue, which precludes a more careful evaluation of the ad's claims	Purchases mediated by the heuristic cue itself; beliefs may also change
Low involvement (Krugman 1965, 1977)	Ad contains the most basic heuristic cue—it identifies the brand (its name, logo, packaging, etc.); brand salience may be enhanced by use of emotion-laden stimuli	Processing of this cue (the brand identification), which is stored in long-term memory—perhaps subconsciously and nonverbally; affective reaction to the ad is also likely	Purchases of the brand mediated solely by a simple choice heuristic: recall or recognition of the brand; beliefs are unchanged

Table 4–2 (Continued)

Theories	*Type of Message (Ad)*	*Predicted Immediate (Proximal) Responses*	*Predicted Delayed (Distal) Responses*
Affective			
Classical conditioning (Gorn 1982; Staats and Staats 1958)	Ad contains a verbal and/or nonverbal positive unconditioned stimulus (USC) assoiated with the brand (CS)	UCS evokes a positive emotional response (UCR) to the ad, which is later associated with the brand (CR), perhaps subconsciously	Brand acquires the capacity to evoke the positive emotional response (CR), producing a more favorable brand attitude and behaviors; beliefs are unchanged
Vicarious learning (Nord and Peter 1980; Bandura 1969)	Ad portrays a role model's reward (or punishment) for using the brand	Identification with the role model, and an emotional reaction like that of the model which is directly related to (exemplifies) the brand's emotional or experimental benefits	Brand acquires the capacity to evoke positive emotional responses, producing a more favorable brand attitude and behaviors; beliefs may also change

of ad immediately after or during exposure (their "proximal" responses) and later, after a delay (their "distal" responses).

Descriptions of the seven most prevalent theories of persuasion are as follows. These descriptions have been included to depict the three different routes to persuasion in greater detail and to demonstrate that all three routes have been substantiated empirically.

Systematic Theories: Systematic theories of advertising, though differing in specific details, all posit a similar process of persuasion. It is assumed that the individual is an active processor of information. Product information is obtained, evaluated, weighted, and integrated with other information. Then a decision is made by systematically comparing the benefits of the various brands available for purchase. Advertising persuades by providing information about functional and/or experiential brand benefits. The persuasion process moves from attention, to comprehension, to evaluation, to some cognitive change or restructuring (that is, changes in brand beliefs and attitudes), and finally to overt behavioral changes. This process is quite like that employed by the traditional rational decision maker of classical economics, although systematic theories of advertising may recognize bounds on rationality.

Many theories of advertising fit this general paradigm, and these systematic theories have tended to dominate research on advertising effects.

Much of the research involving this paradigm has been conducted in laboratory settings with print ads that not only facilitate but encourage such processing of information. There are several well known variants of this paradigm.

Learning Theories: According to Fishbein, (Fishbein 1963; Fishbein and Ajzen 1975), people perceive brands as bundles of attributes. A consumer's overall attitude toward the brand is determined by the following function:

$$A_o = \sum_{i=1}^{n} e_i b_i$$

where A_o is a consumer's attitude toward brand o, n is the number of salient attributes associated with brand o, e_i is an evaluative response or attitude toward brand attribute i, and b_i is a subjective estimation of the probability that the brand actually has attribute i.. Salient attributes (the is) can be functional or experiential in nature.

Fishbein's theory of attitude change posits that an ad can promote a favorable brand attitude either by strengthening b_i, the person's perception of the probability that a brand has some favorable attribute (i), or by changing n, the number of salient attributes associated with brand o. An individual's evaluation of an object attribute (e_i) represents his or her attitude toward that attribute. This evaluation (e_i) can only be altered indirectly by changing the individual's salient beliefs about that attribute's characteristics. Consequently, "in the final analysis, attitude change involves changing a person's beliefs" (Fishbein and Ajzen 1975, p. 398).

A theory of persuasion (McGuire 1972) similar to that of Fishbein began evolving much earlier but has developed relatively independently. McGuire's information-processing paradigm grew out of earlier work in social psychology by the Yale Communication and Attitude Change Program (Hovland, Janis, and Kelly 1953). McGuire's contention is that attitudes can be changed by exposing individuals to information and facilitating the learning and acceptance of this information. McGuire's unique theoretial contribution is his observation that acceptance of a message is facilitated by presenting arguments that support subsequent conclusions. For example, utilizing Fishbein's familiar terminology, McGuire predicts that an effective ad will prove that a product has a particular attribute i (further strengthening b_i) *and also show why this attribute (i) is beneficial* (enhancing e_i by changing beliefs about attribute i).

Cognitive Response Theories: Cognitive response theories suggest that persuasion is mediated by the thoughts generated by the receiver as the communication is received and processed. That is, people are not passively persuaded by information. Rather, they actively evaluate information and in doing so literally persuade themselves.

According to the most parsimonious of these theories (Petty 1981), effective commercials communicate information that is central to the true merits of the brand and elicit verbalizable thoughts reflecting acceptance of this information. Again, a brand's merits can be functional or experiential in nature. Hence Petty's cognitive response theory is similar to the learning theories. The major difference is that Petty predicts one additional proximal effect: he suggests that individuals will evaluate or critique persuasive messages and will therefore generate and remember thoughts in favor of (or opposed to) the advocated position or brand. These thoughts then mediate changes in attitude.

The cognitive response model developed by Olson, Toy, and Dover (1982) offers a somewhat different interpretation of the effects of advertising. Olson and his colleagues predict, and have demonstrated empirically, that exposure to an ad may also spontaneously evoke unexpected idiosyncratic thoughts about the functional or experiential benefits that the advertised brand will or will not be able to deliver (Mitchell and Olson 1981). Furthermore, Olson et al. argue that these idiosyncratic cognitive responses affect people's beliefs and thereby also mediate changes in attitudes. Thus, according to their model, an ad can persuade by stimulating people to remember or infer brand relevant information that is not contained in the ad itself as well as by providing such information directly or explicitly.

Dissonance Theory: Cognitive dissonance theory (Festinger 1957) postulates that "nonfitting" relations among cognitive elements produce aversive dissonance arousal that individuals seek to alleviate. Ray (1982) has proposed that cognitive dissonance is aroused by many consumer purchases because decisions are often made without sufficient information. The cognitive elements that are in a nonfitting relation are the consumer's past experiences (the purchase of brand A rather than brand B) and the consumer's attitudes toward those brands (that he or she feels no more favorably toward A than toward B). In addition, dissonance will be evoked whenever the consumer's favorable attitude toward A is threatened by information that B is superior.

Ray predicts that consumers will alleviate their cognitive dissonance by selective exposure to and acceptance of new information about A's functional or experiential benefits, specifically information provided by A's ads. Therefore A's ads should be designed to provide the information necessary to reduce dissonance. These commercials should strengthen positive beliefs and/or weaken negative beliefs about A and/or strengthen negative beliefs and/or weaken positive beliefs about B. A's ads will thereby produce relatively more favorable attitudes toward A, which both reduces dissonance and increases the purchase probability of brand A in the future.

Thus, in its original formulation, dissonance theory postulates a (behavior) learning-attitude-behavior hierarchy. Although it is based on the same assumptions as other systematic theories of advertising, it is distinguished from the others by its emphasis on yet another unique proximal effect: the reduction of dissonance arousal.

Heuristic Theories: There has been a recent recognition that decision makers do not always, or even usually, engage in effortful and systematic processing of information prior to choice. A growing body of research suggests that decision makers often rely on simple rules of thumb, or heuristics, when making decisions. This is particularly likely when the decision maker is pressed for time, distracted, or unable or unmotivated to engage in effortful systematic processing or when the cost of an incorrect decision is less than the cost of systematic processing (cf. chapter 5). Furthermore, heuristics may yield nearly optimal decisions in many circumstances and in the meantime save the decision maker a substantial amount of time, energy, and effort.

Research on heuristics is of rather recent origin and is only now being applied to the understanding of advertising effects. It appears, however, that when conditions are conducive to heuristic processing, ads with effective cues can persuade consumers to be more favorably disposed toward the advertised brands. Furthermore, such appeals can lead to relatively permanent changes in attitudes and buying patterns, particularly if subsequent experiences with the advertised brands are positive.

Two different heuristic theories have been postulated.

Heuristic Processing: Chaiken (1980) and others (Petty, Cacioppo, and Schumann 1983) have found that relatively permanent attitude changes can occur without systematic processing—without awareness, comprehension, and evaluation of arguments that support the advocated position or brand. All that may be necessary is that people attend to and make decisions on the basis of an ad's heuristic cues. Nonmessage or heuristic cues attempt to persuade, but they are difficult to justify logically. Typical of such cues are the expertise, attractiveness, or trustworthiness of the spokesperson for the advertised brand and whether the argument in favor of the brand appears to be detailed rather than brief.

An ad is processed heuristically if the viewer consciously or subconsciously attends to such a cue and applies a decision heuristic such as "buy what an expert says to buy" or "never buy a brand endorsed by a celebrity." If the ad is persuasive (as in the first example), the viewer acquires a new decision rule that modifies his or her purchase behaviors. When faced with having to choose from among several brands in the same product category, the person will remember and/or decide on the basis of the choice heuristic suggested in the ad. For example, he or she might purchase the advertised brand "because the expert said it was the best" rather than "because I've thought about it, weighed the alternatives, and it is the best."

Commercials use decision heuristics to facilitate the acceptance of their product claims. However, whereas claims that are processed systematically must be substantiated (i.e., logical, believable, and rational assertions about product attributes/benefits), claims that are processed heuristically need not be. The effectiveness of the heuristic cue, not the information itself, is what determines whether the message will be accepted. Thus ads that employ heuristic cues may use puffery or make unsubstantiated assertions that their products are the best or superior. Puffery, if effective, can promote brand sales without changing beliefs about the brand's specific attributes.

Ads are more likely to elicit heuristic processing if they do not contain detailed arguments conducive to systematic processing. Message recipients, however, may choose to implement a decision heuristic even if the ad provides substantive information. A heuristic strategy has the advantage of requiring significantly less cognitive effort. Although a systematic strategy is often a more reliable and accurate method for judging the validity of a claim, consumers may employ a decision heuristic whenever economy of effort predominates.

Low Involvement: The low involvement model is grounded in the hierarchy of effects tradition (Lavidge and Steiner 1961). Krugman (1965, 1977) proposed one of the first modifications of the original learning hierarchy, the low involvement or learning-behavior-attitude hierarchy.

The low involvement model predicts that advertising audiences are often oblivious to all but the simplest of heuristic cues, such as the brand's name, logo, or packaging. Again, the notion is that people rely on such cues when their involvement is low and economy of effort predominates. Often ads use emotion-laden stimuli such as color and imagery to increase the salience of the brand name, logo, and/or packaging (Ray and Batra 1983). Therefore, heuristic processing may also involve the evocation of an emotional reaction to the ad.

Processing of the heuristic brand identification cue restructures the contents of long-term memory. If awareness is conscious, a verbal representation of the brand is stored in memory, facilitating its recall. If awareness is subconscious, nonverbal material (pictures or images) is stored. In the latter case, recall may not be affected since it is a verbal response; however, recognition memory of the brand is strengthened.

Ads that solely evoke heuristic processing by brand identification cues do not influence brand beliefs or attitudes. They stimulate purchase behavior simply because consumers are more likely to remember the advertised brands or to recognize them on store shelves. People buy these brands on the basis of the simplest of choice heuristics: "I'll buy it because it looks familiar to me."

Affective Theories: There has been much discussion of affective advertising, although it is not at all clear what is meant by the term. *Preference, emotion, affect, image,* and *liking* are words that have been used interchangeably in the advertising literature. Unfortunately, despite this keen interest in emotion, appropriate research paradigms for the study of emotional routes to persuasion are seldom used. Instead, most advertising research has been conducted in laboratory settings and with print ads. Since these conditions encourage effortful processing, it has generally been found that research participants are persuaded by the systematic route. There is some evidence, however, that under the appropriate set of conditions, emotional appeals can also produce relatively permanent changes in attitudes and beliefs, even if they are not processed systematically. There are at least two different ways in which emotional appeals can influence attitudes and behaviors.

Classical Conditioning: It has been shown that more favorable attitudes toward objects can be produced by classical conditioning (Plummer and Hecker 1984; Gorn 1982; Mitchell and Olson 1981; Staats and Staats 1958). Ads that contain attractive and gratifying verbal and/or nonverbal stimuli (or unconditional stimuli, the UCS) and evoke pleasant affective responses (the unconditioned responses, or UCR) eventually create associations between the UCS and the advertised brands (the conditioned stimuli, or CS). Initially only the ads themselves will elicit affective reactions. However, if consumers are repeatedly exposed to these ads, eventually the advertised brands themselves will evoke the same pleasant feelings (the conditioned response or CR) or "empathy" (Plummer and Hecker 1984). In effect, consumers will have consciously or subconsciously acquired more favorable brand attitudes and corresponding behaviors even though their brand beliefs have not changed.

Many early studies by social psychologists presumably obtained evidence for the conditioning of attitudes (Staats and Staats 1958). However, the experimental paradigm that was employed has become highly controversial, making it a considerably less attractive research area.

One popular rival hypothesis is that systematic processing rather than classical conditioning occurs. If research participants notice that a brand is repeatedly paired either with a tasteful or a distasteful advertising stimulus, they may infer that the brand has either favorable or unfavorable attributes (Mitchell and Olson 1981). If such is the case, subsequent behavioral changes may be mediated by changes in beliefs rather than by classical conditioning. Unfortunately, this rival hypothesis is difficult to confirm or disconfirm since any observed changes in beliefs may have yet another origin. The very act of explaining one's attitudes or behaviors in an experiment may stimulate information processing (Staats 1969). For example, research participants are likely to construct beliefs, perhaps unintentionally, in order to rationalize attitudes that were initially conditioned (Gorn 1982).

Another criticism of studies that claim to have conditioned attitudes is that people recognize the experimental paradigm and pretend that their attitudes have changed because they wish to be cooperative (Page 1969). However, others have shown that demand characteristics are not necessary to persuade through classical conditioning (Zanna, Kiesler, and Pilkonis 1970; Berkowitz and Knurek 1969). Proponents also point out that classical conditioning may have occurred even if subjects noticed the UCS-CS pairings (Coleman and Gormezano 1979; Staats 1969). Simply being aware of the experimental contingencies does not preclude conditioning and may be inevitable if subjects are highly involved in the experiment.

Despite substantial historical controversy, the classical conditioning of attitudes remains a viable and useful theory for understanding the effects of advertising. One of the reasons classical conditioning has such potential is because it and low involvement theory are the only theories that explain how commercials use emotion to influence purchase behavior without necessarily implying that the products themselves will provide emotional, experiential, or psychosocial benefits.

In classical conditioning, the advertising stimuli that evoke an emotional response need not be logically related to the advertised brand in order for this emotion to transfer to the brand. All that is necessary is that the evocative stimuli and the advertised brand be temporally related, as they inevitably will be in a thirty-second commercial. For example, an ad that is entertaining or heartwarming presumably can enhance more favorable brand attitudes by classical conditioning even if there is no indication that use of the brand itself will be entertaining or heartwarming. Many ads that use emotion apparently do so simply to create a good feeling about the brand regardless of whether one of the brand's most salient benefits is emotional.

Vicarious Learning: Vicarious learning or modeling describes a process whereby people acquire new (by observational learning), stronger (by response facilitation), or weaker (by inhibition) attitudes and corresponding behaviors through observation rather than through direct experience or operant conditioning (Petty and Cacioppo 1981; Nord and Peter 1980; Bandura 1969). People are persuaded because they vicariously experience the actions of a model and the consequences of these actions and expect that they will be rewarded or punished in a similar manner.

In advertising, vicarious learning is generally produced through the following process: Viewers vicariously experience the emotional reaction of a model who is rewarded (or punished), associate the reward (or punishment) with use (or disuse) of the advertised brand, and thereby acquire more favorable brand attitudes and behaviors. If there is conscious awareness of the brand's positive effects, attitude change may be mediated by changes in brand beliefs. If learning is subconscious, persuasion is mediated solely by a positive (or negative) emotional response rather than by changes in beliefs.

It is important to note that in order for vicarious or observational learning to occur, the emotional response evoked by the ad must be brand related. That is, the viewer's emotional reaction must be in response to his or her observation that the model has derived an experiential benefit from the advertised brand. Correspondingly brand attitudes are more favorable after exposure to the ad because the ad has effectively demonstrated the brand's experiential benefits. In contrast, classical conditioning can occur even if the emotion that is evoked does not exemplify such benefits.

Commercials frequently use modeling to demonstrate their products' experiential, social, or psychological benefits. Admittedly, some commercials demonstrate product uses or their objective, functional benefits. However, the theory stipulates that learning must be mediated by an emotional response. Although initially only the model experiences the pain- or pleasure-producing stimulation, "his affective expressions, in turn, serve as the arousal stimuli for the observer" (Bandura 1969, p. 167). It is improbable that people will vicariously experience a model's emotion simply by observing that a product provides functional benefits such as convenience or economy. Hence vicarious learning is also improbable in such situations.

Multidimensionality: Empirical Foundations

Prior Research

Doubts about the adequacy of a simple, undimensional classification of ads (rational versus emotional) initially stemmed from problems encountered in previous research. Stewart and Furse (1986) made an attempt to classify more than a thousand television commercials for consumer packaged goods into one of three categories: rational, emotional, or mixed appeals. Commercials were classified by four raters according to the following operational definitions:

> A fairly straight-forward presentation of the product's attributes and claims is a rational appeal. An emotional appeal does not appeal to reason, but appeals to feelings. A balanced or mixed appeal contains both rational and emotional elements.

It was subsequently determined that this classification scheme had three major shortcomings. First, it was not particularly informative because most of the ads (64 percent) fell into the same rather poorly understood category of mixed or balanced appeals. Second, interrater reliability was relatively low. Twenty-one percent (219) of the ads were not reliably classified. Finally, a cross-tabulation was done in which type of appeal was crossed with each of the 156 message and executional variables that had been coded in the initial study. The results of this analysis further substantiated that most ads contain a heterogeneous set of stimulus elements. Many of the ads classified as primarily emotional appeals explicitly described brand benefits. And many of the ads categorized as "primarily rational appeals" contained emotion-laden stimuli and had emotional overtones. (See appendix 4A.)

Methodology of Present Study

Our study was undertaken to explore why the classification of ads as rational, mixed, or emotional was so problematic and to develop a more appropriate classification scheme. The same data set was reanalyzed, with one minor modification: ads that were not reliably classified were excluded.

Analysis of these data proceeded as follows: First, the cross-tabulation results were used to determine which of the 156 message and executional variables best discriminated among rational, mixed, and emotional appeals. Approximately 70 variables were identified. (These variables are listed in appendix 4A.) Second, a factor analysis was employed to reduce the redundancy in these 70 variables. This factor analysis produced 25 content factors accounting for 62 percent of the variance in the data. Finally and most importantly, a discriminant analysis was conducted to test the proposition that more than one dimension was required to differentiate between these three types of appeals. That is, the matrix of factor scores by cases (ads) was analyzed to identify which dimension or dimensions best discriminated the rational, mixed, and emotional appeals from one another.

Hypotheses

It was hypothesized that the discriminant analysis would yield two underlying or latent dimensions rather than just one. Specifically it was predicted that cognition and emotion would emerge as two distinct and bipolar dimensions rather than as opposite poles of the same dimension. The cognitive or systematic dimension would have a positive pole indicating high information content conducive to systematic processing and a negative pole indicating such low information content that viewers would be encouraged to attend to heuristic cues rather than to engage in systematic processing. Correspondingly, the experiential or affective dimension would have a positive pole indicating the presence of emotionally charged verbal and nonverbal stimuli capable of evoking an emotional response and a negative pole indicating the absence of emotion-laden stimuli.

It was hypothesized that rational appeals would, on average, be positioned in the high systematic–low affective quadrant. Emotional appeals would, on average, be positioned in the high affective–low systematic quadrant. Balanced ads would be positioned in one of the other two quadrants.

Discriminant analysis was used because the null hypothesis of only one underlying dimension (a rational-emotional continuum) could be submitted to a test of statistical significance. Thus the null hypothesis was falsifiable. In contrast, other data reduction techniques such as cluster analysis offer no test of the statistical significance of the resulting dimensions.

It was postulated that a two-dimensional solution would be required in order to discriminate ads designed to persuade viewers by the heuristic route.

Admittedly, coders had not been given the opportunity to classify ads with salient heuristic cues as heuristic appeals per se. At the time these ads were coded, the traditional classification scheme was still considered sufficient. As a result, coders had the option of labeling "heuristic appeals" either as "primarily rational," "primarily emotional," or "mixed." Of these three categories, "mixed" was clearly the most open-ended, as well as the most appropriate for heuristic appeals. Therefore, it was assumed that commercials that had evoked heuristic processing had been classified as mixed or balanced appeals by default.

In one-dimensional space, commercial appeals must be positioned along a continuum ranging from highly rational to highly emotional. In reference to such a continuum, rational ads can be readily distinguished from emotional ads. Rational or systematic appeals on average will be positioned along the high systematic–low affective pole. Emotional or affective appeals on average will be positioned along the high affective–low systematic pole. In contrast, it is not possible to classify the heuristic appeals accurately since they are characterized by low systematic (or heuristic) processing and affective processing ranging from from high to low. Obviously, neither of the two poles is an appropriate location. Nor is the origin, since the origin of this unidimensional space corresponds to moderate systematic and moderate affective processing. Thus, a two-dimensional space is required to discriminate heuristic appeals accurately.

Results

Table 4–3 summarizes the results of the discriminant analysis. As predicted, two discriminant functions were statistically significant: a high systematic–low systematic (or heuristic) processing dimension and an experiential or emotional benefits dimension. The systematic processing dimension explained 77 percent of the between-groups variance. The experiential or emotional benefits dimension explained 23 percent of this variance. The two functions accurately classified 80 percent of the rational appeals, 75 percent of the mixed appeals, and 64 percent of the emotional appeals.

Rational Systematic Appeals: The classification of rational appeals by the two discriminant functions was consistent with initial hypotheses (see figures 4–1 and 4–2 and appendix 4B). Rational ads on average received large positive scores on the systematic processing dimension (group centroid = 1.45) and negative scores on the emotional benefits dimension (group centroid = −.33). Furthermore, the description of a rational appeal that emerged conformed to its stimulus-based definition, which derives from the learning, cognitive response, and dissonance theories of persuasion. These commercials contained stimuli that would be likely to stimulate systematic processing rather than heuristic or affective processing. Specifically, these ads tended to emphasize

Table 4–3
Discriminant Analysis of the Factors

Canonical Discriminant Functions Summary Table

Function	*Eigenvalue*	*Percent of Variance Explained*	*Cumulative Percent*	*Canonical Correlation*	*After Function*	*Wilks' Lambda*	*Chi-squared*	*Degrees of Freedom*	*Significance*
1	0.99	76.9%	76.9%	0.71	0	0.39	780.2	48	0.00001
2	0.30	23.1	100.0	0.48	1	0.77	214.5	23	0.00001

Classification Results

		Predicted Group Membership		
Actual Group	*Number of Ads*	*Rational*	*Mixed*	*Emotional*
Rational	238	191 (80.3%)	46 (19.3%)	1 (0.4%)
Mixed	536	75 (14.0%)	404 (75.4%)	57 (10.6%)
Emotional	63	0 (0.0%)	23 (36.5%)	40 (63.5%)
	837			

Note: Percentage of ''grouped'' cases correctly classified: 76.0.

The ad describes objective product attributes and/or benefits, with the message usually delivered by a user or product champion. Included are demonstrations of the product in use and of the results of using the product.

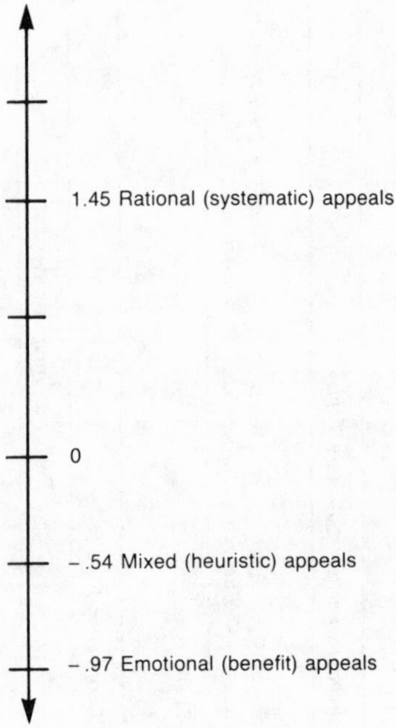

The ad offers limited objective product information. It uses heuristics such as puffery, product reminder messages (sometimes involving emotion-laden stimuli), and the development of brand empathy.

Figure 4–1. Systematic-Heuristic Processing Dimension: Discriminant Function 1

heuristic or affective processing. Specifically, these ads tended to emphasize product components, contents, or ingredients. They also generally described and/or demonstrated the tangible or objective benefits or product usage but not the emotional benefits. Finally, they typically featured product champions, usually actors posing as ordinary consumers. The latter finding was not expected but is completely logical. Rational appeals emphasize objective or tangible product benefits, and the most obvious way to demonstrate or prove that brand X provides benefit Y is to show an "average consumer" (such as

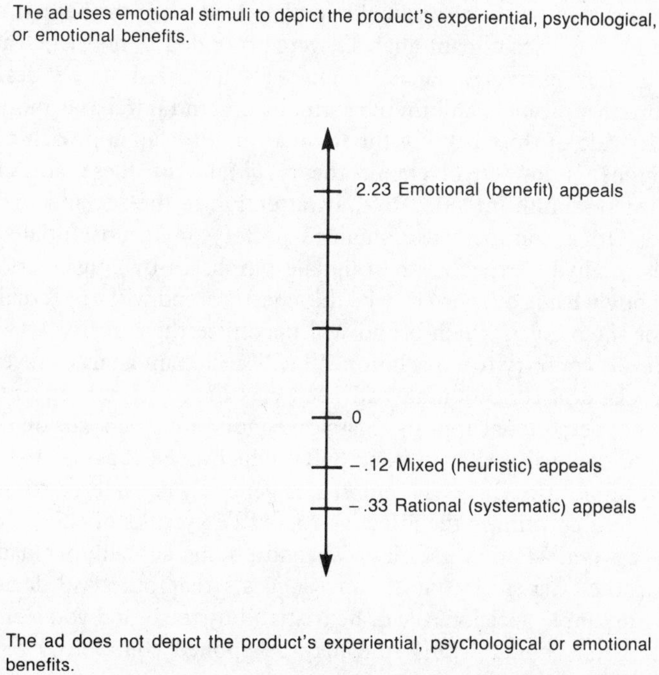

Figure 4–2. Emotional Benefits Dimension: Discriminant Function 2

a housewife) who uses brand X (a no-wax floor cleaner) and thereby obtains benefit Y (a shinier floor).

It would have been highly problematic if these results had not been obtained. Coders were specifically instructed to classify an ad as a rational appeal if it "contained a fairly straightforward presentation of the product's attributes and claims (i.e., benefits)." These data simply substantiate that coders followed the instructions.

Balanced (Heuristic) Appeals: The classification of balanced appeals by the two discriminant functions was fairly consistent with initial hypotheses. (Again see figures 4–1 and 4–2 and appendix 4B). As expected, balanced appeals on average received large negative scores on the systematic processing dimension, indicating that they evoked heuristic processing (group/centroid = –.54), and low scores (close to zero) on the emotional benefits dimension (group centroid = –.12). Thus, as expected, coders apparently classified heuristic appeals as "balanced appeals" because no more appropriate label was made available to them.

Also consistent with the original hypotheses, some of the heuristic appeals identified by the discriminant analysis were grounded in heuristic theories of persuasion. For example, some commercials appeared to be designed to increase brand awareness and thereby stimulate brand purchases motivated by the popular rule of thumb "buy the familiar brand," an approach consistent with Krugman's low involvement theory. Many of these ads contained emotion-laden stimuli intended to draw attention to the ad, and therefore to the brand. Other commercials contained puffery or unsubstantiated claims. These ads might be expected to stimulate purchases by consumers who are willing to buy what is purported to be the "best" brand without actually determining for themselves which brand will maximize their utility.

However, contrary to expectations, the discriminant analysis revealed that ads using classical conditioning had been classified as balanced or heuristic appeals, not as emotional appeals. Classical conditioning depends on the evocation of an emotional response (the UCR), which is later associated with the advertised brand (the CR). Therefore, it is generally considered to be a mode of persuasion that utilizes the affective route. The results of this study, however, suggest that ads that use classical conditioning actually persuade by the heuristic route. Classical conditioning suggests that purchase decisions are based on the simple decision rule or heuristic "buy the brand you feel empathy toward or good about." This rule may be applied consciously or subconsciously.

Some types of persuasion by the heuristic route involve both heuristic and affective processing. What, then, is the difference between these heuristic appeals and emotional benefit appeals? *Affect-laden heuristic appeals* evoke an emotional reaction *to the commercial itself rather than to the advertised brand.* In classical conditioning, this emotion eventually becomes associated with the advertised brand but only after repeated pairings of the ad and the brand. According to low-involvement theory, the emotion that is evoked functions solely to get viewers to pay attention to the commercial and will never become associated with the advertised brand. In contrast, *emotional benefit appeals* elicit emotional responses that are *logically related to the advertised brands.* In fact, the emotions evoked exemplify the advertised brands' psychological, experiential, or emotional benefits. Hence heuristic and emotional benefit appeals use emotion in two very different ways.

Experiential or Emotional Benefit Appeals: As expected, ads classified as emotional appeals on average received very large positive scores on the experiential or emotional benefits dimension (group centroid = 2.23) and large negative scores on the systematic processing dimension (group centroid = −.97). (Refer to figures 4–1 and 4–2 and appendix 4B).

It had been anticipated that ads classified as emotional appeals would employ either classical conditioning or observational learning. Instead it was found that only observational learning was used. Specifically, these commercials featured role models who were shown to obtain emotional, psychological, or experiential (taste, feel, smell, and so on) benefits from using the advertised brands. The emotional benefits portrayed included greater excitement and variety in life, enhanced sex appeal, and an improved self-image. Viewers of these commercials were expected to experience vicariously the emotional (or experiential) benefits derived by the role models, "learn" that the advertised brands could provide these benefits, and subsequently purchase the brands to obtain these benefits.

According to the results of this study, it is rather uncommon for an advertiser of consumer packaged goods to promote a brand's experiential or emotional benefits by observational learning, particularly if the brand has a tangible and verifiable attribute or benefit that makes it superior to that of a competitor (such as "more pain relief"). For example, of the 837 ads in the data set, only 63 were classified as primarily emotional appeals. Of these, only 40 were correctly classified by the discriminant analysis; the other 23 were incorrectly classified as mixed appeals.

Conclusions and Recommendations

Summary of Findings

There is considerable evidence that it is not possible to classify commercials as either rational or emotional since most commercials contain heterogeneous or mixed stimuli. A more appropriate classification scheme must be adopted. This chapter describes one such scheme. It is proposed that in order to meaningfully categorize and then evaluate the effectiveness of a commercial (in terms of improving brand attitudes, purchase intentions, and sales), the stimuli it contains and the responses it evokes must be classified along two dimensions: a systematic-heuristic dimension and an emotional (or experiential) benefits dimension. That is, based on the type of cognitive processing it evokes, an ad should be classified along a continuum ranging from primarily systematic appeals to primarily heuristic appeals. Based on the extent to which it elicits a vicarious experience of the brand's emotional benefits, an ad should also be classified along a continuum ranging from primarily experiential or emotional benefit appeals to appeals that do not portray such benefits.

Finally, an ad should be categorized using a two-stage process, first based on the stimuli it contains and then based on the proximal (or mediating) responses it evokes. If the stimuli do not produce the expected proximal response, the ad must be reclassified. For example, if an ad that is classified as primarily a heuristic appeal (because it contains a dominant heuristic cue) is not processed heuristically, it should be reclassified based on the stimuli to which the majority of viewers are actually attending. In other words, a manipulation check should be done to verify what type of ad elicited the observed outcome or distal response (attitude, intention, and/or behavior). Otherwise it will not be possible to determine causality—that is, to rule out other rival hypotheses regarding why the ad produced the observed distal effect.

Purely systematic appeals are what have in the past been referred to as rational appeals. It is recommended that these commercials be labeled systematic instead of rational to avoid implying that other types of commercials encourage irrational behavior. Systematic appeals present logical arguments in favor of the advertised brand by describing objective brand attributes and benefits. Persuasion occurs by the systematic route; affective processing is minimal. The learning theories, cognitive response theories, and dissonance theory offer different but related explanations of how these appeals influence attitudes and purchase behaviors. (Cacioppo and Petty in chapter 5 refer to these as non-affect-laden appeals processed by the central route.)

Purely heuristic appeals are targeted at consumers who do not have the time, skill, or motivation to evaluate the attributes and benefits of their various choice alternatives. Persuasion occurs by the heuristic route; systematic processing is minimal. Some types of heuristic appeals also evoke an emotional response, but this emotion is not directly related to the advertised brand. The emotion is a response to the commercial as a whole. Classical conditioning involves both heuristic and affective processing, while appeals grounded in low involvement theory may or may not involve both. Finally, the traditional heuristic theory of persuasion describes ads that probably evoke only heuristic processing. (Cacioppo and Petty in chapter 5 concur that persuasion by the heuristic route can be promoted by either affect-laden or non-affect-laden peripheral cues, as do Chaiken and Stangor 1987.)

Purely experiential or emotional benefit appeals are grounded primarily in observational learning principles. These commercials can produce relatively permanent changes in attitudes and/or behaviors, without necessarily requiring consumers to engage in effortful systematic processing. Emotional or experiential benefit appeals evoke emotional responses to the advertised brands, creating emotional states that exemplify the brand's emotional, psychological, or experiential benefits. It is expected that consumers will purchase the advertised brands to obtain these benefits. An experiential or emotional benefit appeal seemingly can be persuasive no matter what type of cognitive processing it evokes. (However, Cacioppo and Petty in chapter 5 apparently assume that affect-laden appeals of this type are processed solely by the central or systematic route.)

Future Research Implications

These empirical findings are consistent with the hypotheses of Cacioppo and Petty (chapter 5), which suggest that the benefits portrayed in an ad can be objective (functional) or emotional (experiential) and that the heuristics used may or may not be affect laden. That is, both this chapter and chapter 5 suggest that there are two (rather than one) relevant dimensions along which ads differ: a systematic-heuristic processing dimension and an affective-nonaffective dimension. Further research is still needed to substantiate this proposition. In particular, although the methodology employed in this study precluded their identification, other relevant dimensions may also exist. For example, it may be more appropriate to treat the various types of heuristic appeals or the emotional versus experiential benefit appeals as qualitatively different.

In the meantime, it is probably inadvisable for advertisers and advertising researchers to continue trying to determine the relative effectiveness of rational versus emotional appeals. Instead two more relevant questions must be addressed:

1. Under what circumstances are ads that evoke systematic processing more or less persuasive than ads that evoke heuristic processing? Under what circumstances are ads that evoke affective processing more or less effective than ads that do not? That is, how does the effectiveness of an appeal interact with variables such as the broadcast environment, the broadcast medium, the product category, the brand, and the viewers' knowledge of and interest in the brand?
2. Given that the circumstances are conducive to a particular type of appeal, which of the specific executional or message elements characterizing this type of appeal are most effective?

In order to investigate these issues through research, it will be necessary to identify or create prototypical ads containing rational or systematic appeals, affect-laden heuristic appeals, non-affect-laden heuristic appeals, and experiential or emotional benefit appeals. This can best be done by employing theory-based operational definitions such as those outlined in tables 4-1 and 4-2. Advertising appeals should be categorized according to the theories of persuasion in which they are grounded. The advantage of this approach is that theories provide both stimulus-based and proximal response-based operational definitions, and often both types of definitions must be used.

If a researcher is interested in studying the effectiveness of a particular type of advertising appeal, exposing research participants to test ads that contain the appropriate stimuli is probably not going to be sufficient. The problem is that most ads are heterogeneous or mixed stimuli rather than pure types. As a result, the researcher will also need to simulate an appropriate exposure environment, one conducive to the type of processing the test ad is expected to elicit. It may be difficult to construct this environment, especially one conducive to heuristic and/or affective processing rather than purely systematic processing (Chaiken 1985). If this is the case, the researcher must verify that the test ads actually evoked in viewers the proximal responses that were anticipated. Thus manipulation checks are indispensable in this field of research. Only through appropriate manipulation checks is it possible to ascertain the process or causal link that leads from stimulus exposure to more distal responses (such as attitudes, intentions, and behaviors).

It is likely that entirely new research paradigms are needed in order to study the persuasiveness of heuristic and experiential or emotional benefit appeals (Chaiken 1985). The research paradigm that is currently most widely used involves showing people print ads in a laboratory setting and measuring their cognitive responses. Under these circumstances, the demand characteristics are such that ads will almost inevitably be processed systematically and little affect is likely to be evoked. This probably explains why systematic theories of persuasion have received the most empirical support (Wright 1980).

It appears that an appropriate exposure environment for studying heuristic and affective appeals must have the following characteristics: the social and/or broadcast environment must be distracting and/or the viewer must not be interested in and/or motivated to evaluate systematically the brand's objective or functional benefits (Wright 1981). In fact, the most valid research paradigm for studying persuasion by means of the heuristic or affective route is likely to be a simulation of the natural broadcast (television or radio) viewing environment. It is suspected that if appropriate research methodologies are developed, it will be determined that many broadcast ads persuade by evoking heuristic and/or affective processing rather than by stimulating purely systematic processing.

References

Agres, Stuart J., and Bernstein, Morty. 1984. "Cognitive and Emotional Elements of Persuasion." In David W. Stewart, ed., *Proceedings of the Division of Consumer Psychology*, pp. 1–2. APA 1984 Annual Convention, Toronto, Canada.

Bandura, A. 1969. *Principles of Behavior Modification*. New York: Holt, Rinehart, and Winston.

Berkowitz, L., and Knurek, L.A. 1969. "Label-mediated Hostility Generalization." *Journal of Personality and Social Psychology* 13:200–206.

Chaiken, Shelly. 1980. "Heuristic versus Systematic Information Processing and the Use of Source versus Message Cues in Persuasion." *Journal of Personality and Social Psychology* 39:752–766.

———. 1985. Personal communication.

Chaiken, Shelly, and Stangor, Charles. 1987. "Attitudes and Attitude Change." In *Annual Review of Psychology* 38:575–630. Palo Alto, Calif.: Annual Reviews.

Cacioppo, John, and Petty, Richard. 1988. "The Elaboration Likelihood Model: The Role of Affect and Affect-Laden Information Processing in Persuasion." In Alice Tybout and Pat Cafferata, eds., *Affective and Cognitive Responses to Advertising*. Lexington, Mass.: Lexington Books.

Choi, Young, and Thorson, Esther. 1983. "Memory for Factual, Emotional, and Balanced Ads under Two Instructional Sets." In D.W. Jugenheimer, ed., *Proceedings of the 1983 American Academy of Advertising,* Lawrence, Kansas, pp. 160–164.

Coleman, S.R., and Gormezano, I. 1979. "Classical Conditioning and the 'Law of Effect': Historical and Empirical Assessment," *Behaviorism* 7:1–33.

Copeland, Melvin T. 1924. *Principles of Merchandising.* New York: A.W. Shew Co.

Festinger, L. 1957. *A Theory of Cognitive Dissonance.* Stanford: Stanford University Press.

Fishbein, M. 1963. "An Investigation of the Relationships between Beliefs about an Object and Attitude toward the Object." *Human Relations* 16:233–240.

Fishbein, M., and Ajzen, I. 1975. *Belief, Attitude, Intention, and Behavior.* Reading, Mass.: Addison-Wesley.

Golden, Linda L., and Johnson, Karen A. 1983. "The Impact of Sensory Preference and Thinking versus Feeling Appeals on Advertising Effectiveness." In A. Tybout and R. Bagozzi, eds., *Advances in Consumer Research,* vol. 10. Ann Arbor: Association of Consumer Research.

Gorn, Gerald J. 1982. "The Effects of Music on Choice Behavior: A Classical Conditioning Approach." *Journal of Marketing* 46:91–101.

Hovland, C.I.; Janis, I.L.; and Kelly, J.J. 1953. *Communication and Persuasion.* New Haven: Yale University Press.

Kisielius, Jolita. 1982. "The Role of Memory in Understanding Advertising Media Effectiveness: The Effect of Imagery on Consumer Decision Making." In A. Mitchell, ed., *Advances in Consumer Research,* vol. 9. Ann Arbor: Association for Consumer Research.

Krugman, Herbert E. 1977. "Memory without Recall, Exposure without Perception." *Journal of Advertising Research* 17:7–12.

———. 1965. "The Impact of Television Advertising: Learning without Involvement." *Public Opinion Quarterly* 29:349–356.

Lavidge, Robert J., and Steiner, Gary A. 1961. "A Model for Predictive Measurements of Advertising Effectiveness." *Journal of Marketing* 25:53–62.

McGuire, W.J. 1972. "Attitude Change: The Information Processing Paradigm." In C.C. McClintock, ed., *Experimental Social Psychology.* New York: Holt, Rinehart and Winston.

Middlestadt, Susan, and Fishbein, Martin. 1987. "Non-Cognitive Effects on Attitude Formation and Change: Fact or Artifact?" Paper presented to the Sixth Annual Advertising and Consumer Psychology Conference, Chicago.

Mitchell, Andrew A., and Olson, Jerry C. 1981. "Are Product Attribute Beliefs the Only Mediator of Advertising Effects on Brand Attitude?" *Journal of Marketing Research* 18:318–332.

Nord, Walter R., and Peter, Paul J. 1980. "A Behavior Modification Perspective on Marketing." *Journal of Marketing* 44:36–47.

Olson, Jerry C.; Toy, Daniel R.; and Dover, Philip A. 1982. "Do Cognitive Responses Mediate the Effects of Advertising Content on Cognitive Structure?" *Journal of Consumer Research* 9:245–262.

Page, M.M. 1969. "Social Psychology of a Classical Conditioning of Attitudes Experiment." *Journal of Personality and Social Psychology* 11:177–186.

Paivio, Alan. 1978. "A Duel Coding Approach to Perception and Cognition." In I. Pick and E. Saltzman, eds. *Modes of Perceiving and Processing Information.* Hillsdale, N.J.: Erlbaum Assoc.

Peterson, R.A.; Hoyer, W.D.; and Wilson, W.R. 1987. *The Role of Affect in Consumer Behavior: Emerging Theories and Applications.* Lexington, Mass.: Lexington Books.

Petty, Richard E. 1981. "The Role of Cognitive Responses in Attitude Change Processes." In Richard E. Petty, Thomas M. Ostrom, and Timothy C. Brock, eds., *Cognitive Responses in Persuasion.* Hillsdale, N.J.: Erlbaum Associates.

Petty, Richard E., and Cacioppo, John T. 1981. *Attitudes and Persuasion: Classical and Contemporary Approaches.* Dubuque, Iowa: William C. Brown Company.

Petty, Richard E.; Cacioppo, John T.; and Schumann, David. 1983. "Central and Peripheral Routes to Advertising Effectiveness: The Moderating Role of Involvement." *Journal of Consumer Research* (September): 135–146.

Plummer, Joseph T., and Hecker, Sidney. 1984. "Consumer Empathy and Advertising." In David W. Stewart, ed., *Proceedings of the Division of Consumer Psychology*, pp. 3–4. APA 1984 Annual Convention, Toronto, Canada.

Ray, Michael L. 1982. *Advertising and Communication Management.* Englewood Cliffs, N.J.: Prentice-Hall.

Ray, Michael L., and Batra, Rajeev. 1983. "Emotion and Persuasion in Advertising: What We Do and Don't Know about Affect." In A. Tybout and R. Bagozzi, eds., *Advances in Consumer Research,* vol. 10, pp. 543–548. Ann Arbor: Association for Consumer Research.

Rossiter, John R., and Percy, Larry. 1980. "Attitude Change Through Visual Imagery in Advertising." *Journal of Advertising* 9:10–17.

Runyon, Kenneth, and Stewart, David W. 1987. *Consumer Behavior and the Practice of Marketing.* 3d ed. Columbus, Ohio: Charles E. Merrill Publishing Co.

Sentis, Keith P. 1984. "Targeting Advertisements to the Emotional Self." In David W. Stewart, ed., *Proceedings of the Division of Consumer Psychology,* pp. 9–10. APA 1984 Annual Convention, Toronto, Canada.

Staats, Arthur W. 1969. "Experimental Demand Characteristics and the Classical Conditioning of Attitudes." *Journal of Personality and Social Psychology* 11:187–192.

Staats, Arthur W., and Staats, Carolyn K. 1958. "Attitudes Established by Classical Conditioning." *Journal of Abnormal and Social Psychology* 57:37–40.

Stewart, David W., and Furse, David H. 1986. *Effective Television Advertising: A Study of 1,000 Commercials.* Lexington, Mass.: Lexington Books.

Stout, Patricia, and Leckenby, John D. 1984. "The Rediscovery of Emotional Response in Copy Research." Paper presented to the Annual Conference, American Academy of Advertising, Denver.

Thorson, Esther, and Friestad, Marian. 1984. "Emotion and the Recall of Television Commercials." In David W. Stewart, ed., *Proceedings of the Division of Consumer Psychology,* pp. 7–8. APA 1984 Annual Convention, Toronto, Canada.

Wright, Peter. 1981. "Cognitive Responses to Mass Media Advocacy." In Richard E. Petty, Thomas M. Ostrom, and Timothy C. Brock, eds., *Cognitive Responses in Persuasion.* Hillsdale, N.J.: Erlbaum Associates.

Zanna, M.P.: Kiesler, C.A.; and Pilkonis, P.A. 1970. "Positive and Negative Attitudinal Affect Established by Classical Conditioning." *Journal of Personality and Social Psychology* 14:321–328.

Zielske, Hubert A. 1982. "Does Day-after Recall Penalize 'Feeling' Ads?" *Journal of Advertising Research* 22:19–24.

Appendix 4A: Results of the Cross-Tabulation Analysis

	Classification		
Variables	*Rational*	*Mixed*	*Emotional*
Information content			
Quality		+	
Economy/savings	+		
Sensory		+	+
Aesthetic		+	+
Components/ingredients	+		
Availability		+	+
Safety	+		
Nutrition/health	+		
Company image/reputation			+
Results of using	+		
Superiority		+	
New product or feature	+		
Use occasion			+
Brand and product identification			
Visual brand sign-off	+		
Auditory brand sign-off	+		
Congruence of commercial elements			
Brand name reinforces product benefits		+	+
No setting	+		
Visual devices			
Scenic beauty			+
Beauty of principal character			+
Graphic displays	+		
Visual tagline	+		+
Auditory devices			
Memorable rhyme/mnemonic			+
Promises, appeals, or selling propositions			
Attributes/ingredients	+		
Product performance/benefits	+		
Psychological benefits			+
Product reminder		+	+

A plus sign (+) indicates that ads classified as such were significantly more likely to contain this variable.

Variables	*Classification*		
	Rational	*Mixed*	*Emotional*
Psychological appeals:			
Sex appeal			+
Safety appeal	+		
Enjoyment of life			+
Social approval			+
Self-esteem		+	+
Excitement/variety			+
Emotional tones			
Cute/Adorable		+	+
Warm/Caring		+	+
Modern/contemporary		+	
Technical/futuristic	+		
Conservative/traditional	+		
Old-fashioned/nostalgic			+
Happy/fun loving			+
Somber/serious	+		
Relaxed/comfortable		+	+
Glamorous			+
Humorous			+
Comparisons			
Direct comparison	+		
Indirect comparison	+		
Unsubstantiated claim		+	
Commercial structures			
Opening surprise/suspense		+	+
Commercial format			
Slice of life			+
Testimonial of user	+		
Product demonstration			+
Demonstration of results	+		
Comedy/satire			+
Animation/cartoons		+	
Mood or image dominant		+	+
Problem and solution	+		
Music and dancing			
Music present		+	+
Music carries message			+
Music creates mood			+
Continuing music theme			+

Variables	*Classification* *Rational*	*Mixed*	*Emotional*
Commercial characters			
Principal character is a minority			+
Actor plays an ordinary person	+		
An animal is the primary character		+	+
No principal character	+		
Background cast		+	+
Animal in minor role			+
Voice over announcer			+
On camera announcer	+		
Setting			
Outdoor setting			+
No setting	+		
Commercial approach			
Negative appeal	+		
Mixed appeal		+	
Positive appeal	+		+
Brand differentiating			
Message	+		
Timing and counting items			
Length of ad		+	
Time until brand name identification	+		
Number times brand name/logo is shown		+	
Time package on screen	+		
Number on-screen characters			+
Other variables			
Total information	+		
Total number of psychological appeals			+
Total number of emotional tones			+

Appendix 4B: The Discriminant Functions

Factors Correlated with Discriminant Function I

Factor	Correlation between Factor I and Function	Correlation between Factor II and Function	Variable Description	Factor Loading	Ads Containing Variable
Uses surprise and puffery and not ordinary people	−.54	−.12	Does not have a conservative, traditional tone	−.73	(20%)
			Uses opening surprise/suspense	.72	77
			Has a modern, contemporary tone	.58	25
			Product declared best without specifying criterion (puffery)	.50	58
			Brand name provides product information	.43	22
			Actor does not play role of an ordinary person	−.40	(45)
			Product reminder is the ad's primary objective	.34	26
			Does not show testimonial by product user	−.31	(14)
Evokes warmth and comfort; uses puffery	−.33	.07	Has a relaxed, comfortable tone	.68	18
			Attempts to create a desire for the product by appealing to the viewer's emotional/sensory involvement in the ad	.58	31
			Has a warm, caring tone	.52	5

			Product declared best without specifying criterion (puffery)	.27	58
Describes components, ingredients	+.22	.02	Provides information on components, contents, or ingredients	84	60
			A main focus is on how the product is made or its ingredients	.81	55
			Provides information on nutritional or health-related characteristics	.65	28
Uses sign-offs	+.17	.22	The brand name is stated as the ad ends	.76	71
			The brand name or package is visible as the ad ends	.71	95
Describes results or benefits	+.15	−.22	Describes results of using the product	.76	55
			Results of using the product are demonstrated	.75	24
			A main focus is on product performance or its benefits	.70	68
			Uses a problem-solution format	.65	18
			Does not describe a sensory experience associated with the product	−.48	(49)
			A main focus is not about enjoying life	−.32	(10)
			Product reminder is not the ad's primary objective	−.30	(26)

Appendix 4B (Continued)

Factor	*Correlation between Factor I and Function*	*Correlation between Factor II and Function*	*Variable Description*	*Factor Loading*	*Ads Containing Variable*
Shows an ordinary person	+.15	.04	An animal is not the principal character	−.65	(8)
			The ad is not animated	−.61	(7)
			The principal actor plays the role of an ordinary person	.46	45
			Entire audio message is delivered by on-camera characters	.40	7
			Does not have a cute or adorable tone	−.39	(8)
Uses large cast; is outdoors	−.14	.02	There is a background cast	.82	27
			There are many on-screen characters	.81	
			The ad is set outdoors	.48	23
			Portrays a conceivable real-life situation	.27	32
Stresses safety	+.14	.03	A main focus is on being free from physical danger	.79	1
			Provides information concerning the product's safety	.76	4
			The principal character is a racial or ethnic minority	.29	1

Factors Correlated with Discriminant Function II					
Uses music, glamour, and high tech to create excitement	+.35	.11	Uses background music to create a mood or emotion	.74	2
			Has a technological, futuristic tone	.55	2
			Has a glamorous tone	.31	1
			Uses music	.28	42
			A main focus is on adding excitement and variety to life	.23	1
Focuses on excitement and enjoyment	+.30	.05	A main focus is on adding excitement and variety to life	.57	1
			Refers to the company's image/reputation	.48	3
			A main focus is about enjoying life	.43	10
			The principal character is not a racial or ethnic minority	−.36	(1)
			The brand name provides product information	.31	22
Focuses on sex appeal	+.30	.09	Suggests an appropriate use occasion for the product	.76	1
			A main focus is one's sex appeal	.62	1
			A main focus is the psychological or subjective benefits of product ownership	.26	1
			Has a warm and caring tone	.25	5

Appendix 4B (Continued)

Factor	*Correlation between Factor I and Function*	*Correlation between Factor II and Function*	*Variable Description*	*Factor Loading*	*Ads Containing Variable*
Uses cute comedy	+.27	.01	Ad is written to be funny; uses comedy or satire	.78	2
			Has a humorous tone	.73	5
			Has a cute, adorable tone	.39	8
Uses a continuing music theme and slogan	+.23	−.01	Uses a recognized continuing music theme	.72	2
			Uses a nonmusical rhyme, slogan, or other memory device	.67	8
			Lyrics of the music carry product message	.57	12
			Refers to the company's image/reputation	.36	3
			Has a happy, fun-loving tone	.36	5
			Uses music	.28	42
Uses sign-offs	+.22	.17	See factors correlated with function I		
Describes results/benefits	−.22	.15	See factors correlated with function I		
Describes sensory benefits	+.20	−.10	Demonstrates the product in use and/or product benefit	.71	60
			Describes a sensory experience associated with the product	.51	49

			A main focus is about enjoying life	.39	10
			Makes a comparison but does not name the competitor	−.44	(11)
			Does not explicitly state a unique product benefit	−.34	(44)
			Uses music	.32	42
Makes direct, lighthearted comparison	+.20	.05	Visually presents new information at the end	.73	1
			Makes a comparison and names competitor	.35	11
			Has a happy, fun-loving tone	.31	5
			Does not show a user testimonial	−.27	(14)
Shows beauty of outdoors	+.18	−.00	Ad shows scenes of natural beauty	.70	2
			Animals are used in minor roles	.62	2
			The ad is set outdoors	.23	23
			Has a warm, caring tone	.26	5
Focuses on self-image	+.17	−.07	A main focus is on improving one's self-image	.68	3
			A main focus is the psychological or subjective benefits of product ownership	.56	1
			Has a glamorous tone	.47	1
			A main focus is one's sex appeal	.39	1

Part II
Theoretical Processes Underlying Cognitive and Affective Responses to Advertising

5
The Elaboration Likelihood Model: The Role of Affect and Affect-Laden Information Processing in Persuasion

John T. Cacioppo
Richard E. Petty

> The physiologists who, during the past few years, have been so industriously exploring the functions of the brain, have limited their attempts at explanation to its cognitive and volitional performances. . . . But the *aesthetic* sphere of the mind, its longings, its pleasures and pains, and its emotions, have been so ignored in all these researches that one is tempted to suppose that . . . the matter lay for them among the problems of the future, only to be taken up after the simpler ones of the present should have been definitively solved. (James 1884, p. 188)

William James's observations over a century ago that affect and emotion were relatively ignored applies equally well to the field of advertising and consumer psychology today. Inspection of the first three volumes of Division 23 conferences on advertising and psychology, for instance, reveals that the concepts of affect and emotion are considered only infrequently, whereas the concepts of cognition and deliberation are pervasive. This book, with its focus on affect and affect-laden information processing, marks an important departure from this tradition (see also Peterson, Hoyer, and Wilson 1986).

Our purpose in this chapter is twofold. We begin by reviewing briefly several questions and concerns shared by the other contributors to this book, noting not only common themes and approaches but also differences in conceptualization that are often disguised in the literature by similarities in terminology. Second, we outline a general theoretical framework to integrate the seemingly contradictory findings in the field and account for attitude persistence, attitude resistance, and attitude-behavior correspondence. Specifically, we outline the role of affect and affect-laden information processing in the Elaboration Likelihood Model (ELM; Petty and Cacioppo 1981, 1986). In addition, we address several questions and apparently contradictory empirical findings reported in this book in light of the ELM.

The research reported in this chapter was supported by National Science Foundation Grant BNS-8414853 to John T. Cacioppo

Themes, Conceptualizations, and Nomenclature

The contributors to this book represent diverse theoretical and methodological perspectives. Some have employed advertising stimuli to achieve an ecologically valid means of investigating what attributes make communications attention getting, emotional, memorable, and persuasive (Srull, chapter 7; Calder and Gruder, chapter 12). Others have attempted to identify cognition and emotion as they appear in advertising (see Holbrook and Westwood, chapter 16; Coulson, chapter 3). Despite this diversity, all deal with one-way persuasive communications transmitted through print, audio, or audiovisual channels; all adopt an intrapersonal-process orientation; and all seek ultimately to specify lawful relations between advertising input, affective response, and consumer behavior.

There are at least three problems relating to nomenclature and referents in the research of affect and affect-laden information:

1. The different ways in which the terms *affect, attitudes,* and *arousal* are used.
2. The concept that physiological arousal is necessarily a component of affect and emotion.
3. The concept that attitudes and affect are equatable.

Usage of Terms: Affect, Attitude, *and* Arousal

The different ways in which *affect, attitudes,* and *arousal* are used in the various chapters and in the field generally are problematic. *Affect* has been used to refer to preferences, reported emotional state, evaluations, undifferentiated arousal tagged with an emotional label, any kind of positive or negative orientation toward a stimulus, and "feeling states." The term *attitude* has been used to refer to affect, evaluations, and the tripartite of affect, cognition, and behavior. *Arousal* has been used to refer to reported (symptomatologic) bodily activation, autonomic activation (such as skin conductance changes), diffuse physiological arousal, cortical activation, alpha blockage, and behavioral activation.

The variation in conceptual referent for these terms is a problem because there is often little evidence that the different referents are marking the same phenomena. If fact, just the opposite is the case. Consider, for instance, the low convergent validity for conceptualizations of "arousal." There are subtle distinctions among some of the early arousal theories (Duffy 1957; Lindsley 1951; Malmo 1959). The basic premise of these theories can nevertheless be succinctly summarized: behavioral processes are viewed as consisting of a directional component, which represents the orientation of the person toward a goal, and an intensive component, which specifies the concomitant degree of energy expenditure. The construct of generalized physiological arousal refers to the intensity of physiological functioning. Moreover, the intensive component is viewed as being synonymous with the level of neural activity in the central nervous system (CNS) and as exerting an effect on performance.

According to arousal theory, behavioral efficiency increases as arousal increases to some optimal level. Beyond that point, behavioral efficiency decreases as arousal continues to increase (cf. Yerkes and Dodson 1908). There is an intuitively sensible arousal-affect model that might be postulated: Liking for a stimulus increases as the excitatory impact of the stimulus increases up to some optimal level, after which point liking for the stimulus decreases as its effect on organismic arousal continues to increase.

As appealing as these models might be, the task of moving the concept of arousal from hypothetical construct to intervening variable has been more complicated than typically recognized in theoretical and empirical investigations. The finding and mapping of the reticular formation (Moruzzi and Magoun 1949), which initially appeared to serve as a general organismic arousal mechanism, once provided a physiological locus for the construct of arousal. But the reticular formation is not as homogeneous as was first believed. For instance, it is a collection of nuclei that can have specific effects depending on the intensity of stimulation (see Van Toller 1979). This suggests that even if a noninvasive measure of reticular activation was feasible, it might not be a sufficient index of a general and diffuse state of physiological, reportable, and behavioral arousal.

The theory-driven assumption regarding arousal measurement has been that although some general measure of the level of excitation characterizing the CNS would be best, any measure of the extent to which the sympathetic dominated the parasympathetic nervous system would serve as a valid and sensitive measure. For instance, the degree of activation of an autonomic (for example, heart rate), somatic (for example, muscle tension), or cortical (for example, alpha blocking) measure could serve as a convenient, indirect measure of arousal within the CNS.

Among the problems confronting this conceptualization, however, are the distinctions found between tonic and phasic physiological responses. Briefly, Wilder (1957) proposed what he termed the "law of initial values," which states the magnitude and direction of a response (such as skin resistance response) within an individual varies inversely with the prestimulus level of arousal within that response system (such as skin resistance level). The implication worth noting is that whether an organism appeared to become more aroused, less aroused, or showed no change in arousal could be simply a function of the degree to which the target response (for example, cardiovascular, eccrine) system was activated prior to the stimulus of interest (cf. Cacioppo and Petty 1983).

Moreover, dissociations were soon found within and between response systems thought to serve general and diffuse physiological arousal. For instance, behavioral and cortical arousal were found to be directly related when the ranges of arousal being compared were quite wide, as when contrasting deep sleep and waking states (cf. Lindsley 1951). But even here inverse relationships were soon realized, as when people are in the paradoxical sleep-stage of rapid eye movement (REM) or when people are "paralyzed" in fear. Cortical arousal is sometimes directly related to autonomic arousal, as during REM and high fear states, and sometimes inversely related, as in sensory deprivation (Zuckerman 1969).

The Laceys (1959, 1967) also provided evidence that the physiological effectors within a single system (such as the autonomic nervous system) are not highly correlated. Lacey and coworkers (1963), for instance, found that when people performed a task requiring them to monitor flashing lights, heart rate declined and electrodermal activity increased. The response fractionation found across and within physiological systems constitutes yet another problem for arousal theory. Whether subjects are labeled more or less aroused depends entirely on the process measure selected rather than on the stimulus-response conditions.

Finally, the concept of response fractionation has also been found when comparing autonomic and verbal measures of arousal following an excitatory stimulus or event. Cantor, Zillmann, and Bryant (1975), for instance, found that felt (reportable) arousal subsides more quickly than do the increases in heart rate and blood pressure that follow exercise. We recently replicated this result showing that exercise-induced cardiac activity remains significantly elevated when subjects ceased to report feeling aroused due to the exercise. In addition, psychophysical scaling of overall arousal level was used to demonstrate that the state of residual arousal is imperceptible rather than simply misreported (Cacioppo, Tassinary, Stonebraker, and Petty, in press). Clearly the psychological significance of the term *arousal* cannot be assumed to be the same across these various types of activated (or disinhibited) bodily response.

Physiological Arousal as It Relates to Affect and Emotion

A second problematic conceptualization is that physiological arousal is necessarily a component of affect and emotion (Schachter and Singer 1962). Although emotionally arousing situations and stimuli can be and perhaps often are both autonomically and behaviorally arousing, there are at least two reasons (besides those outlined above) to question conceptualizations of advertising effects in which affect and arousal are equated. First, the affective states such as those evoked by mildly pleasant and unpleasant stimuli found in advertisements can be accompanied by rudimentary muscle action potentials over the muscles of emotional expressions that are detectable using electromyography (EMG) even in the absence of reliable increases in electrodermal or cardiac activity (Cacioppo, Petty, Losch, and Kim 1986). This line of research implies that the absence of autonomic or behavioral changes should not be interpreted as the absence of affect. Second, a variety of cognitive as well as emotional stimuli have been found to evoke autonomic activation (Lacey et al. 1963; Cacioppo and Sandman 1978; Lynn 1966).

Relationships between Attitudes and Affect

A third quagmire, in our view, are conceptualizations in which attitudes and affect are equated. *Affect* is a term commonly used to refer to an emotional reaction that has a high probability of changes in awareness, expressive display, overt behavior, and physiological functioning (Tomkins 1981). The pleasantness-unpleasantness dimension of emotional experience is sometimes emphasized in conceptualizations of affect, whereas others have included dimensions such as activation and control (Osgood 1966). Affect is used here as the superordinate construct that encompasses moods as well as emotions. It is distinguished from cognition by its rudimentary manifestation in neonates, its potential to arouse feelings rather than facts, and its motivational consequences (Izard 1977; Zajonc 1980).

Consistent with Bower (1981), each distinct affective state can be conceived as having a specific node in memory, connected by associative pointers to other aspects of the emotion (some of which are not cortical). For instance, propositions describing products, advertisements, and events from one's life during which a particular affect was activated would be linked with varying associative strength to the corresponding functional affect-unit. When an affect-unit is activated, by whatever means (external stimuli, proprioceptive, or interoceptive stimuli), excitation is transferred in a continuous flow to nodes responsible for autonomic arousal, expressive behavior, socialized display rules governing emotional expressions and behavior, and associated memory structures. The effects of this excitation at each of these nodes can range from subthreshold to superthreshold activation. Depending on the level of activation and the criterion level, only a subset of the features that are thought to characterize intense emotional states (such as autonomic arousal, verbal report, expressive behavior, and mood congruence effects) may be evident in any particular instance in which affect is evoked.

By *attitude*, on the other hand, we mean a global and enduring evaluation of some attitude object—that is, a propositional representation rather than an affect.[1] Attitude objects can be defined at varying levels of specificity (for example, natural foods versus brand X granola bars). A person's general evaluations or attitudes can be based on a variety of behavioral, cognitive, and affective events and are capable of guiding behavioral, cognitive, and affective processes.

More specifically, attitudes are conceptualized as a specific node in memory connected by associative pointers to other aspects of the knowledge schema (such as thoughts, images, and emotions), but they represent a particular class of memorial (learned) categories rather than an organismic affect-unit. For instance, the memorial network underlying an attitude is conceived in cognitive terms and of a cortical locus, whereas the memorial network underlying an affect is conceived in cognitive and somatovisceral terms of a cortical and subcortical locus (Cacioppo, Petty, and Geen, in press).

Activation of an affect-unit need not spread so far as to invoke extensive somatovisceral activation. Moreover, whereas attitudes are generally conceived as being global and enduring evaluations of a stimulus (Petty and Cacioppo 1981; Zanna and Rempel 1986), affective reactions can be transient and specific (James 1905; Zajonc 1980). We have been using phasic physiological reactions such as evoked facial EMG responses to track these affective reactions. Our findings indicate that tasks requiring individuals to form an evaluation of a stimulus are accompanied by a different profile of facial EMG and autonomic response than tasks that evoke an affective response (Cacioppo, Petty, Losch, and Kim 1986; Cacioppo, Petty, and Morris 1985; see Cacioppo, Losch, Tassinary, and Petty 1986).

The underlying theory in our psychophysiological research on attitudes is that (1) attitudinal processing consists of a finite set of processing elements or operations; (2) qualitative differences in verbal, behavioral, and/or physiological response patterns suggest distinctive psychological operations (for example, due to a distinctive input, processing element, or set of processing elements); and (3) similarities in response patterns provide converging evidence for similar psychological operations (Cacioppo and Petty 1986). This approach has revealed support for the notions that similar general and enduring evaluations of stimuli (attitudes) can be based on and activate different psychological operations and that attitudes and affect can be differentiated. In recent pilot testing, for instance, we observed facial EMG activity to vary as a function of the positive or negative feelings a person has toward an attitude object, even when the person's general evaluation of the attitude object was held constant. One individual indicated that she held equally positive attitudes toward twenty-four-hour banking and lasagna, the former because of its high instrumental value to her and the latter because of its delicious consumatory value (cf. Millar and Tesser 1986). When the subject was asked to ruminate about these attitude objects, recordings of facial EMG activity revealed that rumination about the consumatory attitude object, which was liked because of the way lasagna made her feel, was accompanied by a stronger pattern of facial efference characteristic of positive emotional states (for example, elevated EMG activity over the region of the zygomaticus major muscle) than was rumination about the instrumental attitude object. These pilot observations are tentative but illustrate graphically the conceptual distinctions psychophysiological research supports as existing among attitudes, beliefs, and affect.

Whether attitudes and facial EMG covary depends on a number of factors. For example, when people are left to think about a generally counterattitudinal versus proattitudinal topic, the stream of attendant affective reactions as one considers the topic might vary so dramatically and consistently that facial EMG could differentiate the individuals in these conditions (see Cacioppo and Petty 1979). But the same general factors mitigating attitude-behavior correspondence when comparing a general measure of attitude with a specific measure of behavior can also be expected to vitiate the correspondence between a person's general and enduring attitude toward a stimulus and the facial efference associated with transient, specific, and possibly issue-irrelevant (perhaps the speaker's facial expression; cf McHugo et al. 1985) affective reactions.

These observations led us to reconsider the evidence for the tripartite conceptualization of attitudes by which attitudes are viewed as consisting of affect, cognition, and behavior (Rosenberg et al. 1960). The conceptualization of attitudes as global and enduring evaluations is theoretically more parsimonious only if the data thought to support the attitude tripartite can be explained equally well by the view that attitudes represent global and enduring evaluations of stimuli.

Two aspects of the evidence purported to favor the tripartite model are therefore noteworthy. First, the evidence consists essentially of multitrait, multimethod studies in which attitude measures based on verbal responses from the affective, cognitive, and behavioral domains were found to exhibit convergent and discriminant validity. Second, in every study supporting the attitude tripartite distinction, the indexes of "cognition," "affect," and "behavior" have been scaled to reflect evaluations of the attitude objects. For example, Breckler (1984) obtained thought listings about an attitude object. However, rather than using the total number of issue-relevant thoughts (or some other cognitive structure index) as a measure of the cognitive component, he had each thought rated along an evaluative dimension and used the ratio of the favorable to unfavorable thoughts about the attitude object as an index of the cognitive component. The research purported to support the tripartite over the unidimensional model therefore may have resulted from the scaling of originally orthogonal, mutually exclusive, and exhaustive dimensions of experience along a common evaluative continuum. Indeed, this is exactly what one might expect based on Fishbein's (1963) model of attitudes (see also Cullen 1968).

If this reasoning is correct, then other independent dimensions representing a stimulus, such as activity and potency, may yield the same pattern of results found in research purported to support the attitude tripartite once the ratings constituting these orthogonal representations of the stimulus have been rescaled in terms of evaluation. Activity and potency dimensions of attitude objects might be particularly interesting to examine because previous research (Osgood, Suci, and Tannenbaum 1957) has shown them to provide independent representations of stimuli and to be orthogonal to people's evaluations of the stimuli and because no one has ever argued that activity and potency are attitude components. Hence, if activity and potency representations of attitude stimuli were subsequently rated along an evaluative dimension (in much the same manner as did Breckler [1984] when calculating the cognitive-response measure to index the "cognitive" component of attitudes) one might get what appeared to be evidence for a multidimensional conceptualization of attitudes. More parsimoniously, the data would simply reflect the fact that evaluative ratings of any large enough set of stimulus attributes could be aggregated to yield a measure of attitudes.

Consistent with this reasoning, Geen (1986) found that activity and potency ratings of attitude objects yielded two orthogonal representations of each attitude object, whereas transformations of these ratings along the evaluative dimension produced a pattern of results similar to that found in previous research on the attitude tripartite. Moreover, structural equation analyses (LISREL) of the transformed activity and potency data indicated that a two-component model was superior to a unidimensional model of attitudes, but in this case the "components" of attitudes would be activity and potency.

More parsimoniously, these data indicate that the conceptualization of attitudes as global and enduring evaluations of stimuli can account for the evidence cited in support of "multidimensional" attitude conceptualizations. As Ostrom (1969), the first to use the multitrait-multimethod approach to provide what he believed was unique support for the tripartite conceptualization of attitudes, acknowledged:

> For the tripartite distinction to be of value, it must be demonstrated that evaluative responses within each component share a unique set of determinants distinct from those for the other components. If no unique determinants can be established, it would be conceptually unparsimonious to invoke a distinction which had no effect at the empirical level. (pp. 13–14)

But our research demonstrated that the evaluative responses within even initially orthogonal dimensional representations of a stimulus can yield the same pattern of data. Hence such a pattern does not provide support for the value of the tripartite distinction.

On the positive side, the separation of constructs of attitudes and affect renders more manageable a number of what otherwise appear to be perplexing issues regarding discrepancies between expressed attitudes and affect, between attitudes toward the ad and attitudes toward the brand, and between the ability of a particular ad execution to evoke affect and its ability to influence consumer attitudes and behavior. It is to some of these issues, and in particular to the role of affect in attitude change, that we turn.

Integrating Knowledge about Affect, Communication, and Persuasion

The major goal of an advertising appeal, whether to stem nuclear proliferation or to sell soap, is to influence the behavior of an audience. Behaviorists have long known that physical reinforcement and punishment can achieve this end, and various marketing strategies are designed to capitalize on these principles (coupons, rebates, and discounts, for example). It has, however, also long been recognized that the actual application of rewards and punishments was very limited. Hence attention turned to the task of developing general and enduring attitudes (for example, using mass communication) that would exert a corresponding influence on behaviors toward the attitude object (Thurstone 1928; Hovland, Lumsdaine, and Sheffield 1949). In the half-century of research that followed, theories of persuasion proliferated within psychology and advertising.

After reviewing the empirically supported communication and persuasion theories and the literature on attitude persistence, we concluded that the many different empirical findings and theories in the field might profitably be viewed as emphasizing one of just two relatively distinct routes to persuasion (Petty and Cacioppo, 1981, 1986; for a review of related follow-up work, see Pechmann and Stewart, chapter 4). The first route is that which likely occurs as a result of a person's careful and thoughtful consideration of the true merits of the information presented in support of an advocacy (central route). The second type of persuasion is that which more likely occurs as a result of some simple cue in the persuasion context that induced change without necessitating scrutiny of the central merits of the issue-relevant information presented (peripheral route).

Our Elaboration Likelihood Model (ELM) encompasses these two routes to persuasion. Before outlining the manner in which affect fits into the ELM, we briefly review a few of the basic postulates of the model. The ELM has typically been presented in graphic form (figure 5–1), but the fundamental postulates of the model have also been outlined (Petty and Cacioppo 1986).

The processes of attention, comprehension, elaboration, and integration are components of the ELM. Given people's limited capacity for processing information and the large number of daily exigencies, communications, and persuasive appeals to which individuals are exposed, it is little wonder that advertising researchers are concerned about capturing an audience with their appeals. Although the aspects of the ELM outlined in figure 5–1 presume attention and comprehension have been achieved, our first postulate addresses the underlying motivation leading individuals to expend their limited cognitive resources on persuasive appeals. Following Festinger (1954), it is postulated that people are motivated to hold correct attitudes. Correct attitudes help

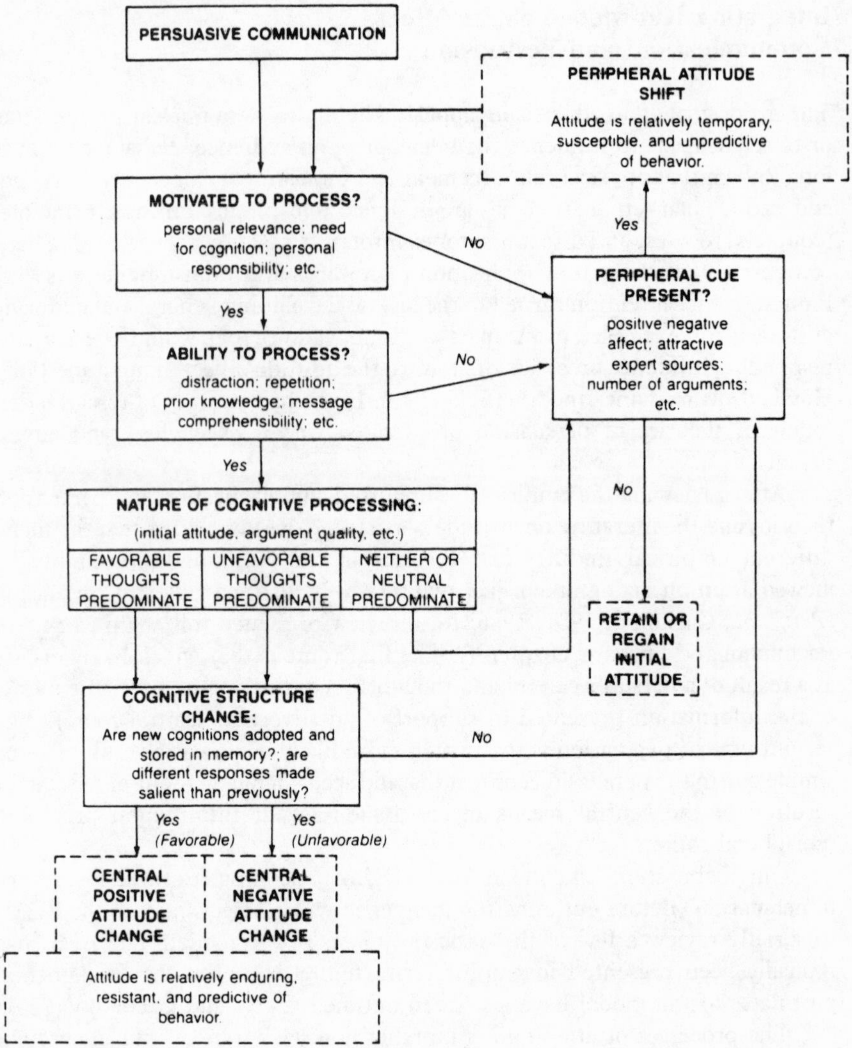

Note: Schematic depiction of the two routes to persuasion. This diagram depicts the possible end points after exposure to a persuasive communication according to the ELM. (Central attitude change, peripheral shift, no change) (from Petty & Cacioppo, 1986).

Figure 5-1. Central And Peripheral Routes To Persuasion. This Figure Depicts The Two Anchoring Endpoints On The Elaboration Likelihood Continuum

individuals make sense of themselves and their world, respond and adapt effectively to the changing events around them, and garner the fruits of social interaction (Cacioppo et al., in press).

It is further postulated that although people want to hold correct attitudes, the amount and nature of issue-relevant elaboration in which they are willing or able to engage to evaluate a message varies with individual and situational factors. By elaboration, we mean the extent to which a person thinks about issue-relevant information, bits of knowledge that can be activated by or heavily imbued with affect. A discussion of the developmental trends in elaboration and the distinctions between the concept of elaboration in the ELM and the concepts of automatic versus controlled processing, mindfulness-mindlessness, cognitive effort, and levels of processing can be found elsewhere (Petty and Cacioppo 1986, chap. 1). However, it may be instructive to survey briefly the determinants of elaboration likelihood.

The likelihood that argument elaboration occurs can be viewed as being a function of the separable elements of motivation and ability (figure 5-2). Motivation refers to the factor that propels and guides people's information processing and gives it its purposive character. What variables affecting motivation seem to have in common is that they act on a directive, goal-oriented component, which might be termed *intention,* and a nondirective, energizing, information-processing component, which might be termed *effort* or *exertion.* Many variables can influence a person's intention to think about a message or issue, whether they are conscious or deliberative about the influence of these variables on intention. The task variables of personal relevance and responsibility, the individual difference variable of need for cognition, and the contextual variable of number of sources all influence an individual's intention to think about the persuasive communication presented.

Intention is not sufficient for motivation, however, since one can want to think about a message or issue but not exert the necessary effort to move from intending to trying. Little research has been directed explicitly at specifying what variables influence this stage, but hypothetically the excitatory strength of a persuasive appeal, as in advertisement, is related curvilinearly to this intensity (trying) component. That is, organismic arousal increases to some optimal level; the persuasive appeal evokes attention and exploration, comprehension, elaboration, and integration; as the arousal increases beyond this optimal level, there is a decrement in integration, elaboration, comprehension, and, ultimately, in attention as well. However, the conceptualization of arousal data obtained using measures of autonomic, cortical, reportable, and behavioral activation has not provided clear support for a physiological connection, and the status of arousal in the present context is only as a hypothetical construct. Interesting questions remain regarding exactly which variables

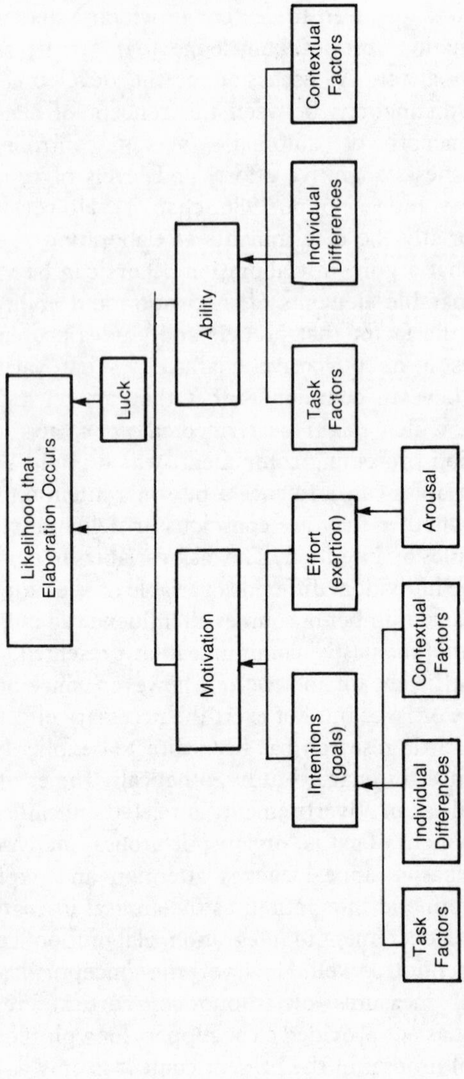

Figure 5–2. Schematic Depiction of Factors Affecting the Likelihood of Elaboration

Source: Petty and Cacioppo 1986.

act on message elaboration and whether more sophisticated conceptualizations and measures of arousal, such as "wakefulness" (cf. Cacioppo and Petty 1983b) will yield evidence for this hypothetical link.

As specified in figure 5–2, message elaboration also requires that individuals have the ability to process the message. Task factors (such as comprehensibility), individual difference variables (such as IQ), and contextual variables (such as opportunity variables, distraction) are again germane because they can influence ability (see Petty and Cacioppo 1986 for a recent review of motivational and ability variables that influence elaboration likelihood).

Figure 5–2 does not address what happens when motivation and ability are low or high, but the ELM does. The third postulate of the ELM concerns how variables in a persuasion context can determine the extent and amount of attitude change. It states that variables can affect the amount and direction of attitude change by serving as persuasive arguments, serving as peripheral cues, and/or affecting the extent or direction of issue and argument elaboration. The ELM is unique in that variables in an advertising context can serve in more than one of these capacities.

Persuasive Arguments as a Basis for Attitude Change

Persuasive arguments represent bits of information relevant to a person's subjective determination of the true merits of the advocated position. What kind of information is relevant to evaluating the central merits of a product or issue may vary from situation to situation or from person to person. The assessment of information is not assumed always to be rational, nor is affect viewed as necessarily irrelevant to the merits of a product or issue. That is, in the ELM, the term *arguments* refers to any information contained in a communication that permits a person to evaluate the message target along whatever target dimensions are central for that person.

Although persuasion researchers over the past few decades have focused on the cognitive foundations of attitudes (see McGuire 1969), investigators are beginning to show renewed interest in the affective bases of attitudes and persuasion (Cacioppo and Petty, 1981; Cacioppo, Petty, and Geen in press; Clark and Fiske 1982; Zajonc and Markus 1982). The ELM holds open the same possibilities for affect that it does for the other source, message, recipient, and context variables that have been the traditional focus of persuasion researchers. For example, for some people or in some situations, a determination of the central merits of an attitude object might entail an analysis of one's feelings rather than one's beliefs or behaviors. Thus the affective state (such as attraction or excitement) induced by an attitude object (perhaps another individual) might serve as a persuasive argument for or against the merits of the object when the elaboration likelihood is high (for example, if the individual is one's potential spouse)—a process most likely when the affect is perceived to be directly relevant to the central merits of the object or issue under consideration—(for example, the salivating joy one feels when considering the merits of consuming a sizzling steak when famished or the disgust one feels after sensing the steak is rancid).

In short, according to the ELM, relevant affective states should serve as persuasive arguments or help in assessing the cogency of arguments when the elaboration likelihood is high (as when fear may contribute to a person's assessment of the danger inherent in not following a specific recommendation). When the elaboration likelihood is high but irrelevant affective states are induced, it is postulated that the affect will have little to no effect on attitudes and that any influence it does have will be to bias issue-relevant thinking by making affectively consonant thoughts and ideas more accessible in memory (Bower 1981; Clark and Isen 1982; see chapter 1).

Peripheral Cues as a Basis for Attitude Change

Peripheral cues in the ELM represent stimuli in the context that can affect attitudes without necessitating processing of the message arguments. Affect has the potential to operate as a peripheral cue. Indeed, one of the distinguishing characteristics of the ELM is the postulate that in addition to stimuli that can act as cues because they invoke guiding rules (such as balance) or inferences (such as self-perception) that are not inherently linked to the attitude object, stimuli that trigger relatively primitive affective states (whether relevant or irrelevant to the central merits of an attitude object) can become associated with it and serve as peripheral cues.

According to the ELM, the conditions under which affect operates in each of these capacities differ. In contrast to the postulated impact of affective states when the elaboration likelihood is high, affect, whether relevant or irrelevant, serves as a simple peripheral cue when people are either relatively unmotivated or unable to engage in the cognitive work necessary to evaluate the central merits of an attitude object or issue. As a cue, affect should enhance attitudes when it is pleasant but have a negative effect when it is unpleasant, unless, of course, the cue is so distal or weak that it has no effect whatsoever.

Several studies in consumer literature support this postulate. For instance, Gorn (1982) investigated the power of a simple affective cue to modify attitudes toward a product when the personal relevance of an advertisement was low. Before viewing any advertisements, subjects in the high-relevance conditions were told that their task was to advise an advertising agency as to whether they should purchase time on television. In addition, they were told that they would later get to choose as a gift one of the advertised pen packs. In the low-relevance conditions, subjects were provided with little reason to think about the advertisements. They did not expect to advise the ad agency nor did they expect to receive pens as a gift prior to their exposure to the advertisements. All subjects were exposed to two different advertisements for a pen. One ad was attribute oriented and provided relevant information about the pen (such as "never smudges"); the other ad featured pleasant music rather than information. About one hour following their exposure to the advertisements, subjects were given a choice between the two brands of pens. The majority of the subjects in the high-relevance condition chose the pen advertised with the information, whereas the majority of the subjects in the low-relevance condition chose the pen advertised with pleasant music.

In a conceptually similar study, Srull (chapter 7 to this book) provided evidence that simple affective cues may be a more important determinant of attitudes when prior knowledge is low rather than high. Srull had subjects rate their general knowledge about automobiles. Following a positive, negative, or neutral mood-induction procedure, they were exposed to an attribute-oriented advertisement for a new car. Respondents then evaluated the advertised product. The results revealed that the attitudes of low-knowledge subjects were significantly affected by the mood induction, whereas the attitudes of high-knowledge subjects were not influenced by this simple and irrelevant affective cue. Together the Gorn and Srull studies demonstrate that affect can act as a simple persuasion cue and influence attitudes as outlined in figure 5-1 when people's motivation and/or ability to engage in issue-relevant thinking (their elaboration likelihood) is low (see also Batra and Ray 1985).

Extent or Direction of Elaboration as a Basis for Attitude Change

The third way in which a variable can affect persuasion is by influencing the direction and amount of issue-relevant thinking in a relatively objective or biased manner. According to the ELM, affect has the potential to serve in this capacity as well. It does so when people are uncertain as to whether they should think extensively about a persuasive communication (a moderate elaboration likelihood). Specifically affective states alter the amount of issue-relevant thinking through the influence of the associated changes in arousal on cognitive and behavioral effort (see figure 5-2) and possibly through a direct tendency of euphoric states to lead to greater cognitive effort than dysphoric states. Given that elaboration is thereby enhanced, affect may also alter the direction of issue-relevant thinking by making affectively consonant thoughts and ideas more accessible in memory ("mood congruence"; see chapter 6). Mood congruence is the mechanism postulated to explain, for instance, the increased negative thinking that occurs when a message is repeated an excessive number of times, even when the message arguments were initially effective (Cacioppo and Petty, 1985; see also chapter 8).

In conclusion, according to the ELM, affect is a variable that can have multiple effects on issue-relevant thinking and persuasion. One important implication of this analysis is that simply contrasting "rational" with "emotional" advertisements will ultimately prove equally as frustrating as prior attempts to conceptualize other factors in a persuasion context (such as source credibility) as acting in a simple and uniform manner across persuasion contexts (see Petty and Cacioppo 1986, chap. 8).

According to the ELM, both attribute-oriented and emotional appeals can lead to attitude change by the peripheral route when people's motivation to think about the message is low. Conversely, both rational and emotional appeals may lead to attitude change by the central route if the elaboration likelihood is high, and the appeals provide information that strikes to the core of an attitude objects' utility to recipients. Those attitudes achieved through the central route, whether through rational or emotional argumentation, have been shown to be more persistent (Petty and Cacioppo 1986), more resistant to counterpropaganda (Petty and Cacioppo 1986), and more predictive of behavior (Cacioppo, Petty, Kao, and Rodriguez 1986; Petty, Cacioppo, and Schumann 1983).

Although it may be possible to produce attitudes by the peripheral route that have some of the same characteristics (such as persistence and accessibility) as those produced by the central route, more messages and cue exposures should be required to achieve these results (Weber 1972). Of course, if the intended audience does not have the motivation to think carefully about the merits of a product, then repeated presentations of a positive cue with the product may be one of the few ways to induce the audience to try the product. Reinstatement of a positive cue at the point of purchase should also be helpful when an advertising campaign has operated through the peripheral route. Once individuals have made an initial product purchase, however, they are in a position to evaluate the central merits of the product based on their own experiences with it.

Answers to two questions are important from the perspective of advertising: whether a specific feature in an ad will serve as a message argument or peripheral cue and whether an affect provoked by an ad will be relevant. The answers to these questions, guided by and coupled with the ELM, should provide direction for advertising strategies and executions. However, these answers may be idiosyncratic to the audience or product (Snyder and DeBono 1985). This suggests the possible utility of psychographic profiles of the target audience and possible in-depth primary research to learn more about specific motivators and product relevance.

Finally, a little-studied but interesting theoretical issue arises regarding the differential effects that can be expected from attitudes changed because individuals considered carefully the cogent rational (such as instrumental) versus cogent emotional (such as consumatory) arguments for adopting a particular position; that is, when attitudes have been achieved through the central route as the result of affect-laden versus non-affect-laden thought about the attitude object. One can conceive of such attitudes that are equally positive, enduring, and accessible. Many aspects of the cognitive (such as vertical and horizontal) structure underlying these attitudes could also be quite similar. The major difference in these attitudes, then, would be the memories, thoughts, and associations evoked by the attitude objects (the associated nodes in memory), as well as the associative pointers linking attitudes based on emotional appeals to one or more affect-units.[2]

Attitudes achieved through the central route are postulated to be more enduring, more resistant to counterpersuasion, and more predictive of behavior—in part because the more articulated structure and content of the schema is better able to guide the manner in which incoming information is related to people's previous experiences and knowledge. The content of the relevant knowledge structures and the functions served by the attitudes therefore hold additional information about effective communication and persuasion. Millar and Tesser (1986), for instance, found that attitudes toward puzzles for which affective (consumatory) antecedents were made salient were more predictive of consumatory than instrumental behaviors. Conversely, attitudes toward the same puzzles for which cognitive (instrumental) antecedents were made salient were more predictive of instrumental than consumatory behaviors.

In sum, the interesting theoretical and empirical analyses of affect and advertising provided in this book may at times suggest seemingly conflicting results. We have attempted to reconcile these differences in two ways. First, we have suggested some differences that exist because of the various ways in which terms are conceptualized and/or measured. Included are such fundamental concepts as attitudes, affect, and arousal. Second, we have extended the ELM in an attempt to place other conflicting results in the literature under one conceptual umbrella by specifying the major processes underlying persuasion and indicating how affect can relate to these processes in three separate capacities. Finally, we have examined how affect can influence the memorial (structural) basis of attitudes and thereby influence the stimuli that access the attitudes, the behaviors that are deemed relevant, and the comprehension and elaboration of subsequent incoming information.

Notes

1. Ephemeral, transitory, or self-presentational expressions of global evaluation would not be considered expressions of attitude, because they would not be reliable and enduring. To say that attitudes are enduring, however, is not to say that they are not subject to various processes of change. An attitude can endure for varying lengths of time, just as learned information can endure for varying lengths of time. Hence the term *enduring* is used in the same sense as it is in learning and memory.

2. For didactic purposes, we are depicting attitudes formed in response to rational appeals as if they were solely the consequence of rational information processing and

the attitudes formed in response to emotional appeals as if they were solely the consequence of affect-laden, issue-relevant thinking. This is an oversimplification. Attitudes formed in response to rational appeals can also involve considerable affect-laden thinking, and the difference is likely to be more a matter of degree rather than presence or absence. Hence many attitude structures are likely to include associative pointers linking the attitude nodes to affect-units, although the strength of these links (and the excitation needed to activate the affect-links) should differ as a function of the emotional antecedents and consequences of the attitudes.

References

Batra, R., and Ray, M. 1985. "How Advertising Works at Contact." In L. Alwitt and A. Mitchell, eds., *Psychological Processes and Advertising Effects: Theory, Research and Application.* Hillsdale, N.J.: Erlbaum.

Bower, G.H. 1981. "Mood and Memory." *American Psychologist* 11:11–13.

Breckler, S.J. 1984. "Empirical Validation of Affect, Behavior, and Cognition as Distinct Attitude Components." *Journal of Personality and Social Psychology* 47: 1191–1205.

Cacioppo, J.T.; Losch, M.E.; Tassinary, L.; and Petty, R.E. 1986. "Properties of Affect and Affect-laden Information Processing as Viewed Through the Facial Response System." In R.A. Peterson, W.D. Hoyer, and W.R. Wilson, eds., *The Role of Affect in Consumer Behavior: Emerging Theories and Applications,* pp. 87–118. Lexington, Mass.: Lexington Books.

Cacioppo, J.T., and Petty, R.E. 1979. "Attitudes and Cognitive Response: An Electrophysiological Approach." *Journal of Personality and Social Psychology* 37:2181–2199.

———. 1981. "Electromyograms as Measures of Extent and Affectivity of Information Processing." *American Psychologist* 36:441–456.

———. 1982. "The Need for Cognition." *Journal of Personality and Social Psychology* 42:116–131.

———, eds. 1983a. *Social Psychophysiology: A Sourcebook.* New York: Guilford Press.

Cacioppo, J.T. and Petty, R.E. 1983b. "A Contrasting Frame of Reference: Soviet Contributions of Social Psychophysiology." In. J.T. Cacioppo and R.E. Petty, eds., *Social Psychophysiology: A Sourcebook,* pp. 693–730. New York: Guilford Press.

———. 1985. "Central and Peripheral Routes to Persuasion: The Role of Message Repetition." In A. Mitchell and L. Alwitt, eds., *Psychological Processes and Advertising Effects.* Hillsdale, N.J.: Erlbaum.

———. 1986. "Social Processes." In M.G.H. Coles, E. Donchin, and S. Porges, eds., *Psychophysiology: Systems, Processes, and Applications,* pp. 646–679. New York: Guilford Press.

Cacioppo, J.T.; Petty, R.E.; and Geen, T.R. (In press). "Attitude Structure and Function: From the Tripartite to the Homeostasis Model of Attitudes." In A.R. Pratkanis, S.J. Breckler, and A.G. Greenwald, eds., *Attitude Structure and Function.* Hillsdale, N.J.: Erlbaum.

Cacioppo, J.T.; Petty, R.E.; Kao, C.; and Rodriguez, R. 1986. "Central and Peripheral Routes to Persuasion: An Individual Difference Perspective." *Journal of Personality and Social Psychology* 51:1032–1043.

Cacioppo, J.T.; Petty, R.E.; Losch, M.E.; and Kim, H.S. 1986. "Electromyographic Activity over Facial Muscle Regions Can Differentiate the Valence and Intensity of Affective Reactions." *Journal of Personality and Social Psychology* 50:260–268.

Cacioppo, J.T.; Petty, R.E.; and Morris, K. 1985. "Semantic, Evaluative, and Self-Reference Processing: Memory, Cognitive Effort, and Somatovisceral Activity." *Psychophysiology* 22:371–384.

Cacioppo, J.T., and Sandman, C.A. 1978. "Physiological Differentiation of Sensory and Cognitive Tasks as a Function of Warning, Processing Demands, and Reported Unpleasantness." *Biological Psychology* 6:181–192.

Cacioppo, J.T.; T.B. Stonebraker, L.G. Tassinary; and Petty, R.E. (In press). "Self-Report and Autonomic Measures of Physiological Arousal: Fractionation during Residual Arousal." *Biological Psychology.*

Cantor, J.R., Zillmann, D., and Bryant, J. 1975. "Enhancement of Experienced Sexual Arousal in Response to Erotic Stimuli through Misattribution of Unrelated Residual Excitation." *Journal of Personality and Social Psychology* 32:69–75.

Clark, M.S., and Fiske, S.T., eds. 1982. *Affect and Cognition: The Seventeenth Annual Carnegie Symposium on Cognition.* Hillsdale, N.J.: Erlbaum.

Clark, M.S., and Isen, A.M. 1982. "Toward Understanding the Relationship between Feeling States and Social Behavior." In A. Hastorf and A. Isen, eds., *Cognitive Social Psychology.* New York: Elsevier-North Holland.

Cullen, D.M. 1968. "Attitude Measurement by Cognitive Sampling." Ph.D. dissertation, Ohio State University.

Duffy, E. 1957. "The Psychological Significance of the Concept of 'Arousal' or 'Activation.'" *Psychological Review* 64:265–275.

Festinger, L. 1954. "A Theory of Social Comparison Processes." *Human Relations* 7: 117–140.

Fishbein, M. 1963. "An Investigation of the Relationships between Beliefs about an Object and the Attitude toward That Object." *Human Relations* 16:233–240.

Geen, T.R. 1986. "A Comparison of the Tripartite and Unidimensional Conceptualizations of Attitude Structure." Master's thesis, University of Iowa.

Gorn, G. 1982. "The Effects of Music in Advertising on Choice Behavior: A Classical Conditioning Approach." *Journal of Marketing Research* 46:94–101.

Hovland, C.I.; Lumsdaine, A.; and Sheffield, F. 1949. *Experiments on Mass Communication.* Princeton, N.J.: Princeton University Press.

Izard, C.E. 1977. *Human Emotions.* New York: Plenum.

James, W. 1884. "What Is Emotion?" *Mind* 9:188–204.

———. 1905. *The Principles of Psychology,* vol. 2. New York: Holt. Originally published, 1890.

Kahneman, D. 1973. *Attention and Effort.* Englewood Cliffs, N.J.: Prentice-Hall.

Lacey, J.I. 1959. "Psychophysiological Approaches to the Evaluation of Psychotherapeutic Process and Outcome." In E.A. Rubinstein and M.B. Parloff, eds., *Research in Psychotherapy,* vol 1. Washington, D.C.: American Psychological Association.

———. 1967. "Somatic Response Patterning and Stress: Some Revisions of Activation Theory." In M.H. Appley and R. Trumbull, eds., *Psychological Stress: Issues in Research.* New York: Appleton-Century-Crofts.

Lacey, J.I.; Kagan, J.; Lacey, B.; and Moss, H.A. 1963. "The Visceral Level: Situational Determinants and Behavioral Correlates of Autonomic Response Patterns." In P.H. Knapp, ed., *Expression of the Emotions in Man.* New York: International Universities Press.

Lindsley, D.B. 1951. "Emotion." In S.S. Stevens, ed., *Handbook of Experimental Psychology.* New York: Wiley.

Lynn, R. 1966. *Attention, Arousal, and the Orientation Reaction.* Oxford: Pergamon Press.

Malmo, R.B. 1959. "Activation: A Neurophysiological Dimension. *Psychological Review* 66:367–386.

McGuire, W.J. 1969. "The Nature of Attitudes and Attitude Change." In G. Lindzey and E. Aronson, eds., *The Handbook of Social Psychology,* vol. 3, 2d ed. Reading, Mass.: Addison-Wesley.

McHugo, G.; Lanzatta, J.T.; Sullivan, D.G.; Masters, R.D.; and Englis, B. 1985. "Emotional Reactions to a Political Leader's Expressive Displays." *Journal of Personality and Social Psychology* 49:1513–1529.

Millar, M.G., and Tesser, A. 1986. "Effects of Affective and Cognitive Focus on the Attitude-Behavior Relation." *Journal of Personality and Social Psychology* 51: 270–277.

Moruzzi, G., and Magoun, H.W. 1949. "Brainstem Reticular Formation and Activation of the EEG." *Electroencephalography and Clinical Neurophysiology* 1:455–473.

Osgood, C.E. 1966. "Dimensionality of the Semantic Space for Communication via Facial Expressions." *Scandinavian Journal of Psychology* 7:1–30.

Osgood, C.E.; Suci, G.J.; and Tannenbaum, P.H. 1957. *The Measurement of Meaning.* Urbana: University of Illinois Press.

Ostrom, T.M. 1969. "The Relationship between Affective, Behavioral, and Cognitive Components of Attitude." *Journal of Experimental Social Psychology* 1:12–30.

Peterson, R.A.; Hoyer, W.D.; and Wilson, W.R., eds. 1986. *The Role of Effect in Consumer Behavior: Emerging Theories and Applications.* Lexington, Mass.: Lexington Books.

Petty, R.A., and Cacioppo, J.T. 1981. *Attitudes and Persuasion: Classic and Contemporary Approaches.* Dubuque, Iowa: Wm. C. Brown.

———. 1986. "The Elaboration Likelihood Model of Persuasion." In L. Berkowitz, ed., *Advances in Experimental Social Psychology,* vol 19. New York: Academic Press.

Petty, R.A.; Cacioppo, J.T.; and Schumann, D. 1983. "Central and Peripheral Routes to Advertising Effectiveness: The Moderating Role of Involvement." *Journal of Consumer Research* 10:134–148.

Rogers, R. 1983. "Cognitive and Physiological Processes in Fear Appeals and Attitude Change: A Revised Theory of Protection Motivation." In J.T. Cacioppo and R.E. Petty, eds., *Social Psychophysiology: A Sourcebook.* New York: Guilford Press.

Rosenberg, M.J., Hovland, C.I., McGuire, W.J., Abelson, R.P., and Brehn, J.W., eds. 1960. *Attitude Organization and Change.* New Haven: Yale University Press.

Schachter, S., and Singer, J.E. 1962. "Cognitive, Social, and Physiological Determinants of Emotional State." *Psychological Review* 69:379–399.

Snyder, M., and DeBono, K.G. 1985. "Appeals to Image and Claims about Quality:

Understanding the Psychology of Advertising." *Journal of Personality and Social Psychology* 49:586–597.

Thurstone, L.L. 1928. "Attitudes Can Be Measured." *American Journal of Sociology* 33:529–544.

Tomkins, S.S. 1981. "The Quest for Primary Motives: Biography and Autobiography of an Idea." *Journal of Personality and Social Psychology* 41:306–329.

Van Toller, C.V. 1979. *The Nervous Body: An Introduction to the Autonomic Nervous System and Behaviour.* New York: Wiley.

Weber, S.J. 1972. "Opinion Change Is a Function of the Associative Learning of Content and Source Factors." Ph.D. dissertation, Northwestern University.

Wilder, J. 1957. "The Law of Initial Values in Neurology and Psychiatry: Facts and Problems." *Journal of Nervous and Mental Disease* 125:73–86.

Yerkes, R.M., and Dodson, J.D. 1908. "The Relation of Strength of Stimulus to Rapidity of Habit Formation." *Journal of Comparative Neurology and Psychology* 18:459–482.

Zajonc, R.B. 1980. "Feeling and Thinking: Preferences Need No Inferences." *American Psychologist* 35:151–175.

Zajonc, R.B., and Markus, H. 1982. "Affective and Cognitive Factors in Preferences." *Journal of Consumer Research* 9:123–131.

Zanna, M.P., and Rempel, J.K. 1986. "Attitudes: A New Look at an Old Concept." *Proceedings of the Conference on Social Psychology of Knowledge.*

Zuckerman, M. 1969. "Variables Affecting Deprivation Results." In J.P. Zubek, ed., *Sensory Deprivation: Fifteen Years of Research,* pp. 47–84. New York: Appleton.

6
Some Ways in Which Affect Influences Cognitive Processes: Implications for Advertising and Consumer Behavior

Alice M. Isen

A growing body of research suggests that affect can substantially influence social behavior and cognitive processes such as memory, judgment, decision making, and problem solving. The purpose of this chapter is to explore the nature of these effects in order to improve our understanding of how they occur, some of the circumstances under which they might be expected to occur, and some of the ways in which they may impact consumer decision making and behavior. To this end, I will present a brief overview of the effects of affect that have been observed, followed by a more detailed consideration of some of the issues arising from these findings. The issues to be discussed in detail are the impact of affect on memory, the asymmetry between positive and negative affect in influence on memory and behavior, and the influence of positive affect on cognitive organization. These issues have implications regarding the effects of different kinds of advertising strategies in various situations, and they suggest some intriguing possibilities for new consumer research.

Overview

Recent studies indicate that mild elation, induced in a variety of simple ways, can influence social behavior and cognitive processes that may play a role in consumer decision making and behavior. The kinds of events used to induce affect in this research have been simple, common, seemingly small, and unimportant occurences such as finding a dime in the coin return of a public telephone, receiving a useful free sample worth under fifty cents, or winning a computer game. These apparently insignificant events are capable of influencing our thoughts, motivations, and behavior, in both social and nonsocial domains.

In general, positive affect can be said to be associated with increased helping, generosity, sociability, and friendliness (for example, Batson et al. 1979; Gouaux 1971; Isen 1970; Isen and Levin 1972; Veitch and Griffitt 1976; Weyant 1978). However, it also appears to induce a motivation to maintain the positive state and an increased sensitivity to losses generally (Isen, Nygren, and Ashby 1985; Isen and Simmonds 1978). For example, in one study (Isen and Simmonds 1978) people in whom positive affect had been induced were found to be *less* helpful than control subjects when the helping task clearly threatened their positive feelings (although a similar group was more helpful than control subjects when the task did not pose a threat to the positive state). Thus although people who are feeling happy may tend, in general, to be more helpful, less aggressive (Baron 1984; Baron and Ball 1974), and more cooperative (for example, in negotiation; Carnevale and Isen 1986), there are circumstances under which these tendencies may be overridden by considerations relevant to self-protection.

Similarly some studies suggest that positive affect may lead to greater receptiveness to persuasive communication (Galizio and Hendrick 1972; Janis, Kaye, and Kirschner 1965), but there is reason to believe that this may not hold true under all circumstances. In particular, if persons are threatened by a stimulus or in some other way are already negatively disposed toward it, positive affect may not promote cooperativeness or receptiveness toward that target (Forest et al. 1979; Isen and Simmonds 1978). Thus the evidence suggests that positive affect promotes two behavioral tendencies possibly of interest to students of consumer behavior: a positive, cooperative approach to others, but a positive orientation to oneself and one's good feeling state and a sensitivity to losses or clear danger.

These same kinds of simply induced affective states can influence *cognitive* processes that may be relevant to consumer behavior and to the effectiveness advertising. Memory, judgment, decision making, and problem solving have been seen to be influenced by positive feelings, as have even more fundamental processes such as cognitive organization (the perceived relatedness of ideas). For example, there is evidence that mild positive affect can facilitate recall of positive material in memory and can influence judgments regarding neutral material. Studies have shown, for instance, that people who are happy demonstrate better recall of positive material (for example, Isen et al. 1978; Laird et al. 1982; Nasby and Yando 1982; Teasdale and Fogarty 1979). Other research further suggests an impact of positive feelings on judgment. In a study conducted in a shopping mall, people who were unaware that they were subjects in an experiment were approached and given a small free-sample note pad or nail clipper from a person claiming to be a company representative. Subsequently when these subjects participated in a consumer opinion survey being conducted by a different person at another place in the mall, they evaluated the performance and service records of their automobiles and television sets more positively than did a control group whose members had not been given the free sample (Isen et al. 1978). This effect of feelings on evaluation has been attributed to the influence of feelings on memory. Tversky and Kahneman (1973, 1974) have pointed out that judgments are likely to be influenced by the thoughts that come to mind most easily. Since positive affect can serve as a retrieval cue for positive material in memory, making it more likely that positive thoughts will come to mind, positive affect may thus be able to influence judgment.

Later we will consider the impact of affect on memory in more detail. At that time two points will be discussed more fully because they appear to have both theoretical and practical implications. First, there seems to be an asymmetry between positive and negative affect (especially sadness) in effects on memory. Most studies investigating the influence of sadness find that it does not facilitate the recall of negative material comparably with the way in which positive affect facilitates the recall of positive material. Second, investigation of the impact of feelings on memory suggests that the effect tends to be one at time of retrieval, mediated by the meaning of the material to be recalled, rather than a state-dependent-learning effect. This distinction has theoretical and practical implications, which we will consider.

Positive affect has also been found to influence the way in which people go about making decisions and solving problems. In particular, mild, positive affect has been shown to promote simplification of complex tasks under some circumstances (Isen 1987; Isen and Means 1983; Isen et al. 1982). For example, there are times when positive affect appears to make the use of heuristics in decision making more likely. Such task simplification may relate to consumer behavior and response to advertising because it implies that simplified, heuristic approaches might be more effective when a person is feeling happy than at another time.

Researchers studying the factors that influence persuasion have identified two kinds of processes that can occur: central or algorithmic and peripheral or heuristic (see chapter 5; Chaiken 1980, for fuller discussion of these concepts). If positive affect promotes the use of heuristics or reliance on peripheral factors under some circumstances, this suggests that such aspects of the persuasion situation might be relatively more important to the decision process when a person is experiencing positive affect than at another time. Some research has begun to investigate this question directly (Worth and Mackie 1987).

Use of heuristics and task simplification can lead to either impaired or improved task performance and to either poorer or more efficient decision making, depending on the situation and the requirements of the task. In one series of studies (Isen et al. 1982), for example, subjects in positive-affect conditions were more likely than those in control conditions to use an intuitive solution and a heuristic in solving two different types of problems (a physics timer-tape problem used to study time-rate-distance relationships and a relative frequency judgment). In these problems, simplifying the situation and using a heuristic or an intuitive answer led to incorrect answers; therefore a subject's performance was impaired by the presence of positive affect. In other situations, however, it may be that the ability to find a heuristic to use on an otherwise unsolvable task might improve performance. Additional aspects of the task situation also may play a role in whether performance will be impaired or improved by positive affect. For example, it has been pointed out that these situations provided no feedback to the subjects as to the correctness of their answers, and it has been suggested that this absence of feedback may have been a factor in the impaired performance that resulted.

For an illustration that positive affect can lead to improved performance under some circumstances, consider the results of a study in which subjects were asked to choose a car for purchase. In this complex decision-making task, there were six cars that differed along each of nine dimensions, such as purchase price, resale value, fuel economy, and interior roominess. Subjects in whom positive affect had been induced (by report of success on an unrelated task) were more efficient in reaching a decision than were control subjects (Isen and Means 1983). The cars chosen by the two groups did not differ on average, but the experimental subjects reached a decision more quickly (in eleven minutes, as contrasted with the control group's mean of nineteen minutes), eliminating unimportant dimensions from the material to be considered and engaging in less rechecking of information that had already been considered.

The findings of these two types of studies (car choice and heuristics in problem solving) are completely compatible, though the two showed different effects on performance (one indicated what might be called improved performance, the other impaired; see Isen et al. 1982, and Isen 1987, for a fuller discussion of this issue). Together they suggest that people who are feeling happy may sometimes tend to simplify at least some types of decision or problem-solving situations.

It should also be noted, however, that these were complex tasks, not readily solved or answered. The car-choice problem, for example, presented a large amount of information, and subjects who did not simplify the problem had difficulty getting through it. Thus the tendency that was observed for positive-affect subjects to simplify decision tasks may occur only in complex, otherwise unmanageable situations. More research is needed not only on the tendency of people in positive-affect conditions to use heuristics and otherwise simplify tasks but also more generally on the decision-making processes of persons who are feeling happy.

Induced good feelings have also been observed to influence categorization, to result in more unusual first associates to neutral words, and to facilitate creative problem solving as represented by tasks such as Duncker's candle task and the Mednick's Remote Associates Test (Isen and Daubman 1984; Isen, Daubman, and Nowicki 1987; Isen, Johnson, Mertz, and Robinson 1985). These results suggest that cognitive organization—patterns of association and perceived interrelatedness of ideas—may be influenced by affective state. Later we will consider these findings, including their possible relevance to advertising and consumer behavior, in greater detail.

Positive affect has also been found to influence people's preferences and behavior in situations of risk or uncertainty. In hypothetical risk situations or where the chance of winning is *high,* positive affect appears to be associated with risky behavior relative to that of a control group. However, where meaningful loss is possible and salient, positive affect is associated with increased sensitivity to loss and with behaviors that protect against loss (such as cautiousness), relative to a control group. In one study, subjects were given the opportunity to gamble with chips representing fractions of their credit for participating in the experiment (a real loss), and the only bet open to them was a high-risk bet (17 percent chance of winning). Under these circumstances, persons in whom positive affect had been induced bet less than control subjects (Isen and Patrick 1983). In another study in which the dependent measure was acceptable probability level for placing a predetermined bet of one, five, or ten chips (again representing fractions of participation credit), subjects in whom positive affect had been induced, relative to controls, required a higher probability of winning before they were willing to bet five or ten chips (but not for one chip). In these conditions, experimental subjects also expressed a higher percentage of thoughts about losing than did control subjects, in a thought-listing task (Isen and Geva 1987). Findings from these two studies suggest that positive-affect subjects tend to be more cautious than control subjects where the potential for loss is high.

Another study has indicated that positive affect influences the subjective negative utility of losses, making possible losses seem worse than they normally might (Isen, Nygren, and Ashby 1985). This study used a procedure devised by Davidson, Suppes, and Siegel (1956) to estimate perceived utility while holding probability constant, by having subjects indicate their preferences over a series of gambles. Results indicated that potential losses held greater negative utilities for subjects who had received a small free gift than for those in a control situation.

This finding is compatible with those showing increased cautiousness among positive-affect subjects, and it suggests that the effect may be mediated by an impact of positive feeling on perceived utility (aversiveness) of loss (independent of any influence of affect on subjective proability of an event's occurrence). That is, it suggests that losses may seem worse to people who are feeling good. Thus it indicates that for people who are feeling happy, avoidance of loss and affect maintenance may be more of a factor in decisions posing risk and potential loss. These findings are compatible with the idea that positive affect promotes mood protection as well as more outgoing tendencies and that sometimes countervailing tendencies generated by positive feelings will need to be reconciled in order to predict behavior under conditions of positive affect.

These findings regarding the influence of affect on people's preferences in situations of risk may be of great interest to marketers and to students of consumer behavior generally. Potentially they relate to consumers' reactions to advertisements involving risk or safety, their reactions to products themselves involving risk or safety, and the ways in which people may use products. Because advertisements sometimes induce positive affect, the risk-preference data may suggest some important considerations regarding the compatibility of certain kinds of ads and products. These are all topics for continued research.

In summary, these and related findings suggest that mild affective states may influence processes relevant to consumer decision making and behavior in a wide variety of ways. I have selected three of the research findings presented in this overview to discuss in more detail: (1) the influence of affect on memory, (2) the asymmetry between positive and negative affect in effects on memory, and (3) the fact that positive affect appears to change patterns of association and to promote a relatively broad cognitive organization. These findings may help us to understand better how affect influences cognitive processes relevant to consumer decision making and behavior.

Affect and Memory

One influence of affect on memory that has been found rather consistently is an effect of positive feelings at time of *retrieval* (attempted recall). People who are made to feel happy show facilitated recall of positive material learned during the experimental session, relative to other material learned then, and relative to people not exposed to positive-affect-inducing treatments (Isen et al. 1978; Laird et al. 1982; Nasby and Yando 1982; Teasdale and Fogarty 1979; Teasdale and Russell 1983). This suggests that positive feelings can cue material that is organized in the mind as relevant to positive affect.

To understand this effect it is helpful to consider the concepts of "accessibility" and "priming" (Brown 1979; Neely 1976, 1977; Tulving and Pearlstone 1966). Accessibility refers to the ease of retrieving learned material under particular conditions of recall. (Tulving and Pearlstone 1966 distinguished this concept from "availability," which refers to whether material has been learned at all.) Several studies have demonstrated that the presence at time of attempted recall of a cue that "primes" the material (that is, makes one think of something related to the material to be recalled) facilitates recall of the material. For instance, Tulving and Pearlstone (1966) found that subjects could recall more words from a list of learned words when presented with the name of the category appropriate to those words at time of retrieval than when not given this cue. For example, if subjects had learned a list of words and one of them was *Texas*, their recall might be better if they were presented with the word *states* at the time of attempted recall than if not given that cue. Those authors interpreted this finding as evidence for the difference between availability of material in memory storage and accessibility of that same material under particular conditions of recall. Material of the category was said to be more accessible, and therefore more easily recalled, under conditions of retrieval in which the category was primed. Several other studies have shown that people respond more quickly and easily to words that are related to material to which they have recently responded, whether these are category names, category members, or other related words or social concepts (Higgins and King 1981; Jacobson 1973; Loftus 1973; Loftus and Loftus 1974; Meyer and Schvaneveldt 1971; Posner and Snyder 1975; Srull and Wyer 1979; Warren 1977). Thus, thinking about something or having it brought to mind appears to facilitate responding compatible with that topic.

Similarly it was proposed that positive affect could serve as a retrieval cue for positive material in memory, rendering such material more accessible and facilitating responding compatible with positive affect. There is now considerable evidence that this is the case, and it seems that positive affective state—feelings—can function like category name or other organizing unit as a cue to prime related cognitive material. Thus it appears that feelings, at least positive feelings, can cue material organized in the mind as related to those feelings.

Other studies have reported an *encoding* effect of positive feelings whereby people who are happy at the time of learning later show better recall of positive material in the list of items or paragraph being learned than other material, relative to controls. (This effect has been called "mood-congruent learning" by Bower and his colleagues.) Bower, Gilligan, and Monteiro (1981), using hypnosis to induce affect, found that participants recalled more facts about persons described as happy (more facts compatible with a positive state) when they themselves had been happy while learning the material and that persons who learned material while feeling sad showed a superiority of memory for information compatible with the negative affective state. Nasby and Yando (1982), using fifth-grade children as subjects and nonhypnotic mood induction, also found that a positive encoding mood facilitated learning positive trait adjectives and that anger at time of learning improved later recall of negative material. (However, they did not find a facilitative effect of sadness at time of encoding. Sadness at encoding did not improve recall of negative material but did impair recall of positive information.) Thus people who are happy may find it easier to learn material compatible with their positive state, and this may improve their memory of that material later, even if they are not made happy at the time of recall (Bower, Gilligan, and Monteiro 1981; Nasby and Yando 1982). This finding, like the retrieval effect, suggests that positive material somehow receives preferential treatment in memory when one is happy.

Another type of effect reported in the affect-and-memory literature, but least reliably, is the *state-dependent-learning effect* (called "mood-dependent recall" by Bower and his colleagues). This refers to the facilitation of recall by the matching of affective *states* at time of learning and recall, independent of the content or meaning of the material to be recalled. It refers to the tendency for any material learned in a specific state to be recalled better when one is again in that same state than at another time.

State-dependent-learning effects based on distinctive physiological states, such as alcoholic intoxication, have been reported in humans for some time (Weingartner and Faillace 1971). In these situations, a person's recall is better if he or she is in the same state (intoxicated or not intoxicated) that he or she was in when the material was learned. This effect, small in magnitude and noted more clearly in alcoholics than in normals (Weingartner and Faillace 1971), is conceptually similar to others in the learning (including animal learning) literature suggesting that reinstatement of context can be a slight aid to memory. These studies have shown that by presenting, at time of retrieval, context cues (such as color of the walls of a room or experimental chamber) that were present at time of learning, under some circumstances one can slightly facilitate recall of the material learned in that same context.

A state-dependent effect of positive feelings has been reported by a few authors (Bartlett, Burleson, and Santrock 1979; Bartlett and Santrock 1978; Bower 1981; Bower, Monteiro, and Gilligan 1978), but it has more frequently not been found (Isen et al. 1978; Laird et al. 1982; Nasby and Yando 1982; see Eich and Birnbaum 1982; Isen 1984; Isen et al. 1978, for discussion of this issue). Most recently, Bower and his colleagues (for example, Bower and Mayer 1985), among the primary proponents of affect-based state-dependent learning, have reported repeated failures to obtain this effect and have suggested that it is not reliable.

It appears that a state-dependent-learning effect of feelings is most likely to be observed in situations in which people have few, if any, other or better ways to attempt to recall the material. Since people tend to use the meaning of material as a basis for learning and retrieval where possible (Tulving and Thomson 1973), state-dependent memory in humans may be observed when the material being learned and tested is meaningless and when people therefore cannot use their preferred strategy (meaning) for recall. Another situation in which state-dependent-learning effects based on emotional states may be observed may be where emotions are especially extreme (as in clinical states) or are for some other reason focal in subjects' attention (as in hypnotically induced affective states). These speculations may be addressed in future research. However, the now widely acknowledged difficulty in obtaining state-dependent-learning effects based on feeling states, together with the weakness of the effect even where observed, suggests that this effect may not be very influential in everyday situations.

The fact that retrieval effects of positive feelings appear to be consistently obtained, whereas state-dependent-learning effects based on normal feeling states tend not to be the rule, may have theoretical implications about the role that affect plays in memory. In addition, these findings may hold practical implications regarding the circumstances under which, and the ways in which, one might expect affect's influence to be felt.

One point of theoretical significance is that these findings suggest that affect's influence on memory is mediated by meaning, rather than mechanistically, as a state-dependent-learning effect would imply. The state-dependent-learning effect would suggest that affect functions as a physical context cue, mechanistically cueing anything that happened to be present at the time of the feelings, regardless of the meaning or tone of that material or the way in which the learner had encoded the material. As we have seen, however, the research literature shows that positive material is more readily recalled when one is happy than at another time and that this effect is not usually based on state-dependent learning. Thus the literature suggests that positive affect does not simply act as a physical context cue. Rather, good feelings appear to influence memory through meaning, cueing material that is meaningfully related to positive affect.

Given the encoding-specificity principle (Tulving and Thomson 1973), this suggests that positive affect may be the basis of a cognitive category that is actively used by people in learning, organizing material, and remembering. The encoding-specificity principle (Tulving and Thomson 1973) holds that in order for a cue to be effective in facilitating retrieval, the material to be recalled needs to have been organized and stored in memory as relevant to that cue. Thus in order for positive affect to be capable of cueing words or thoughts, those concepts must be organized in a person's mind as related to positive feelings. Moreover, the encoding-specificity principle suggests that those strategies actively used for learning and remembering will play a role in what is learned and how that material is stored and later retrievable. Thus, a person's choice of strategy for learning influences what is later retrieved and determines the cues that will be effective in prompting memories; the finding that mild positive affect is a readily effective retrieval cue suggests that people use normal, common positive feelings as a way of organizing and remembering experience. Not only do they remember how things made them feel, but the affect-and-memory literature suggests that they often organize cognitive material in terms of how it made them feel. (It may not be the only organizing principle that people use, but it appears to be one.)

This has important implications for the broader role of affect in the cognitive system and in decision making and for the ways in which affect may influence response to communication and behavior based on those responses. It suggests that affect is an important dimension of memory, one that people tend to use, but that not all affects or all material to be remembered may be suitable for each other. Positive affect appears to be quite effective in cueing positive material in memory (material organized in mind as relevant to positive feelings), but attempts to link other kinds of material with positive affect by reinstatement of context (matching affective states at time of learning and recall) may be less successful. Thus efforts to capitalize on the effectiveness of positive affect as a retrieval cue will need to take into consideration the content of the material to be cued.

Applied to advertising and consumer psychology, this suggests that the strategy of using positive affective state as a cue for a product may be more appropriate for some types of products than for others. For example, soft drinks or wine coolers, which may be used on occasions of good times and good feelings, may be good candidates for positive-affect-inducing ads. Relations that are even more specific may be helpful, as implied in several chapters in this book suggesting that specific states or specific topics may be tied cognitively to some material or products (for example, chapter 12). In contrast, strategies based on state-dependent-learning (that is, matching of affective states or other context cues at time of learning and intended recall) may be less successful. Attempts to utilize reinstatement of affective context in order to influence recall of a product or an ad, or to influence purchase and use of the product, may show little effectiveness unless the product is one that lends itself to classification in a positive category and in fact is so classified in people's minds. Thus if one expects people to be happy when buying or using the product and if the product is of a type compatible with those positive feelings, one may attempt to use the knowledge that positive affect cues positive material in order to heighten recall of the product (and presumably use and sales of it) by using advertising that associates the product with positive feelings.

This line of reasoning appears compatible with the research results reported by Calder and Gruder (chapter 12) regarding the role of specific concepts. Both suggest a more schematic and meaning-based cognitive process than is often assumed to characterize thinking. For example, in the network and spreading-activation model of cognition, the operation of the network, and the spread of activation, is often assumed to be automatic and mechanistic. However, the affect data, and other results such as Calder and Gruder's, suggest the importance of interpretation. There may be times when mechanistic or automatic processes do occur but often thought processes are more purposive and schematic. Thus a positive-affect ad (say, one including humor or one showing people having fun at a picnic in a grassy, lush spot) may not be as appropriate for something like a Toro lawnmower as it would be for a new brand of wine cooler. Although the Toro may be associated with grass, the grass present at the picnic may not make one think of one's Toro. (If it does, that is probably because of some problem that has occurred, and these thoughts will not be compatible with positive affect.) This may be because enjoying grass or playing on grass may not be schematically related to cutting the grass (yard work). In contrast, the wine cooler is more schematically and meaningfully related to a positive-affect state and therefore should be more readily cued by such a state. The purpose of the positive-affect ad in this case might be to associate the name of the brand with the product and the affective state.

One point that needs to be considered is whether all products in a positive general product class such as "soft drink" might be cued by positive feelings and thus benefit from positive-affect advertisements. If this is so, then every positive-affect ad for Coke is an ad for Pepsi and every other soft drink (or even related beverages such as beer), and the whole enterprise might be seen as self-defeating. Research is needed to determine the extent to which related products benefit from successful advertising campaigns and, if so, whether this effect follows a generalization gradient or tends to be more schematic (see chapter 11 for a discussion of related issues). To some extent successful campaigns for specific products probably can sometimes increase sales of an entire product class. However, it is also likely that there are ways to target the effects of positive affect a bit more specifically.

For example, overall, this analysis suggests that focus must be on the brand name rather than the general product type, unless the target brand already is the leading, best-liked, best-known brand in the field, with no close competitors. For a well-known, leading brand *with* close competitors this analysis suggests that a good strategy might be to identify the product (brand name) with a particular, distinctive (but common) positive affective state (such as the youthful exhilarated infatuation depicted in the Michael J. Fox Pepsi ads). This may be one reason that advertisers sometimes try to give a popular product an image, and it suggests that it might often be wise to include a positive affect component in this image.

For less well-known products, the main problem is that the product name must be remembered. Advertisers planning a positive-affect campaign for a product in a positive domain must take care to associate their product name with the ad and the affect. Affect commercials for soft drinks, beer, and wine seem designed to capitalize on the natural association that these products have with positive affect, but they often run into exactly the problem mentioned: although the ad may be enjoyable, if the product is not sufficiently highlighted, the consumer at point of purchase may not be able to recall the particular product that was supposed to be cued by the affect. Instead he or she may recall the ad and the positive affect but not the product. In such cases, a clever or very appealing ad may serve to increase sales of the best-known brand rather than of its own product. Thus it would be important to provide memorable references to the brand name, as well as memorable generation of affect. It might also be useful to include point-of-purchase reminders that the popular ad is for that product.

A recent ad campaign that seems to have taken many of these considerations into account is that for Bartles and Jaymes wine cooler. This was initially a campaign for a new or little-known product in a domain with positive-affect potential. The ad campaign used positive affect (humor) but was distinctive and identified the product name centrally in the ad. By identifying the humorous characters as the very product name itself, as well as displaying the package prominently in the ad, the advertisement made it more likely that consumers would recall the name of the product and associate it with the positive-affect generated. The effectiveness was increased by following through with larger posters of these characters in stores, which immediately reminded potential purchasers of the ad and the name of the product.

Thus it appears that understanding the way in which positive affect can be used as a retrieval cue can enable more effective message communication and may keep us from making certain kinds of mistakes in planning communications. Research into specific issues such as distinctiveness and carryover among similar products, as well as ways of creating new schemata or bringing new products into existing schemata, would seem important in this context.

Throughout this discussion it has been noted that negative affect is a less successful memory device than positive affect. In the next section we examine this situation in more detail.

Asymmetry between Happiness and Sadness in Effects on Memory

Most of the studies that attempt to investigate simultaneously the influence of comparable happiness and sadness on recall of affect-compatible material, whether describing encoding (Nasby and Yando 1982), retrieval (Isen et al. 1978; Nasby and Yando 1982; Teasdale and Fogarty 1979), or state-dependent-learning effects (Bartlett et al. 1982; Bartlett and Santrock 1979), report a nonsymmetrical effect of sadness and happiness. That is, while positive affect facilitates the recall of positive material, sadness either fails to facilitate the recall of negative material or facilitates it in a much attenuated way compared to the effect of positive feelings. This implies that attempts to use negative affect as a retrieval cue at the very least will have to be carefully constructed and in fact may be ill fated in most cases.

Understanding the cause of the asymmetry between positive and negative affect in influence on memory may help us to determine how to approach negative feelings and/or negatively regarded material. It has been suggested that this asymmetry may reflect an asymmetry in the way in which negative and positive material are stored in or accessed from memory (Isen 1985). That is, the structures of negative and positive material in mind may be different, perhaps varying in size and/or in internal consistency (variety of material included within the structure) and interrelatedness with other material. The structure associated with positive affect appears to be relatively broad and extensive, whereas that associated with negative affect may be smaller, narrower, less well interconnected with other material, and more specific to the particular state induced or even the way in which it was induced. This suggestion would be compatible not only with the asymmetry that has been observed between negative and positive affect in ability to cue material of generally like valence but also with the fact that negative affect has been found to impair access to positive material (Nasby and Yando 1982).

Another possible interpretation of the asymmetry noted is that it may reflect differences in the ways in which negative and positive material are accessed from memory. This may say something about peoples' strategies for coping with, or enjoying, their affective states. That is, people may want to remain in a positive state and therefore may encourage or foster their own access to compatible material, but they may want to change a negative state, especially sadness. Thus unless instructed to maintain their induced negative states, as in some of the studies in which symmetrical effects of happiness and sadness were reported (Bower 1981; Bower, Gilligan, and Montiero 1981; Bower, Montiero and Gilligan 1978), people who are feeling sad may not try to access negative material or may even purposely try to access other kinds of material.

The distinction between structure and process is not absolute; these two possibilities are not mutually exclusive (see, for example, Mandler 1979, 1984, for discussion of this issue). Habitual and continued use of certain strategies or processes can lead to the creation of certain kinds of cognitive structures, and the existence of structural differences can give rise to different processes and can promote the use of different strategies. Most likely, both influences are important in most situations. More research is needed on the kinds of motivations and strategies that may be introduced by the presence of affective states and on the kinds of material cued by various affective states.

Thus the observed asymmetry may result from people's motivations to avoid negative states, or it may reflect differences in the cognitive structures related to these two broad classes of material, or both. In either case, the observed asymmetry between negative and positive affect in effects on memory suggests that negative affect may be relatively narrowly and specifically organized or represented in memory, and the individual negative affects (such as anger or sadness) may be differentiated still further in this way. This implies that negative material will either be virtually impossible to cue by means of common, everyday feelings, under normal circumstances, or the situation and materials will have to be carefully constructed to be completely and specifically compatible.

Furthermore, this asymmetry between negative and positive affect in ability to serve as a retrieval cue must be viewed in conjunction with the fact that the influence of affect on memory is mediated by meaning and by people's strategies for remembering rather than simply on the basis of physical stimulus properties and as a result of automatic association. This suggests not only that the affect state induced and the material to be cued may have to match precisely if the negative state is to cue the material but also that there must be reason to expect that in the learning situation people would have used the negative affect as a way to organize the material for memory storage. At present very little is known about the circumstances under which people might be expected to do this.

Some advertisers seem tempted to use affect in the negative context, either as a cue for recall in negatively valenced situations or as a means of improving message recipients' feelings toward disliked products or material. Therefore it might be helpful to speculate a bit further about the kinds of cautions that the experimental literature suggests might be in order when using negative affect in advertising.

One type of situation in which advertisers seem tempted to use reinstatement of context, with negative-affect cueing, is in advertising products such as pain relievers. For example, advertisers might attempt to induce a mildly painful state while providing information about their pain reliever, believing that in the future, when the message recipient is experiencing the pain of a headache, the pain will cue the material learned while in the simulated pain state, and the person will therefore be more likely to think of the advertised product and message. (Farfetched as this may seem to some readers, I have seen ads that I think must have been based on this or a related principle.)

There are several reasons, however, that this strategy may not be wise. First, the existing research suggests that in humans, reinstatement of context (the state-dependent-learning effect) generally tends to have, at best, only a slight effect in facilitating recall and that there is little evidence for any facilitative effect at all when mild negative feelings are used as the contextual factor.

Second, while the possibility remains that pain may be different from other negative states in its effectiveness as a cue, research is needed on the influence of pain in a learning situation. Not only would it be important to know how effective pain is as a retrieval cue for material learned while in simulated pain, but also it would be necessary to know something about how well people learn while in pain. This is because the strategy described involves putting people in mild pain at the time of learning so that later pain will cue the material learned. However, if little is learned while in pain, then the cue at retrieval will not facilitate recall of much material even if it is determined that pain can be an effective cue. Moreover, if it is true for pain, as it may be for some other negative affect states, that an effective retrieval cue will have to be precisely relevant to the negative material to be recalled, then advertisers may have to be careful that their ad induces pain and not other negative feeling states such as anger.

Finally, in order for this strategy to be sensible, there would have to be reason to expect that people would organize the material to be learned in terms of the pain cue in the ad (or caused by the ad). Recall that the research literature suggests that active processes involving meaning and interpretation (rather than automatic processes) figure most often in human learning. Thus it does not seem that any negative "arousal" alone (which people often assume accompanies negative affect) should be expected to facilitate learning and recall under most circumstances. Rather, in order to expect any facilitative effect of the negative feelings (pain), there would have to be reason to expect people to use the unpleasant cue as a way to organize their thoughts. The circumstances under which people may be likely to use such a strategy for memory are not yet well explored. For all of these reasons, the research literature suggests caution in attempting to use negative affect as a memory cue.

This raises the issue of why negative (annoying) ads appear to work and therefore continue to be used. I have been told by advertising executives that some ads that are widely viewed as annoying, such as the old "ring around the collar" ads for Wisk, nonetheless are effective in stimulating sales. In these cases, however, it is not clear how the advertiser established that it was the ad in particular that boosted sales of the product. It may be that Wisk sold in spite of the obnoxious ad rather than because of it. For example, if the product is of high quality, is well packaged, and is promoted in other ways (such as by coupons and pricing) besides use of the ad, these factors may override the unpleasant ad in influencing sales. This kind of an explanation is compatible with the theoretical points already raised because the latter suggest that any mild negative affect engendered at the time of viewing the ad might not be used as a way of encoding information about the product and therefore may not figure prominently at recall or point of purchase. Thus if for some other reason the person thinks to purchase the product, the mildly negative ad may not interfere. It is not clear whether this would be true of extremely negative affect, as it appears to be for mildly negative feelings.

Another negative context in which advertisers may be tempted to try to use affect is one in which they are dealing with a product that has a bad image or generates negative feelings. However, it may be difficult to use affect to change people's feelings about negatively valenced items. For example, if it is determined that a product has an image problem, some may attempt to remedy this through association with positive affect. They might attempt to use a classical conditioning paradigm to relate the negatively valenced item to something positive, hoping to change the negative reaction to a positive reaction. But the research literature suggests that such a technique might not be successful. First, positive affect does not appear to extend its influence to negative material. For example, positive feelings were found to influence the rating of neutral or ambiguous material rather than to influence the rating of more clearly valenced material (Isen and Shalker 1982; Schiffenbauer 1974). For another example, positive affect led to more unusual word associations to neutral words as stimuli but not to negative words as stimuli (Isen et al. 1985). Thus there is reason to believe that attempts to associate negative and positive items, or a negative item with positive feelings, might not be successful.

There is another reason that it might not be advisable to try to use positive affect directly in coping with negatively viewed material. Studies indicate that people in whom positive affect had been induced were less helpful to a disliked cause than were control subjects (Forest et al. 1979). This suggests that attempts to improve the image of a disliked product by means of attaching positive affect to it may backfire. That is, in the studies described, there was evidence that people in whom positive affect had been induced demonstrated more freedom to express their thoughts and to behave as they pleased. Thus if people are generally negatively disposed toward a product, inducing positive affect in consumers by means of a humorous ad, for example, may cause recipients of the message to denigrate the disliked product further. It may be necessary to change the attitude toward a disliked product first, say by means of information, before any attempt at increasing positive feelings toward it through positive affect is attempted. Together these results and this line of analysis suggest that negative affect may have to be approached very carefully and that affect may not be the best dimension to use where there is negative affect.

In summary, some products or advertisements may not lend themselves to recall enhancement by means of affect. Positive feeling is much more effective than negative as a memory aid, and not all kinds of products are likely to become associated with positive affect. Generally, negative affect may be a relatively ineffective type of cue, so that products associated with negative feelings may be difficult to prime by means of affect, under normal circumstances. Moreover, products associated with negative feelings may not easily be transformed into favorites simply by means of association with liked items or good feelings. It might be better to use another, nonaffective, approach altogether with such material. This issue merits further investigation.

Positive Affect and Cognitive Organization

The third point to be considered is the fact that positive affect tends to influence cognitive organization in such a way that it facilitates creativity, remote associations, perception of relatedness among cognitions, and in general a more integrated and flexible thinking style. Positive material itself is extensive and well interconnected, in contrast with negative material. Further, recent studies on the influence of positive affect on tasks such as categorization, word association, and creative problem solving suggest that positive affect may result in more flexible thinking and a more integrated organization of even neutral material. This means that for a person who is feeling happy, patterns of association and perceived interrelatedness may be changed from what they are for persons in a neutral state. A person in a positive feeling state may see implications that others do not see and may interpret communications differently.

For example, in one series of studies, persons in whom positive affect had been induced tended to categorize a wider range of stimuli together, whether measured by a rating task or a sorting task (Isen and Daubman 1984). In the rating task (similar to that used by Eleanor Rosch to study prototypicality) people were asked to rate on a scale from 1 to 10 the degree to which they felt an item was a member of a category. Those in whom positive affect had been induced rated fringe exemplars (that is, words like *purse, cane,* and *ring* in the category "clothing") as better exemplars of the category than did persons in a control condition. In a sorting task in which subjects were asked to sort the stimuli into collections of items that could be grouped together, people in whom positive affect had been induced made larger groupings (said more items could go together) than did control subjects (Isen and Daubman 1984). In a more recent study, it has also been found, however, that relative to controls positive-affect subjects sort stimuli into more different groupings if given multiple trials and asked how many different ways the items can be organized (Isen and Daubman 1986). Thus persons who are feeling happy seem more cognitively flexible and more able to make associations and see potential relations among stimuli than do persons in a neutral state.

This suggestion of change in cognitive organization as a function of positive affect is also supported by studies of word association and creative problem solving. Several recent studies show that persons who are happy, compared with controls, give more unusual and more diverse first associates to neutral stimulus words in a word-association task (Isen et al. 1985). For instance, to the stimulus word *house,* whose most common associate is *home,* persons in positive-affect conditions tended more than control subjects to respond with related but uncommon words such as *residence* or *apartment.* The unusual responses of persons in the positive-affect conditions suggest that their associations to the target words were more far-ranging and their thoughts more flexible.

Studies of creative problem solving also offer support for the proposition that positive affect can influence cognitive organization. (By "creative," I mean the useful combination of elements that are not usually related to each other; Koestler 1964; Mednick 1962.) Several recent studies indicate that persons in whom positive affect has been induced are better able to solve two tasks usually considered to require creativity, Duncker's candle task and the Mednick's Remote Associates Test (Isen, Daubman, and Nowicki 1987). In the candle task, subjects are shown a candle, a box of tacks, and a book of matches and are asked to affix the candle to the wall (a cork board) in such a way that it will burn without dripping wax on the table or floor. (The problem can be solved if the tacks are removed from the box and the box is tacked to the wall and used as a platform for the candle.) The Remote Associates Test is an individual-difference measure of creativity designed by M.T. Mednick, S.A. Mednick, and E.V. Mednick (1964), based on S.A. Mednick's (1962) associative theory of creativity. Subjects are given three words and asked to think of a fourth word that relates to each of the other three.

These findings suggest that positive affect may influence cognitive organization (the patterns of relatedness perceived among stimuli) and, by implication, the inferences that people may make from material presented. This may have important potential implications for consumer psychology. The effects of positive feelings on cognitive organization may be relevant at either the point of seeing an advertisement or at the point of purchase and/or use of a product. For example, at point of purchase, consumers who are feeling good may be more likely to see more potential uses for products or to see the connection between a product and some desired outcome. At the point of viewing or hearing an ad, positive affect may lead to a more complete grasp of the persuasive situation, the implications of what is being conveyed, the communicator's intent, and so forth. These points suggest that the use of humor or free gifts, for example, in advertising might be especially appropriate to certain kinds of products (for example, those for which one hopes a consumer will find increased application and occasion for use) or in certain situations (for example, those in which one is trying to increase consumers' enjoyment and use of a product). The recent ad campaign for Bartles and Jaymes wine cooler, mentioned above, is also a good example of advertising that seems to make use of this association between positive feelings and innovation. In several of the spots, the intent of the ad seems to be to extend the use of wine cooler (for example, to bagel-and-lox breakfast), and it uses humor effectively to make the suggestion.

These points regarding the effect of positive feelings on cognitive organization also suggest, however, that people who are feeling happy may think and behave in nontypical ways. Therefore attempts to communicate with elated persons or to affect their memories may have to take an approach different from the usual. In addition, sometimes the relationship between positive affect and innovation may raise unexpected concerns, such as improper use of products.

One area of concern to advertisers may be potential misuse of products by consumers in ways that can result in product liability suits. The work indicating that positive affect may result in more understanding of implied messages and in more innovative use of products suggests that positive-affect ads may need to be especially careful not to suggest or imply endorsement of dangerous practices and to make a special effort to clarify any hidden danger in any practices that they do illustrate or tend to promote. (The data indicating that positive-affect subjects are especially sensitive to potential loss and tend to be protective of themselves suggest that clarifying the possibility of danger may help protect against consumer injury.)

A recent positive-affect ad for Mountain Dew soft drink was criticized by community health personnel for showing happy picnickers diving head-first into a mountain stream. The combination of the positive affect generated by the ad, the nonobviousness of the danger of diving head-first into water of unknown depth (the danger is spinal cord injury), and the implication in the ad that such a practice was safe and appropriate was especially problematic. The ad was removed in response to the objection. While it is not clear that advertisers or product manufacturers could be held liable for injury resulting from unsafe practices by consumers, nevertheless, it would be beneficial if advertisers used their awareness of the likely consequences of messages to plan the safest ads possible.

In addition, positive affect may have an impact on the social influence process generally, and therefore persuasive communications designed to influence elated or amused persons may need to be prepared with this possibility in mind. Elated persons may be more receptive to persuasive communications under some circumstances, but they may be more independent under other circumstances. Moreover, they may go beyond the information given and make more inferences than the advertiser intended, possibly inferences regarding the communicator's goals or characteristics. Research is needed to determine how these effects might influence people's responses to ads designed to utilize positive affect.

Concluding Comments

The points made in this chapter have important implications for understanding the ways in which affect may influence response to communication and the decision processes and behavior, including consumer behavior, that result from communications. Most important, they point to the role that meaning, interpretation, and purposive cognitive strategies play in memory and decision making. Rather than suggesting that most learning and response is automatic, the data indicate that people's responses may often depend on how they organize the material to be learned and how they interpret the learning and response situations. Understanding how this interpretation and organization are likely to be done and the circumstances under which automatic versus more interpretive processes are likely to be employed may help communicators to achieve their goals.

For example, it might be concluded on the basis of associative models that all stimuli present at the time of an affective state will be associated with that affective state. This assumption underlies the expectation of affect-based state-dependent-learning effects, but the data on the influence of affect on memory suggest otherwise. They indicate that such effects, while perhaps not impossible, are small, unreliable, and dependent on the absence of superior methods of learning. They suggest that everything present at time of positive affect is not equally likely to become associated with positive feelings, as if automatically; rather, some material appears to be more fitting for this association. The connection seems to be the result of a learning strategy aimed at organizing relevant material in memory rather than of an automatic associative process.

Results of studies on cognitive processes generally, and on the role of affect in cognition in particular, suggest that both automatic and interpretive processes occur together to influence memory, recall, and thinking. In order to design maximally effective communications, advertisers, like other communicators, need to be aware of both kinds of processes, the ways in which they work, and the circumstances under which one type is more likely to occur than the other.

One need not assume that affect, or something learned about one product, will necessarily spread to all other related products. While there is potential for this to occur, there may be ways to construct the communication so as to foster or circumvent this likelihood. Communicators can attempt to use conceptual material to try to highlight similarities or differences (depending on the communicators' goals) among products, situations, or practices. To the extent that associations are not automatic but rather are mediated by meaning, communicators can work with concepts to convey their intended message and structure the material to be learned and used most effectively. More research is needed to learn about the processes that people use in thinking and decision making and, in particular, the interplay between automatic and strategic processes in thinking.

The importance of learning strategies is also illustrated by the asymmetry between negative and positive affect in influence on memory. If memory processes were typically automatic, one might expect negative affect to have an impact parallel with that of positive, as indeed was suggested by proponents of a network and spreading-activation theory of the influence of affect on cognition. In contrast, the absence of symmetry between positive and negative affect is compatible with the suggestion that active processes are involved in memory, if one assumes that under most circumstances people may not want to use negative affect as a way to organize their minds.

Further, the effectiveness of positive feelings as a retrieval cue indicates not only that meaning or interpretation plays an important role in memory but also that positive feelings tend to be used by people as a way to categorize material. These results suggest that when exposed to material, people are likely, without prompting, to organize it and remember it according to how it makes them feel, especially if it makes them feel good. It is important to note that the positive affect dimension tends to be used by people, even without prompting. (It is also possible that this tendency is increased further when a cue, such as positive affect, is present at time of encoding and does prompt organization in terms of affect. This suggestion is supported by the data showing effects of positive affect at time of encoding.) Later people can recall this material more easily when the feeling cue is present (that is, when they feel good) because of the way in which they had learned and stored it (not because of an automatic association between material learned and recalled in the same state).

The fact that positive affect is more often used than negative affect as a cue may also reflect the importance of purposive cognitive processes in memory in a slightly different way. Positive affect may be preferred for what might be called motivational reasons—that is, because it makes a person feel good. Or it may be used as a way to organize material simply because it is salient or because it is a large, broadly encompassing category. In summary, people seem to use categories to organize material for memory, in most cases, rather than to rely on automatic, simple contextual association; and positive affect appears to be a readily used category if it is present. According to these points, any salient category present in the material might likely be used to organize it. We must also consider the fact that positive affect may be used instrumentally, for purposes of affect improvement or maintenance. There is evidence that this can be the case, but an important question remains as to the circumstances under which this occurs. Clearly people cannot always think only about what makes them happy.

These points suggest that although automatic associations may sometimes occur, associationistic models of memory, in particular of the way in which affect influences cognition, may be in need of refinement or supplementation. They are helpful up to a point but do not account for all of the data. Thus the network and spreading-activation account of the way in which affect influences memory and decision making may be incomplete. Supplementary conceptualizations may be helpful to understanding the effects of feelings on cognitive processes. Unsupplemented, associative views of the way in which affect influences memory encounter problems in dealing with the findings mentioned thus far (the difficulty in observing state-dependent-learning effects based on affect and the asymmetry between negative and positive affect in ability to cue related cognitive material) because the findings imply that people actively organize material for memory. Moreover, there are additional findings that point to the need to supplement purely associative models of learning and memory.

For example, associative propositions alone also find it problematic that positive affect appears to be such an effective retrieval cue. The literature suggests that everyday, mild, positive affect is effective in cueing positive material and therefore potentially important in influencing cognitive processes. This, in and of itself, may be something of a problem for associationist models such as network and spreading-activation theory because, according to such theories, mild, everyday, positive feelings are so common that they should not function very effectively as memory cues. It is assumed in these theories that such common cues spread their cue potential automatically among all stimuli present and therefore lose the ability to signal discriminatively some of those stimuli. These theories do not consider, or at least do not emphasize, that some stimuli may inhere better to the cue and therefore may be facilitated by the cue even though other material is also present to be associated with the cue.

As noted by Ger (chapter 11), associative models also have difficulty with results showing an absence of gradients in effects of feelings on expectations (Johnson and Tversky 1983). Sometimes gradients in the effects of feelings have been observed, but, as Ger suggests, it is important to be able to predict when global effects (no differential effects based on a gradient of similarity to the target) will be obtained, as contrasted with the circumstances under which local or gradient effects are to be expected. To make this possible, it may be necessary to learn more about the knowledge structures associated with domains of interest. Further, if one wishes to understand how affect will spread (influence cognition and behavior), this will require learning more about the cognitive structures associated with various affective states.

Moreover, the finding that positive affect influences (broadens) cognitive organization and interpretation of material seems unanticipated by associationist models. In addition, these models have difficulty in dealing with the fact that positive affect broadens associations to neutral words but not to positive or negative ones (Isen et al. 1985). The influence of positive affect on cognitive organization therefore also suggests again that associative models do not present a complete picture of the way in which feelings influence cognitive processes; consequently, from this perspective too, it appears that a supplement to associative views would be helpful.

This does not mean that associationistic models of memory, or of the way in which affect influences cognition, should be rejected completely. Rather these points call attention to the imcompleteness of those models in accounting for all of the phenomena observed and the need to develop ideas to supplement the associationistic conceptualization. Clearly these models can be a useful tool, but equally clearly, some of their predictions seem not to hold for the influence of affect. Moreover, influences of affect that are not predicted by the network and spreading-activation model have been observed. Further exploration of these models, their implications, and alternative views seems warranted.

Sometimes people do learn automatically, but many times purposive processes, strategies, plans, and interpretation play a role in what is learned, recalled, or considered (see Isen 1984, 1987 for further discussion of these theoretical issues). Some associative models do have a conceptual component, as well as an automatic component. They do provide for the activation of concepts related by meaning, but the relationship between automatic and conceptual processes often is not made clear, so that it is difficult to know exactly what to expect. The relationship between conceptual and automatic processes, as well as questions of the circumstances under which automatic, as opposed to interpretative or motivated processes occur, and of how these kinds of processes interact to influence thinking, are important for further study.

I have also noted a difference between positive and negative affect in influence on memory and behavior. This asymmetry calls attention to the fact that positive and negative affect are not necessarily polar opposites, a common assumption. Instead it is apparent that they do not always produce equivalent, symmetrical, opposite, or parallel effects. Rather, their effects on memory and decision making seem to depend on what they make people think about and the cognitive and motivational processes that result. This situation reinforces the call for research into the cognitive structures associated with various affective states.

Finally, the material presented in this chapter addresses the question of the functional relationship between affect and cognition. It should be clear from this work that, functionally, affect and cognition influence one another. Thus they need not necessarily be juxtaposed with one another, as if they were opposite poles in a human system, or processes that precluded each other. That is, it is not necessary to presume that people *either* think *or* feel in response to a communication such as an ad. It is likely that they do both in most situations. Indeed the evidence suggests that rather than causing people not to think, affect (at least some affects) can influence thought by influencing what people think about, how they relate things to one another, what they try to accomplish, and how they go about solving problems. Thus feelings can have a substantial influence on thought processes and resultant behavior. Exploration of these effects is an exciting area for continued research.

References

Aderman, D. 1972. Elation, depression and helping behavior. *Journal of Personality and Social Psychology* 24:91–101.

Aderman, D., and Berkowitz, L. 1970. Observational set, empathy, and helping. *Journal of Personality and Social Psychology* 14:141–148.

Baron, R.A. 1984. Reducing organizational conflict: An incompatible response approach. *Journal of Applied Psychology* 69:272–279.

Baron, R.A., and Ball, R.L. 1974. The aggression-inhibiting influence of non-hostile humor. *Journal of Experimental Social Psychology* 10:23–33.

Bartlett, F.C. 1932. *Remembering: A study in experimental and social psychology.* New York: Cambridge University Press.

Bartlett, J.C.; Burleson, G.; and Santrock, J.W. 1982. Emotional mood and memory in young children. *Journal of Experimental Child Psychology* 34:59–76.

Bartlett, J.C., and Santrock, J.W. 1979. Affect-dependent episodic memory in young children. *Child Development* 50:513–518.

Batson, C.D.; Coke, J.S.; Chard, F.; Smith, D.; and Taliaferro, A. 1979. Generality of the "Glow of goodwill": Effects of mood on helping and information acquisition. *Social Psychology Quarterly* 42:176–179.

Batson, C.D.; Duncan, D.B.; Ackerman, P.; Buckley, T.; and Birch, K. 1981. Is empathic emotion a source of altruistic motivation? *Journal of Personality and Social Psychology* 40:290–302.

Bower, G.H. 1981. Mood and memory. *American Psychologist* 36:129–148.

Bower, G.H.; Gilligan S.G.; and Montiero, K.P. 1981. Selectivity of learning caused by affective states. *Journal of Experimental Psychology: General* 110:451–473.

Bower, G.H., and Mayer, D. 1985. Failure to replicate mood-dependent retrieval. *Bulletin of the Psychonomic Society* 23:39–42.

Bower, G.H.; Montiero, K.P.; and Gilligan, S.G. 1978. Emotional mood as a context for learning and recall. *Journal of Verbal Learning and Verbal Behavior* 17:573–585.

Bransford, J.D. 1979. *Human cognition.* Belmont, Calif.: Wadsworth.

Brown, A. 1979. Priming effects in semantic memory retrieval processes. *Journal of Experimental Psychology: Human Learning and Memory* 5:65–77.

Carnevale, P.J.D., and Isen, A.M. 1986. The influence of positive affect and visual access on the discovery of integrative solutions in bilateral negotiation. *Organizational Behavior and Human Decision Processes* 37, 1–13.

Chaiken, S. 1980. Heuristic vs. systematic information processes and the use of source vs. message cues in persuasion. *Journal of Personality and Social Psychology* 39: 752–776.

Davidson, D.; Suppes, P.; and Siegel, S. 1956. *Decision making: An experimental approach.* Stanford: Stanford University Press.

Dunker, K. 1945. On problem-solving. *Psychological Monographs* 58, whole no. 5.

Eich, J.E., and Birnbaum, I.M. 1982. Repetition, cueing and state-dependent memory. *Memory and Cognition* 10:103–114.

Forest, D.; Clark, M.S.; Mills, J.; and Isen, A.M. 1979. Helping as a function of feeling state and nature of the helping behavior. *Motivation and Emotion* 3:161–169.

Fried, R., and Berkowitz, L. 1979. Music hath charms . . . and can influence helpfulness. *Journal of Applied Social Psychology* 9:199–208.

Galizio, M., and Hendrick, C. 1972. Effect of musical accompaniment on attitude: The guitar as a prop for persuasion. *Journal of Applied Social Psychology* 2:350–359.

Gouaux, C. 1971. Induced affective states and interpersonal attraction. *Journal of Personality and Social Psychology* 20:37–43.

Griffitt, W.B. 1970. Environmental effects on interpersonal affective behavior: Ambient effective temperature and attraction. *Journal of Personality and Social Psychology* 15:240–244.

Higgins, E.T., and King, G. 1981. Accessibility of social constructs: Information processing consequences of individual contextual variability. In N. Cantor and J.F. Kihlstrom, eds., *Personality, cognition, and social interaction.* Hillsdale, N.J.: Erlbaum.

Isen, A.M. 1970. Success, failure, attention and reactions to others: The warm glow of success. *Journal of Personality and Social Psychology* 15:294–301.

———. 1984. Toward understanding the role of affect in cognition. In R. Wyer and T. Srull, eds., *Handbook of social cognition.* Hillsdale, N.J.: Erlbaum.

———. 1985. The asymmetry of happiness and sadness in effects on memory in normal college students. *Journal of Experimental Psychology: General* 114, 388–391.

———. 1987. Affect, cognition, and social behavior. In L. Berkowitz, ed., *Advances in experimental social psychology.* New York: Academic Press.

Isen, A.M., and Daubman, K.A. 1984. The influence of affect on categorization. *Journal of Personality and Social Psychology* 47:1206–1217.

———. 1986. Manuscript. University of Maryland.

Isen, A.M.; Daubman, K.A.; and Nowicki, G.P. 1987. Positive affect facilitates creative problem solving. *Journal of Personality and Social Psychology* 52:1122–1131.

Isen, A.M., and Geva, N. 1987. The influence of positive affect on acceptable level of risk: The person with a large canoe has a large worry. *Organizational Behavior and Human Decision Processes* 39:145–154.

Isen, A.M.; Johnson, M.M.S.; Mertz, E.; and Robinson, G. 1985. Positive affect and the uniqueness of word association. *Journal of Personality and Social Psychology* 48: 1413–1426.

Isen, A.M., and Levin, P.F. 1972. The effect of feeling good on helping: Cookies and kindness. *Journal of Personality and Social Psychology* 21:384–388.

Isen, A.M., and Means, B. 1983. The influence of positive affect on decision-making strategy. *Social Cognition* 2:18–31.

Isen, A.M.; Means, B.; Patrick, R.; and Nowicki, G. 1982. Some factors influencing decision-making strategy and risk-taking. In M.S. Clark and S.T. Fisk, eds., *Affect and cognition: The Seventeenth Annual Carnegie Symposium on Cognition.* Hillsdale, N.J.: Erlbaum.

Isen, A.M.; Nygren, T.E.; and Ashby, F.G. In press. The influence of positive affect on the subjective utility of gains and losses: It's not worth the risk. *Journal of Personality and Social Psychology.*

Isen, A.M., and Patrick, R. 1983. The effect of positive feelings on risk-taking: When the chips are down. Organizational Behavior and Human Performance 31, 194–202.

Isen, A.M., and Shalker, T.E. 1982. Do you "accentuate the positive, eliminate the negative" when you are in a good mood? *Social Psychology Quarterly* 45:58–63.

Isen, A.M; Shalker, T.; Clark, M.; and Karp, L. 1978. Affect, accessibility of material in memory and behavior: A cognitive loop? *Journal of Personality and Social Psychology* 36:1–12.

Isen, A.M., and Simmonds, S.F. 1978. The effect of feeling good on a helping task that is incompatible with good mood. *Social Psychology* 41:345–349.

Jacobson, J.Z. 1973. Effects of association upon masking and reading latency. *Canadian Journal of Psychology* 27, 58–69.

Janis, I.L.; Kaye, D.; and Kirschner, P. 1965. Facilitating effects of "eating while reading" on responsiveness to persuasive communications. *Journal of Personality and Social Psychology* 11:181–186.

Jenkins, J.J. 1974. Remember that old theory of memory? Well, forget it! *American Psychologist* 29:785–795.

Johnson, E., and Tversky, A. 1983. Affect, generalization and the perception of risk. *Journal of Personality and Social Psychology* 45:20–31.

Koestler, A. 1964. *The act of creation.* New York: Macmillan.

Laird, J.D.; Wagener, J.J.; Halal, M.; and Szegda, M. 1982. Remembering what you feel: The effects of emotion on memory. *Journal of Personality and Social Psychology* 42:646–657.

Levin, P.F., and Isen, A.M. 1975. Something you can still get for a dime: Further studies on the effect of feeling good on helping. *Sociometry* 38:141–147.

Loftus, E.F. 1973. Activation of semantic memory. *American Journal of Psychology* 86: 331–337.

Loftus, G.R., and Loftus, E.F. 1974. The influence of one memory retrieval on a subsequent memory retrieval. *Memory and Cognition* 2:467–471.

Mandler, G. 1979. Organization, memory, and mental structures. In C.R. Puff, ed., *Memory organization and structure.* New York: Academic Press.

———. 1984. *Mind and body.* New York: Norton.

Mednick, M.T.; Mednick, S.A.; and Mednick, E.V. 1964. Incubation of creative performance and specific associative priming. *Journal of Abnormal and Social Psychology* 69:84–88.

Mednick, S.A. 1962. The associative basis of the creative process. *Psychological Review* 69:220–232.

Meyer, D.W., and Schvaneveldt, R.W. 1971. Facilitation in recognizing pairs of words: Evidence of a dependence between retrieval operations. *Journal of Experimental Psychology* 90:227–234.

Mischel, W.; Coates, B.; and Raskoff, A. 1968. Effects of success and failure on self-gratification. *Journal of Personality and Social Psychology* 10:381–390.

Mischel, W.; Ebbesen, E.; and Zeiss, A. 1973. Selective attention to the self: Situational and dispositional determinants. *Journal of Personality and Social Psychology* 27:129–142.

———. 1976. Determinants of selective memory about the self. *Journal of Consulting and Clinical Psychology* 44:92–103.

Moore, B.S.; Underwood, W.; and Rosenhan, D.L. 1973. Affect and altruism. *Develmental Psychology* 8:99–104.

Nasby, W., and Yando, R. 1982. Selective encoding and retrieval of affectively valent information. *Journal of Personality and Social Psychology* 43:1244–1253.

Neely, J.H. 1976. Semantic priming and retrieval from lexical memory: Evidence for facilitatory and inhibitory processes. *Memory and Cognition* 4:648–654.

———. 1977. Semantic priming and retrieval from lexical memory: Roles of inhibitionless spreading and activation and limited-capacity attention. *Journal of Experimental Psychology: General* 106:226–254.

Posner, M.I., and Snyder, C.R.R. 1975. Attention and cognitive control in R.L. Solso, ed., *Information Processing and Cognition: The Loyola Symposium.* Hillsdale, N.J.: Erlbaum.

Riskind, J. 1983. Nonverbal expressions and the accessibility of life experience memories: A congruence hypothesis. *Social Cognition* 2:62–86.

Schiffenbauer, A. 1974. Effect of observer's emotional state on judgments of the emotional state of others. *Journal of Personality and Social Psychology* 30:31–36.

Srull, T.K., and Wyer, R.S. 1979. The role of category accessibility in the interpretation of information about persons: Some determinants and implications. *Journal of Personality and Social Psychology* 37:1660–1672.

Teasdale, J.D., and Fogarty, S.J. 1979. Differential effects of induced mood on retrieval of pleasant and unpleasant events from episodic memory. *Journal of Abnormal Psychology* 88:248–257.

Teasdale, J.D., and Russell, M.L. 1983. Differential aspects of induced mood on the recall of positive, negative and neutral words. *British Journal of Clinical Psychology* 22:163–171.

Teasdale, J.D.; Taylor, R.; and Fogarty, S.J. 1980. Effects of induced elation-depression on the accessibility of memories of happy and unhappy experiences. *Behavior Research and Therapy* 18:339–346.

Thomson, D.M., and Tulving, E. 1970. Associative encoding and retrieval: Weak and strong cues. *Journal of Experimental Psychology* 86, 255–262.

Tulving, E., and Pearlstone, Z. 1966. Availability versus accessibility of information in memory for words. *Journal of Verbal Learning and Verbal Behavior* 5:381–391.

Tulving, E., and Thomson, D.M. 1973. Encoding specificity and retrieval processes in episodic memory. *Psychological Review* 80:352–373.

Tversky, A., and Kahneman, D. 1973. Availability: A heuristic for judging frequency and probability. *Cognitive Psychology* 5:207–232.

———. 1974. Judgments under uncertainty: Heuristics and biases. *Science* 185:1124–1131.

Veitch, R., and Griffitt, W. 1976. Good news—bad news: Affective and interpersonal effects. *Journal of Applied Social Psychology* 6:69–75.

Warren, R.E. 1977. Time and the spread of activation in memory. *Journal of Experimental Psychology: Human Learning and Memory* 4:458–466.

Weingarten, H., and Faillace, L.A. 1971. Alcohol state-dependent learning in man. *Journal of Nervous and Mental Disease* 153:395–406.

Weyant, J.M. 1978. Effects of mood states, costs, and benefits of helping. *Journal of Personality and Social Psychology* 36:1169–1176.

Worth, L.T., and Mackie, D.M. 1987. Cognitive mediation of positive affect in persuasion. *Social Cognition* 5:76–94.

Part III
Cognitive Processing Issues

7

Advertising and Product Evaluation: The Relation between Consumer Memory and Judgment

Thomas K. Srull

The purpose of this chapter is to consider carefully the relationship between consumer memory and judgment from a psychological perspective. Most psychological theories assume implicitly that there should be a close correspondence between the specific facts that can be recalled about an object and any global evaluation made of that object. This is true in most theories of attribution, impression formation, and other areas of social judgment. In general, the person is assumed to recall specific episodic events involving the target and then determine the implications of these events for the judgment to be made.

Theorists differ on how elaborate the intervening combinatorial process is hypothesized to be, but there is almost universal agreement that there should be a strong relationship between the evaluative implications of whatever events are recalled and the extremity of any evaluative judgment that is made. The extent of this agreement is so strong that Hastie and Carlston (1980) have referred to this as the traditional model.

Evidence for the Traditional Model

Theorists have been nearly universal in painting a picture of what should happen, but empirical examinations have come out quite differently. For example, approximately fifty published experiments in the psychology literature have examined the relationship between memory and judgment (Hastie and Park 1985). The typical procedure is to present subjects with information, wait for some period of time, and then ask them to recall as much of the information as possible and make an evaluative judgment of the target. The average evaluative implication of each item recalled is then correlated across subjects with the judgments made. Do subjects who recall the most favorable information make the most favorable judgments? Usually not; the correlations are invariably quite small and seldom statistically different from zero.

From the perspective of current psychological theory, it is surprising that one would ever find such a lack of correspondence between the specific facts recalled and the judgments made. It is even more surprising when one considers how general and robust this finding appears to be. For example, in a classic impression formation study, Anderson and Hubert (1963) provided subjects with trait adjectives. Their essential finding was that there are strong primacy effects in impression formation but reasonably large recency effects in recall. The authors concluded that the impression judgments and memory for the trait adjectives must be independently stored and accessed in memory.

In a later study, Dreben, Fiske, and Hastie (1979) replicated these effects and also found that temporal delays produced a large effect on recall but only modest changes in impression ratings. They also concluded that there must be some independence between episodic memory and abstract evaluative impressions (see also Riskey 1979).

There is also a long line of persuasion studies that have found a weak relationship between memory for information in a persuasive communication and attitude formation and attitude change. A good illustration is a classic set of studies reported by Greenwald (1968). Subjects were presented with arguments concerning two separate controversial issues. They first received an opinion pretest, followed by the presentation of the communication. Upon reading the communication, subjects were asked to write a one-sentence reaction to the main point of the paragraph. Their opinions were again assessed, followed by an unexpected recall test. After one week, the opinion posttest and the recall test were unexpectedly readministered. Greenwald found no correlation between posttest opinion and retention of communication content at either of the delay intervals. He concluded that memory for information in a persuasive communication is not a mediating variable of subject attitude change. A number of other studies are also consistent with this general conclusion (see Insko 1964; Miller and Campbell 1959; Watts and McGuire 1964). These failures to find the predicted relationship ultimately led to the cognitive response approach to the study of persuasion that is so dominant now (Petty, Ostrom, and Brock 1981).

The same essential conclusion has been reached in the study of attributions of causality. For example, Fiske and coworkers (1979) conducted a series of studies examining whether imagery accounts for the effects of empathy on attributions. No correlation between what was remembered and the attributions that were made was observed in any of these studies. Similar to many other experiments, there was no evidence for any recall-attribution link. These researchers concluded that these results parallel those found in the other domains, a conclusion also reached in more recent reviews (Hastie and Park 1985; Lichtenstein and Srull 1985).

A similar situation exists in the psychology of advertising (Beattie and Mitchell 1985; Edell and Staelin 1983; Lichtenstein and Srull 1985). Most theories have assumed that there should be a close correspondence between the specific facts recalled about a product and any general evaluative judgment made of that product. For this reason, recall has become one of the most popular measures of advertising effectiveness. Again, however, the empirical evidence is quite different. In four separate reviews, the relationship between recall and judgment within an advertising context has been found to be very small, and only in rare cases was it significantly different from zero (Gibson 1983; Ross 1982; Stout 1981; Young 1972).

Seldom do theory and data stand in such stark contrast. Is it possible for so many theorists to be misguided on such a fundamental issue? It may be possible, but it is also doubtful. In the following discussion, recent advances in cognitive psychology are used to explicate the conditions under which a strong correspondence between memory and judgment should and should not be expected on conceptual grounds. In the process, a general model that can be used to conceptualize the judgment process will be outlined. Several lines of empirical evidence bearing on the model will then be summarized, and the data from several recent experiments will be reported.

A Preliminary Model

The model proposed is based on a more comprehensive theory of information processing developed by Wyer and Srull (1986). Although the theory is relatively complex and well beyond the scope of the present discussion, two aspects of it are of particular importance. First, the theory suggests that the mental representation of product information will often differ as a function of the initial processing objectives of the consumer. The importance of differing mental representations in understanding the recall-judgment relationship will soon become apparent. The second noteworthy aspect of the Wyer and Srull theory concerns its broad scope. Because it is intended to trace the flow of information from the initial encoding stage to the final response stage, it makes specific statements about how any given mental representation should be reflected in various performance measures. Although different representations may look the same on the basis of some dependent measures (such as overall levels of recall), they can be differentiated on the basis of others (for example, probe reaction time or the type of judgments made). The underlying assumption is that understanding of the recall-judgment relation will be best advanced by considering several aspects of performance simultaneously.

An additional virtue of the Wyer and Srull theory is that it incorporates the distinction between retrieval and computational processes. Imagine that a consumer is asked, "Is the Ford Thunderbird a luxury automobile?" A retrieval model would suggest that, at least for some people, the answer to such a question has already been determined and stored in memory. Thus one would simply need to retrieve it from memory in order to answer such a question.

In contrast, a computational model would suggest that, at least for some consumers, the answer to such a question has not already been determined. That is, the mental representation of Ford Thunderbird does not contain any propositional knowledge indicating a value along some luxury dimension (or membership in some luxury-related category). In order to answer such a question, one would need to retrieve as much information as possible about the Ford Thunderbird, compare it to one's referent for luxury automobile, and then compute, or figure out, an answer on the spot. Of course, if one were asked the same question again, he or she would not need to recompute an answer but simply retrieve the previous judgment (Wyer and Srull 1986).

Although the distinction between retrieval and computational processes is not often discussed, a number of researchers in both social cognition (Allen and Ebbesen 1981; Ebbesen and Allen 1979) and consumer behavior (Bettman 1979; Burke 1980; Brucks and Mitchell 1981; Mitchell and Smith 1982; Smith, Mitchell, and Meyer, 1982) have recently found it to be useful. This distinction also turns out to be crucial in understanding when there will and will not be a relationship between recall and judgment. In particular, the model proposed suggests that the consumer's information-processing objectives or goals are a critical mediating variable that determines the nature of the relationship between recall and judgment. The reason is that such processing objectives often determine whether product evaluations have been prestored or need to be computed on the spot.

The model postulates that when a consumer acquires ad information with the (implicit or explicit) objective of making an evaluative judgment of the product, the global evaluation will be made at the time of information acquisition and stored in memory separately and independently from the specific episodic facts learned. If the consumer is later asked to make a specific judgment, the evaluation will have already been computed and will simply be accessed at that time. This is consistent with a large body of literature that suggests self-generated evaluations are much more accessible in memory than externally presented information (Johnson and Raye 1981; Ostrom et al. 1980; Slamecka and Graf 1978). Thus, under these conditions, there is no reason to expect any strong relationship between the specific facts recalled and the global evaluation made. This is a straightforward retrieval model in which the previous judgment and the specific episodic facts on which it is based are independently stored and accessed. It is a process consistent with the conceptualizations outlined by Anderson and Hubert (1963) and Dreben, Fiske, and Hastie (1979).

Sometimes an alternative process will apply. Specifically, when a person acquires ad information with no specific objective in mind or only a very general objective such as to comprehend the information being presented, a global evaluation of the product will not be made at the time of information acquisition (that is, when the ad is seen, heard, or read). Thus no evaluation will be incorporated into the resulting mental representation. If later asked to make a specific judgment, the consumer will be forced to retrieve the previously acquired information, or some subset of it, and use it as a basis for an evaluative judgment of the product. In other words, a judgment will have to be computed on the spot. Under these conditions, a strong relationship would be expected between the global evaluation and the evaluative implications of the information recalled.

Empirical Evidence Bearing on the Model

Summary of Preliminary Research

As an initial test of the model, Lichtenstein and Srull (1985) presented undergraduate students with simulated print ads that were as complex as possible in the sense that they contained a large amount of attribute information and pertained to products with which the subjects were likely to have little prior familiarity. Three separate stimulus replications were used. Half the subjects, who participated in an on-line processing condition, were told to read the ad with the purpose of forming an evaluation of the product so that they would later be able to judge how desirable it would be relative to other competing brands. The other half, participating in a memory-based processing condition, were told that the ad was written by an undergraduate advertising major. Their task was to read the ad in order to judge how grammatical, coherent, and interesting it was.

After reading the ad, there was either a five-minute or a forty-eight-hour delay. Then subjects were asked to recall as much of the information as possible and make a general evaluative judgment of the product, half of the subjects completing the recall task first and the other half beginning with the judgment task.

The typical way to analyze such data is to have a separate group of subjects rate the evaluative implication of each proposition, or idea unit, in the ad. Then the mean evaluative rating for each proposition recalled by any given subject is determined. These values are then correlated, across subjects, with the product evaluation ratings.

Lichtenstein and Srull (1985) found in all twelve independent comparisons that the correlation between recall and judgment was higher in the memory-based than on-line conditions. Moreover, the correlations in the memory-based conditions were universally large and statistically different from zero. The mean correlation across twelve conditions was .64 in the memory-based condition and .22 in the on-line condition. These data are consistent with what the model predicts.

Hastie and Park (1985) replicated these effects by using a slightly different paradigm. The on-line condition was very similar to that of Lichtenstein and Srull. However, for a memory-based condition, they had subjects anticipate making one judgment but later asked them for a different, unrelated judgment. Across four separate experiments, the average correlation between recall and judgment was .51 in the memory-based condition and .16 in the on-line condition.

These findings are very strong and replicate across a variety of laboratories, stimulus sets, content domains, and delay intervals. They suggest that past studies have consistently found only a weak relationship between recall and judgment because subjects have tended to use some type of on-line processing strategy (that is, subjects are told explicitly that they will be asked to form an impression, rate the product, evaluate the ad, and so on).

In the few studies that have included memory-based conditions, however, a strong correspondence between recall and judgment has indeed been found. For example, Sherman and colleagues (1983) provided subjects with current information about two historically rival football teams. In one case, the goal was to remember the information as well as possible. In another case, the goal was to form an impression of the potential outcome of an upcoming game between the two teams. Sherman et al. found a very weak relationship between memory for the information and subjects' judgments of the outcome when they had formed their impressions at the time of information acquisition. However, this relationship was quite strong among subjects who had initially been given a memory set. The authors suggest that the "availability" of information in memory will affect judgments only when they are initially unanticipated. A similar finding was also reported by Reyes, Thompson, and Bower (1980).

Experiment 1

Although support for the model appears strong, it is also indirect. There appear to be two difficulties in interpreting the results of past research within the context of advertising. The first concerns the nature of the stimuli used. In order to obtain the largest correlations possible, past researchers have included both positive and negative attributes in their descriptions of the target. Yet this is seldom true in actual advertisements. Even in the Lichtenstein and Srull (1985) study, the only one specifically conducted within an advertising context, the stimuli were not real ads.

The second complication involves the orienting task used. Nearly every past study has contrasted a memory set with some type of impression formation set. It seems reasonable to assume, however, that in many contexts, consumers simply want to comprehend what is occurring in the environment. This circumstance may not be equivalent to a memory set or an impression formation set. Thus there is a need to study processing motivated by normal comprehension goals.

The present study was designed to address both of these issues. Three actual print ads were used as stimuli (for the Motorola KDT hand-held computer, Haverill's navigator watch, and Pella storm window improvement doors). Each was fairly long and chosen because it presented substantial attribute information, all of it verbatim. Each subject saw all three ads, in an order randomized separately for each subject.

The design was a 3 x 2 x 2 completely balanced factorial. Three different processing objectives were examined. A product evaluation set was used as a pure on-line processing task. Subjects in this condition were told to read each ad with the purpose of forming an evaluation of the product so that they would later be able to judge how desirable it would be relative to other competing brands. Two other sets were assumed to invoke memory-based processing. One was a standard memory set in which subjects were told they were participating in a memory experiment; their ostensible task was to remember the information presented in the ads as well as possible because later they would be asked to recall it. Other subjects were given a comprehension set in which they were simply told to pay attention to the information that would be presented. In each case, subjects paced themselves through the three ads.

Two other independent variables pertained to the length of the delay before the recall and judgment measures were obtained and the order in which the two measures were assessed. Specifically, subjects were tested after either five minutes or forty-eight hours and completed the recall task either before or after the judgments were collected. For each ad, subjects were asked, "Assuming you wanted to purchase a product similar to the __________, how desirable do you think this particular brand would be?" Subjects made one rating for each product on a scale ranging from 0 ("very undersirable") to 20 ("very desirable").

The mean within-cell correlations in each condition are presented in table 7-1. In each case, zero-order correlations were obtained under the product evaluation set. The correlation between recall and judgment was substantial under the comprehension set, with the correlations under the memory set being moderate in size. This same general pattern held for each of the three

Table 7-1
Within-Cell Correlations Obtained in Experiment 1

	Five Minutes		*Forty-eight Hours*	
Processing Set	*Recall-Judgment*	*Judgment-Recall*	*Recall-Judgment*	*Judgment-Recall*
Product evaluation	.07	.09	.11	.03
Memory	.21	.26	.18	.21
Comprehension	.52	.42	.58	.56

ads. As reported by Lichtenstein and Srull (1985), neither the order in which the recall and judgment measures were assessed nor the length of the delay had a systematic effect.

Theoretically the results of this study can be accounted for as follows. The product evaluation set is a processing objective that encourages on-line processing. As a result, the evaluation of the product is made at the time of information acquisition (when the ad is read) and stored in memory independent of the specific episodic facts that are learned. At some later time, either five minutes or forty-eight hours, there is no relationship between the evaluation made of the product and whatever episodic facts happen to be recalled.

In contrast, the comprehension set encourages memory-based processing. Theoretically the product evaluation is not made at the time of information acquisition but only at the time of judgment. As a result, the specific facts recalled at the time of judgment are strongly related to the judgment made.

The memory set data are slightly more difficult to account for. It was expected that this set would also elicit pure memory-based processing, and the results would thus mirror those obtained under the comprehension set. It is possible, however, that memory set subjects (or some percentage of them) actually formed an evaluation of the product at the time of input. There are two reasons to believe this. First, because subjects did not know in advance how many ads they would read, they may have formed a general evaluative impression to use as a mnemonic strategy in recall. Second, similar effects have recently been reported in other domains (Hastie and Park 1985; Lichtenstein and Srull 1985), particularly when multiple information sets are provided.

Experiment 2

The purpose of the second experiment was twofold: to elucidate the findings obtained earlier with memory set instructions and, more important, to tap directly into the intervening processes that are postulated by the model. The presumed difference between a product evaluation group (who theoretically are forming their evaluations on-line) and a comprehension group (who theoretically are not) is in the amount of computational activity required at the time of judgment. This should be reflected in the amount of *time* required to make a judgment.

Subjects in the second experiment were presented with a series of twelve print ads, each from a different product class. One group was told to read the ads and form an evaluation of each product described. Another group was told simply to pay attention and comprehend the information presented. The third group was told to remember all of the information as well as possible. The judgment task was then administered either five minutes or forty-eight hours later. The subject sat in front of a computer screen and was probed with, "Please rate the desirability of each of the following products." On each of the twelve trials, the screen displayed after a rest interval the brand name and a ten-point rating scale, ranging from 0 ("very undesirable") to 9 ("very desirable"). The time interval between stimulus onset and response was recorded on each trial.

The results are presented in figure 7-1. The mean reaction time for the product evaluation group was approximately five seconds in the five-minute delay condition, and approximately six seconds under the forty-eight-hour delay condition. In contrast, the mean reaction time for the comprehension group was approximately ten seconds in the five-minute delay condition and nearly twenty seconds in the forty-eight-hour delay condition. As suggested by the analysis offered earlier, the mean reaction time for the memory set group is intermediate under both conditions.

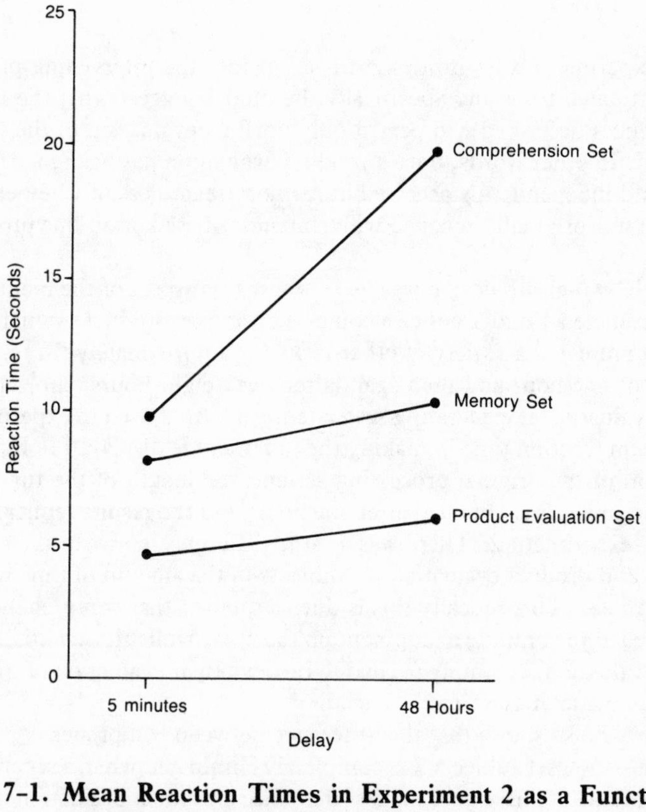

Figure 7-1. Mean Reaction Times in Experiment 2 as a Function of Orienting Task and Delay Interval

The most parsimonious interpretation of these results is that the on-line processing group formed their evaluations of the product at the time of information acquisition. At the time of judgment, they simply needed to access the appropriate evaluation in memory. It took them slightly longer after forty-eight hours than after five minutes, but they were very rapid in both cases. In contrast, the memory-based group must retrieve the episodic facts that were learned, or at least some subset of them, integrate the facts retrieved into a global evaluative judgment, and finally make an overt response. These subjects took twice as long as the on-line group to make their judgments after five minutes and nearly four times as long after forty-eight hours.

In short, these data provide strong support for the proposed model. The large reaction time differences presumably reflect differing amounts of mental activity at the time a judgment is requested. As the model suggests, the cognitive demands are much greater when the ad was originally encoded under a memory-based, as opposed to on-line, processing set.

Experiment 3

The final experiment was also designed to tap into the intervening processes that are postulated to occur. Specifically the model suggests that the reaction time differences described will persist only until an evaluation of the product is computed. In other words, once a product evaluation has been made, it will be stored and independently accessed in memory regardless of whether the ad information was originally encoded with a memory-based or on-line processing strategy.

A simple two-group design was used to test this aspect of the model. Subjects read a single ad under either a comprehension or product evaluation set. They then completed a variety of other tasks for approximately fifty minutes. At the end of one hour and then again after forty-eight hours, subjects made a product evaluation along a rating scale identical to that used in experiment 2.

The mean reaction time in making the judgment is displayed in figure 7–2 as a function of the original processing set and the length of the time delay. The first judgment was obtained after one hour, and the results replicate those obtained in experiment 2. There was a large difference between the comprehension set and product evaluation set subjects in the amount of time required for the judgment. Theoretically this is due to the fact that comprehension set subjects needed to compute a judgment on the spot, while those initially given a product evaluation set simply needed to retrieve their evaluation of the product that was made at the time of encoding.

Figure 7–2 also shows that the difference between comprehension set and product evaluation set subjects was completely eliminated when a second judgment was obtained. These data suggest that once a product evaluation is made, that evaluation is stored in memory and is available for use later in making any subsequent judgment (Loken and Hoverstad 1985).

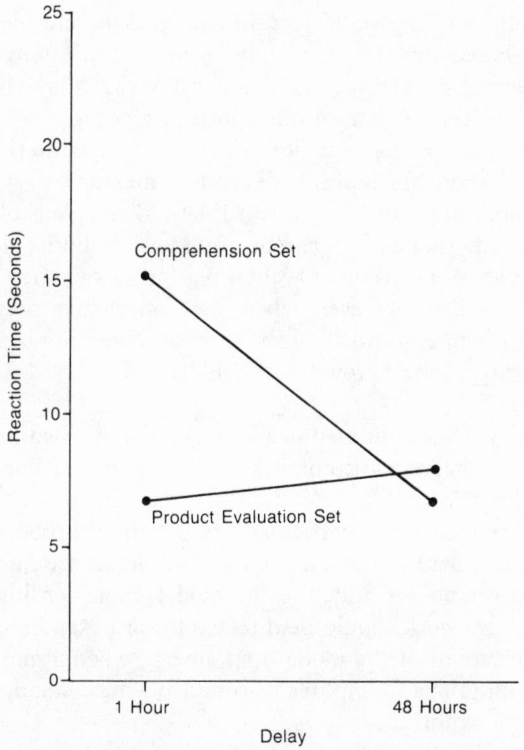

Figure 7–2. Mean Reaction Times in Experiment 3 as a Function of Orienting Task and Delay Interval

Conclusions

One of the most perplexing problems in advertising research over the past several decades has been the general failure to find any consistent relationship between memory for information presented in an ad and product evaluation. These failures have been met with surprise and discouragement, and some have even used them to question why researchers need to be concerned with memory processes in the first place. The research presented here should help to frame the problem in a somewhat new perspective.

From a metatheoretical point of view, three assumptions are central to the present approach. First, it is assumed that different types of mental representations can be distinguished only by simultaneously examining several different aspects of performance. The reason is that different underlying representations will often react to experimental manipulations in the same way. Thus mental representations may appear to be the same even when they are not. In one study reported by Lichtenstein and Srull (1985), for example, the overall levels of recall and the overall levels of judgment were identical for on-line and memory-based subjects. It is only by looking at a range of measures that one can discover converging evidence for how the underlying mental representations must be different from one another.

The second assumption is that theories must be developed to the point at which they have implications for multiple dependent measures if they are going to be distinguishable empirically (see Srull 1984). While plausible alternative interpretations of any single effect can be numerous, building alternative, internally consistent theories capable of accounting for a large array of data is much more difficult. Moreover, even when such alternative accounts are devised, subsequent attempts to distinguish between them are nearly certain to produce substantial theoretical growth (see Srull and Wyer 1984 for an elaboration of this point).

Third, the model we have outlined is a very general one, within which a variety of more specific theoretical commitments can be made. For example, the exact format of knowledge representation has been left unspecified, and no commitment has been made to a particular type of retrieval process. At this level of analysis and for these purposes, such commitments are unnecessary. However, as new constraints are added to the model, more sensitive predictions will emerge. Future work should be directed toward examining some of the more subtle implications of the model that emerge when a more specific set of theoretical assumptions is imposed. From a practical standpoint, this suggests two implications for advertisers:

1. Interpretations of recall measures could be ambiguous unless researchers have some indication of whether individuals were processing on-line or in a memory-based fashion when viewing the ads.
2. If we can understand when recall and attitude will or will not be related, advertisers could use this information to develop strategies for influencing processing at the time of exposure.

References

Allen, R.B., and Ebbesen, E.B. 1981. Cognitive processes in person perception: Retrieval of personality trait and behavioral information. *Journal of Experimental Social Psychology* 17:119–141.

Anderson, N.H., and Hubert, S. 1963. Effects of concomitant verbal recall on order effects in personality impression formation. *Journal of Verbal Learning and Verbal Behavior* 2:379–391.

Beattie, A.E., and Mitchell, A.A. 1985. The relationship between advertising recall and persuasion: An experimental investigation. In L.F. Alwitt and A.A. Mitchell, eds., *Psychological processes and advertising effects.* Hillsdale, N.J: Erlbaum.

Bettman, J.R. 1979. *An information processing theory of consumer choice.* Reading, Mass.: Addison-Wesley.

Brucks, M., and Mitchell, A. 1981. Knowledge structures, production systems, and decision strategies. *Advances in Consumer Research* 8:750–757.

Burke, R. 1980. A preliminary model of consumer cognition. Unpublished manuscript. Gainesville: Center for Consumer Research, University of Florida.

Dreben, E.K: Fiske, S.T.; and Hastie, R. 1979. The independence of item and evaluative information: Impression and recall order effects in behavior-based impression formation. *Journal of Personality and Social Psychology* 37:1758–1768.

Ebbesen, E.B., and Allen, R.B. 1979. Cognitive processes in implicit personality trait inferences. *Journal of Personality and Social Psychology* 37:471–488.

Edell, J.A., and Staelin, R. 1983. The information processing of pictures in print advertisements. *Journal of Consumer Research* 10:45–61.

Fiske, S.T.; Taylor, S.E.; Etcoff, N.L.; and Laufer, J.K. 1979. Imaging, empathy, and causal attribution. *Journal of Experimental Social Psychology* 15:356–377.

Gibson, L.D. 1983. Not recall. *Journal of Advertising Research* 23:39–46.

Greenwald, A.G. 1968. Cognitive learning, cognitive response to persuasion, and attitude change. In A.G. Greenwald, T.C. Brock, and T.M. Ostrom, eds., *Psychological foundations of attitudes.* New York: Academic Press.

Hastie, R., and Carlston, D. 1980. Theoretical issues in person memory. In R. Hastie, T.M. Ostrom, E.B. Ebbesen, R.S. Wyer, D.L. Hamilton, and D.E. Carlson, eds., *Person memory: The cognitive basis of social perception.* Hillsdale, N.J: Erlbaum.

Hastie, R., and Park, B. 1985. The relationship between memory and judgment depends on whether the judgment task is memory based or on-line. Unpublished manuscript. Evanston, Ill.: Northwestern University.

Insko, C.A. 1964. Primacy versus recency in persuasion as a function of the timing of arguments and measures. *Journal of Abnormal and Social Psychology* 69:381–391.

Johnson, M.K., and Raye, C.L. 1981. Reality monitoring. *Psychological Review* 88:67–85.

Lichtenstein, M., and Srull, T.K. 1985. Conceptual and methodological issues in examining the relationship between consumer memory and judgment. In L.F. Alwitt and A.A. Mitchell, eds., *Psychological processes and advertising effects: Theory, research, and application.* Hillsdale, N.J.: Erlbaum.

Loken, B., and Hoverstad, R. 1985. Relationships between information recall and subsequent attitudes: Some exploratory findings. *Journal of Consumer Research* 12: 155–168.

Miller, N., and Campbell, D.T. 1959. Recency and primacy in persuasion as a function of the timing of speeches and measurements. *Journal of Abnormal and Social Psychology* 59:1–9.

Mitchell, A.A., and Smith, T.R. 1982. The applicability of computational process models for representing consumer behavior. *Advances in Consumer Research* 9: 125–131.

Ostrom, T.M.; Lingle, J.H.; Pryor, J.B.; and Geva, N. 1980. Cognitive organization of person impressions. In R. Hastie, T.M. Ostrom, E.B. Ebbesen, R.S. Wyer, D.L. Hamilton, and D.E. Carlston, eds., *Person memory: The cognitive basis of social perception.* Hillsdale, N.J.: Erlbaum.

Petty, R.E.; Ostrom, T.M.; and Brock, T.C., eds. 1981. *Cognitive responses in persuasion.* Hillsdale, N.J.: Erlbaum.

Reyes, R.M.; Thompson, W.C.; and Bower, G.H. 1980. Judgmental biases resulting from differing availabilities of arguments. *Journal of Personality and Social Psychology* 39:2–12.

Riskey, D.R. 1979. Verbal memory processes in impression formation. *Journal of Experimental Psychology: Human Learning and Memory* 5:271-281.

Ross, H.L. 1982. Recall versus persuasion: An answer. *Journal of Advertising Research* 22:13–16.

Sherman, S.J.; Zehner, K.S.; Johnson, J.; and Hirt, E.R. 1983. Social explanation: The role of timing, set, and recall on subjective likelihood estimates. *Journal of Personality and Social Psychology* 44:1127–1143.

Slamecka, N.J., and Graf, P. 1978. The generation effect: Delineation of a phenomenon. *Journal of Experimental Psychology: Human Learning and Memory* 4:592–604.

Smith, T.R.; Mitchell, A.A.; and Meyer, R. 1982. A computational process model of evaluation based on the cognitive structuring of episodic knowledge. *Advances in Consumer Research* 9:136–143.

Srull, T.K. 1984. Methodological techniques for the study of person memory and social cognition. In R.S. Wyer and T.K. Srull, eds., *Handbook of social cognition,* vol. 2. Hillsdale, N.J.: Erlbaum.

Srull, T.K., and Wyer, R.S. 1984. Progress and problems in cognitive social psychology. In J.R. Royce and L.P. Mos, eds., *Annals of theoretical psychology,* vol. 1. New York: Plenum Press.

Stout, R.G. 1981. Copy testing is only part of advertising research. Paper presented at the Twelfth Annual Conference of the Association for Consumer Research.

Young, S. 1972. Copy testing without magic numbers. *Journal of Advertising Research* 12:3–12.

Watts, W.A., and McGuire, W.J. 1964. Persistency of induced opinion change and retention of the inducing message contents. *Journal of Abnormal and Social Psychology* 68:233–241.

Wyer, R.S., and Srull, T.K. 1986. Human cognition in its social context. *Psychological Review* 93:322–359.

8

Strategies for Designing Persuasive Messages: Deductions from the Resource Matching Hypothesis

Punam Anand
Brian Sternthal

During the past decade, it has become apparent that principles of memory operation offer a promising explanation for persuasive communication effects. It has been shown that the persuasive effects of source credibility, repetition, threat, humor, discrepancy, and other communication variables can be interpreted in terms of memory operation principles (Petty and Cacioppo 1981; Sternthal and Craig 1982). The main contention is that people represent message information by a process of cognitive elaboration. This process typically involves the association of message information with people's prior knowledge that is relevant to the appeal. It is the elaboration of message information in memory that facilitates its retrieval at the time of judgment. And because messages are designed with the intent to persuade, the retrieval of message information enhances the likelihood of advocacy-consistent judgments.

A basic premise underlying this depiction of message influence is that it requires an internal commodity or input, which we shall refer to as cognitive resources. It is also hypothesized that message influence is enhanced when there is congruence between the cognitive resources required for message processing and those available for the task. Clearly, however, such congruence does not always occur. In some situations, the resource requirements for message processing may exceed those available because people are not sufficiently motivated to evoke more substantial resource levels. And even if people are highly motivated to process a communication, the resources required may exceed their capacity limitation (Calder, Insko, and Yandell 1974). In other situations, the resources available for processing may exceed those required. Message persuasion under these conditions of mismatched resources can also be interpreted in terms of memory operation principles.

Consider a situation in which too few resources are available for message processing. The lack of resources is likely to lead to impoverished processing of message information and thus limit persuasion. Alternatively, for some stimuli, people can cope with their resource limitation by engaging in heuristic processing. This entails invoking some strategy that reduces the information considered in making judgments. For example, a heuristic is employed when judgments are made on the basis of some cue peripheral to the message such as the spokesperson or the number of arguments advanced in support of the advocacy rather than on the basis of the information content of the message.

A different type of cognitive dynamics is expected when the resources available to the processor exceed those required for message processing. Here it is anticipated that people will employ surplus resources to engage in cognitive elaboration of message-related issues. As the disparity between resource requirements and resource availability increases, more of the elaboration is expected to be of personal or idiosyncratic associations, and less of the elaboration will pertain to information presented in the message. These idiosyncratic associations are not necessarily unfavorable to the message advocacy; however, in persuasive communication settings, they are likely to be less favorable than direct message associations because stimulus messages are specifically designed with the intent to persuade. Thus the availability of greater resources than are needed for message processing is hypothesized to limit persuasion.

The view emerging from this analysis is that message processing and persuasion are enhanced by matching the resources available for elaborating upon the communication content and the resources required for this task. When too few resources are available, impoverished processing of the appeal may limit persuasion. When available resources exceed requirements, message recipients' idiosyncratic associations to the communication may undermine persuasion. We shall refer to this view as the resource-matching hypothesis.

In this chapter we examine evidence relevant to the judgment process under varying conditions of resource availability and resource requirements. The perspective is that of the communication strategist whose objective is to enhance the persuasive impact of a message. We first consider research that offers some insight about the types of strategies likely to enhance message influence when the resources available for message processing are exceeded by the requirements of the communication task. Next, we assess ways of enhancing persuasion when there is a surplus of resources given the demands of the processing task. This is followed by a more mechanistic analysis of human resource allocation and its strategic implications as suggested in recent research pertaining to hemispheric lateralization. Finally we summarize the theoretical and practical implications emerging from our analysis.

In reviewing the literature, we focus on experimental studies that manipulated indicators thought to represent the resources available and/or those required for stimulus processing and measured subjects' evaluations of the stimulus. Such investigations are most directly germane to making causal inferences about the effects of resource allocation on judgments prescribed by the resource matching hypothesis. Given our strategic perspective, we also favored studies for review when they suggested interventions that could be adapted to enhancing message persuasion in applied settings. As a consequence of following these criteria, many of the studies we examine here are our own and have yet to appear in professional journals.

Increasing Message Processing with Resources Limited

Suppose people do not evoke sufficient resources to elaborate on the message content, and as a result they are not highly persuaded by the communication advocacy. The resource matching hypothesis suggests two types of strategies to enhance persuasion in this situation. One is to reduce the resources required for message processing so that they more closely approximate the resources likely to be available. Alternatively, in some situations, it may be possible to motivate people to access the resources necessary for message elaboration.

Reducing Resource Requirements

Two factors can account for message recipients' failure to allocate the resources necessary to process a communication. It may be that the resources required to process the message exceed people's resource capacity. This might occur if the message is complex and presented at a pace dictated by the communicator. Or it may be that people have the resources necessary to process a message but are not motivated to access them. In either event, it is possible to increase the persuasive impact of a message by reducing the resources required so that they correspond to the resources people do make available for the processing task.

Directing Limited Resources: One strategy for reducing the resources required for message processing might be to direct people's limited resources to selected aspects of the appeal that are likely to be particularly persuasive. Research reported in the linguistic literature offers an approach to implementing this strategy. The notion is that the content of a message can be conveyed in the form of given and new information (Chafe 1976). Given information refers to the message content the communicator assumes is already processed; new information is message information that is being activated for the first time. For example, in the sentence, "It is Tide that cleans clothes better" "cleans clothes better" is the given information, and "Tide" is the new information. The distinction between given and new is important because it is hypothesized that, to the extent message recipients detect new information, they will direct their resources to elaborating upon it.

Assuming for the moment that this contention is valid, the issue becomes one of developing procedures that vary the ease with which the new information presented in a communication can be detected. The linguistic literature suggests that the extent to which new information is detected can be varied by altering the syntactical structure of an assertion. For example, the use of a pseudo-cleft structure is thought to be a powerful means of making new information readily distinguishable from given information (Hornby 1974). This structure is illustrated in the sentence, "The product that cleans clothes better is Tide." Here, Tide would be easily detected as new information. By contrast, it is less apparent what constitutes new information when the same thought is conveyed using a standard active structure as in, "Tide cleans clothes better." As a result, message recipients would be more likely to allocate their available resources to processing the brand name *Tide* when the pseudo-cleft structure is used than when a standard active construction is employed.

Saliba (1987) applies these notions in a persuasive communication context. He reasoned that when people have too few resources to elaborate upon all of the message information, the variation in syntactical structure will affect message processing. If the syntactical structure caused people to focus their limited resources on the information that presented persuasive arguments for the advocacy, their judgments would be more favorable toward the message position than if the syntactical structure provided no such focus. Without the focus induced by the syntax, message recipients might process the entire appeal in a cursory fashion, or they might focus on aspects of the message that were not particularly persuasive.

To test this hypothesis, Saliba (1987) constructed a persuasive message for a clock radio that contained a description of several attributes common to this product, as well as one favorable feature unique to the brand advocated. Two versions of the unique feature were presented to different groups of subjects. In one condition, the following pseudo-cleft construction was used to focus message recipients' resources on the unique attribute, the direct-reflecting speakers: "The thing that gives it greater musical clarity than comparably priced radios is the patented direct-reflecting speakers." In the other condition, subjects' resources were not focused. This was achieved by using a standard active construction in this statement: "The patented direct-reflecting speakers give it greater musical clarity than comparably priced radios." Both messages were presented by tape recorder at a pace that did not allow subjects to elaborate upon all of the message information.

After exposure to one of these messages, subjects were administered the dependent measures. Half of the subjects first evaluated the product on a series of bipolar adjective scales and then listed their thoughts relevant to the product. The remaining subjects were administered these measures in the reverse order, a condition intended to prompt the activation of additional resources to elaborate on the message information in relation to the resources available when evaluation immediately followed message exposure. Thus the experimental design was a 2 × 2 factorial. The manipulation of the syntactical structure was conceived of as a means of directing or not directing message recipients' resources to certain aspects of the message. The order of dependent variable administration manipulation was intended to vary the resources available for message processing.

The findings indicated that the use of a pseudo-cleft induced greater persuasion than the use of a standard active message when product evaluations immediately followed the communication. Apparently focusing subjects' resources on the segment of the message that presented new or unique arguments for the advocacy enhanced its persuasiveness. It was also found that when product evaluation followed the thought-listing measure, the product evaluations in response to the pseudo-cleft were less favorable than they were when evaluations were administered first. This outcome may have occurred because the combination of directing resource allocation to particular message information and increasing the resources available to elaborate upon it may have induced the activation of more resources than were required for message processing.

Message Simplification. Another approach to reducing the resources required for message processing is to simplify the communication by eliminating some of the message content or by making the appeal easier to follow. The expectation is that persuasion will be enhanced if the resources required for message processing are reduced to a level where they better match the resources available for the task.

A recent study reported by Yalch and Elmore-Yalch (1984) is relevant to this prediction. Subjects were exposed to an audiovisual communication attributed to either a highly credible or moderately credible source. The presentation of the message arguments favoring the advocacy were varied so that they were qualitative or quantitative. The findings suggested that subjects relied on message information to render their judgments when the message arguments were qualitative. By contrast, the credibility of the source affected subjects' judgments when the message arguments were quantitative. The highly credible source induced greater persuasion than the moderately credible spokesperson.

These data are congenial to the resource matching hypothesis if it is assumed that the processing of qualitative arguments is a less resource-demanding task than the processing of quantitative arguments. More specifically, it can be argued that the resources required to process qualitative message information approximated the resources subjects made available, and so the message information guided their judgments. By contrast, the processing of quantitative arguments required more resources than subjects had available.

As a result, subjects resorted to the use of a less resource-demanding source cue in making their judgments.

Yalch and Elmore-Yalch's findings suggest two alternative approaches to enhancing the persuasive impact of an appeal when inadequate resources are available for message processing. One approach is to reduce the resources required to process a message by making it easier to follow and less encumbered with factual detail. Even if this simplification strategy fails to reduce the resource requirements for message processing to the level corresponding to available resources, people may be persuaded if the cues peripheral to the message imply that the communication is compelling. This second approach is less preferred because it is thought that persuasion based on peripheral cues will not involve the elaboration of arguments favoring the advocacy and as a result will be less persistent than persuasion based on the processing of message content (Petty and Cacioppo 1981).

The contention that simplifying a message can enhance persuasion has also received support in several other studies. Anand and Sternthal (1987a) found that a single exposure to a read version of a message induced greater persuasion than exposure to a version in which the same message was sung to music. Presumably eliminating the singing and musical accompaniment reduced the resources required for message processing and thus enhanced persuasion. Similarly Smith and Dorfman (1975) observed that a single exposure to a colored pattern varying in complexity induced more favorable evaluations when the pattern was simple rather than complex. Again it appears that reducing resource requirements for message processing can enhance persuasion.

Increasing Resource Availability

The strategies considered to this point involve adapting the resource requirements for message processing to accommodate the resources communication recipients happen to make available for the task. The logic of these strategies is that the persuasive impact of a message will be greater if people are induced to process some limited amount of message information than if they were not so stimulated. However, it would seem that even greater levels of persuasion might be possible if people were motivated to process extensive amounts of information relevant to an advocacy, perhaps by introducing devices that increase the resources available for message processing.

We consider three strategies that are viable means of increasing resource availability: increasing the incongruity between the message and expectations, increasing personal relevance of the message information, and increasing exposures to the message. In accord with the resource-matching hypothesis, these strategies are expected to enhance persuasion if message recipients have the cognitive capacity to increase resource availability and the resources made available do not exceed those required for message processing. The availability of surplus resources is likely to stimulate idiosyncratic associations and thus undermine persuasion.

Message Incongruity: Consider a persuasive communication in which features of a product are described. If people are familiar with this message content, it would seem judicious for them not to elaborate upon the content again. Rather, it would seem more appropriate for people to conserve these cognitive resources for the processing of information that would make a more profound contribution to their knowledge. This situation might occur if the information conveyed in a message is incongruent with people's prior knowledge. If people recognized this incongruity, they might be motivated to allocate the resources necessary to reconcile it. The act of increasing the resources available to elaborate upon message information would be expected to enhance persuasion.

A study conducted by Sujan (1985) suggests that a message can stimulate resource availability when it is incongruent with communication recipients' prior expectancies. Sujan classified subjects as experts or novices on the basis of their knowledge about a specific product category, cameras. Subjects were exposed to a message in which the headline identified the product as either a basic or advanced camera and the body copy described the camera's features. Congruity was varied by whether the type of camera specified in the headline matched the description presented in the body copy. Subjects' reaction times and their associations to the message served as the critical dependent variables.

Sujan found that subjects' responses depended on their prior knowledge of the category. Experts exhibited faster reaction times and fewer associations related to the contents of the message when the headline and body copy were congruent than when they were not. Stated another way, experts appeared to engage in a more detailed consideration of the information describing the product when it was incongruent with their expectations about the camera implied by the headline. Novices, on the other hand, appeared not to elaborate upon the body copy regardless of its congruity with the headline; their responses seemed to be confined to the use of the information presented in the headline.

These findings suggest that information incongruent with prior expectations motivated people who were knowledgeable about a product category to activate the resources necessary to engage in detailed processing of the message. People with minimal category knowledge were not so motivated by incongruent information. This outcome occurred even though novices appeared to recognize the disparity between the headline and the body copy. Apparently this knowledge was not sufficient to prompt novices to activate the resources necessary for message processing. It may be that interventions not dependent upon novices' knowledge of the product would be more reliable means of prompting detailed processing. One such intervention is personal relevance.

Personal Relevance: In an extension of Sujan's research, Maheswaran (1987) assessed whether varying the personal relevance of the message would affect experts' and novices' processing strategies and judgments. Personal relevance was varied by telling subjects that they were among a small number of people who would be asked to judge the product and that their judgments would affect management's disposition toward launching the product or that they were among a large number of respondents whose opinions would be averaged. The intent of this intervention was to manipulate subjects' motivation to process the message information in detail. As in Sujan's experiment, subjects were exposed to a headline and body copy that were congruent or incongruent. subjects' associations to the product and their evaluative judgments served as dependent measures.

Maheswaran's findings under conditions of low personal relevance were consistent with those found by Sujan. Experts reported more message associations in the incongruent condition that in the congruent condition, whereas novices had few associations to the message content regardless of the congruity between the headline and body copy. By contrast, stimulating personal relevance motivated both experts and novices to generate a relatively large number of associations to the message content.

Thus it appears that experts can be motivated to invoke the resources necessary for message processing either by the presence of incongruity in the message information or by enhancing the personal relevance of the appeal. In contrast, for novices, enhancing the personal relevance of the appeal is more likely than message incongruity to induce detailed message processing. Further, whether the processing of message information enhances or undermines persuasion seems to depend on the contents of the appeal. Maheswaran found that judgments were more favorable when subjects processed an appeal describing a superior product than when the message described a parity product.

Maheswaran also found that the nature of detailed message processing differs between experts and novices when the information presented is personally relevant. Experts tend to retrieve message information in relation to their evaluation of that information, whereas novices primarily generate verbatim recalls of the message content. This observation suggests that caution is necessary in introducing interventions to motivate experts' activation of resources for message processing. Strong motivations of this type may induce the activation of idiosyncratic associations in the form of counterarguments to the message advocacy and thus undermine persuasion. This problem is less likely to be manifested in novices because they are unlikely to have the prior knowledge necessary to engage in counterargumentation.

The effectiveness of personal relevance as a means of stimulating message processing has also been examined in a series of studies conducted by Petty, Cacioppo, and their associates (Petty and Cacioppo 1984; Petty, Cacioppo, and Goldman 1981; Petty, Cacioppo, and Schumann 1983). Representative of this research is the study reported by Petty, Cacioppo, and Schumann (1983). They exposed subjects to a persuasive message that featured either strong or weak arguments for a particular advocacy. The message was attributed to either a highly credible source or a less credible communicator. These manipulated variables enabled a detection of the information that subjects used in rendering their judgments. The resources subjects were likely to make available for message processing were manipulated by making the communication issue personally relevant to the subjects or not. Thus the experimental design was a 2 x 2 x 2 factorial with two levels of message strength, two levels of source credibility, and two levels of personal relevance. Judgments of the message advocacy served as the criterion measure.

The findings indicated that the personal relevance of the message determined the information subjects used to render judgments. When personal relevance was low, judgments were based on the credibility of the source; the highly credible spokesperson induced more favorable judgments than the less credible source. This reliance on peripheral cues to make judgments under conditions of impoverished resources is the same phenomenon observed by Yalch and Elmore-Yalch (1984). By contrast, when personal relevance was high, subjects relied on the strength of the arguments as a basis for their judgments and were more favorable when the message arguments were strong. Similar results were reported by Petty and Cacioppo (1984) in another study. They found that people relied on the message information under conditions of high personal relevance and used the number of arguments advanced in the message to render judgments when the appeal was not made personally relevant.

Langer, Blank, and Chanowitz (1978) offer additional testimony for the contention that increasing resource availability by enhancing the personal relevance of a message increases its processing. They approached people who were using a copy machine with a request to reproduce either five or twenty pages. This variable can be conceived of as a manipulation of personal relevance in that the large request would be more consequential than the smaller one. The specific form of the request was also varied to detect the information on which subjects based their responses. In one condition, the request was followed by an appropriate rationale: "May I use the Xerox machine because I'm in a rush?" In a second condition, the appeal had the same structural elements—that is, a request followed by a rationale. But in this case the rationale was placebic; it did not provide a compelling reason for making the request. The appeal was, "May I use the Xerox machine because I have to make copies?" In a third condition, the request was made without a rationale. Thus the design varied in the magnitude of the request and the way in which the request was made. The proportion of subjects in each condition who complied with the request was the dependent measure.

Langer et al. found that compliance with these requests was affected by the magnitude of the request. When the request was to use the machine to reproduce five pages, subjects were highly compliant if the rationale was appropriate or placebic but not if it was absent. Apparently under conditions of low personal relevance, subjects did not process the appeal in sufficient detail to distinguish between a rationale that was compelling and one that was placebic. The presence of either rationale enhanced compliance.

A different pattern of compliance was observed when the personal relevance of the request was heightened by asking to copy twenty pages rather than five. Here compliance was greater when the rationale was appropriate than when it was placebic or absent. Under conditions of high personal relevance, people processed the request and rationale in detail and were more likely to comply when an appropriate reason for the request was offered.

Increasing Exposure: An alternative strategy to stimulate message processing is to increase exposures to the message. As Cacioppo and Petty (1979) have noted, at least up to some point, increasing exposures to a message increases "the available time to think about the message arguments, generate new topic relevant thoughts, and so forth." (p. 106) In turn, the presence of additional resources to elaborate upon the message information is likely to enhance persuasion. Beyond this point, however, additional exposures to the message are likely to make available surplus resources and thus activate idiosyncratic associations that undermine persuasion.

An experiment conducted by McCullough and Ostrom (1974) is illustrative of the enhancing effect of repetition. Multiple print advertisements for a brand were presented in the context of a magazine. The ads differed from each other in terms of the headline and illustration, as well as the phrasing and order of arguments. The findings indicated that evaluation of the brand was enhanced as the number of exposures mounted. Similar effects of repetition have been found by other investigators when there was a delay between the time of stimulus exposure and the completion of the persuasion measures (Johnson and Watkins 1971; Wilson and Miller 1968).

There is also evidence that beyond a certain point, increasing the number of message exposures can undermine the persuasive impact of a message. Cacioppo and Petty (1979) varied the number of times subjects were exposed to a written persuasive message and then measured subjects' agreement with the advocacy, associations to the message, and recall of the communication. Their results indicated that increasing exposures from low to moderate levels enhanced agreement, replicating the effect reported by McCullough and Ostrom (1974). Further exposures, however, caused agreement to decline. Categorization of subjects' message associations into positive, negative, and neutral thoughts revealed that the number of negative thoughts declined and then increased as exposures mounted, whereas the opposite pattern was obtained for positive thoughts. Neutral thought increased with repetition. Finally, it was shown that repetition enhanced the recall of message content.

These outcomes can be explained in terms of the resource matching hypothesis. Initial message exposures increased the resources available to elaborate upon the message. Such elaboration would entail positive thoughts because the message was designed to be persuasive. Hence message influence increased. Further exposures provided more resources than were needed to process the appeal. The surplus resources may have been used to generate idiosyncratic associations rather than associations closely linked to the message information. Because idiosyncratic associations are likely to be less favorable than message information, which is designed to be highly favorable to the advocacy, persuasion declined. Recall may have been enhanced with increased exposure because the idiosyncratic associations activated at high exposure levels provided additional cues to retrieve message information when subjects' task was to recall the communication content.

It would also seem that manipulating the duration of exposure to a stimulus would be a means of varying resource availability. Longer exposure durations might provide the opportunity to engage in fuller elaboration of the stimulus information and thus enhance its persuasive impact. Evidence germane to this line of reasoning has been reported in a study by Seamon, Marsh, and Brody (1984). They exposed subjects to irregular polygons for durations ranging from zero milliseconds (ms) to 48 ms via a tachistoscope. Subjects' recognition of the stimuli and affect toward them served as dependent measures. They found that affect increased and then reached an asymptote as exposure duration increased. A similar pattern was observed for recognition, though recognition levels above the chance level occurred only at higher levels of exposure duration. In effect, the pattern of response was such that the increase in affect occurred at chance levels of recognition. The important finding for the present discussion is that duration of exposure and the number of exposures to a stimulus appear to be viable means of increasing resource availability and enhancing influence.

Summary

The investigations reviewed suggest that there are a variety of strategies to enhance message influence when persuasion is limited by impoverished resource availability. Syntactical constructions can focus individuals' limited resources on critical stimulus information. Alternatively, the message can be simplified so that the resources required for processing better match the resources people are likely to have available for the task. These strategies have the virtue of being viable whether the limited availability of resources is attributable to active resource conservation by message recipients or to a limitation in their resource capacities.

When people have the capacity to increase the resources devoted to message processing, several other strategies become viable. One is to motivate people to increase the resources activated. This can be achieved by presenting internally incongruent message information or by emphasizing the personal relevance of the information to message recipients. Increasing personal relevance is preferred when the processor is unlikely to have the expertise necessary to detect the incongruity in message information. Alternatively, one can increase the duration or number of exposures as a means of enhancing the resources available for processing. In pursuing this latter strategy, caution is warranted because resource availability is nonmonotonically related to persuasion. Possibly too many resources will become available, and persuasion will decline. In the following section, we assess strategies to enhance persuasion under conditions of surplus resource availability.

Enhancing Message Processing When Resources Are Excessive

From a strategic perspective, the finding that persuasion is undermined when the resources available for message processing exceed those required would seem to imply the need to reduce message exposures. In applied settings, however, this strategy is often not appropriate. When competitors are spending heavily against their products, an advertiser risks low product awareness and message influence if frequency is not sustained at substantial levels. To resolve this dilemma, strategies are needed that allow the advertiser to maintain a strong presence through repeated exposure without incurring the adverse effects on persuasion caused by high levels of message repetition.

In this section we assess the value of three strategies for enhancing persuasion when the level of message exposures is substantial. First, we consider the use of multiple messages that share the same content but differ in execution as a means to reverse the adverse effects of high exposure levels. This is the approach most commonly used by advertisers. Then we consider two strategies implied by the resource matching hypothesis: alteration of the resources required for message processing and variation in the resources available for the processing task.

Changing the Execution

Perhaps the predominant commercial approach to addressing the problem of surplus resources is to develop a campaign in which the sales proposition remains constant across message exposures, but the advocacy is presented in different situations. For example, a pool of commercials for a beer might emphasize the brand's superior taste, with the commercials differing in the consumption contexts shown. One commercial execution might depict consumption after work, another after sports participation, and still another in the context of a camping trip. The premise underlying this pool-out strategy is that changing the spokespeople or setting in which an advocacy is presented will motivate people to sustain their processing of message information.

The resource matching hypothesis, however, suggests that this strategy is unlikely to be effective in forestalling the decline in persuasion. Changing the spokespeople or setting might sustain people's motivation to elaborate upon the message, but because the arguments supporting the message advocacy are invariant across exposures, such elaboration would likely be in the form of idiosyncratic associations that limit persuasion.

Calder and Sternthal (1980) conducted a study to investigate this issue. Subjects were exposed to one, three, or six television programs. The viewing of the multiple programs was spaced over time. Within each program, subjects saw a series of twelve commercials presented at the same intervals as in prime-time programming. Of particular interest were subjects' evaluations of a product that was advertised three times within each program they viewed. The messages were varied so that the same commercial message was presented three times or this commercial was shown once along with two others that had the same message but differed in the setting and spokespeople represented in the appeals. Thus subjects in the one program condition were exposed to the same commercial for a product three times or to three different commercials for the product. Subjects in the three-program condition either saw the same commercial for the product of interest nine times or were exposed three times to each of three different commercials. And those viewing six programs saw the same commercials for the product eighteen times, or they saw three different commercials six times each.

The findings were in accord with the resource matching hypothesis: message persuasion declined with increasing frequency. This outcome occurred whether the same message execution was presented or three different executions were shown. Thus changing the execution was not an effective means of forestalling the decline in persuasion that occurs under high levels of message exposure.

Varying Resource Demands for Message Processing

A more viable strategy for enhancing persuasion under high levels of message exposure is to increase the resources required for message processing. Smith and Dorfman (1975) varied the complexity of a colored pattern configuration and the number of times subjects were exposed to it. They found that as exposures were increased, judgments of the complex configuration became more favorable, and judgments of the moderately complex configuration first became more favorable and then less so. It was also found that judgments of the simple configuration became less favorable, though this trend was reversed at the highest exposure level.

These data are generally congenial with the resource matching hypothesis if one interprets complexity of the configuration as an indicator of the resources required for processing. Viewed from this perspective, the favorableness of judgments was enhanced when the configuration was complex because adequate resources for processing this stimulus information became available only when the exposure level was high. For the moderately complex configuration, the observation that a moderate number of exposures maximized the favorableness of judgments is explained by noting that this exposure level created a match between resources required for processing and those available. Finally, for the simple configuration, it appears that surplus resources became available as the exposure level was increased, idiosyncratic associations were generated, and thus the favorableness of the judgments declined. Moreover, at the highest exposure level, the availability of resources may have so exceeded the requirements for message-related processing that subjects' pool of idiosyncratic associations was depleted and message information was elaborated anew. The increase in the favorableness of judgments is consistent with this explanation.

A similar experiment was conducted by Anand and Sternthal (1987a) in a persuasive communication context. Subjects were exposed to a persuasive appeal presented auditorially either three, five, or eight times. This manipulation was intended to represent the resources available for message processing. The resources required for processing were manipulated by the message format. In the read condition, subjects heard a persuasive message for a product that was read by an actor. In the sung condition, the same message was sung to a musical accompaniment. And in the hook condition, a statement describing the product's focal attribute was read and was followed by the same message as was presented in the sung condition. Manipulation check measures suggested that the hook condition would require more resources to process than the read appeal, perhaps because it included a message sung to music. The manipulation check measures also suggested that the hook required fewer resources to process than the sung message, perhaps because it was preceded by a read message that described the product characteristic later promoted in the sung portion of the appeal. Subjects' message associations and evaluations of the product served as the criterion measures.

Anand and Sternthal found that the effect of varying message exposures on message associations and product evaluations depended upon the type of message presented. Increasing exposures to the sung message stimulated an increase in the number of message-related associations and the persuasiveness of this appeal. For the hook message, increasing exposures caused idiosyncratic associations in the form of counterarguments to decline and then increase and caused message-related associations as well as the favorableness of judgments to increase and then decline. Finally, increasing exposures to the read message initially enhanced and then reduced counterargumentation, reduced and then enhanced the number of message associations, and caused persuasion to decline and then increase.

These outcomes can be explained in terms of the resource matching hypothesis. Increasing exposures made available the resources required to process the sung message, first provided too few and then a surplus of resources in the hook condition, and introduced more resources than were required to process the read appeal. And as Smith and Dorfman found for their least resource-demanding stimulus, the substantial resource surplus that occurred in the read condition at the highest level of exposures seemed to have prompted the depletion of subjects' counterarguments and the renewed activation of message associations.

The data reported by Smith and Dorfman (1975) and Anand and Sternthal (1987a) suggest that when more resources are available than are required for message processing, persuasion can be enhanced by increasing the resources required to process the stimulus. Operationally this has been achieved without compromising the frequency of exposures by increasing the complexity of the communication. In accord with the resource matching hypothesis, it should also be possible to enhance persuasion by reducing resource availability so that there is a better match with the resource requirements of the processing task.

Varying Resource Availability

The communication literature suggests three interventions that can be used to reduce the availability of resources for message processing without compromising the frequency of message presentation: increasing the rate of message presentation, including a distractor during the presentation of an appeal, and presenting a distractor prior to the communication.

The effect of varying the rate of message presentation has been investigated by Kisielius and Sternthal (1984). They had subjects process a message at either a slow or a fast rate. In accord with Seamon et al.'s (1984) findings, this intervention can be conceived of as a manipulation of the resources available for message processing. Kisielius and Sternthal also varied the resource demands of the processing task by manipulating the richness of message information: either the verbal message was accompanied by pictorial analogs, or the verbal message was presented alone. Subjects' evaluations of the product promoted in the communication served as the dependent measure.

Kisielius and Sternthal found that the rate of message presentation and the type of message had an interactive effect on persuasion. When the rate of message presentation was relatively slow, the verbal message accompanied by pictorial analogs induced less persuasion than the presentation of the verbal information alone. This outcome can be explained by hypothesizing that message recipients activated idiosyncratic associations in response to the pictorial stimuli. Increasing the rate of message presentation enhanced the persuasiveness of the pictorial message but had no effect on the impact of the verbal message, perhaps because increasing the rate of presentation reduced the resources available for generating idiosyncratic associations activated by the picture during the slower presentation. Furthermore, because few, if any, idiosyncratic associations were likely to have been generated in response to the verbal message, increasing its rate of presentation had no effect on the impact of this message.

The use of distractors during the presentation of a communication offers another means of reducing resource availability (see Baron, Baron, and Miller 1973). Moderate levels of distraction appear to reduce the resources available for processing to a level that inhibits the generation of idiosyncratic associations without impairing the elaboration of associations closely related to the message content. As a result, persuasion is enhanced by moderate distraction. High levels of distraction, however, appear to inhibit the elaboration of message associations and thus undermine message persuasion.

A study conducted by Petty, Wells, and Brock (1976) illustrates the procedures employed to examine distraction effects on persuasion. Subjects heard a message that included either weak or strong arguments for an advocacy. While listening on headphones to the message, subjects were asked to monitor an unrelated stimulus projected in one of four quadrants on a screen. Distraction was varied by manipulating the frequency with which this unrelated stimulus appeared. The findings suggested that increasing distraction from low to moderate levels reduced elaboration. Moreover, the effect of this reduced elaboration depended on the strength of the arguments to which subjects were exposed. When message arguments were weak, increasing distraction appeared to reduce the resources that would otherwise be used to generate unfavorable thoughts, and thus persuasion was enhanced. By contrast, increasing distraction appeared to reduce the resources available for activating favorable thoughts in response to the strong message arguments, and therefore persuasion declined.

Distractions prior to the message also can serve as a means of reducing the resources available for processing. In a follow-up to the study reported earlier, Anand and Sternthal (1987b) exposed subjects to either the read or hook message three times. This manipulation was intended to vary the resources demanded for message processing. Prior to each presentation of the message, a program segment was presented. Subjects heard either the same program segment three times or three different program segments so that the extent to which subjects were distracted from processing the message varied. Specifically it was thought that three exposures to the same program segment would enable subjects to elaborate on its contents, whereas a single exposure to three different program segments would be too resource demanding to stimulate elaboration. This assumption was supported empirically in a preliminary study by showing that the program received greater processing when the same segment was presented than when the program segments differed. Subjects' thoughts about the product described in the message and their evaluations of it served as the dependent measures.

The findings indicated that the types of message and program had interactive effects on subjects' responses. Increasing the program distraction enhanced the persuasiveness of the read message, replicating an outcome observed by other investigators (Soldow and Principe 1981). It was also found that increasing program distraction enhanced the proportion of message thoughts and reduced the proportion of idiosyncratic thoughts in the form of counterarguments that occurred in response to the read appeal. By contrast, increasing the program distraction increased the proportion of counterarguments and reduced the persuasive impact of the hook appeal.

When the message required relatively few resources for processing, as was likely to be the case for the read message, increasing program distraction reduced the resources available for evoking idiosyncratic associations and thus enhanced persuasion. By contrast, increasing program distraction may have left too few resources available to process the relatively resource-demanding hook message, causing persuasion to decline.

Summary

The evidence reviewed suggests that it is possible to provide message recipients with surplus resources and in the process undermine persuasion. The simplest solution to this problem may be to reduce the frequency of message exposure, but this strategy may compromise brand awareness and message influence, especially if the product category in which a brand competes is heavily advertised.

Alternatively an attempt may be made to sustain the resources required for message processing by varying the spokespeople and settings presented in a message while holding the information communicated constant. This strategy is questionable not only because of the substantial cost of producing multiple executions but also because it has been shown that changing executions is not an effective means of forestalling the decline in persuasion when there are surplus resources. In resource matching terms, changing the execution still leaves message recipients with more resources than they need to process the persuasive message content, which is constant across executions. As a result, changing executions does not forestall the generation of idiosyncratic associations that cause a decline in persuasion.

Strategies implied by the resource matching hypothesis offer a more promising means of overcoming the decline in persuasion associated with the availability of surplus resources. One strategy is to increase the resources required to process the message. Operationally this can be achieved by increasing the richness and detail of the stimulus information. Another strategy is to reduce the resources available for message processing by increasing the rate of message presentation or introducing distractors prior to or during the message presentation.

Resource Matching and Hemispheric Operation

The analysis of persuasive communication effects in terms of the resource matching hypothesis has been based on several assumptions. One is that a single pool of resources is available to the processor. This pool can be increased by introducing a variety of motivational devices and reduced by directing resources to nonfocal tasks. It is also assumed that the resources required for processing are dictated by features of the stimulus information, such as its complexity. A variety of persuasive communication effects can be explained by invoking these assumptions. But despite this explanatory power, there are grounds for questioning the generality of the resource matching hypothesis as it is currently formulated. Work in hemispheric lateralization challenges both the notion of a single resource pool and the notion that stimulus features are the sole determinants of resource requirements. In this section we examine research in hemispheric lateralization that is relevant to the resource matching hypothesis.

Hemispheric Resource Allocation

Recent research pertaining to hemispheric operation offers a description of how resources might be allocated in memory to process information and render judgments. Two observations advanced in this literature are particularly germane to the current discussion. One is that the left and right hemispheres in the human brain are specialized to perform different functions: the left hemisphere for language processing and the right for wholistic processing, including the processing of music (Gates and Bradshaw 1977; Moore and Haynes 1980). It is also thought that each hemisphere operates on a pool of resources inaccessible to the other (Herdman and Friedman 1985). This implies that if the resources of one hemisphere were exhausted in processing some stimulus information, additional resources could not be transferred from the other hemisphere to facilitate processing.

One procedure commonly used to investigate these notions of hemispheric lateralization is a dichotic listening task. Subjects attend to distractor information presented in one ear while information critical to judgments is presented in the other ear. Because the information presented is represented primarily in the contralateral hemisphere, the resources available for processing and those required can be varied by manipulating what is presented in each ear.

In a study reported by Anand and Sternthal (1987c), a dichotic listening task was used to investigate the role of resource allocation in the judgment process. Subjects heard a verbal message transmitted by headphones to the right ear, which was therefore processed initially in the left hemisphere. Depending on the treatment to which subjects were assigned, the distractor task was to repeat the passage and simultaneously correct errors in a transcription of the passage, only repeat the passage, or only correct errors in the transcription. This manipulation was intended to vary the resources required in the left hemisphere such that repeating the passage and correcting errors in the transcript required the most left hemisphere resources and correcting errors required the fewest. Stated another way, the resources available in the left hemisphere after processing the distractor task should be fewest in the repeat-and-correct condition and most abundant in the correct-only condition.

Anand and Sternthal also varied the information presented in the left ear and initially processed in the right hemisphere. This information was presented as subjects performed the distractor task. The information was composed of three melodies presented five times in the left ear. Two treatments were designed. In the massed condition, each melody was presented five times before the next melody was played. In the spaced condition, the three melodies were presented contiguously, and this pattern was repeated five times. This manipulation was based on the premise that regardless of whether the stimulus information was massed or spaced, it would be processed by the right hemisphere, to which it was originally sent. Whether this information would also be processed by the left hemisphere would depend on the resources available in that hemisphere in relation to those required. And because the left hemisphere is thought to be more efficient in processing information of the sort presented in the massed condition than that presented in the spaced condition (Tucker and Williamson 1984), it was anticipated that greater left hemisphere resource availability would be required for processing of the information presented in the spaced condition.

Several types of dependent measures were administered to assess subjects' responses to the experimental manipulations. Of particular interest here are the measures pertaining to recall of the distractor communication and evaluation of the melodies. It was found that recall of the distractor was superior in the massed condition than in the spaced condition. This outcome is consistent with the premise that fewer left hemisphere resources were required in the massed condition than in the spaced condition. As a consequence, more left hemisphere resources were available to elaborate upon the distractor message in the massed condition.

The data also indicated the presence of an interactive effect of the treatments on evaluation of the melodies (figure 8-1). These findings can be explained as follows: the task of processing the melodies presented in the spaced condition required substantial resources, which were available when the distractor task was moderately resource demanding—that is, in the

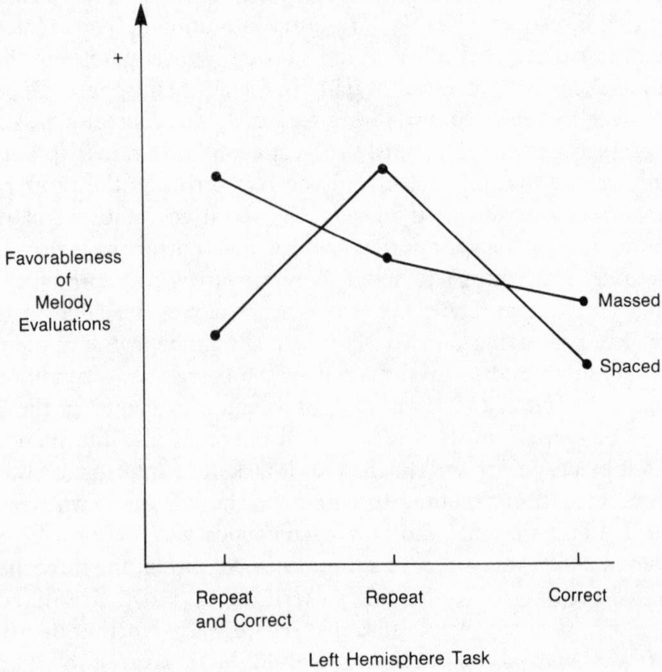

Source: Anand and Sternthal 1986c.

Figure 8–1. Effects of Varying Left and Right Hemisphere Tasks on Melody Evaluations

repeat condition. As a consequence of this match between the resources required and those available, judgments in the spaced melodies condition were relatively favorable. The less favorable judgments in the other two distractor task conditions can be explained by arguing that too few left hemisphere resources were available to process the spaced melodies when the distractor task involved repeating and correcting, and too many left hemisphere resources were available when the distractor task entailed correcting errors in a transcript of the passage.

The same theorizing can account for the judgment effects found in response to the massed-melodies condition. Relatively few left hemisphere resources are thought to be required to process such melodies, and these resources appeared to be available when the distractor task was to repeat and correct, thus accounting for the relatively favorable judgments observed. By contrast, the other distractor conditions provided more resources than were required to process the massed musical stimuli. As a consequence, judgments were less favorable in these distractor conditions than in the repeat-and-correct conditions.

Further evidence implicating hemispheric resource allocation in the judgment process was found in a follow-up study conducted by Anand and Sternthal (1987c). The experimental procedure already described were replicated and extended by switching the hemispheres to which the distractor information and the information critical to judgment were sent. The findings replicated the pattern of judgments shown in figure 8–1 when the distractor information impinged on the left hemisphere and the critical stimulus information impinged on the right hemisphere. By contrast, there were no treatment effects on judgments of the melodies under the switched condition.

These outcomes are consistent with the notions of hemispheric lateralization. Presentation of the distractor passage to the right hemisphere inhibited its processing because this hemisphere cannot efficiently process linguistic information. To perform the distractor task, the information impinging on the right hemisphere would have to be represented in the left hemisphere. This activity would be likely to use the resources that might otherwise be allocated to processing the information critical to judgment. This impoverished resource availability explains why the experimental treatments did not affect the evaluation of the melodies.

The research on hemispheric lateralization provides additional testimony for the resource-matching hypothesis. Like persuasive communication studies, lateralization research implies that the favorableness of judgments is undermined by the availability of more resources or fewer resources than are required for the processing task. Hemispheric lateralization research extends the analysis of resources matching by suggesting that stimulus complexity is not the only factor affecting resource requirements. It also appears that the hemispheres differ in how efficiently they process certain types of information and that this efficiency is a determinant of resource requirements. The observation that the same stimulus information required varying levels of resources to process depending on whether it was massed or spaced is consistent with the notion that processing efficiency affects resource requirements. The observation that varying the ear to which critical information was sent affected its processing offers additional evidence for this view.

Conclusion

The view emerging from this analysis is that persuasion is determined by the congruence between the resources required for message processing and those available for this task. When the number of exposures to an appeal is too few to provide the resources necessary for encoding the message content, persuasion is limited. And when the number of exposures to a message provides more

Table 8–1
Strategies for Enhancing Persuasion under Various Resource Conditions

Situation	*Strategy*	*Comments*
Resources required exceed resources available for message processing	Reduce resources required for processing Focus limited resources Simplify message content	These strategies can be effective regardless of whether resource limitation or resource conservation is responsible for resource inadequacy. Limitation of these strategies is that persuasion must be based on relatively little information.
	Increase resources available for processing Use incongruous messages Emphasize personal relevance Increase exposures to message	Advantage of these strategies is that they provide an opportunity to convey substantial amounts of information as a basis for judgments. These strategies are based on the assumption that adequate resources are available, but people are not motivated to invoke them without special incentive.
Resources available for message processing exceed requirements	Increase resource requirements for message processing Increase message complexity	
	Reduce resource availability Increase rate of message presentation Use a distractor during message presentation Use a distractor prior to message	Caution is warranted in using these strategies because substantial increases in resource requirements or substantial reductions in resource availability may limit message processing and thus undermine persuasion.

resources than those required for message processing, individuals use their surplus resources to activate idiosyncratic associations. Because these associations are likely to be less favorable than more direct message associations, persuasion declines. These observations imply that matching resources available for message processing and those required for this task should enhance communication effectiveness.

This account of the judgment process raises questions about the mechanism by which resource matching might occur. From a strategic perspective, it would be useful to anticipate the factors that affect resource requirements for message processing, as well as factors that influence resource availability. Recent research pertaining to hemispheric operation is useful in this regard. It suggests that the left and right hemispheres of the human cortex perform different tasks with greater efficiency. The left hemisphere appears to be particularly efficient in processing linguistic and redundant information, whereas the right hemisphere is relatively efficient in processing wholistic and novel stimuli. Moreover, the resources available in each hemisphere are thought to be independent.

The implications of these notions for designing persuasive messages are summarized in table 8–1. As the table suggests, strategies for dealing with impoverished and surplus resource availability involve manipulations of the resource requirements for message processing and the resources available for the task; however, the specific devices useful in each of these circumstances differ. To remedy problems associated with inadequate resource availability, a choice must be made between strategies that require relatively few resources to be available but foster the processing of highly limited amounts of information and strategies that require increasing resource availability to stimulate substantial information processing. In situations where surplus resources are available, the strategies chosen require careful calibration. Although increasing resource requirements or reducing resource availability to some extent is likely to enhance persuasion, overzealous use of either of these strategies may undermine message processing and limit persuasion.

References

Anand, P., and B. Sternthal. 1987a. "Resource Matching as an Explanation for Repetition Effects on Persuasion." Unpublished manuscript. New York University.

———. 1987b. "Persuasion under Varying Conditions of Resource Requirements and Resource Availability." Unpublished manuscript. New York University.

———. 1987c. "The Effect of Cognitive Resource Availability on Affective Judgments." Unpublished manuscript. New York University.

Baron, R.S., P.H. Baron, and N. Miller. (1973). "The Relation between Distraction and Persuasion." *Psychological Bulletin* 80:313–323.

Cacioppo, J.T., and R.E. Petty. 1979. "Effects of Message Repetition and Position on

Cognitive Response, Recall and Persuasion." *Journal of Personality and Social Psychology* 37:97–109.

Calder, B.J., C. Insko, and B. Yandell. 1974. "The Relation of Cognitive and Memorial Processes to Persuasion in a Simulated Jury Trial." *Journal of Applied Social Psychology* 4:62–93.

Calder, B.J., and B. Sternthal. 1980. "Television Commercial Wearout: An Information Processing View." *Journal of Marketing Research* 17:173–186.

Chafe, W.L. 1976. "Givenness, Contrastiveness, Definiteness, Subjects, Topics, and Point of View." In C.N. Li, ed., *Subject and Topic,* pp. 25–55. New York: Academic Press.

Gates, A., and J.L. Bradshaw. 1977. "The Role of the Cerebral Hemispheres in Music." *Brain and Language* 4:403–431.

Herdman, C.M., and A. Friedman. 1985. "Multiple Resources in Divided Attention: A Cross-Modal Test of the Independence of Hemispheric Resources." *Journal of Experimental Psychology: Human Perception and Performance* 11:40–49.

Hornby, P.A. 1974. "Surface Structure and Presupposition." *Journal of Verbal Learning and Verbal Behavior* 13:530–538.

Johnson, H.H., and T.H. Watkins. 1971. "The Effects of Message Repetition on Immediate and Delayed Attitude Change." *Psychonomic Science* 22:101–103.

Kisielius, J., and B. Sternthal. 1984. "Detecting and Explaining Vividness Effects in Attitudinal Judgments." *Journal of Marketing Research* 21:54–64.

Langer, E.J., A. Blank, and B. Chanowitz. 1978. "The Mindlessness of Ostensibly Thoughtful Action: The Role of "Placebic' Information in Interpersonal Interaction." *Journal of Personality and Social Psychology* 36:635–642.

Maheswaran, D. 1987. "Piece Meal versus Heuristic Processing Strategies by Novices and Experts." Unpublished manuscript. Northwestern University.

Moore, W.H., and W.D. Haynes. 1980. "A Study of Alpha Hemisphere Asymmetries for Verbal and Nonverbal Stimuli in Males and Females." *Brain and Language* 9:338–349.

McCullough, J.L., and T.M. Ostrom. 1974. "Repetition of Highly Similar Messages and Attitude Change." *Journal of Applied Psychology* 59:395–397.

Petty, R.E., and J.T. Cacioppo. 1981. *Attitudes and Persuasion: Classic and Contemporary Approaches.* Dubuque, Iowa: W.C. Brown.

———. 1984. "The Effects and Involvement on Response to Argument Quantity and Quality: Central and Peripheral Routes to Persuasion." *Journal of Personality and Social Psychology* 46:69–81.

Petty, R.E., J.T. Cacioppo, and R. Goldman. 1981. "Personal Involvement as a Determinant of Argument-based Persuasion." *Journal of Personality and Social Psychology* 41:847–855.

Petty, R.E., J.T. Cacioppo, and D. Schumann. 1983. "Central and Peripheral Routes to Advertising Effectiveness: The Moderating Role of Involvement." *Journal of Consumer Research* 10:135–146.

Petty, R.E., G.L. Wells, and T.C. Brock. 1976. "Distraction Can Enhance or Reduce Yielding to Propaganda: Thought Disruption versus Effort Justification." *Journal of Personality and Social Psychology* 34:374–384.

Saliba, S. 1987. "The Persuasive Effects of Linguistic Variation in Message Structure." Ph.D. dissertation, Northwestern University.

Seamon, J.G., R.L. Marsh, and N. Brody. 1984. "Critical Importance of Exposure Duration for Affective Discrimination of Stimuli That Are Not Recognized." *Journal of Experimental Psychology: Learning, Memory, and Cognition* 10:465–469.

Smith, G.F., and D.D. Dorfman. 1975. "The Effect of Stimulus Uncertainty on the Relationship between Frequency of Exposure and Liking." *Journal of Personality and Social Psychology* 31:150–155.

Soldow, G.F., and V. Principe. 1981. "Response to Commercials as a Function of Program Context." *Journal of Advertising Research* 21:59–66.

Sternthal, B., and C.S. Craig. 1982. *Consumer Behavior: An Information Processing Perspective.* Englewood Cliffs, N.J.: Prentice-Hall.

Sujan, M. 1985. "Consumer Knowledge: Effects on Evaluation Strategies Mediating Consumer Judgments." *Journal of Consumer Research* 12:31–46.

Tucker, D.M., and P.A. Wiliamson. 1984. "Asymmetric Neural Control Systems in Human Self-Regulation." *Psychological Review* 91:185–215.

Wilson, L.R., and H. Miller. 1968. "Repetition, Order of Presentation, and Timing of Arguments and Measures as Determinants of Opinion Change." *Journal of Personality and Social Psychology* 9:184–188.

Yalch, R.F., and R. Elmore-Yalch. 1984. "The Effect of Numbers on the Route to Persuasion." *Journal of Consumer Research* 11:522–527.

9
Advertising Art: Cognitive Mechanisms and Research Issues

Fairfid M. Caudle

A work of art is by convention acknowledged to have been created for the sake of form, beauty, and design and needs no other justification for its existence. One way in which a work of art considered to be great, such as a painting, acquires this status is through recognition of the work's ability to evoke a response in the viewer that endures and grows rather than being diminished by continued or frequent contemplation. In contrast, an illustration is considered to have a lesser scope: to be decorative, created for a particular occasion, and perhaps put aside when its occasion has passed. To be sure, many works that originated as illustrations or for purely decorative purposes have since acquired the status of work of art; however, the distinction still holds.

One might argue that the vast majority of art created for advertising, particularly magazine advertising, falls into the category of illustration. As a magazine is read, the reader pays attention primarily to its written content; advertisements are scanned during this process but are not necessarily intentional focal points. Within this context, the art contained within an advertisement must make its impact on the viewer not in the luxuriously long periods of focused contemplation expected when examining a recognized work of art

---

An extended version of a portion of this chapter was presented at the American Psychological Association Annual Convention in Anaheim, California, in August 1983, under the title "Mechanism, Form and Style in Advertising Art: An Appraisal." A revision was presented at the International Conference on Psychology and the Arts at the University of Wales in Cardiff in September 1983 under the title "Psychological Aspects of Art in American Magazine Advertising." This chapter consists of a further revision of this second version, together with the addition of material concerning theoretical aspects of cognitive mechanisms in the effectiveness and persuasiveness of advertising art and suggestions for further research.

I would like to thank students in my course on the psychology of advertising for bringing to my attention several examples employed in this chapter. The assistance of Danna L. Givot of Research Resources Inc., both in obtaining permission to reproduce examples of advertisements, as well as in meticulously attending to myriads of details, has been invaluable and is greatly appreciated. Finally, I would like to thank Pat Cafferata and Alice Tybout for their many thoughtful comments and suggestions.

but in the brief moments of perusal spent by the typical magazine reader, together with the additional exposure gained through the repeated placement of the advertisement in a number of publications. It should not be surprising, therefore, that the art found in advertising achieves this condensed impact by relying on a number of mechanisms employed in "real" art (even to the extent of incorporating well-known works of art into the advertisement) and employing several basic techniques that tap into the ways we attend to and process information.

Information processing has long been of interest to those researching advertising effectiveness. However, the great preponderance of such studies has been concerned with verbal processes. (For exceptions, see the reviews by Alesandrini, 1983, and Rossiter and Percy, 1983.) Bettman (1986) has noted that "despite the importance of the issue of visual processing, relatively little empirical work has been done. This is an area of research that deserves much more emphasis" (p. 276). Thus this chapter suggests possible cognitive mechanisms through which visual content in advertising achieves its impact, an analysis that will draw on illustrations of some of the relationships and parallels between art found in advertising and the classical and modern art found in museums. This discussion is intended both to provide a source of ideas and stimulation for those who create advertising and to identify research issues for those with empirical concerns. Finally, it is hoped that by selectively examining the visual content of advertising as art rather than as illustration, readers will discover a new source of aesthetic enjoyment and that works of art otherwise destined to be put aside once the page has been turned might begin to be given the recognition they deserve.

Advertising, Communication, and Cognitive Mechanisms

Advertising exists to communicate. Whatever the particular medium chosen, the major goals of virtually all advertising are to capture the viewer's or listener's attention, to establish the identity of a product while differentiating it from others in its class, and to establish a motive for buying the product. While there are many methods of achieving these goals, this chapter considers only those in which visual content may in some way be instrumental in providing an avenue of communication. The major premise to be explored is that three cognitive mechanisms appear most frequently in magazine advertising art—association, visual incongruity, and metaphorical symbolism—and that further research is needed to assess their impact on advertising memorability and persuasiveness. While it is certainly the case that each of these mechanisms can operate through either verbal or visual media, discussion will focus on their pictorial expression by first illustrating them in general advertising contexts and then considering them with regard to their specific roles in advertising art.

The Association of Ideas

To establish the identity of a product, advertising relies on imparting desirable and distinctive associations to that product. One might almost say that meaning is association in the sense that the meaning of a word or object consists of the associations that it elicits. Long ago Aristotle categorized associations as falling into three categories. *Association by similarity* occurs when one idea brings to mind similar ones (for example, the thought of ice cream might bring to mind thoughts of pudding, yogurt, or gelatin, all foods sharing similar characteristics). *Association by contrast* occurs when one idea triggers its opposite (thinking of the roughness of sandpaper might, for example, make one think of the smoothness of marble or glass). Terms such as *concept, schema,* and *category* may be used to describe the mental organization of information based on similarity or contrast.

Aristotle's third category, *association by contiguity,* will be of particular interest here. In this instance, ideas become associated simply by being paired together. Try this simple experiment: announce to any group of people that you are going to count to three and then say a word. Everyone is to say immediately the first word that comes to mind. Then count to three and say *table.* It is likely that most people will say the word *chair* (as you very likely thought to yourself in reading these instructions). Why should this occur? The simplest explanation is that "table" and "chair" are experienced together (contiguously) so often that when we think of one, we think of the other. (For an extended discussion of association based on similarity, contrast, and contiguity, see Caudle, 1988.)

When association by contiguity is employed in advertising, the product is depicted together with something that already evokes desirable feelings, associations, or attitudes. If the advertisement is effective, these associations can be transferred, in the mind of the consumer, to the product, service, or institution being advertised, thus allowing attitudes and product choices to be influenced.

When considering association, why should association by contiguity be of particular interest? The answer lies in the fact that there need be no inherent connection or similarity in the ideas in order for an association to be formed; the association can be quite arbitrary and still be powerful. Thus when one desires to establish the meaning or identity of a product, association by contiguity can provide a highly effective tool because of the enormous range of objects or meanings that can be associated with a product.

Later in the chapter, we will see how advertising art can provide a locus within which the product and the desired association may be brought together. However, let us look first at a straightforward example of association by contiguity and consider an advertisement for a brand of men's underwear (figure 9–1). The objective of this advertisement is to establish a connection (association) between the product, Great Looks Men's Fashion Underwear, and the model, who is powerful enough to control the sleek and fierce black panther.

Figure 9-1. Illustration of the Association of Ideas through Contiguity. This advertisement contains a number of associative links between the product and a powerful, animal nature. (Reproduced by permission of Fruit of the Loom, Inc.)

The wild or savage quality of the model-panther combination is reinforced by placing the advertisement in an outdoor setting. The association between the name of the product and the powerful animal is strengthened by including an animal "growl" in the title of the product: "GRRREAT LOOKS." Thus, by depicting the product contiguously with this particular setting, this advertisement provides several associative links between the product and the ideas of masculinity, power, jungle, and animal nature, none of which is necessarily present when considering the product alone.

Visual Incongruity

Another cognitive mechanism often employed in magazine advertising is the use of visual incongruity, which can be defined as the combination of images or parts of images that do not ordinarily belong together. There are numerous ways of achieving incongruity, ranging from the use of distorted size relationships to the fusion of parts from normally incompatible sources to form a new whole. Visual incongruity provides a potentially effective technique because it captures the viewer's attention by presenting a puzzle that must be examined further in order to identify the source of the discrepancy. One example of visual incongruity is in the shadow technique employed in figure 9-2, an advertisement for a brand of instant coffee. Normally an object's shadow conforms in general outline to the object itself. However, in this instance, the object (a jar of instant coffee) casts a shadow having the outline of a coffee pot rather than a jar. This discrepancy between what should be there and what is there is intended to capture the viewer's attention and to establish for the product the highly desirable association of freshly ground perked coffee.

Metaphorical Symbolism

The use of visual metaphor provides a means of communicating symbolic meanings and associations. For example, in an advertisement for perfume, a snake is entwined around a woman's neck. One could argue that this symbolically represents a woman being sexually embraced by a man. The head of the snake is directed toward the bottle of perfume, symbolizing the paradise to be gained by the union of male and female. The use of the snake also achieves great dramatic impact.

One might suppose that the perfume advertisement is just another example of twentieth-century preoccupations with sexual themes and their symbolic representation within a psychoanalytic framework. However, such visual metaphors appeared in art long before they were discovered by advertisers. For example, the painting entitled *Profile of Simonetta Vespucci* (figure 9-3; see Berenson 1968) by Piero di Cosimo (1462–1521) also depicts a young maiden with a snake entwined around her neck. I am not proposing that there is a

Figure 9–2. An Illustration of Visual Incongruity. Note the discrepancy between the product and its shadow. (Reproduced by permission of Nestlé Foods Corp.)

Figure 9-3. ***Portrait of Simonetta Vespucci.*** **LAC 159724, Piero di Cosimo.** Chantilly, Musée Conde. This painting symbolically communicates meanings through the use of visual metaphor, an approach that is also employed in magazine advertising. (Reproduced with the permission of Giraudon/Art Resource, New York.)

Introducing Quorum. A cologne for the other man lurking inside you.

Figure 9-4. Advertisement Combining the Association of Ideas, Visual Incongruity, and Metaphorical Symbolism. (Reproduced with the permission of Ogilvy & Mather Advertising, and Compar, Inc.)

direct connection between these two works but rather that, consciously or unconsciously, both artists were employing highly charged symbols with multiple levels of meaning in order to communicate.

Having examined examples of how the visual content of an advertisement can employ the association of ideas, visual incongruity, or metaphorical symbolism in order to communicate meanings, let us look at one example that illustrates how all three of these cognitive mechanisms can be combined. Figure 9–4 is an advertisement for a man's cologne. The visually incongruous shadow technique is used to associate the metaphorical symbol of the devil with the model, giving visual meaning to the caption: "A cologne for the other man lurking inside you." This is but one example of the many intricate and powerful ways that the pictorial content of an advertisement can establish product meanings or reinforce verbal messages.

Now that these cognitive mechanisms have been defined and illustrated within general advertising contexts, let us consider them within the context of advertising art. For purposes of discussion, advertising art will be viewed broadly as including paintings, photographs, and retouched photographs that go beyond the simple depiction of the product and its use.

Use of Art in Establishing Associations

Art has enormous value and prestige within today's society. Therefore recognized works of art can possess numerous associations of value to the advertiser in establishing the identity of a product and in reaching its target population. One frequently employed strategy attempts to link a product with a recognized work of art so that the product will, by association, acquire some of the status and prestige of the art work. There are four most commonly employed ways in which the cognitive mechanism of association is employed: using art as a background or setting; associating a company with socially desirable values by presenting art to the public; comparing the product with a recognized work of art; and depicting the product itself as a work of art.

Art as a Setting for the Product

There are many ways in which art is used to provide a setting for a product. Some examples follow.

Reproduction of Art with Desirable Associations: Perhaps the simplest way to use art as a setting is to select a well-known work of art with themes appropriate to the advertisement. For example, the background for an advertisement for Toujours Moi perfume reproduces Pierre Cot's *The Storm,* which shows a man grasping a young woman around the waist and sheltering her with his cloak. The only copy in the ad states, "The French call such thoughts fantasy.'' Thus, the painting is used to depict a fantasy centering on male pursuit and protectiveness.

Paintings portraying meals in progress have been employed as focal points by Rice a Roni Savory Classics to illustrate headlines and to attract attention to the main message of the advertisement. For example, the headline ''Before Savory Classics, a delicious side dish in 10 minutes took a miracle'' is illustrated with the 1655 painting *Old Woman Saying Grace,* by Nicolaes Maes, in which a woman is seated before a simple meal with her eyes closed and hands held to say a blessing. A somewhat more dramatic painting, Edouard Manet's *Luncheon on the Grass* (1863), has been employed to illustrate the point: ''Before Savory Classics, people went to extremes to make meals interesting.'' This well-known painting showing a picnic attended by two men and one woman, fully clothed, and a second, nude woman, created a scandal in its day.

Use of Art to Create a Distinctive Room: An advertisement for Paco Rabanne cologne depicts a man in his bedroom, and a conversation with his girlfriend is reproduced in the ad's copy. Surrounded by many works of art on the walls, the man is portrayed as worldly and sophisticated. In this instance, the use of art creates a setting of earthy elegance. This example also provides a complex and interesting display of spaces within spaces, since many paintings are shown. The reader is thus drawn into the space of the room and may spend more time examining it.

A setting of cool sophistication is achieved by an advertisement for Estee Lauder Private Collection Perfume, which depicts a model clad in an evening gown and seated graciously in an elegant drawing room filled with its own ''private collection.'' Thus the perfume is given the associations of exclusivity and understated wealth.

Reproduction of Art Directly Related to the Product: Occasionally the setting created by art is used to establish more direct associations. For example, an advertisement for Smirnoff Vodka employs a portrait of someone we presume to be a Russian czar, thus giving the vodka (which is made in the United States) highly desirable associations of prerevolutionary Russia. The same approach was employed in an advertisement for Courvoisier. To strengthen the association of the product as ''the cognac of Napoleon,'' a portrait of Napoleon is placed just behind a bottle of the product and a filled glass. A lit candle (the lighting source in Napoleon's day) evokes feelings of warmth and provides a mellowed color tone to the entire advertisement.

Presentation of Art to the Public

Becoming involved in some way with the presentation of art to the public can provide an advertising vehicle that will enhance a company's image. For example, Sotheby's, a well-known auction house, often reproduces in its advertisements examples of works that have been sold there. One advertisement reproduced a painting by Cézanne to illustrate the point made in the ad's copy that "Sotheby's is the forum where great works of art meet serious collectors." Similarly, Philip Morris Incorporated reproduced several works from a touring exhibit of art from the Vatican collections in an advertisement informing the reader that the company was one of the exhibit sponsors. IBM frequently reproduces paintings from exhibits it has sponsored and actually maintains its own gallery of science and art, from which paintings are borrowed for use in its advertisements. And although it is not involved directly with the presentation of art to the public, the Stanhope Hotel has capitalized on its location directly across the street from the Metropolitan Museum of Art in New York (certainly association by contiguity in its most literal sense) with a series of advertisements, each reproducing a painting from the museum.

Figure 9-5 illustrates how the presentation of art to the public can both enhance a company's image and associate the company with meaningful and powerful metaphors. This advertisement for the *Arizona Republic/Phoenix Gazette* was directed toward potential advertisers in the newspaper. It reproduces a contemporary painting, *Phoenix in Flight* (from its own collection), to reinforce the point that the city of Phoenix, like its mythological predecessor, rose from the "ashes" of several Indian cities and now is "soaring higher than any other major market." The city is portrayed as a market to be considered seriously, and the newspaper is depicted as an appropriate vehicle for the placement of ads to reach that market.

Comparisons between the Product and a Recognized Masterpiece

An analogy is a form of reasoning in which similarities are pointed out in relationships between objects which are otherwise dissimilar. For example, one might say that "duck" is to "pond" as "deer" is to "forest." In both instances, there is a relationship between an animal and its habitat, though the animals themselves are quite dissimilar. Analogies can be effective advertising strategies because they can establish equivalency within a class.

If one considers the general category of masterpieces, there are masterpieces of art, literature, and other media. By making the point that a product is a masterpiece in its own class, just as is a recognized work of art, an association is established that influences the consumer to view the two objects, the product and the art work, as having an equivalent status. This approach is illustrated in the advertisement for Perugina chocolates in figure 9-6 which portrays an equivalency between Michelangelo's statue of David and the product.

Numerous additional examples of this technique might be cited, such as

Bird on the wing.
Phoenix is soaring higher than any other major market in population growth.
Over the past decade, Phoenix has been a major beneficiary of the ongoing migration from the northern states to the sunbelt.
The Phoenix market now ranks 25th in population. And the last census figures show a 55% increase in population.
The new Phoenix residents tend to be younger, better educated, and more affluent than the norm. They're attracted to Phoenix by its vitality, its healthy economy, and its wide-open spirit.
Today, over 1.6 million people call the Phoenix market their home. And most share a strong commitment to personal and financial growth.
Their median age is 30.8 years—younger than the national average of 31.1. Almost half of all Phoenix adults are college-educated. And 58% enjoy annual household incomes of $25,000 or more.
More than seven out of ten of these affluent adults are reached with an average daily issue of The Arizona Republic/The Phoenix Gazette. Across the nation, few major markets offer such a decidedly upscale audience.
And, few major metro newspapers deliver comparable media dominance. When you buy us, you own Phoenix.
Phoenix. It's a rare bird indeed.
THE ARIZONA REPUBLIC/The Phoenix Gazette

Figure 9–5. Advertisement for *Arizona Republic/Phoenix Gazette*. It reproduces a commissioned work of art, *Phoenix in Flight,* by Doug Danz, © 1984. Phoenix Newspapers Inc. (Reproduced by permission. Permission does not imply endorsement by the newspaper.)

Figure 9–6. Advertisement Establishing an Analogy between a Product and Recognized Work of Art. (Reproduced with the permission of Perugina Chocolates & Confections Inc.)

a series of advertisements for Tanqueray Gin. Each Tanqueray ad pairs the product with a work of art, such as a jade figurine, to support the statement, "Why go halfway around the world to find a masterpiece, when you can acquire one right around the corner." The same technique has been employed by Kodak. However, rather than reproducing the work of art, the advertisement compares the signature of the artist, Rembrandt, with the name *Kodak* in photoprocessing. Showing only Rembrandt's signature and the Kodak logo, the copy reads: "In Dutch painting the Rembrandt signature says it's the genuine article. In photoprocessing this signature says it's the genuine article," reminding readers to check that film receives genuine Kodak processing. At the same time this analogy reinforces associations implying that colors and textures in the photograph will be reproduced as accurately as if the photographs were works of art.

Product as a Work of Art

Occasionally, instead of pairing the product with a work of art in some other medium, the product itself is depicted as having the quality and the aesthetic characteristics of a work of art. For example, figure 9–7 contains a photograph that at first glance appears to be of a modern sculpture. Upon reading the text, however, one discovers that the photograph is, in fact, the "precisely-crafted engine intake frame" for a U.S. Navy plane. By presenting a high-precision object in an aesthetically satisfying way, the manufacturer gains the status of being an artist of sorts.

The impact of this concept is increased through the use of a series of similar advertisements, each representing as an art form some aspect of the advanced technology manufactured by this corporation. A spherical form that resembles a beautiful vase turns out to be a photograph of a gyroscope bearing, which is in actuality no larger than a pea. In another example, what appears to be a kinetic sculpture turns out to be an antenna undergoing testing; another in this series depicts intriguing patterns of shadow and light—in reality, the airflow pattern in an engine inlet duct. The heat plume generated by an engine takes on the appearance of a painting in still another example. The cumulative impact of these advertisements helps to create associations of precision, quality, and beauty that enhance the image of the company.

Portraying the Product with an Artist's Tools: Brushes, Palette, or Frame: There are numerous other ways in which a product can be represented as a work of art. For example, a product that provides a colorful display can be associated with the idea of art simply by employing an artist's palette and brushes as props. Or the product can be "framed" as if it were a work of art within a larger setting. This strategy was employed in a series of advertisements for Burlington Socks. In one example, a man is shown sitting in a

Precisely crafted engine intake frame for the U.S. Navy F/A-18A Hornet. Producing advanced technology products efficiently demands the most modern plants and equipment. This year Northrop will invest more than $120 million in new tools and facilities to assure a continuing capability to develop innovative approaches to emerging customer requirements.
NORTHROP
Making advanced technology work.

Figure 9–7. Presentation of a Product as a Work of Art. (Reproduced with the permission of the Northrop Corporation).

darkened room. Light shining through the door behind him falls on a "painting" on the wall, which is in reality a collection of colors and patterns reproduced from those used in the design of socks.

Another example that "frames" the product as if it were a painting can be found in an advertisement for designer shirts and ties. The advertisement shows a room with various items of clothing strewn in a line along the floor. A snobbish-looking butler is carrying two martinis on a tray, presumably to the owners of the discarded clothing. The ad is dominated by an enormous painting on the wall, which shows part of a shirt, collar, and tie, and the painting is signed by the designer. The copy informs us that the pattern of the shirt and tie is one of a series by the same designer. While not part of the scenario depicted in the ad, the "painting" nevertheless dominates the ad and gains attention, if for no other reason than its relative size.

Absolut Vodka has depicted its product as an "Absolut Masterpiece" by showing a nearly completed painting of a bottle of the product, together with the artist's hand holding a paintbrush. By showing the product as worthy of being painted, associations of status and prestige are created.

Incorporating the Product into a Commissioned Work of Art: Yet another way in which the product can be portrayed as a work of art is by incorporating it in some way into an original painting commissioned from a recognized artist and reproduced within the advertisement. This approach was employed by a fabrics company that commissioned artists to create original paintings of interiors utilizing the company's products. This strategy has also been employed by the designer Halston, who commissioned a series of original paintings by Andy Warhol. Each "painting" consists of a collage incorporating clothing and cosmetics carrying the Halston name. An advertisement for Cracker Barrel Cheese placed a round cracker containing a square of cheese on an original painting in such a way that, at first glance, the patterns formed by the surface and contours of the cheese and cracker seemed part of the content of the abstract painting.

The Container as a Work of Art: Sometimes the container rather than the product itself is depicted as a work of art. The obvious association is that the product must indeed be very special in order to be worthy of such an outstanding container. One cosmetics company has portrayed the compact for its powder as a "work of art," and a Finnish brand of vodka has presented its unusually textured bottle noting that "you don't put a common vodka in a bottle that's a work of art."

The goal of each of the preceding strategies was to link a product with art in some form in order for the product to acquire some of the positive associations to art presumably held by the target audience. The following section illustrates yet another means of employing well-known works of art to establish desirable associations and to attract the viewer's attention.

Incongruity, Association, and Metaphor through Synthetic Art

When recognized works of art are altered in some way in order to incorporate the representation of a product, the result is a kind of synthetic art that both associates the product with a prestigious work of art and provides a powerful attention-getting stimulus through the resulting visual incongruity. Since the most striking combinations are achieved by employing the most widely recognized paintings, it is not surprising that one of the more frequent choices for such synthetic creations is Leonardo da Vinci's portrait of Mona Lisa. Among the many advertising examples that have reproduced this painting in some way is an advertisement for a food product used to make "Mona Lindsay's olive meatloaf" (figure 9–8). The incongruity of seeing what appears at first glance to be possibly the world's most recognizable painting altered to hold a platter of food is a powerful attention-getting stimulus. In a statement framed as if it were a painting, the viewer is informed, "Now you can create your own Italian masterpiece." An association evoked by the combination of Mona Lisa and food is that this is the source of the famous Mona Lisa smile. Another example employing the Mona Lisa that alludes directly to this association shows her wearing a pair of earphones and asks: "Ever wonder why she's smiling?" An advertisement for a computer accessory shows Leonardo da Vinci using his computer to create the Mona Lisa with different looks, with the caption, "Let's see how it looks with a smile, Mona."

The alteration of well-known works of art to make a statement occurred in the art world long before being employed as advertising strategy. The Dada movement was a protest against traditional art forms and the rigid rules governing what was and was not considered to be acceptable. In creating his "Dada Manifesto," Marcel DuChamp embellished the Mona Lisa with a mustache (figure 9–9) and was well aware of the shock value that such an act would have.

Each ad in a delightful series of advertisements for Levolor Blinds not only displays a well-known painting but actually reconstructs the painting and incorporates the product into the background. These ads combine this synthetic reconstruction with the use of analogy to remind consumers to watch out for imitations. For example, figure 9–10A notes that "if it's really a painting by Whistler, it says Whistler. If it's really a Riviera Blind by Levolor, it says Levolor" and presents a reconstruction of *Whistler's Mother.* Other paintings in this campaign reconstruct well-known paintings by Fragonard, Renoir, and Goya.

Figure 9–8. Example of Synthetic Art Based on the *Mona Lisa*.
(Reproduced with the permission of Lindsay Olive Growers.)

Figure 9-9. ***Mona Lisa*** **with a Moustache, by Marcel Duchamp,** L.H.O.O.Q. (Reprinted with permission of The Bettman Archive, Inc., New York)

If it's really a painting by Whistler, it says Whistler.
If it's really a Riviera Blind by Levolor, it says Levolor.
Watch out for imitations. Make sure it's a signed original from the Levolor Riviera™ Collection. Custom made for your windows in hundreds of colors and prints. Levolor Blinds come in a variety of slat widths including the elegant, slim new Levolor Micro Blind. At fine stores everywhere.
LEVOLOR FOREVER NEVER WORRY WARRANTY
Lift a Levolor

Figure 9–10A. Four Levolor Lorentzen, Inc., Ads. Each features a well-known painting (by Whistler, Fragonard, Renoir, and Goya and incorporates the product. (Reproduced with the permission of Levolor Lorentzen. Inc. and Muller Jordan Weiss. "LEVOLOR and RIVIERA" are registered trademarks of Levolor Lorentzen, Inc.)

LEVOLOR
If it's really a painting by Fragonard, it says Fragonard.
If it's really a Micro Blind by Levolor, it says Levolor.
LEVOLOR FOREVER NEVER WORRY WARRANTY
Lift a Levolor

Figure 9–10B

If it's really a painting by Renoir, it says Renoir.
If it's really a Pleated Shade by Levolor, it says Levolor.
Watch out for imitations. Make sure it's a signed original from the Levolor Pleated Shade Collection
In pastels and neutrals. Stripes, solids and patterns. Sheer and semi-opaque fabrics.
At fine stores everywhere.
Lift a Levolor

Figure 9–10C

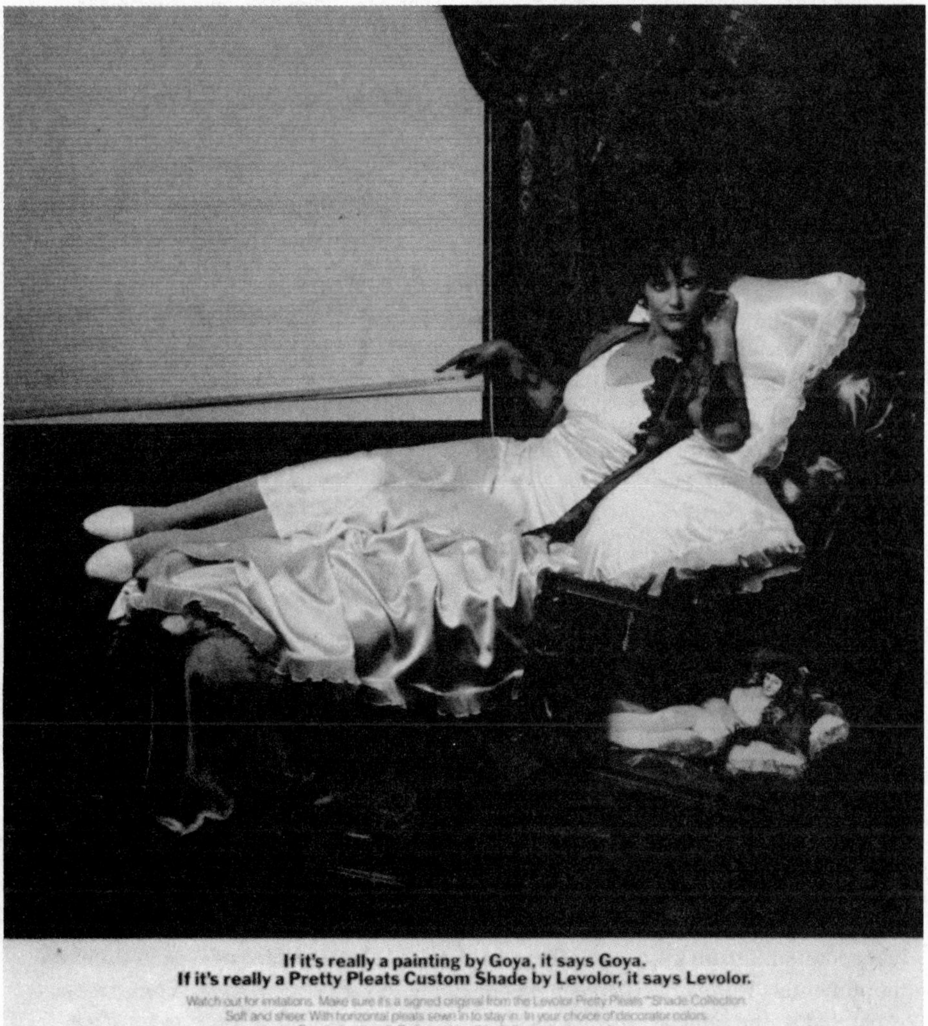

If it's really a painting by Goya, it says Goya.
If it's really a Pretty Pleats Custom Shade by Levolor, it says Levolor.
Watch out for imitations. Make sure it's a signed original from the Levolor Pretty Pleats™ Shade Collection. Soft and sheer. With horizontal pleats sewn in to stay in. In your choice of decorator colors. Beaded side-pull. Rolls up smoothly. At fine stores everywhere.
Lift a Levolor

Figure 9-10D

Another highly recognizable painting that has given rise to a number of advertising clones is Grant Wood's *American Gothic*, which shows an unsmiling man and woman standing before a church, the man holding a pitchfork with its tines pointing upward. Figure 9–11 shows a version of this painting in which the pitchfork has been replaced by a Casio musical computer, and the woman holds one as well. The incorporation of the modern calculator into this 1930s painting results in an anachronistic visual incongruity. In addition, an incongruity of content results from the combination of the caption, which refers to "making beautiful music together," and the stern, grim expressions of the couple, for whom one would think that music making would be the furthest thought from their minds. It is of interest to note that the artist conceived the original painting as being a man and his unmarried daughter, not his wife. However, so ingrained is the perception of the man and woman as husband and wife that they have always been interpreted in this way in the frequent advertisements based on this painting. A number of additional examples have been reproduced in the catalog for an exhibition of Grant Wood's work (Corn 1983).

Other ingenious examples of synthetic art deserve mention. A painting by the French impressionist painter Edgar Degas (1834–1917), *Dance Foyer at the Opera*, depicts a ballet master and dancers in a ballet studio. The open space in the painting's foreground was filled by incorporating a Renault car in such a way that the dancers appear to be looking at it (figure 9–12). The car is presented as an "affordable masterpiece," equating it with the painting in terms of real, rather than financial, worth. The advertisement provides startling incongruities (a car within a room; a modern car within a century-old context) and associates the product with a prestigious work of art and the desirable characteristics of "Frenchness" and the precision, balance, grace, and control of ballet.

A more subtle use of the same technique is provided by the advertisement for Ile de France Brie (figure 9–13) in which a picture of the product has been incorporated into an approximation of a detail of Georges Seurat's (1859–1891) monumental *A Sunday Afternoon on the Island of La Grande Jatte.* The cheese is painted in the same pointillist style as the original painting, both as an attentional mechanism and to impart the associations of Frenchness and masterpiece quality.

Similarly, *The Luncheon of the Boating Party* by Pierre-Auguste Renoir (1841–1919) represents a group of friends around the table of a pleasure garden on the banks of the Seine. In an advertisement reproducing this painting, the background of vegetation and sailboats on the river, and the canopy overhead, have been altered to fade into the textured background of an American Express card (figure 9–14). The sharp-eyed observer will also note that the same credit card has been inserted into the hand of one member of the party. The copy notes, "There are many kinds of meal, but the nicest of all is surely the long,

Figure 9-11. A "Revision" of Grant Wood's *American Gothic*.
(Reproduced with the permission of Casio, Inc.)

The affordable masterpiece. Renault 18i.
The Renault 18i. Engineering that demonstrates why Renault is the world leader in front wheel drive. Fuel injected for a hwy est. of 41 MPG and EPA est. MPG of 29.* Performance tailored by 5-speed overdrive or 3-speed automatic transmission options.
The Renault 18i. The perfect balance of handling and comfort. Rack and pinion steering, sway bars front and rear, Michelin radials and biomechanical seats all come standard. And every 18i is covered by American Motors' Buyer Protection Plan®
with its full 12-mo./12,000-mi. warranty.† Renault 18i. A masterpiece you can afford.
Deluxe sedan under $7,900.**
Deluxe wagon under $8,400.**
RENAULT
American Motors

Figure 9–12. Synthetic Art Employing Edgar Degas' *Dance Foyer at the Opera*

leisurely relaxed dinner at a favourite restaurant with a group of good friends," and goes on to name a number of such restaurants in Europe. The painting supports this copy by representing just this sort of meal. At the same time, it provides a single image associating a leisurely meal with representations of the product.

The technique of synthetic art has also been used with paintings not so readily identifiable. One advertisement for shoes showed a painting of a man (which I eventually tracked down to be a detail from Michaelangelo's fresco of the Sistine Chapel) embracing a woman. All that is visible are the woman's legs, clad in shiny red high-heeled shoes, and her fingers with matching red nail polish grasping the man's back. The juxtaposition of Renaissance and modern motifs, of softer and vivid colors, as well as the incomplete representation of the shoe-wearing woman, provided vivid and interesting incongruities. The relative effectiveness of sources for the creation of synthetic art that have different degrees of familiarity is an issue that requires further research.

Figure 9–13. Advertisement for Ile de France Brie depicted as a detail of Georges Seurat's *A Sunday Afternoon on the Island of La Grande Jatte*. (Ile de France is a registered trademark of Universal Foods Corporation, Milwaukee, Wisconsin. Reproduced by permission of Schratter Import, a division of Universal Foods Corporation.)

The creation of synthetic art is not limited to paintings; statues and sculpture can also provide effective media, especially where humor is intended. One need only recall the numerous times Auguste Rodin's (1840–1917) *The Thinker* has appeared in various contexts to illustrate or reinforce some copy point.

Figure 9–14. ***The Luncheon of the Boating Party*, by Auguste Renoir, in an Updated Version.** The meal is being paid for by credit card. (Copyright American Express. Reproduced with permission.)

Similarly, the Statue of Liberty has appeared in many guises and contexts, with one of the most ingenious being an advertisement within a medical journal for an ointment to relieve itch. The Statue of Liberty is shown from the back (which most people never see), and her left arm appears to be reaching up to scratch her back. This example provides a vivid visual image likely to elicit at least a chuckle (and a closer look) from the reader.

Another example in which a well-known sculpture provides the basis for an advertising image is an ad appealing for funds to support the arts. The statue (itself based on a photograph), depicting the planting of the United States flag on Iwo Jima during World War II, was transformed into a struggling group of men in modern dress trying to "plant" an enormous paint brush. The ad provided a striking visual metaphor.

In general, creations of synthetic art provide compelling visual incongruities and anachronisms by utilizing a work or style of art that is so well known as to be recognizable instantly. The actual persuasiveness of such approaches is a subject that needs further research, as does the general topic of the characteristics of those works of art that have become so immediately identifiable, even when altered, that they have assumed the status of a kind of cultural icon.

Form in Advertising Art

In classical art, three of the most frequent forms of paintings are the portrait, the still life, and the scene or landscape. Modern art has added, among others, the abstract composition and the collage. In creating these forms, the artist employs such tools as color, contrast, composition, perspective, balance, and texture to create a harmonious whole. The same forms are employed in the art found in advertising; however, in advertisements, the goal is to focus attention on the product in a way that produces positive associations and enhances memory.

The Portrait

In advertising, as in art in general, the portrait provides a powerful medium for making statements. The most successful portraits are those that can be interpreted at several levels and seem to give some insight into the inner nature of a person, going beyond the simple portrayal of physical features. As employed in advertising, the portrait, which could be a painting or a photograph, might represent an example of someone who uses the product.

Portrait of a Well-Known Person: Cutty Sark has presented a series of striking portraits of successful persons such as the contemporary American composer Philip Glass. He is shown with a forthright, unwavering gaze, looking directly at the reader and holding a handful of musical notes. Because the strong, successful person in the portrait is portrayed as being a devotee of this brand of scotch, status and prestige are imparted to the product, and the consumer may unconsciously and in varying degrees feel that, by using this product, he or she acquires some aspect of status.

Portrait of a Professional Model. Metropolitan Life insurance company wished to make the point that time passes quickly as a child becomes an adult and that it is necessary to take steps to secure the child's future. The effective focal point of the advertisement is a portrait of a child that simultaneously captures the qualities of "little girl" and, with the serious and contemplative facial expression, "woman." The portrait, with its caption, "A child is someone who passes through your life, and then disappears into an adult," provides a powerful context for the message contained in the advertisement's copy.

Portraits are often the means to communicate the graciousness and elegance to be obtained by using particular products. An advertisement for Raffinée perfume used veiling and lighting contrasts together with downcast eyes to achieve a mysterious and feminine quality in the portrait associated with the product.

Reclining Portrait: Just as reclining figures have been frequent subjects in classical art, so also have they been employed in advertising. One such portrait in an advertisement for Opium perfume evokes associations of opulent sensuality, the same sorts of associations evoked, for example, by Renoir's painting *Odalisque* (figure 9-15) in which a woman is shown reclining, leg bent, with a sultry, almost challenging expression. Numerous additional examples of well-known paintings of reclining figures by Goya, Manet, and others have had their echos in advertising.

Portrait of the Product: It is not necessary to confine the use of portraits to persons. A portrait of the product itself can be created, as in figure 9-16, a portrait by Andy Warhol of Absolut Vodka. This painting uses nonrealistic color and imprecise contours and goes far beyond the simple representation of the product to elicit associations of meaning, substance, depth, and presence.

The Still Life

In a classical still life, the artistic impact comes from both the selection and arrangement of the objects and the way they are portrayed. As employed in advertising, the portrayal of the object has tended to be scrupulously realistic (although this need not be the case), and emphasis is placed on the product within an aesthetically pleasing arrangement of objects chosen for their positive associations. An advertisement for Booth's Gin consists of a grouping

Figure 9-15. *Odalisque,* by Auguste Renoir. Portraits of reclining figures are often created for magazine advertisements. (National Gallery of Art, Washington; Chester Dale Collection)

that includes a martini, a bottle of the product, a bowler hat, and a folded newspaper, which appears to be the *London Times*. The arrangement is visually satisfying and balanced, and the hat and paper provide associations of London. The only copy in the advertisement reproduces a British accent saying "Ved-d-dy ved-d-dy dry."

An advertisement for Godiva Chocolates that provides another example of a still life employs an arrangement of chocolates and berries. The arrangement is carefully balanced and proportioned and associates the product, chocolates, with the flavors of the berries contained within them. The caption, "Berried Treasures," uses a pun to indicate that the berries are "buried" inside the chocolates.

In still another example, a department store advertisement for terra cotta serving pieces displays two bowls, a sugar pot, a corked bottle, a marmalade pot, and a butter dish in a beautifully designed arrangement, augmented by a few vegetables. If the copy were removed, one could easily envision this photograph in a museum collection because of its qualities of balance and soothing serenity. Advertisements for glassware, wine, ceramics, and similar objects provide many opportunities for creating a still life rather than just an ordinary arrangement of products, especially since such objects have often been the subjects of paintings by classical artists.

Figure 9–16. Example of a Product Portrait: Absolut Vodka by Andy Warhol. (Reproduced with the permission of Carillon Importers Ltd.)

The Landscape

When a landscape is employed in advertising, it is usually chosen to provide a context for the product and to provide positive associations to it. Sometimes the product is incorporated into the landscape as in a series of advertisements for J&B Scotch. These ads do not show the product in its entirety. Instead portions of the label are embedded within the setting of a soothing, peaceful lake. The caption, "It whispers," adds to the association of smoothness, a highly desirable association for scotch whisky. An identical technique has been employed by E&J Brandy, incorporating the product label into a snow scene or lake surface.

Cutty Sark whisky has employed a series of advertisements in which a giant bottle of the product is incorporated into a scene such as the New York skyline at sunset. The Cutty Sark boat on the label is made to appear as if it is sailing along the horizon line.

A landscape or scene can also be used to provide associations of romance, mystery, or other emotions, as in a wine advertisement that included a scene of bare, fog-shrouded trees, with a couple as one small part of the scene.

Other Forms

The abstract composition has not been employed in advertisements as often as other art forms, but it can be stunning in its impact. An advertisement for watches laid out the watches vertically and horizontally in a composition (figure 9–17) that seemed to be a realization of a detail from one of the Dutch painter Piet Mondrian's paintings (figure 9–18), which are often elegant patterns of straight lines, sometimes framing areas of solid colors. The collage is another approach that has been employed less frequently but can also provide a highly pleasing and interesting medium. In a collage commissioned by the IBM Company, elements related to computers were combined with portions of a profile to create an intriguing composition.

Style in Advertising Art

Artistic style plays an important role in the overall impact of advertising art in capturing attention and in providing positive associations for a product. An area needing further research concerns the extent to which different artistic styles may be particularly compatible with the cognitive mechanisms already described. Although advertising draws upon numerous artistic styles and has created many of its own, only two of the styles most often employed will be discussed here: impressionism and surrealism.

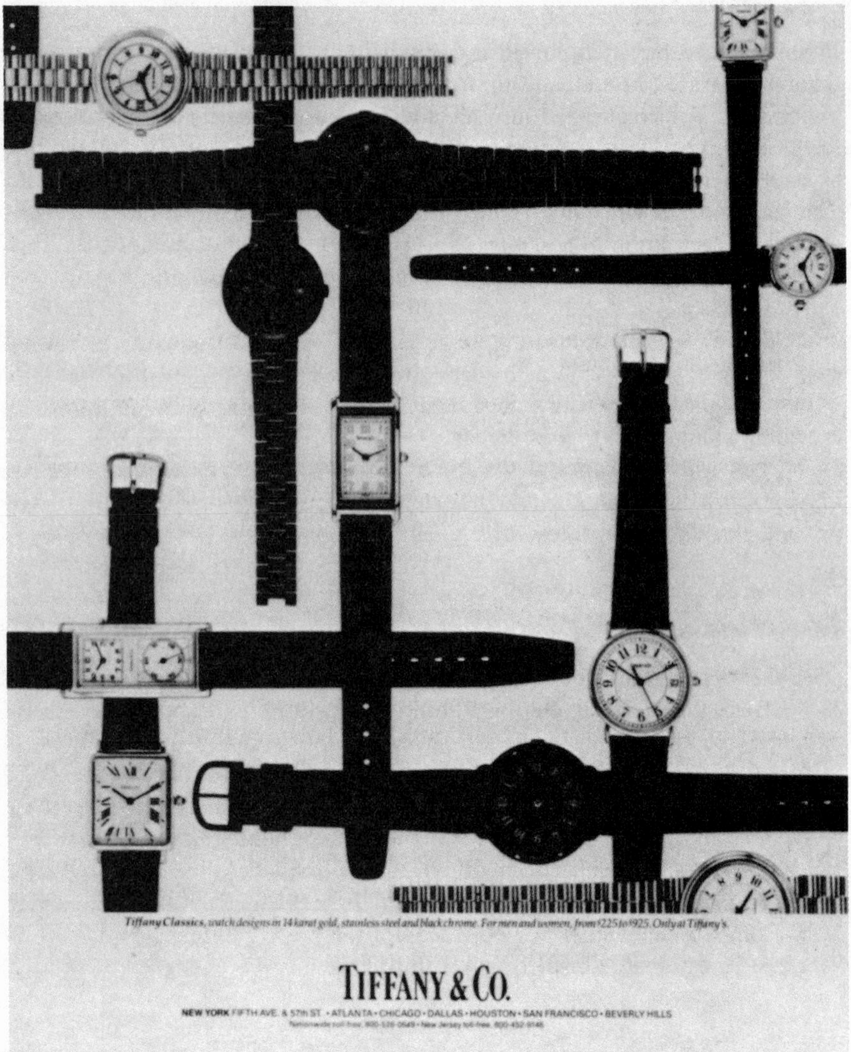

Figure 9-17. Abstract Composition Composed of Watches. Note its similarity to a fragment of figure 9-18, one of many abstract compositions by Piet Mondrian. (Reprinted with the permission of Tiffany & Co.)

Figure 9–18. *Composition 7* by Piet Mondrian (1913). (Solomon R. Guggenheim Museum, New York; Photo: Robert E. Mates)

Impressionism

As impressionism evolved as a style, it focused on emphasizing the immediate and purely visual impression of the subject of a painting, with much less emphasis on detail, form, or outline. Definition was achieved largely through color, with perspective minimized and the representation of depth often hazy and indistinct (Réalités 1973). One writer describing a painting by Degas noted that "Degas . . . has diminished the distance between his model and the viewer. The proximity, the disturbing warm colors, the haziness, the unusual position . . . , all enable him to enter the model's 'territory.' " p. 71).

We might apply many of these comments to the art taken from an advertisement for L'Air du Temps perfume (figure 9–19), which associates the

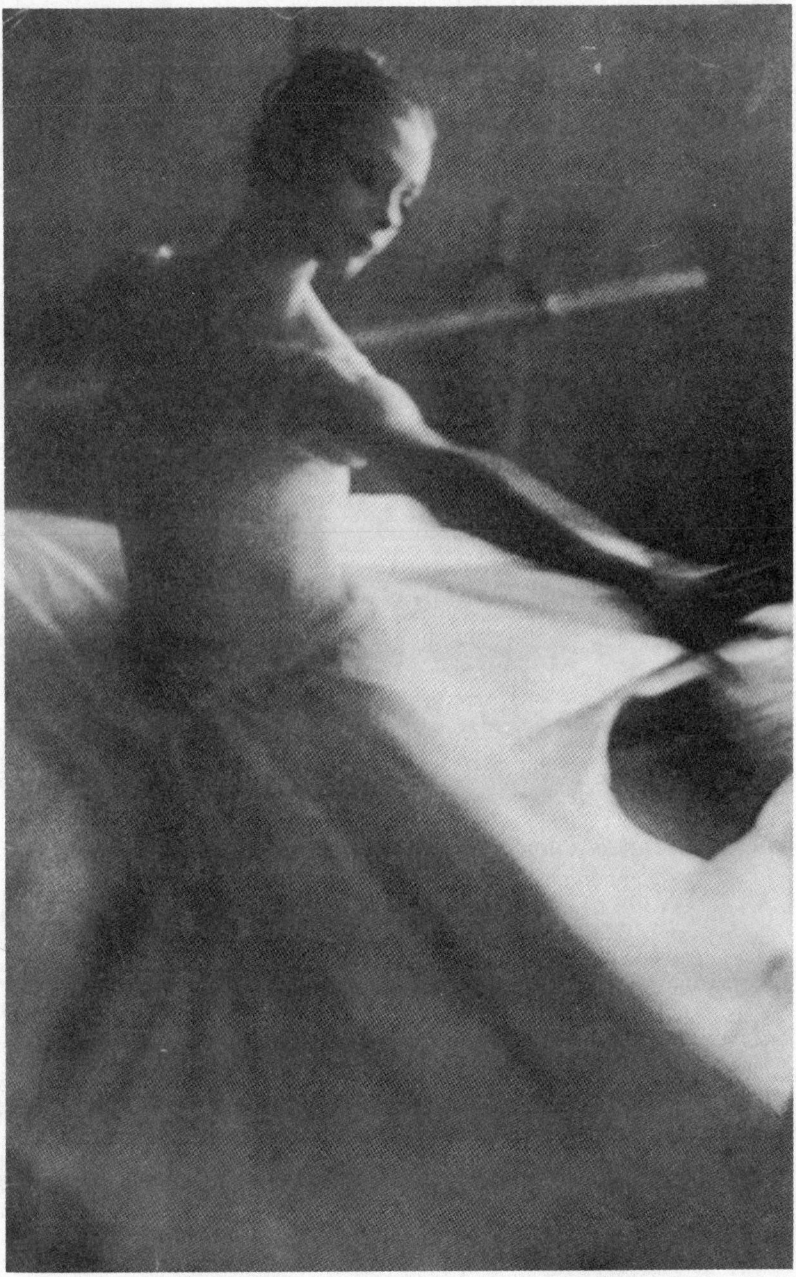

Figure 9-19. Example of the Impressionist Style in Advertising Art. Shown is the Nina Ricci ballerina, from an advertisement for L'Air du Temps perfume. (Reproduced with the permission of Nina Ricci.)

product with a romantically hazy portrayal of a ballerina. The subject, the lighting, the transparency, and the captured moment in motion are all evocative of the impressionist style, which, as employed in this example, creates associations of grace, beauty, and elegance.

A similar approach was employed in an advertisement for Vanderbilt perfume that centered on a swan in flight, just leaving the surface of the water. The swan has associations of grace and elegance, which were reinforced by the impressionistic treatment in the advertisement. One might speculate that the style of impressionism creates a viable means for operationalizing the mechanisms of association and metaphor in advertising art.

Surrealism

The most prominent characteristic of surrealism as a style is its emphasis on the nonrational and nonlogical. Situations and objects are shown that could not exist in the real world. Often dramatic visual incongruities are incorporated into paintings, as if to emphasize even more strongly the conflict between what is real and what is not. The movement, greatly influenced by Freud and psychoanalysis, explored the unconscious mind. Writing about this movement, Wilson (1975) notes:

> In the *Manifesto of Surrealism,* André Breton wrote, "We are still living under the rule of logic. . . . The absolute rationalism which remains in fashion allows the consideration of facts relating only narrowly to our experience. . . . Under the banner of civilization, under the pretext of progress we have managed to banish from the mind anything which could be accused, rightly or wrongly, of being superstition or fantasy, and to banish also any method of seeking the truth which does not conform to tradition." The alternative he proposed was the exploration of the irrational part of the human mind, the unconscious; "If the depths of the mind contain strange forces capable of reinforcing or combating those on the surface it is in our greatest interest to capture them." (p.3.)

A number of artists employed various approaches and styles within the larger movement of surrealism. One who has been especially influential in advertising art is the Belgian artist René Magritte (1898–1967). Wolfram (1972) has pointed out, "In the skillful hands of Magritte, illogical ideas, hitherto unconnected in the mind, are opened up with new meanings which had been hidden, lost and forgotten through overfamiliarity with things which we just take for granted" (p. ii). One of Magritte's most famous paintings is *The Red Model* (figure 9–20), which shows a pair of shoes that merge into feet. Wilson (1975) has described it as

> one of the paintings in which Magritte combines objects in such a way as to produce an "impossible" new object which because it is painted in a conventional representational way is nevertheless there, existing before the specta-

Figure 9-20. René Magritte's Surrealist Painting *The Red Model.* Compare with the visual metaphor in figure 9-21. (Reprinted with permission of the Moderna Museet, Stockholm, Sweden)

> tors' eyes. The effect of such an image is to produce an intense sense of shock, bafflement and frustration: however hard you look the object refuses to resolve itself entirely into its components—boot and foot in this case—although both are clearly there. (p.9)

Compare Magritte's *The Red Model* with figure 9–21, an advertisement directed toward potential advertisers in *Texas Monthly.* This advertisement also produces an "impossible new object" in the fusion of the western boot and the buildings that have begun to march over the Texas landscape. Instead of presenting an enigma, however, here the fusion is meant to convey the message that although one object has physically displaced the other, both are still influential as traditions. As with Magritte's work, the visual incongruity produces intense involvement in the ad. This example illustrates how a surrealistic style may be particularly appropriate when utilizing visual incongruity as a cognitive mechanism, especially when the result provides a visual metaphor.

Among the other examples of Magritte's work that have been particularly influential is his *Time Transfixed.* Perhaps his best-known painting, it shows a fireplace with a clock on the mantlepiece. Coming out of the fireplace is a locomotive, stationary, as if caught in a moment of time. Magritte, in describing this painting, noted, "As for the locomotive I made it loom out of a dining-room fireplace in place of the usual stovepipe" (Larkin 1972, p. 2.) There are thus two obvious visual incongruities: the combination of a train with a fireplace, together with the fact that the train appears suspended above the floor. There are a number of parallels between this painting and an advertisement for table linens that shows a table covered with a cloth and food, including a plate and a bowl of fruit. The entire table appears to be flying through the air at an angle over the sea. Although the tablecloth seems to be flapping in the breeze, all the items on the table stay in place. While the subject matter is certainly different, this advertisement is also producing multiple visual incongruities and impossible situations: a flying table, a table over the sea, objects remaining in place although in reality they would fall off were the table actually in motion. In addition to the attention-riveting images, the painting is aesthetically pleasing and would be worthy of placement in a museum in its own right.

Magritte's *The Titanic Days* depicts another impossible object: a man and a woman merged into one being, with contours that make one body. A medical advertisement used the same visual metaphor—a photographic collage of two bodies merged into one. The advertisement was for a medication for a sexually transmitted disease that, in order for treatment to be successful, had to be taken by both members of a couple. In this advertisement, as in the Texas magazine advertisement, the visual metaphor was directly related to the message in the copy and served to illustrate it.

Magritte was particularly fond of smudging the distinction between what is real and what is unreal. One of his favorite techniques was to paint the view

Figure 9–21. Example of the Surrealist Style in Advertising. (Reproduced with the permission of *Texas Monthly*. Illustration by Ignacio Gomez.)

from a window in which the distinction is unclear between a surface, such as the glass of the window, and the view through the window. However, on the shards of broken glass below the window can be found the same image of the sun, as if it had somehow merged with the object through which its light passed. In *Euclidian Walks*, a painting of a scene resting on an easel is shown before a window opening onto the same scene. Where the painting ends and the real scene begins is apparent only through close inspection, thus making unclear which is the real scene and which is the painted one.

Similar contradictions between whether a scene is real or merely a two-dimensional representation of something real have been effectively employed in advertising. For example, each in a series of advertisements for a luggage company depicted what appeared to be a realistic picture of sky and clouds; however, there was a broken hole in the sky, through which the realistically depicted product was shown as if it had just hurtled through. Thus, the products, not the sky, is real. Similarly, an advertisement for beer shows a small town street scene. In the "sky" a disproportionately large can of beer is shown penetrating the scene, with jagged edges of torn paper surrounding it. Thus the product becomes the "real" object rather than the scene.

This discussion of impressionist and surrealist styles has illustrated a number of characteristics that appear in advertising art, delineating still further the many links between the art of the museum and the art of the advertisement. An impressionist style may be particularly useful when employing association through similarity or contiguity; surrealism, predicated on incongruity, provides a way of operationalizing that mechanism. Both styles can be employed in creating visual metaphors.

Thus far, comparisons and analyses have been made primarily from an aesthetic point of view. What remains is to begin to consider these relationships from a different research perspective and to draw on the existing theoretical and empirical literature in order to suggest tentative hypotheses concerning ways in which art may influence advertising effectiveness. In the process a number of additional directions for future research will be suggested.

Cognitive Mechanisms in Advertising Art: Historical Background and Issues for Further Research

The discussion thus far has focused on providing a review and analysis of the many relationships between advertising art and the art of the museum. However, little is known about the specific effects of advertising art or how the cognitive mechanisms, forms, or artistic styles utilized in advertising may affect memorability or persuasiveness. Now we will examine preliminary steps that can be taken toward specifying more concretely some of the possible ways in which advertising art may achieve its effects. Several seemingly disparate topics will be considered separately and then jointly so that their possible interactions can be proposed: historical conceptions of cognitive processes, relevant psychoanalytic concepts, possible physiological processes relevant both to cognitive processes and psychoanalytic concepts, and parallels with contrasting advertising styles. Finally, the relationship of each of these topics to selected contemporary research findings will be described as they may pertain to the three basic mechanisms of advertising art already described.

Contrasting Views of the Mind

Associative versus Wholistic Conceptions: The history of psychology has been replete with controversies concerning the basis and nature of mental processes. As psychology was developing into a science in the latter part of the nineteenth century, it drew upon the early conceptualizations of Aristotle, as well as those of such 17th–19th century philosophers as John Locke, David Hume, and J.S. Mill. These philosophers viewed associative processes as the links through which mental elements could be joined, resulting in more complex ideas and higher mental processes. This view of the mind led to its being considered as somewhat similar in function to a kind of telephone switchboard in which the mind served as the central point at which incoming and outgoing messages could be processed and new connections formed (through association). Perception and thought were viewed as a kind of "sequential and associational assembly of bits from simple to complex" (Horowitz 1970).

In the early twentieth century, this view was challenged by Gestalt psychology, which proposed that perception is wholistic, not the putting together of smaller units. According to Gestalt psychology, perceptions are organized into figure-ground relationships, and patterns are perceived as wholes rather than as parts or elements. Beginning with the perception of the illusion of movement (the Phi phenomenon, as seen, for example, in the apparent movement of lights around a theater marquee, a perceptual experience that cannot be analyzed into individual elements in motion since it is an illusion with no actual movement), the Gestalt psychologists went on to demonstrate that wholeness and organization are fundamental to the entire spectrum of cognitive processes, including problem solving, memory, perception, thinking, and imagining.

These contrasting conceptions of the mind, a sequential, associative model, and a model based on the simultaneous perception and processing of organized wholes have continued to shape twentieth-century experimental psychology, appearing and reappearing in various guises.

Psychoanalytic Tradition: At the same time, the psychoanalytic tradition originated with Sigmund Freud has continued to be a prominent influence within the domain of clinical psychology and personality theory. Centering around the concept of the unconscious mind and the interplay among unconscious motives, ideational content and defense mechanisms, and their influence on and expression in thought and behavior, the psychoanalytic framework has enriched and broadened our understanding of the significance of metaphor and symbolism in creative thought and particularly in art (Kris 1952).

Contrasts in Cognitive Functioning between Left and Right Hemispheres: More recently, a series of discoveries about the organization and functioning of the human brain has provided tantalizing experimental evidence that ultimately promises to lead to a resolution of the controversy between the differing conceptions of mind just described and to shed light on a possible physiological basis for unconscious processes. These discoveries may also aid in clarifying responses to art of the sort already discussed.

Comparisons between left and right brain hemispheres in humans have indicated that the two hemispheres are specialized for different cognitive functions. These studies were initially conducted with patients who had undergone split-brain surgery (in which the corpus callosum, a bridge between the cerebral hemispheres, is severed in order to prevent an epileptic seizure from involving both hemispheres). Later, testing situations were devised to enable hemispheric differences to be studied in normal subjects. (Among those who have described these findings in detail are Hansen 1981 and Springer and Deutsch, 1985.)

Although each hemisphere is able to learn and remember, as well as to initiate behavior and to feel emotion, the two hemispheres function and process information in greatly differing ways. The left hemisphere thinks in a linear, sequential manner. It controls language (which itself involves a sequential flow of information in which linear order is important to meaning), is analytical, and is able to focus on details. It also thinks logically (again, a form of processing in which order and sequence are essential).

In contrast, the right hemisphere seems to think primarily in images rather than words and in an intuitive rather than logical manner. It responds wholistically (that is, to wholes rather than by analyzing details) and thus processes many inputs simultaneously rather than sequentially. The right hemisphere is far better than the left hemisphere at spatial tasks, such as the perception of complex geometric patterns. Its special capacities become clearer when we think of the process of facial recognition. In recognizing a face, one perceives and recognizes the entire face (a spatial type of information with all of it processed simultaneously) rather than analyzing it into details (we do not start at the left eyebrow and view each detail until the face is recognized). The (mostly) nonverbal right hemisphere is the more emotional half of the brain and seems to play a special role in imagery and dreaming, as well as in music and other creative abilities.

Although the hemispheres may be specialized for different functions, they interact continuously. Levy (1985) has noted, for example, that in reading a story, the right hemisphere may be more involved in appreciating humor or metaphor, while the left hemisphere may play a special role in such activities as understanding syntax. The integrated functioning of both hemispheres contributes to the overall understanding of the story.

Physiological Basis for Contrasting Conceptions of the Mind: In comparing the capacities of the two hemispheres, there would seem to be compelling parallels between the two opposing theoretical modes of mental functions: a sequential and associative mode and a wholistic, spatial one. While these views of the mind developed long before these physiological discoveries were made, each view of mental functioning nevertheless seems to be related to dominant processes in one or the other hemisphere. However, instead of either-or dichotomies such as sequential versus wholistic, verbal versus nonverbal, or associative versus Gestalt, the as-yet-incomplete study of hemispheric interactions suggests that we must begin to think of complementary modes of cognition and to develop theories that deal with their interactions. (Arieti 1976 has taken an enormous step in this direction.)

Hypothesis Concerning the Physiological Basis of Certain Unconscious Processes: How might we tie in the psychoanalytic point of view? We can add to our listing of either-or dichotomies the one proposed by Freud, who distinguished between primary process thought, which is the dominant mode of the unconscious mind and of dreams and some forms of mental illness, and secondary process thought, which is the logical thinking of the waking mind.

Galin (1974) has pointed out that "certain aspects of right hemisphere functioning are congruent with the mode of cognition psychoanalysts have termed primary process" (p. 574). To support this hypothesis, he notes the right hemisphere's primarily nonverbal mode of representation, presumably through images, and its nonlogical reasoning. In addition, he notes that when words are used in mental constructions by the right hemisphere, their meanings depend on context and can shift when seen as parts of a new pattern (p. 574), giving rise to such forms as puns and metaphors.

Galin also notes the possibility that the two hemispheres can simultaneously experience conflicting emotions and motivations, with those experienced by the hemisphere dominant at the time being expressed through thought or action. According to Freud, repression is one of the defense mechanisms through which primary process thought becomes inaccessible to secondary process thought. Noting parallels between the functioning of the isolated right hemisphere and those mental processes that are repressed and thus unconscious, Galin has proposed in addition that there may well be a physiological mechanism involving the corpus callosum through which ideational content in one hemisphere might be dissociated or isolated from the other hemisphere. That is, Galin has hypothesized a physiological mechanism for repression in which what is unconscious is not verbalized but can nevertheless be represented through imagery, metaphor, and symbol.

Logical-Verbal and Emotional-Nonverbal Modes of Advertising: It is a long conceptual leap to move from a discussion of parallels between the dichotomy of secondary and primary process thought and that of the logical-verbal left hemisphere and emotional-nonverbal right hemisphere to a consideration of advertising strategies, and yet there have been intermediate steps in this direction. As Martineau (1971) pointed out, it becomes apparent that, for much of its history, advertising was essentially a verbal medium that presented logical reasons for product purchase. In the 1950s there was a shift toward emphasis on nonverbal, pictorial communication designed to appeal to unconscious emotions, needs, and motives.

One might argue that the left hemisphere is more involved in processing logical verbal advertisments, whereas the right hemisphere may be more involved in responses to pictorial, nonverbal advertisements that appeal to emotions. Figure 9–22 is an automobile advertisement targeted toward the special characteristics of each hemisphere. Half of the advertisement is in words and is directed toward the left half of the brain; the other half is a picture of the automobile hugging the road, which we see in several fragments in a complex spatial configuration. The copy notes that this is a car for both sides of the brain, thus appealing to logical and spatial responses. Note, however, that little is known about how such intentional construction of an advertisement translates into greater persuasiveness or memorability.

Cognitive Mechanisms Reconsidered

What has all this to do with possible cognitive mechanisms in the effectiveness of advertising art? The impact of advertising content, whether verbal or visual or combined, is very likely related in some as yet undefined ways to the characteristics and limitations of the hemisphere more involved in processing it, as well as to the resulting interactions between right and left hemispheric modes of thought and the effects of repeated exposure over time. In the discussion of advertising art, three mechanisms were considered as potentially of importance: the association of ideas by pairing the product with something already

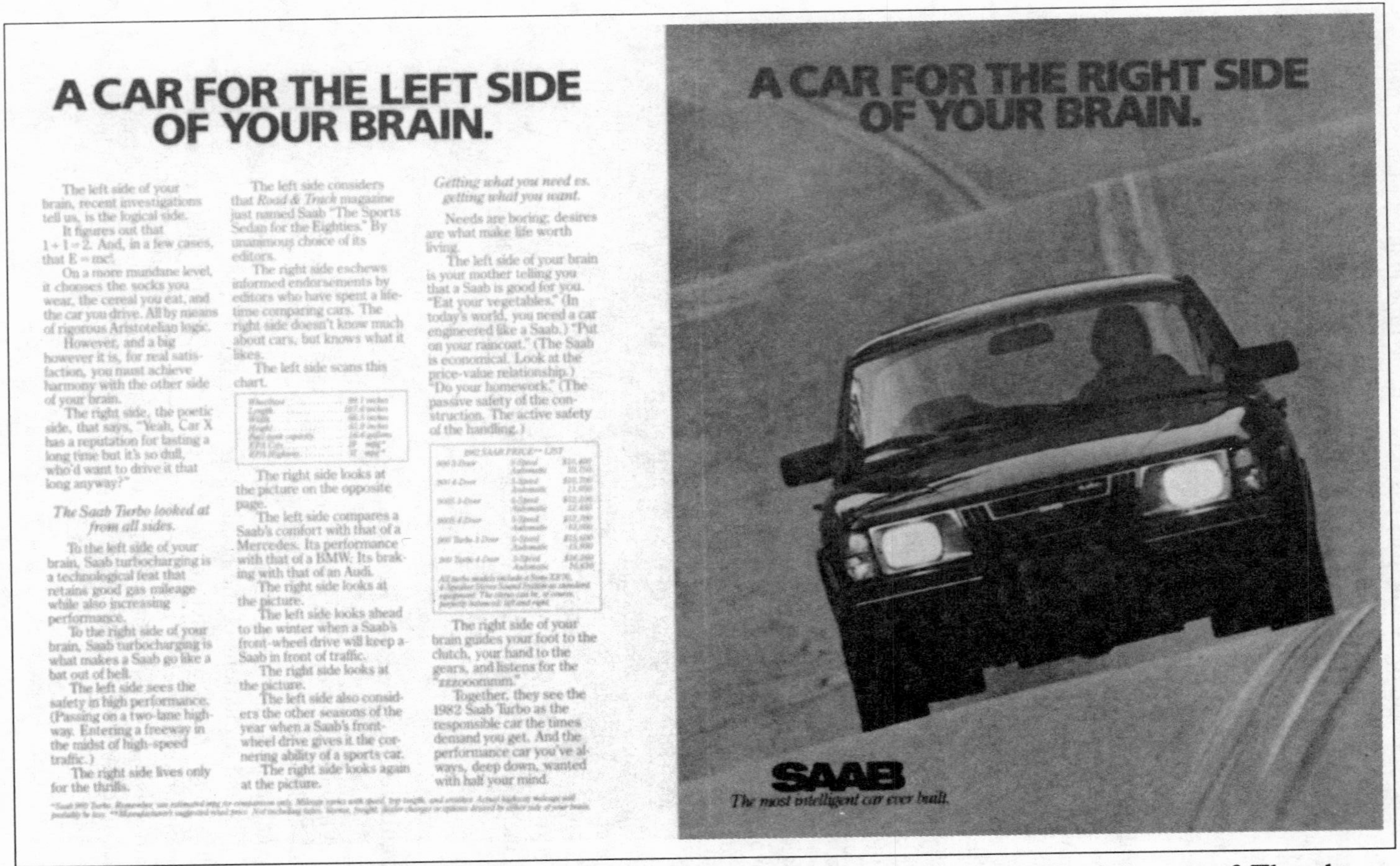

Figure 9–22. Advertisement Designed to Appeal to Verbal-Logical and Spatial-Emotional Aspects of Thought. (Reproduced with the permission of Saab-Scania of America, Inc.)

having desirable associations; the use of visual incongruity, in which something is presented that could not exist in reality; and the use of metaphorical symbolism, in which meanings are communicated visually through representations whose referent may be disguised and which may simultaneously have multiple meanings. Let us consider each of these three strategies in the light of the contrasting verbal and visual modes of thought discussed and in relation to certain theories and empirical findings.

Association of Ideas and Memory

Memory requires storage of information by the brain. A moment's reflection should indicate that we store both verbal information (for example, begin reciting to yourself the U.S. pledge of allegiance to the flag), and visual information (imagine a U.S. flag waving in the breeze; imagine the colors, the patterns, the location of the flagpole). There are, to be sure, individual differences in the effectiveness of one mode or the other, but, nevertheless, one's naive experience supports this idea of storage of different forms of information.

Comparisons of Memory for Verbal and Visual Information: The majority of research studies on memory have dealt with verbal memory and the formation of verbal associations. Although many models of verbal memory have been proposed, it has generally been established that the processing of verbal information involves a series of stages, the most prominent of which have been labeled short-term memory (STM) and long-term memory (LTM). I will highlight one generally accepted characteristic of short-term verbal memory that has many implications for advertising effectiveness: its limited capacity to hold information in an acoustic, verbal code unless that information is rehearsed or organized in some way. STM can hold a maximum of about seven pieces of information. (This number has become immortalized in Miller's article, "The Magical Number Seven, Plus-or-Minus Two: Some Limits on Our Capacity for Processing Information" published in 1956.) While capacity can be increased by "chunking" and organizing information, nevertheless the number of "chunks" that can be processed remains fixed. Even when verbal information has successfully been stored in LTM, we are limited in the amount of verbal information retrieved at any moment.

Does this limitation hold as well for visual information stored in memory? The saying that "a picture is worth a thousand words" may in fact contain some truth. The evidence is somewhat tentative but suggests the possibility that visual information can be held in STM and passed into LTM without the need for rehearsal that applies to verbal material. Referring to Haber (1970) and other studies, Klatzky (1980) notes that "the possibility of a specialized code for visual information in LTM is suggested in part by experiments indicating that people have a vast capacity for storing visual details" (p. 199).

Horton and Mills (1984), reviewing recent studies of learning and memory, have noted that "one of the recurrent findings in studies which compare memory for pictures and words is that pictures are remembered better than words" (p. 381). A number of studies support this view that pictures and words may be handled differently in memory (Deffenbacher, Carr, & Leu 1981; Childers and Houston 1984).

Horton and Mills (1984) also have noted that the theoretical explanation most frequently given for the superiority of pictures over words in memory has been Paivio's dual coding theory, which proposes that pictures are more likely to be stored in both verbal and image memory systems (that is, to receive dual coding) than are words and thus are remembered better. (See Paivio 1969 for a full exposition of this theory, and see Klatzky 1980 for a summary, pp. 202ff.) In addition to the assumption of two memory systems (in this case referred to as verbal and imaginal systems) the theory proposes that information that can be represented in both systems at the same time will be remembered better. Evidence to support this point comes from studies comparing memory of concrete and abstract words. Lists of concrete words that can be readily visualized (such as *elephant*) are remembered better than lists of abstract words that are difficult to visualize (such as *truth*). Together this point of view and related findings suggest that pictorial material in advertising may be remembered better than verbal material.

If visual, pictorial modes of communication result in greater memorability of information, do they automatically increase the persuasiveness of an advertisement? Not necessarily, according to Kisielius and Sternthal (1984), who examined circumstances under which vivid stimuli enhanced message persuasiveness. These authors found that in some instances, verbal statements produced greater persuasion when presented alone than when accompanied by a pictorial analog but that in other circumstances, the reverse effect was found. They proposed that persuasiveness was influenced more by the type of cognitive elaborations evoked rather than verbal or visual dimensions of information.

The effects of visual material on persuasiveness were also studied by Mitchell (1986), who sought to determine the effects of affect-laden photographs on attitudes toward an advertisement and brand attitudes. Results indicated that positively evaluated photographs created more favorable attitudes in both instances than did negatively evaluated photographs though the photographs had no direct relationship to advertising copy. In addition, Mitchell presented findings suggesting that verbal and visual information may have independent effects on brand attitudes.

The somewhat contradictory findings of these two studies suggest that much remains to be learned concerning the role of visual content in advertising memorability and the relationship between memorability and persuasiveness. And with regard to advertising art, the findings of these and other studies assessing the relative influence of verbal or visual stimuli suggest an additional topic that needs greater attention when designing research: the structural or aesthetic characteristics of visual stimuli that may inadvertently influence experimental results. It is of interest that Kisielius and Sternthal (1984) employed line drawings, whereas Mitchell (1986) employed photographs. In research comparing verbal and visual effects, it has generally been considered sufficient simply to construct a visual stimulus of one sort or another. Little is known of ways in which characteristics of visual stimuli may affect experimental findings. Indeed visual information is given so little emphasis in reporting research that one looks in vain for reproductions of visual stimuli in most journal articles and finds only unrelenting statistical tables and graphs and the occasional diagram or flowchart.

It seems clear, then, that in addition to the need for greater attention to the role of visual information in memorability and/or persuasiveness, another problem for research concerns the effects of various aesthetic and artistic characteristics of visual stimuli employed. It would certainly be of interest to compare effects of visual stimuli that range from minimal line drawings to artistic and aesthetically pleasing representations in color of the same objects, persons, or situations. Such visual materials might be created through cooperative arrangements with, for example, a university art department.

Another issue for research concerns the effects of presenting multiple visual stimuli in sequence. Often an advertisement will show several scenes that together tell a story. The implicit assumption is that such visual information will be processed in a logical sequence much as verbal information would be. Is this in fact the case? It may well be that a single, organized visual entity is more effective than a sequence of scenes, in part because of the differing ways in which the human mind processes verbal and visual information. This is an additional dimension that may have had some effect on studies. Kisielius and Sternthal (1984) employed multiple, sequentially presented visual stimuli, with one line drawing for each statement of copy, whereas Mitchell (1986) presented individual photographs to accompany verbal copy. These comments are not intended as criticisms of these studies but rather as illustrations of the need to clarify the effects of such stimulus dimensions as "multiple and sequential" versus "individual and organized" on experimental findings.

Let us examine this idea of organization of visual content by considering some relevant research findings concerning the effects of organization in imagery and how artistic forms may provide a means of enhancing organization and cohesiveness in the visual content of advertisements.

Organization of Visual Information: Among the components that contribute to the aesthetic characteristics of a visual work is its organization. One issue that needs to be considered is whether, and if so, how, the organization of visual material affects its memory retrieval and its persuasiveness. One potential direction for such research is suggested by studies of the effect of imagery in visual memory.

Imagery has been found in a number of studies to be an effective mnemonic mechanism in learning. In general, lists of concrete nouns that are mentally associated through images constructed by experimental subjects are remembered more effectively than the same objects memorized as lists of words with no instructions to form images. Of greater interest to the current discussion is the finding that, in learning multiple lists of such words, the construction of a single, ever-increasing complex image is superior to constructing successive, individual images. Furthermore, the more bizarre the image is, the more memorable it is (Bower 1970a, 1970b).

Let us return to the subject at hand—possible cognitive mechanisms in the effectiveness of advertising art. If we consider an advertisement as a means of providing a ready-made image to establish associations and meanings for a product, the discussion suggests that an advertisement that integrates a visual representation of the product and the to-be-associated objects or setting into an organized whole may be more effective than visual information presented successively as separate images or pictures within the body of the advertisement. Among the examples we have examined, the various art forms of still life, portrait, landscape, abstract composition, and collage provide opportunities for this sort of integrated presentation of a single image combining the product with objects, settings, or arrangements that evoke the desired associations. The use of such art forms may facilitate storing information that is relevant to the product and thus may influence the memorability of the advertisement. In addition, the persuasiveness of an advertisement may be influenced by the extent to which objects incorporated into its art already elicit favorable attitudes and associations.

Visual Incongruity, Mental Effort, and Persuasiveness

Synthetic art, which incorporates a product into a recognized work of art, associates the product with a work of art and provides an attentional mechanism through the resulting visual incongruity. Questions arise as to whether (and, if so, why) the use of incongruity produces such an impact and whether it may have positive or negative effects on advertising persuasiveness. Once again, the points to be made are tentative and require further research.

If we consider that well-known works of art (such as the Mona Lisa) are already represented in memory, then we might argue that the incorporation of a product into a previously existing whole is providing a single image that has been further elaborated by incorporation of the product. This new image may provide a unifying link between the product and something already well represented. One could argue that the effectiveness of this approach may depend in part on the extent to which the work of art into which the product is embedded can be viewed as appropriate. (In figure 9–13, it was more appropriate to incorporate French brie into a well-known painting by a French artist.) This brings up the question of the extent of the incongruity and the possible effects of different degrees of disparity in the elements joined.

Degree of Incongruity: In a study of the relationships between schema congruity and incongruity and the evaluation of objects, Meyers-Levy and Tybout (1988) found that moderate schema incongruity led to more favorable evaluation than either schema congruity or extreme schema incongruity. These findings are cited as supporting Mandler (1982), who has proposed that only moderate levels of incongruity are consistently associated with positive evaluation, with more extreme incongruity leading less predictably either to positive or to negative responses. Mandler has proposed that one effect of incongruity is to stimulate further mental activity; however, the greater is the effort required by the cognitive activity taken to resolve an incongruity, the more intense the resulting response will be. An extreme incongruity may lead to feelings of frustration and helplessness and thus to a negative response (Meyers-Levy and Tybout 1988, summarizing Mandler 1982).

Following from this line of reasoning, we might expect more favorable responses to incongruity in synthetic art when it is moderate rather than extreme. In general, this technique has most often been employed by altering works of art that are well known and recognizable to the generally well-educated and knowledgeable target audience for the ads, a circumstance that could be viewed as resulting in moderate incongruity. It remains to be determined whether the visual incongruity resulting from either the alteration of less familiar works, the drastic alteration of familiar works, or the construction of visual metaphors results in differential degrees of persuasiveness.

Incongruity and Novelty: An additional point to consider is that the visually incongruous stimulus represents a novel object or combination that has not been encountered before. Responsivity to novelty seems to be an essential human characteristic, a point of view first developed by Fiske and Maddi (1961). Among the collection of papers in that book is one by Platt (1961), who discussed the role of novelty in the human's response to works of art:

> It is easy to see why we may be pleased and satisfied by the representational elements in art. . . . They resemble our own moments of heightened experience. It is not so easy to see why a full-grown and intelligent adult is deeply satisfied by the formal elements in art. That is, by space and time patterns and the deviations from them, as in the development of the theme in a quartet or in the balancing of the painting by a touch of red in the opposite corner. . . . It . . . appears . . . that the requirements for aesthetic enjoyment

> are simply the requirements for perception itself, raised to a higher degree; and the essential thing in each case is to have *a pattern that contains the unexpected.* (p. 403)

Platt went on to discuss the need for deviations in patterns:

> Modern aesthetic theory says, nevertheless, that formal beauty is more than pattern: what is beautiful is pattern that contains uncertainty and surprise and yet resolves them into the regularity of a larger pattern. I believe that this view can easily be understood in the light of our physiological need for novelty as well as pattern. (p. 421)

Visual incongruity in advertising art may present a novel object or a pattern that elicits greater interest, and thus greater mental effort may be expended in processing it. Such incongruity also presents a logical paradox, and there may well be reward value in identifying the reasons for the paradox and in analyzing the art into its component parts in order to solve the puzzle. Thus a visual incongruity may be responded to more intensely and evoke greater cognitive effort in its perception because its spatial patterns and visual content engage the right hemisphere while its logical contradictions simultaneously challenge the left hemisphere. It should be kept in mind, however, that there may be instances in advertising in which visual incongruity may be a liability rather than an asset because greater mental effort is required to process it. A favorable evaluation of such novel patterns may depend on the degree of incongruity they contain for the audiences to which they are directed. One circumstance in which the degree of incongruity may be particularly relevant concerns the incongruity that frequently results from the construction of visual metaphors.

Metaphorical Symbolism

Metaphor is prominent in surrealistic art, which in turn often reflects the illogical qualities of dream imagery. With its capacity to express multiple meanings, metaphor is also one basis for the symbolic constructions through which the unconscious mind expresses itself. Discoveries concerning the contrasting organization of the brain's two hemispheres have provided additional insights, through the understanding of their possible physiological basis, into Freud's distinctions between primary process, the dominant mode of the unconscious mind, and secondary process, the dominant mode of the logical, waking mind. Now we must ask, How might these concepts contribute to an understanding of possible means through which metaphor may influence the effectiveness and persuasiveness of art in advertising?

Responses to Creative Works: One starting point is to consider our responses to creativity in general. What are the charateristics of creative works that trigger responses to them? Arieti (1976) has taken material from many sources, including wit and humor, poetry, and painting, in order to begin to understand the processes of creativity, why we respond as we do to its products, and the special role of metaphor. In his discussion, Arieti has built on a number of Freud's ideas, extending (and sometimes disagreeing with) them as well. In thought, the metaphor represents something that can simultaneously be interpreted at many levels of meaning, with some thread of similarity connecting all the levels. In his discussion, Arieti points out how level upon level of meaning can be found in the metaphor in a poem, for example, and this can result in constant interplay between primary and secondary process as new meanings are discovered.

Pointing out that "in dreams, thoughts are transformed into visual images" (p. 145), Arieti notes that this provides a kind of "concretization of the concept through imagery" (p. 150). The concrete objects and situations constructed and envisioned during dreams simultaneously embody multiple meanings, some of which may be immediately apparent to the logical mind remembering the dream, while others may be hidden or disguised because their meanings are repressed, buried in the primary process of the unconscious mind. Among the characteristics of dream imagery noted by Freud (and commented upon by Arieti), two deserve special attention: fusion and condensation.

Fusion as a Conceptual Medium: When fusion occurs, parts from disparate wholes are combined to form a new whole. For example a dream image might be of a nonexistent animal that combines parts of several animals. The constructions of Magritte illustrate this approach, such as the fused foot and shoe of *The Red Model* (figure 9–20) and the somewhat similar imagery in the marching boots and buildings of figure 9–21. Why does such fusion involve us? Arieti noted that it is "more the aesthetician's job than ours to determine why such compositions are at times unacceptable or bizarre concoctions and at other times great works of art" (p. 217) but points out nonetheless that "in the great work of art the fusion is accepted visually and conceptually; an element of pleasure is experienced, and whatever seems unnatural from a biological or physical point of view seems very natural in the realm of art" (p. 217). Such a harmonious fusion in modern art

> plunges very deeply into the primary process. But no matter how deeply it plunges, it rises again to attune with the secondary process. What at first seemed a private way of looking at the world receives collective consensus, the details merge into a unity, the parts form a whole, and the concrete becomes the incorporation of the abstract. (p. 223)

With regard to the fused images sometimes employed in advertising art, it may not be possible to extract a formula for generating successful ones. However, Arieti has given some clues: acceptability of the image, pleasure in recognition, an abstraction becomes "concretized," and an appropriateness in the selection of elements joined that is appreciated by the logical mind. All of these are present in the fused boot and building figures of figure 9–21, and the image, while certainly of an unreal object, is nonetheless aesthetically pleasing, involving, and memorable, thus possibly attracting greater cognitive effort in the mental processing of its information. One intriguing possibility for research would be to compare responses, including measures of such variables as immediate and delayed memory, inspection time, and emotional reactions, to created objects and images that do and do not have such qualities. This concept of harmonious fusion is one that may well find applications in such areas as the creation of product personalities and the design and marketing of children's toys, among others.

Condensation in Visual Metaphor: In dreams, condensation occurs when a single image communicates multiple meanings (the meanings are "condensed" into a single image). These may remain unconscious or may be discovered through analysis. The feelings they represent can influence behavior, whether or not they are conscious. Like the dream symbol, the visual metaphor can have a manifest or overt meaning and one or more latent or disguised meanings. Several examples of visual metaphors in advertising, each with such condensed, multiple meanings, have been noted earlier in this chapter, including the snake entwined around the neck of a woman, the devil shadow in figure 9–4, and the phoenix in figure 9–5.

There are a number of questions that need clarification regarding the use of such metaphors in advertising. If the right hemisphere already thinks in such images, can visual symbols provide a sort of direct connection to the thought processes of that hemisphere, including unconscious needs, wishes, or motives? If this is possible, under what circumstances is it desirable to do so? If such symbols are processed by the inaccessible unconscious mind, how does one measure their effects or persuasiveness? This would be difficult, I think, but not impossible if we look to the associative approaches devised by Freud and others to gain access to unconscious thoughts.

The most frequently employed visual symbols in advertising have, not unexpectedly, been related to sexual and aggressive themes, certainly major concerns in Freudian psychoanalytic theory. But there are many positive symbols of power, transformation, growth, and wholeness that are also possible. In particular, the voluminous writings of C.G. Jung, who originally followed Freud and then created his own point of view, represent a relatively unmined lode of rich symbolism.

Final Thoughts

Our explorations have led us to venture along a number of pathways—imagery, memory, creativity, aesthetics, contrasting styles of thought, and the unconscious mind—in examining some of the factors that may affect the impact of art in advertising. This chapter is a first step toward the development of a more comprehensive treatment of this subject. Many areas have not been addressed and must await more extended discussion. In the meantime, the most important suggestion that I can make to those who would wish to "operationalize" any of the points presented here is to study art and become familiar with its history, forms, styles, and aesthetic components, as well as individual responses to these factors. The reader who seriously wishes to explore art as a communicative medium will find much of value in Arnheim's *Art and Visual Perception* (1974).

An additional suggestion might be considered a corollary: when considering an advertisement that is to include the representation of the product and/or its use, consider whether there is an opportunity to go beyond a simple illustration or layout and instead present the product in an aesthetically involving and satisfying way. Perhaps a change in the arrangement of objects can transform something ordinary into a still life or some other form with lasting appeal and interest.

This idea of lasting appeal is important. I believe that if greater attention is paid to the aesthetic values in advertising art, advertising will not only become more effective but also provide a continuing and lasting source of aesthetic enjoyment, interest, and emotional value within society. One purpose of this chapter has been to focus attention on the many existing links and relationships between the art found in advertising and the art found in museums. These relationships could ultimately become the focus of a permanent museum devoted to advertising art—a fusion of sorts between the necessarily transient appearance of the advertising image in a magazine and the permanence of preservation, not only of printed works but of the originals on which they are based. This chapter will have achieved a measure of success, and perhaps have made a small step toward such a long-range goal, if it increases our awareness, enjoyment, and creation of advertising art that endures beyond the printed page.

References

Alesandrini, K.L. 1983. Strategies that influence memory for advertising communications. In R.J. Harris, ed., *Information Processing Research in Advertising*. Hillsdale, N.J.: Erlbaum.

Arieti, S. 1976. *Creativity: The Magic Synthesis.* New York: Basic Books.

Arnheim, R. 1974. *Art and Visual Perception.* Rev. ed. Berkeley: University of California Press.

Berenson, B. 1968. *Italian Painters of the Renaissance,* vol. 2. London: Phaidon Press. Originally published, 1952.

Bettman, J.R. 1986. Consumer psychology. *Annual Review of Psychology* 37:257–289.

Bower, G.H. 1970a. Imagery as a relational organizer in associative learning. *Journal of Verbal Learning and Verbal Behavior* 9:529–533.

———. 1970b. Organizational factors in memory. *Cognitive Psychology* 1:18–46.

Caudle, F.M. 1988. Associative strategies in magazine advertising: An illustrated taxonomy. In L.F. Alwitt, ed., *1987 Proceedings of the Division of Consumer Psychology, Annual Convention of the American Psychological Association.* Washington, D.C.: Division of Consumer Psychology, American Psychological Association.

Childers, T.L., and Houston, M.J. 1984. Conditions for a picture-superiority effect on consumer memory. *Journal of Consumer Research* 11:643–654.

Corn, W.M. 1983. *Grant Wood: The Regionalist Vision.* New Haven: Yale University Press for the Minneapolis Institute of Arts.

Deffenbacher, K.A.; Carr, T.H.; and Leu, J.R. 1981. Memory for words, pictures, and faces: Retroactive interference, forgetting, and reminiscence. *Journal of Experimental Psychology: Human Learning and Memory* 7:299–305.

Fiske, D.W., and Maddi, S.R. 1961. *Functions of Varied Experience.* Homewood, Ill.: Dorsey Press.

Galin, D. 1974. Implications for psychiatry of left and right cerebral specialization: A neurophysiological context for unconscious processes. *Archives of General Psychiatry* 31:572–583.

Haber, R.N. 1970. How we remember what we see. *Scientific American* 222, no. 5: 104–112.

Hansen, F. 1981. Hemispherical lateralization: A review and a discussion of its implications for consumer behavior research. *Journal of Consumer Research* 8:23–36.

Horowitz, M.J. 1970. *Image Formation and Cognition.* New York: Appleton-Century-Crofts.

Horton, D.L., and Mills, C.B. 1984. Human learning and memory. *Annual Review of Psychology* 35:361–394.

Kisielius, J., and Sternthal, B. 1984. Detecting and explaining vividness effects in attitudinal judgments. *Journal of Marketing Research* 21 (February): 54–64.

Klatzky, R.L. 1980. *Human Memory: Structures and Processes.* 2d ed. San Francisco: W.H. Freeman.

Kris, E. 1952. *Psychoanalytic Explorations in Art.* New York: International Universities Press.

Larkin, D. ed. 1972. *Magritte.* New York: Ballantine Books.

Levy, J. 1985. Right brain, left brain: Facts and fiction. *Psychology Today* 19, no. 5: 38–44.

Mandler, G. 1982. The structure of value: Accounting for taste. In M.S. Clark and S.T. Fiske, eds., *Affect and Cognition: The Seventeenth Annual Symposium.* Hillsdale, N.J.: Erlbaum.

Martineau, P. 1971. *Motivation in Advertising: Motives That Make People Buy.* New York: McGraw-Hill.

Meyers-Levy, J., and Tybout, A.M. 1988. Schema congruity as a basis for natural object evaluation. Pre-publication draft.

Miller, G.A. 1956. The magical number seven, plus-or-minus two: Some limits on our capacity for processing information. *Psychological Review* 63, no. 2:81–97.

Mitchell, A. 1986. The effect of verbal and visual components of advertisements on brand attitudes and attitude toward the advertisement. *Journal of Consumer Research* 13 (June): 12–24.

Motherwell, R., ed. 1951. *The Dada Painters and Poets: An Anthology.* New York: George Wittenborn.

Paivio, A. 1969. Mental imagery in associative learning and memory. *Psychological Review* 76:241–263.

Platt, J.R. 1961. Beauty: Pattern and change. In D.W. Fiske and S.R. Maddi, eds., *Functions of Varied Experience.* Homewood, Ill.: Dorsey Press.

Réalités, eds. 1973. *Impressionism.* Secaucus, N.J. Chartwell Books.

Rossiter, J.R., and Percy, L. 1983. Visual communication in advertising. In R.J. Harris, ed., *Information Processing Research in Advertising.* Hillsdale, New Jersey: Erlbaum.

Springer, S.P., and Deutsch, G. 1985. *Left Brain, Right Brain.* Rev. ed. New York: W.H. Freeman.

Wilson, S. 1975. *Surrealist Painting.* London: Phaidon Press.

Wolfram, E. 1972. Introduction to D. Larkin, ed., *Magritte.* New York: Ballantine Books.

10

Gender Differences in Information Processing: A Selectivity Interpretation

Joan Meyers-Levy

The investigation of differences in males' and females' processing of information and rendering of judgments has enjoyed a long tradition. From this a diverse and sizable number of gender effects have emerged. For example, females are often found to be more persuadible (Eagly 1978) but less self-confident (Lenney 1977) than are males. Gender differences also proliferate in communication style (Haas 1979), as well as in the performance of certain cognitive functions. For example, males typically excel in the performance of visual spatial tasks, while females are superior in many linguistic tasks (Maccoby and Jacklin 1974).

Recently, however, a number of researchers have come to regard these and other findings with considerable skepticism (Caplan 1979; Caplan, MacPherson, and Tobin 1985; Deaux 1984; Eagly and Carli 1981; Fairweather 1976). These investigators contend that many gender differences observed in the literature are susceptible to rival interpretations due to the presence of methodological or contextual artifacts. These include sex-typed stimulus materials, small sample sizes, subject selection biases, historical artifacts, and biases associated with researcher gender. Other gender findings are argued to be illusory because they occur only under a limited number of special circumstances. Such observations have led critics to express doubt concerning the fruitfulness of further gender inquiry (Caplan, McPherson, and Tobin 1985; Deaux 1984; Fairweather 1976). As Deaux (1984) contends, "Approaching sex as a subject variable, although a popular pursuit with a long history, may not be the most productive route for understanding gender" (p. 108).

Much of this disenchantment with the study of gender seems to stem from the methodology that abounds in the literature. Most studies have sought reliable main effects of gender that presuppose immutable constancy in males' and females' responses across all situations. Yet the ecological adaptivity of such transfixion would appear to be highly questionable. Hence it is not surprising that the literature reveals both between-studies main effects and null effects concerning gender. Moreover, attempts to interpret such results uniquely are confounded because both the presence and absence of gender effects are susceptible to multiple explanations. Any number of factors associated with either task or situational demands or genuine and substantive gender characteristics can be responsible for these effects.

Given this state of affairs, one manner of pursuit is suggested by Caplan (1979): "What can one do with a body of literature in which contradictory claims are made? One can investigate the possibility that some boundary conditions can explain those apparent contradictions" (p. 78). Boundary conditions detail the precise circumstances that surround effects. Careful examination may uncover commonalities among such conditions that can lead to the development of an encompassing theory of gender. Ideally such a theory would explain a variety of the main effects frequently observed in the literature and also predict the situational variables that will qualify when a particular gender effect will be observed, reversed, or eliminated. To the extent that a single theory is identified that explains a wide variety of gender effects, including interactions, it must be favored over the variety of artifactual explanations that would be required to explain the same body of data.

The objective of this chapter is to propose such a conceptualization of gender differences in information processing. A theory referred to as the selectivity hypothesis is suggested as a unifying framework from which a broad array of observed gender differences can be interpreted. Although this hypothesis may not explain all findings currently in the literature, it appears to provide a more robust and parsimonious explanation than does any other single explanation, artifactual or substantive, that currently is available. The selectivity hypothesis is offered as a starting point from which a more detailed understanding of the mechanisms underlying gender effects can be pursued.

The Selectivity Hypothesis

The selectivity hypothesis is based on the notion that males and females differ in the strategies they use to process information. According to this view, males frequently do not engage in comprehensive processing of all available information as a basis for judgment. Instead they employ various heuristic devices that serve as surrogates for more detailed processing. These heuristic devices are typically ones that involve the use of single cues or cues that convergently imply a single inference. Furthermore males' selective, heuristic mode of processing is often driven by a reliance on cues that are highly available and particularly salient in the focal context. The use of such heuristics has been documented elsewhere in the social cognition literature (Tverskey and Kahneman 1973, 1974). For example, Taylor and Fiske (1978) contend that "instead of reviewing all the evidence that bears upon a particular problem, people frequently use the information which is most salient or available to them, that is, that which is most easily brought to mind" (p. 251).

The selectivity hypothesis suggests that females employ a different approach in processing information. They can be characterized as comprehensive information processors who attempt to assimilate all available cues. Although human processing capacity limitations may at times constrain females from accomplishing such an objective, females generally attempt to engage in a rather effortful, comprehensive, piecemeal analysis of all available information.

According to the selectivity hypothesis, males' characteristic mode of processing is distinguished by greater use of efficiency-striving heuristics, while that of females is marked by more pronounced attempts toward maximizing the comprehensiveness of processing. Because the precise heuristic device males use will be influenced by the nature of the task, selectivity may manifest itself in a variety of responses. However, what is common to these responses and renders them predictable is their reflection of and reliance on subsets of highly available cues. Thus cues typically employed by males are those that are readily available, perhaps by virtue of the high level of contextual salience afforded them or the richly endowed associative network by which they are represented in memory.

Research has demonstrated that information pertaining to the self is represented in memory by a particularly well-developed and elaborate network of associations (Markus 1977; Rogers, Kuiper, and Kirker 1977). Accordingly the selectivity hypothesis holds that males frequently streamline the processing of external world information by focusing on self-related information, which acts as a heuristic device on which to base judgments or behaviors. By contrast, females comprehensively process such information, devoting relatively equal processing to information relevant to the self and to the external world of others.

The notions that underlie the selectivity hypothesis can be traced to explanations for gender effects reported in the literature. For example, congenial with the self versus self and other manifestation of selectivity described previously is a conceptualization of gender differences proposed by Gutman (1970). On the basis of males' and females' responses to a Thematic Apperception Test, Gutmann proposed that males' ego style is allocentric, "distinguished by sharp boundaries between the self and the external world of objects and persons," while females' style is autocentric, implying "ego diffusion or lack of boundaries between self and object" (Kogan 1976). This view concurs that females are more oriented toward relating to the concerns of both self and other, whereas males assume a more self-focused orientation.

Another widely recognized view of gender differences expounded upon by both Bakan (1966) and Carlson (1971, 1972) hypothesizes that the genders differ in psychological orientation along the dimensions of agency and communion. *Agency* refers to the instrumental, self-assertive, self-purposive concerns that characterize males' orientation. By contrast, females' *communal outlook* is characterized by an emphasis on interpersonal relationships, affiliation, and attachment of self and other (Carlson 1971, 1972). This view, too, is readily recast in terms of the more generalized notion of selectivity. The fact that males, who assume an agentic orientation, focus on highly available, self-oriented cues implies that this readily accessed information is used as a heuristic device to streamline processing. By contrast, the relatively communal, self- and other-oriented female appears to focus attention more broadly as she comprehensively considers available cues that pertain both to self and to other.

The selectivity hypothesis is also consistent with the traditional view that gender differences stem from the cultural prescription that males assume the dominant, more forceful social role, while females assume a more submissive, compliant role (Engels 1891; Janeway 1980). It can be reasoned that by virtue of holding the dominant role, males would be free to concentrate their attention on attaining personal goals and desires, with less focus on others' desires. Alternatively, it would be incumbent upon females who hold a submissive role to be observant and accommodative of others' needs, as well as those of self. As Janeway (1980) notes, females learn to survive by understanding and responding to others' states of mind.

Still another explanation of gender differences ascribes a more analytical, logical nature to males and a more subjective, intuitive nature to females (Broverman et al. 1968). For example, drawing on gender principles postulated by Jung (1963) and Wickes (1963), Silverman (1970) proposed a perspective of gender differences in attentional style that is ascribed to be compatible with this view of the genders. Specifically, the more analytic and logical male "cuts away all that does not belong to the defined and often isolated concept" (Wickes 1963, p. 165); hence males are deemed to show more "midrange sensory thresholds, responsiveness to discrete segments of configurations rather than to configurations as wholes, hypoawareness of subtle differences between elements in a configuration, . . . inhibition of responsiveness to irrelevant stimlus attributes in problem-solving" (Silverman 1970, p. 75). Females are purported to show the inverse pattern of these responses.

This view too is in accordance with the selectivity hypothesis. Males may seem to be more logical because they selectively concentrate on the more focal and tangible available cues, while females may appear to be rather subjective because they comprehensively consider seemingly tangential and often subtle cues in concert with those that are more focal and apparent.

This analysis suggests that the selectivity hypothesis is not an entirely novel perspective. Rather the hypothesis is motivated by and can accommodate various views offered in the literature by conceptualizing gender differences at a more abstract level than views that have preceded it. If the selectivity hypothesis can be distinguished from alternative perspectives, it is by virtue of offering a more parsimonious ordering of the gender effects reported in the literature.

The adequacy of the selectivity hypothesis in accounting for a variety of gender effects represented in the literature will be assessed. Considered first is evidence pertaining to the ontogeny and manifestations of gender differences. The plausible developmental path of males' and females' different processing proclivities is traced, and the manifestations of such differences among children and adults are described. The subsequent section considers more rigorous tests of the selectivity hypothesis. These studies examine the preconditions, prescribed by theory, under which gender differences are and are not anticipated. The final section discusses several applications of the selectivity hypothesis.

The Ontogeny and Manifestations of Gender Differences

A sizable stream of theory suggests that gender differences in selectivity may develop due to the alternative levels of structure that are present in the environments of boys and girls. The contention is that males' selectivity may evolve as a consequence of the relatively unstructured environment with which they are left to grapple. Females, encouraged to participate in more highly structured environments, are induced to adopt a sense of interrelated communality with others and thereby are encouraged to process information comprehensively so they can learn and adopt others' structures. Evidence presented in this section traces how high- and low-structure environments produce alternative response patterns that imply differences in the selectivity of processing. This view is bolstered by research that depicts the ways in which social agents both assign the genders to environments that differ in structure and behave in ways that more directly instill selectivity in boys and comprehensiveness in girls. This is followed by an examination of how differences in selectivity are manifested in both children and adults.

Gender Differences in Activity Structure

The theorizing of Carpenter and her colleagues leads to the inference that differences in the inherent structure of activities to which boys and girls are assigned may result in gender differences in selectivity. This theorizing holds that social agents assign children to sex-appropriate activities and that feminine activities contain more structure than do masculine activities. These different levels of activity structure in turn are found to inculcate response patterns that appear to imply differences in the selectivity of processing.

Studies reported in work by Carpenter (1983) serve as the basis for this theorizing. Observations of preschool classrooms that naturally varied in activity structure revealed that girls spent more time in high- rather than low-structure activities. These high-structure activities were characterized by more individual instruction, group feedback, and provision of information due to greater adults accessibility and behavior modeling. Moreover, data indicate that when participating in high-structure activities, children demonstrated greater adult compliance, bids for recognition, and task persistence, which together exemplify structure-conforming behaviors. Boys, however, spent more time in low- rather than high-structure activities, and children in low-structure activities revealed more structure-creating behaviors by exhibiting more task initiations, leadership attempts, aggression, and peer commands. Further, with few exceptions, both boys and girls who selected to play in high- or low-structure activities demonstrated behaviors consistent with that structure, implicating structure rather than gender as the causal agent underlying these effects. Work by Carpenter, Huston, and Holt (1982, cited by Carpenter 1983) corroborates this view.

Analysis of the behaviors that accompany high- and low-activity structures suggests a relationship between the level of activity structure and differences in selectivity. The variety of behaviors that occur in the high-structure settings with which greater female participation is associated can be viewed both as manifestations of communion (that is, greater compliance or conformity) and multiple cue comprehensiveness in processing (that is, structure seeking through requests for help and recognition from adults). Because high-structure settings make available and salient an adult who helps define activity structure by offering direction and task or performance specification, females apparently come to enlist the authority figure in providing further task specification, performance assistance, and performance confirmation. Such information is rich in specifics and is both conducive to and necessary for comprehensive processing of externally defined structures. Thus it appears that the adult authority figure sufficiently reduces and orders available cues that imply response possibilities such that comprehensive processing occurs. In this manner, highly structured environments may encourage participants (typically females) to process available information carefully and comprehensively in an attempt to reproduce adult-modeled behavior or identify rules or criteria that appear appropriate to the situation.

An analysis of the behaviors manifested in low-structure settings also points to a relationship between low activity structure and selectivity. Behaviors more frequently manifested in the low-structure environments, which are inhabited primarily by males, imply greater agency and singular self-assertion (initiation, leadership attempts, peer commands, aggression), which are consistent with a selective orientation. In such contexts, the alternative forms that activity could take are plentiful, but an authority figure who might aid in imposing structure by offering specification for particular activities is minimally suppportive or entirely absent. Seizing on single, highly salient cues may provide low-structure inhabitants a means of coping with the chaos of their environment. Consistent with this reasoning, Mischel (1981) has suggested that "cognitive economies" are demanded when "people . . . are flooded by [unstructured] information that somehow must be reduced and simplified to allow efficient processing and to avoid otherwise overwhelming overload" (p. 14). Thus one might speculate that the script-devoid ambiguity of a low-structure environment necessitates adherence to focused processing of selected cues as a means of simplifying the environment and developing structure. In such a context, comprehensive processing of all cues would likely be overwhelming and dysfunctional because efforts to create structure might be stymied by cues associated with too many alternative structures.

Hence evidence suggests that alternative socialization practices employed with boys and girls may give rise to differences in selectivity in processing, perhaps originating in terms of specific agentic versus communal manifestations. Specifically the unstructured setting confronted by boys may lead them to determine responses on the basis of highly available cues such as those pertaining to self or agentic concerns. Reliance on such single-entity, self-related cues, which represent but one manifestation of selective processing, over time may become highly routinized among males and broaden to a more general reliance on selective heuristic-based processing. Accordingly this mode of processing may come to be employed in numerous domains of activity. Similarly it is speculated that females, immersed in highly structured settings, come to develop more communal concerns regarding self and other. This dual-cue, self and other orientation may expand to encompass a more generalized modus operandi that reflects the relatively comprehensive consideration of multiple entities or cues.

Role of Social Agents in Establishing Structure and Influencing Selectivity in Processing

The genders' considerable experience in high- or low-structured settings may lead to gender differences in selectivity. Still unanswered, however, is the question of why boys and girls acquire more experience in these alternatively structured settings. There is evidence that the greater participation of boys in low-structure settings and girls in high-structure settings may occur because social agents encourage such patterns of behavior and administer different levels of structure to the genders. For example, girls are subject to closer supervision than are boys, play in greater proximity to adults (Carpenter 1983), and, unlike boys, come to engage simultaneously in play and proximal contact with parents (Lewis and Weinraub 1974). Further, mothers are found to be more protective of daughters than of sons (Stewart 1976), thus providing girls greater structure. Finally, girls are more obedient of adults than are boys (Maccoby and Jacklin 1974).

Social agents also influence selectivity by adminstering structure in other ways. Not only are girls more frequently assigned chores that keep them within the highly structured environment of home, but they also receive greater feedback in terms of praise and criticism (Fagot 1978). This feedback would seem both to impose considerable structure and instill greater attentiveness to a variety of specific cues. By contrast, boys are given tasks that take them out of the highly structured home setting (Fagot 1978; Newson and Newson 1976) and are abetted in self-assertion and self-extension strivings (Block 1973), which encourages the creation of one's own structure. Conversely girls receive pressure to conform with others' standards and externally defined structures. Concurrent with these assertions, Fagot (1978) found that girls were encouraged to seek help and to help others perform tasks, presumably instilling in girls a multifocused communal orientation. Boys were discouraged from engaging in these behaviors, thereby encouraging independence and a more single-focused self-oriented mode of behavior.

Parents' nonverbal behavior, too, may convey qualitatively different messages to boys and girls. Frankel and Rollins (1983) found that when performing tasks with their children, parents of both genders behaved cooperatively with their daughters but assumed a more isolationist stance with sons such that parent and child simultaneously worked alone on different parts of the task, with the parent assuming a more directive role. Parents' greater cooperation with girls not only connotes the imposition of more structure, but it also may foster the adoption of a communal orientation that underlies a more comprehensive concern for multiple entities (self and other). The isolationist stance parents assumed with their sons represents the imposition of less structure and may foster males' more single-minded self-concern, which is indicative of their selective orientation.

Frankel and Rollins (1983) found that parents altered their instruction style (global strategic versus specific) and the type of feedback provided depending on whether they interacted with sons or daughters. Parents of both genders seemed to instill selectivity in boys and comprehensiveness in girls through their mode of instruction. They engaged in a larger proportion of specific instructional acts than general strategy behaviors when instructing daughters and used more general problem-solving strategy behaviors than specific acts when teaching their sons. Specific instructions entailed providing concrete suggestions concerning specific stimulus elements ("Put the dog next to the cat"), while global strategy behaviors often encouraged simple categorization of stimulus materials ("Put things together that go together"). Similarly daughters received a larger proportion of specific performance feedback than did sons ("No, that was a dog"), whereas sons were the target of more global approval or disapproval responses ("You did well").

These data indicate that parents' instruction as well as their feedback behaviors were more highly structured and concrete with daughters than with sons. This high level of specificity in instruction and feedback employed with daughters would appear to be conducive to more comprehensive, detailed, item-by-item processing. Parents' more global forms of interaction with sons may contribute to males' use of selective, categorical, and simplified processing strategies by which many diverse aspects of stimuli come to be represented by rather global unitary characteristics.

Manifestations of Gender Differences among Children

If the socialization of boys and girls gives rise to gender differences in the selectivity of information processing, these differences in selectivity should be manifested in children's behavior. Examination in this section focuses on how selectivity is manifested in children's interpretation of information, style of toy or object play, and interaction with others.[1]

Gender Differences in the Interpretation of Information: Theorizing by McGuinness (1976) offers a depiction of how the genders differ in interpreting the external world. Congenial with the selectivity hypothesis, McGuinness (p. 146) contends that males' interpretational mode is largely categorical; they "adapt to the situation by constructing rules, attitudes, laws, etc." Females, she argues, "form judgments of intent" by considering "internal aspects of personal and social situations, [and] asking 'why' questions . . . to determine the specificities and intricacies of the situation." Other researchers' portrayals of the genders converge with this view (Penelope and Wolfe 1983; Smith 1980).

Gilligan's (1982) qualitative analysis of boys' and girls' thoughts in interpreting moral dilemmas supports this characterization of the genders. Drawing on two eleven-year-olds' responses as exemplars, Gilligan observed that the boy "considers the moral dilemma to be sort of like a math problem with humans" (p. 26) and proceeds in a very highly focused, linear, impersonal manner to construct and defend an unequivocal solution. He views the dilemma in a simplified categorical form, regarding it as a conflict of claims and calling upon the principles of law to resolve the conflict. By contrast, the girl reasons comprehensively through possible turns of events and considers in greater detail the interrelated conflicts faced by each actor in the dilemma: "The proclivity of [females] to reconstruct hypothetical dilemmas, . . . to request or supply missing information about the nature of the people and the places where they live, shifts their judgment away from the hierarchical ordering of principles and the formal procedures of decision making" (Gilligan 1982, p. 101). Thus the boy selectively assumes a "highly rational," relatively single-focused logic in addressing the issue, while the girl engages in more comprehensive reasoning that encompasses broader, highly inferential considerations, a woven pattern of contingencies and outcomes.

Gender Differences in Toy and Object Play: Females' greater comprehensiveness relative to that of males is also demonstrated in their tendency toward more broad-range, elaborative thought in play behavior. Relative to boys, girls manifest more ideational play. As toddlers and older, girls pretend more, engage in more acts of fantasy play, and more readily initiate fantasy play without the use of concrete props (Johnson and Roopnarine 1983; McLoyd 1980). In an analysis of childrens' specific communication strategies in play, Haslett (1983) found that while girls made greater use of associative renaming strategies that served to label objects as representing imagined objects (for example, a wooden block serves as a witch's pot), boys were considerably more selective in nature and employed more strategies aimed at protecting, furthering, and maintaining their own interests. Males' rather egocentric strategies were exemplified by comments such as, "I got here first" and "Give me that car; it's mine." Such data suggest that while males pursue a rather selective purview of processing by focusing on self or other stimuli that are apparent and highly available, more comprehensive females are prone to greater inferential, elaborative processing that is likely stimulated by vagaries or tangential aspects of the stimuli and/or context.

Parallel and similarly interpretable gender differences are evident in the way toys are used. Girls consistently have been found to engage in more constructive play that entails the creative use of objects in a sequential organized manner. Boys favor functional play that involves the simplistic and repetitive use of toys in a way that often dramatically satisfies the child's personal desires (Johnson, Ershler, and Bell 1980; Rubin, Watson, and Jambor 1978). Hence because girls' processing of the toy is likely to entail more detailed, elaborative, and comprehensive consideration of toy features and associated dimensions, girls may devise toy uses that extend beyond those that are most obvious. Girls are found to devote more attention to the details of toys in play (Liss 1981) and the details of figures in their artwork (Reeves and Boyette 1983). By contrast, boys' play behavior reflects a relatively narrow consideration of objects that centers on their apparent and readily grasped use.

Gender Differences in Interaction with Others: Examination of the manner in which children interact with others not only provides evidence of gender differences in selectivity but also suggests that these differences become more pronounced with age. This is consistent with earlier arguments. Observations of preschool children by Serbin and coworkers (1982) revealed that boys made more influence attempts than did girls. This outcome occurred largely because boys appeared to make more bold, clearly stated, direct requests than indirect requests, and they tended to make more such direct requests than did girls. Furthermore, boys' use of direct requests and girls' use of indirect requests tended to increase with age. Boys also became less responsive to influence attempts with age, while girls' responsiveness remained constant over age.

The observation that females' requests tended to become increasingly indirect with age may reflect their increasing sensitivity to others' feelings and social setting conventions as greater comprehensiveness and a multiple-cue orientation evolves. By contrast, males' requests became more direct and bold, suggesting a growing selective, single-focused concern with self rather than others. The observation that older boys were more resistant to influence is also consistent with the notion that males' selectivity and self-concerns increase with age as they acquire greater experience in assuming this orientation.

Manifestations of Gender Differences among Adults

The premise that differences in early socialization set the course of development for gender differences in selectivity implies that such gender differences may be especially widespread among adults. This section reviews studies that offer evidence for gender differences in selectivity in numerous facets of adults' behaviors, including the performance of spatial and linguistic skills, conversational style, influenceability, and the determination of self-evaluations. In addition, differences in the structure of the genders' knowledge representations are examined.

Gender Differences in Spatial Skills: A substantial body of evidence suggests that males outperform females in many visual spatial tasks (Maccoby and Jacklin 1974; Guilford 1967; but see Caplan, MacPherson, and Tobin 1985 for a dissenting view). Further, males' relative superiority in visual spatial (VS) functioning is often held to be responsible for their advantage in mathematics (Sherman 1967). Data pertinent to this assertion are supportive but not conclusive (Meece et al. 1982). Spatial skills correlate quite highly and positively with both geometry and quantitative thinking (Bock and Kolakowski 1973), and it has been found that gender differences in math achievement are eliminated when adjustments are made for VS experience (Fennema and Sherman 1977). Moreover, just as males' superiority in VS skills most frequently emerges in adolescence, their advantage in mathematics also does not occur consistently until that time (Meece et al. 1982). This finding not only is consistent with the notion that gender differences in VS skills may underlie those in mathematics, but it also implies that males' superiority in such skills may be evident only after males accumulate considerable practice in honing their VS skills.

Males' superiority in VS tasks may arise due to their greater opportunity to develop spatial skills in childhood. Concordant with Sherman's (1967) suggestion that greater exploratory behavior fosters spatial skills, studies find that boys range farther from home than do girls (Huston 1983) and that children who do so show superiority in spatial skills over those who do not (Munroe and Munroe 1971). Sherman (1967) also has posited that masculine sex-typed toys and activities, such as model construction and aiming games, may facilitate the development of VS skills. Along these lines, preschoolers' participation in masculine but not feminine play has been found to predict performance in spatial tasks (Connor and Serbin 1977; Serbin and Connor 1979), and sex differences in VS skills were observed only in children who preferred appropriate (traditional) sex roles (Nash 1975).

These data suggest that males' superior VS skills are the result of greater experience in activities that foster the development of such skills, implying that with equivalent VS training, the genders' VS task performance should be uniform. Corroboratory evidence supports this inference (Connor, Serbin, and Schackman 1977; Stericker and LeVesconte 1982). Moreover, females frequently show greater improvement after training than do males (Connor, Schackman, and Serbin 1978), suggesting that, at least in part, VS skill deficits may be due to females' inadequate experience with VS tasks.

While greater VS experience may provide males with an advantage in VS tests, it would seem that their tendency toward selective processing may do so as well. Consider the Embedded Figures Test and variants of it that are often employed to assess VS skills. In this test, subjects are shown a simple figure and then asked to locate this target figure when it is embedded within a more complex design (Witkin et al. 1971). Thus a particular figure is made salient to subjects prior to the introduction of the disembedding task. Identification of the target figure requires one to suppress attention to intricate individual elemental shapes that comprise the complex design and instead focus on the single pattern of the target figure, which is composed of a subset of the intricate shapes. This task that requires one to orient toward a singular gestalt pattern would seem to be benefited by males' characteristic mode of selective processing because a selective processor tends to search for and focus on a conceptually single unit of information such as the target figure. Not surprisingly, males typically excel on this task. By contrast, females who behave as comprehensive processors tend to focus on a wider variety of cues. As such, they may be disadvantaged in this task because their processing of intricate nontarget cues and figures interferes with the allocation of resources better devoted to single, target cue processing.

Selective processing also may be advantageous in performing VS tasks that entail mentally rotating or folding a geometric figure such that it matches one or more presented criterion figures. An advantage may accrue to males who, as selective processors, regard the figure as a single holistic configuration during its manipulation to an established criterion. As Bock and Kolakowski (1973) note, VS tasks require one to hold a single image in mind continuously throughout the task. A female comprehensive processor would likely perceive the stimulus as a complex figure and simultaneously attend to all facets or constituent segments of the figure—for example, all individual corners, all angles, and so forth. Their attempts to manipulate these facets to criterion concurrently may increase the task difficulty and exceed resource capabilities, leading to relatively poor task performance.

Hence females' comprehensiveness may be a liability in performing many VS tasks, while males' selective mode of processing may be an asset. This, coupled with males' greater experience in VS tasks, provides a plausible explanation for males' observed superiority in VS tasks. The possibility cannot be dismissed, however, that males' greater experience in VS tasks may contribute to their selectivity, which in turn may result in their superior VS skills.

Gender Differences in Linguistic Skills: Just as a reliance on selectivity may work to males' advantage in VS tasks, females' greater comprehensiveness may provide them an edge in performing a variety of linguistic tasks. These tasks would seem to benefit from the heightened attention to multiple, often detailed cues and the precision with nuances that accompanies comprehensiveness. A spate of studies supports the view that at almost all ages, females exhibit greater facility than do males in numerous linguistic tasks (but see Fairweather 1976 for a dissenting view). Females' display precocity and greater complexity in verbal communication (Haslett 1983), and exhibit superior verbal fluency (Maccoby and Jacklin 1974), better speech articulation, clarity, and quality (Hull et al. 1971), fewer grammatical errors (Smith 1935), more complex and longer sentences (Bennett, Seashore, and Wesman 1956), superior reading skills (McGuinness 1976), and substantially less incidence of reading or language dysfunction (Restak 1979).

Exemplified by each of these linguistic behaviors is attentiveness to and dexterity in manipulating and using multiple detail cues, skills that characterize females' comprehensiveness. For example, comprehensiveness may benefit reading because it requires simultaneously attending to and relating individual letters, spelling, syntax, and semantics (Merritt 1978). Reading skills also should benefit from the consolidation of focal cues with contextual cues and assimilation of intermodal (visual and auditory) cues (Buffery and Gray 1972) that may accompany comprehensiveness. Finally, females' tendency to engage in broadly spanning associative processing also may facilitate reading by relating the literal with the figurative and readily transforming written words into imagery. Indeed in every sense, modality females have been found to engage in more vivid mental imagery than do males (Anastasi and Foley 1949).

Gender Differences in Adults' Interpretation of Information: Haas (1979) contends that females' language reflects an interpretive mode that is subjective and evaluative, while males' language reflects a selective concentration on readily available, objective states (Haas 1979). For example, females are found to use more adjectives than do males (Entwisle and Garvey 1972; Hartman 1976), engage in more creative, associative, imagery-laced interpretation (Wood 1966), and provide greater interpretation of stimuli in terms of feeling and motivation (Gleser, Gottschalk, and Watkins 1959). This interpretive, inferential mode of processing is consistent with a comprehensive processor's tendency to consider a broad scope of information—not only highly available objective attributes but also nonobservable conditions or subjective, perhaps affective considerations that may more thoroughly explain that which is readily discernible. Such findings are reminiscent of those already reported concerning children.

By contrast, males' interpretive style is marked by a focus on clearly identifiable perceptual attributes (Wood 1966) or objective concepts (Gleser, Gottschalk, and Watkins 1959). This more focused attention on objective, readily discernible, and highly available aspects of stimuli is consistent with a selective mode of processing.

Studies of the genders' perceptual preferences produce parallel findings. Poole (1977) found that middle-class males conceptualized items in terms of descriptive labels or physical attributes and seemed to "respond to more external attributes of persons" (p. 249). Females, however, employed more attitudinal or evaluative concepts, apparently basing these on inferential processing.

Gender Differences in Style of Interaction: In conversing with family and friends, evidence suggests that males demonstrate their selectivity by assuming a mode of interaction that suits their own agendas and is less sensitive to others. Conversely females manifest comprehensiveness by drawing out and sharing in others' views. Females' conversation is exemplified by more interactive work such as active and attentive listening, acknowledging and encouraging others' utterances, and sharing emotions (Thorne, Kramarae, and Henley 1983). Females' invitation to others to express their feelings and thoughts in conversation is consistent with their more communal nature and their more comprehensive mode of processing.

The genders' different styles of interaction are clearly demonstrated in studies examining interactions with children. As might be expected of selective processors, males are less concerned with peripheral considerations. Accordingly fathers were found to interrupt their children more than did mothers, and they engaged in more instances of simultaneous parent-child speech (Greif 1980). When interacting with their children, males tend to use more commands and inexplicit directives than do mothers (Bellinger and Gleason 1982). Fathers also are more impolite, use more sophisticated language that reflects less consideration of the child's capabilities, exert more control over conversations, and exhibit greater misunderstanding of their children (Gleason and Greif 1983). By contrast, mothers spend more time interacting with their children, alter their speech more to accommodate the child, and ask more questions to ascertain the child's comprehension of the exchange.

Although neither gender has been found consistently to exhibit greater overall productivity or verbosity (Haas 1979), when differences do emerge, they are compatible with the selectivity perspective. Females are frequently found to be more productive and fluent when they are able to see their conversation partner (Argyle, Lalljee, and Cook 1968; Siegman and Reynolds 1983), while males are more productive and fluent when their partners are concealed (Siegman and Reynolds 1983). Such data suggest that partner visibility enhances females' productivity, presumably because this situation offers more cues for comprehensive processing and discussion than does the absence of visual contact. By contrast, males are more productive when they are not distracted by seeing the person with whom they are conversing, perhaps because this situation allows them to focus selectively on and discuss the topic at hand. The work of Allen and Guy (1977) has established that the presence of visible cues may compromise cognitive processing. Apparently because females have greater experience than do males in comprehensively processing a broad array of cues, the level of visual stimulation at which capacity is overloaded and productivity declines is higher for females than for males.

Gender Differences in Influenceability: A sizable literature has investigated gender differences in influenceability (see Eagly 1978 and Eagly and Carli 1981 for extensive reviews). In a meta-analysis conducted by Eagly and Carli (1981), these social influence studies were categorized into three groups. Persuasion studies included those in which message recipients responded to an influencing agent who presented an advocacy and accompanying supporting arguments. Also identified were conformity studies of two types: those in which an agent advocated a position accompanied by no supporting arguments and was a surveillant as message recipients responded to the advocacy, and those that were identical to the first type except that no surveillance took place. It was found that females were more influenceable than were males in persuasion studies and conformity studies involving surveillance. In conformity studies without surveillance, evidence of gender differences was less certain.

It would seem that these gender differences in influenceability might be interpreted in terms of the selectivity hypothesis in the following manner. In persuasion studies, females as comprehensive processors may process and therefore base their decisions on more of the persuasive supporting arguments than do males, who selectively process a more limited amount of information. Consequently females may be more persuaded than males. Similarly, in conformity studies involving surveillance, females as comprehensive processors may be more attentive and receptive than are males to others' dispositions and the presence of others' surveillance. As such, females may be more accommodative of others when they render their opinions with regard to the advocacy. Finally, limited evidence of gender differences in conformity studies without surveillance would be expected given that in the absence of others' presence or supporting arguments, the amount of information processed by males and females is likely to be similar.

Gender Differences in Self-evaluation: A substantial number of studies have investigated gender differences in the evaluation of one's own abilities. Inquiries of this type can be considered self-evaluation studies. Although females are often found to render lower self-evaluations than do males, a review of the literature by Lenney (1977) identified several variables that typically qualify this effect. These qualifications are compatible with the notion that females as comprehensive processors are particularly sensitive to the available information. For example, females expect to perform less well than do males when clear performance feedback is absent, but no gender differences emerge when performance guidelines are clarified (Lenney, Browning, and Mitchell 1980). This seems to occur because females but not males are sensitive to the availability of such feedback.

Females' but not males' self-evaluations also are contingent on whether a social comparison is at issue (Lenney 1977). Gender differences in self-evaluation are more frequently observed in relative rather than absolute levels of self-evaluation (Lenney, Gold, and Browning 1983).

Finally, females' self-evaluations are dependent on the specific nature of available cues (Lenney 1981; Lenney, Gold, and Browning 1983). In a study conducted by Instone, Major, and Bunker (1983), females' self-evaluations were commensurate with their task-relevant experience, while males reported high self-evaluations regardless of their prior experience. Moreover, females' use of specification cues need not result in self-evaluations that are lower than those of males. Indeed, females in comparison to males exhibited lower relative self-evaluation expectancies only when their partner's ability was expected to be high. When partner ability was expected to be either average or low, females' self-evaluations were equivalent to those of males. Both of these effects occurred because females' judgments were sensitive to partner ability whereas males' were not (Lenney, Gold, and Browning 1983).

The observation that only females' self-evaluations are sensitive to specification cues is consistent with the view that females base their self-evaluations on a comprehensive processing of cues, while males' evaluations are reliant on selective or heuristic-based processing that is generally insensitive to detailed cues. Consequently females' self-evaluations are consistently lower than are males' only when the absence of cues inhibits females from conducting a careful and detailed analysis of their likely performance.

Gender Differences in Structural Organization: The representational structures of the genders would be expected to reflect the genders' different processing approaches. As selective heuristic-based processors, males are claimed to seize upon highly available, often singular cues that eclipse detailed cues. Thus as relatively detail-insensitive processors, males would be expected to possess rather simple, broad, widely encompassing knowledge structures that manifest limited subcategorization and collapse across intricate stimuli distinctions that are relatively inconsequential to males. By contrast, females as comprehensive processors are sensitive to detailed aspects of stimuli, which are apprehended and together come to shape response. Accordingly, females should organize information in a more differentiated manner that represents the more finely tuned discriminations they perceive.

Studies that have employed very different procedures and stimuli uphold these expectations. In color-matching and naming tasks, Nowaczyk (1982) found that males used more basic color terms (such as red and green) than did females, while females correctly matched and generated more elaborate or unusual color words (for example, "a dark, fleshy pink" for the color salmon) than did males. The observation that females' color matches and descriptions were more elaborate than were males' and that females more frequently verbalized finer color discriminations suggests that females' color codes are more differentiated than are males. That is, females have more differentiated structures in which information is stored.

A study by Glixman (1965) supports this view and suggests that relative to males, females establish more subcategories within which they store information. Males and females sorted a large number of statements concerning different topics (such as objects, self, and nuclear war) into groups on the basis of similarity. It was found that regardless of topic, females employed more subcategories in their sortings and exhibited more dispersion of statements across categories than did males. Moreover, Poole (1977, 1982) provided evidence that males and females demonstrate consistency in how they define category boundaries, with females possessing narrower categories and exhibiting more differentiation in grouping items that vary in conceptual similarity. These differences were stronger among middle-class than among working-class subjects.

Studies examining a related concept, bandwidth, provide additional convergent support (Kogan and Wallach 1964; Pettigrew 1958; Wallach and Caron 1959). In these studies, subjects were presented with a standard object and were asked to categorize other, often similar objects into groups that were like or unlike the standard. The data obtained concur that males employ broader, more inclusive categories than do females.

This depiction of the genders' organizational structure is consistent with evidence that pertains to males' and females' manner of encoding cues. Females as comprehensive processors are more attentive to detail than are males and therefore establish more differentiated, narrower, less inclusive category structures to accommodate and organize their finer distinctions. This portrayal is also compatible with evidence that seems to implicate gender differences in information retrieval. Anderson's (1983) model of processing operation suggests that the likelihood of retrieving any individual item within a category is inversely related to the total number of items within that category. This implies that females should manifest a retrieval or memory advantage relative to males because their category structures are narrower. A female memory advantage has been borne out in a number of studies (Guilford 1967; Tyler 1965).

In sum, these findings of gender differences in cognitive representations are harmonious with the selectivity hypothesis. Females who are more comprehensive, detailed processors may make finer distinctions among items and establish a greater number of subcategories, each comprised of fewer items, to order and maintain these distinctions in memory. By contrast, males who are more selective information processors are less attentive to between-item nuances; therefore subcategories are fewer in number and representations are more inclusive of disparate objects.

Summary

The data reviewed suggest that from childhood on, males and females adopt alternative modes of processing that differ in selectivity. The ontogeny of such differences can be traced to the different socialization treatment afforded the genders. Boys, who are exposed to activities low in structure, are encouraged to assume a rather agentic, single-minded approach in mastering their environments through selective processing of stimuli. By contrast, girls, who are steeped in more structured environments, are encouraged to adopt a communal orientation that entails not only greater consideration of others' views but also a concomitant concern with a broad and comprehensive range of cues that facilitate responsiveness to others and their structures. Social agents appear to encourage these alternative processing strategies by assigning boys to low- and girls to high-structured settings and by varying the specificity of instruction and feedback they offer to the genders.

Many manifestations of selectivity and comprehensiveness are observed in children's behaviors and responses. Selectivity is implied by boys' reduced sensitivity to the particulars of events in their interpretation of information. Boys' adherence to selectivity also translates into less fanciful or imaginative play, toy use that follows rather conventional patterns or selectively satisfies self-desires, and the frequent use of direct influence attempts and noncompliance with others' requests. By contrast, girls' comprehensiveness is expressed in their tendency to consider and reason through multiple and multifaceted cues, as is evident in their interpretive style and richly ideational or fanciful play. Further, females' comprehensiveness leads to much responsiveness and sensitivity to others. Thus girls emit requests that are often indirect and attuned to social conventions and others' feelings.

Evidence of gender differences among adults similarly demonstrates that manifestations of these alternative processing modes can take many forms. Yet notions of selectivity and comprehensiveness seem to capture systematic patterns in males' and females' responses. Males' reliance on selectivity is found to enhance their performance on spatial tasks that require focused attention to singular critical forms that are made especially available at task onset. In linguistic tasks, males' selectivity appears to undermine their performance as processing focuses on a relatively constrained set of cues to the exclusion of a variety of other cues germane to the task. Other manifestations of males' selectivity include a focus on salient, objective, categorical states in interpretation, a concentration on self-concerns with limited sensitivity to those of others, undermined facility in conversing when impinging visible cues distract attention away from focal issues, and judgments that display responsiveness to highly available cues but little susceptibility to detailed persuasive or specification cues.

Females' broad, comprehensive allocation of attentional resources to a variety of cues appears to debilitate performance on visual spatial tasks but benefit linguistic performance. Other manifestations of females' comprehensiveness include highly elaborative, inferential, and evaluative interpretations, enhanced information flow in communication due to the encouragement of and sensitivity to others, more facile and fluent conversation when visible cues supply more information, and self- and issue-oriented judgments that reflect the persuasiveness of the arguments and the impact of detail-laden specification cues.

Finally, males' selectivity and females' comprehensiveness seem to foster the development of alternative representational structures that are compatible with these processing modes. Males seem to structure information in broad categories that contain modest subcategorization, while females employ more subcategorized structures that organize the relatively detailed distinctions they perceive.

This wide assortment of gender differences in children's and adults' activities is amenable to a selectivity interpretation, thereby offering testimony to the robustness of this view. This theory is subjected to more severe tests in the following section. A number of predictions that are implied by the selectivity hypothesis and involve interactions of gender and other variables are investigated. In these studies, the selectivity hypothesis is subjected to more stringent scrutiny, while concomitantly greater illumination into the nature of the genders' processing modes is achieved.

Examining the Mechanisms Underlying Selective and Comprehensive Processing

The series of studies in this section examines the predictive accuracy of the selectivity hypothesis under specific circumstances. The initial studies test effects that are predicated on the view that selectivity entails a reliance on a single, highly available, self-oriented cue. Subsequent studies assume progressively broadened positions, first by supplying evidence that selectivity may entail the use of any single cue, regardless of the content of this cue. In turn, this position gives way to a more encompassing perspective that characterizes selectivity as a reliance on single or multiple cues that imply a single inference. Finally, selectivity is conceptualized as a tendency to employ heuristic-based processing.

Selectivity as a Single Cue

The selectivity hypothesis suggests that males base their responses on single cues that are highly available. Cue availability can be enhanced by a variety of factors, including the recency and frequency of prior activation of a construct (Higgins and King 1981). Thus the selectivity hypothesis would predict that if males were confronted with dual cues, they would focus on and use as a basis of response the single cue that was more available. By contrast, females, as comprehensive processors, would be expected to employ both cues in arriving at a response.

A study by Cupchik and Poulos (1984) allows examination of this conjecture. First, subjects were exposed to several affect-evoking stimuli, which they rated in terms of the emotional intensity the stimuli engendered within themselves. Querying subjects about their own reactions or expressivity to the stimuli should enhance the availability of such information. As subjects observed the stimuli, their nonverbal expressivity in response to the stimuli was recorded. Then subjects were shown a slide depicting another person's reaction to each stimulus, and they judged the intensity of the other person's reaction.

As anticipated on the basis of the selectivity hypothesis, males' judgments reflected the use of the single, more highly available cue: their own expressive reaction to the stimuli. Males classified as high expressives judged others' reactive intensity to be high, while low-expressive males judged others' intensity to be low. By contrast, females based their assessments on more effortful, discriminative processing. They compared others' reactions to their own manifested expressivity. High-expressive females rated others' intensity to be low, while low-expressive females rated others' intensity as high. Hence although subjects were exposed to dual, self-, and other-oriented cues, males relied on the single more available self-relevant cue in making judgments of others, while females' judgments reflected the use of both cues, regardless of the cues' salience.

Evidence indicates that gender differences in selectivity need not be confined to contexts in which self and/or other cues are present. In a study by Cupchik and Leventhal (1974, experiment 1), males and females were exposed to cartoons that varied in quality (poor or good) and whether they were accompanied by canned laughter. Subjects' attitudinal evaluations of the cartoons and their expressive behavior as they observed the cartoons were measured. The findings indicated that in the absence of canned laughter, both genders' evaluations showed an effect due to the cartoon quality. Good-quality cartoons were evaluated more favorably and induced more positive behavioral responses than did poor ones. A different pattern of outcomes was observed, however, when the cartoons were accompanied by canned laughter. In this case, males' attitudes and behaviors were affected by only one of the available cues, whereas females' attitudes and behaviors seemed to be responsive to both the cartoon quality and the canned laughter manipulations.

These data are concordant with the selectivity hypothesis. Like females, males' responses manifested an effect due to the quality manipulation when no canned laughter was present—that is, when quality was the only available cue. When cues pertaining to both quality and canned laughter were present, however, males selectively used only one of the available cues, presumably the more salient cue, while females' responses reflected the comprehensive use of both cues.

Other evidence offered by Cupchik and Leventhal supports this interpretation. When two cues were present—canned laughter and good-quality cartoons—females' attitude-behavior consistency was high and correlations were significant, but males' consistency correlations were low and nonsignificant. Examination of the available data suggests why males showed little consistency. It appears that in this dual-cue condition, males' behavioral responses were determined on the basis of the behavioral induction, the canned laughter cue, which apparently was more pertinent or available with regard to determining behavior. Their evaluative responses, however, were determined on the basis of the evaluative quality characteristic of the cartoons, which was more germane to the determination of an evaluative response. This suggests that males, who selectively based their responses on highly available or salient cues, not only employed different cues as a basis of determining attitudinal and behavioral responses but also used cues that were most fitting or salient with regard to the nature of the particular response.

These observations raise the possibility that when engaging in multiple responses, males may in fact employ multiple cues. In accordance with selectivity notions, however, each individual response will be based on only a single cue. Moreover, this cue may be the one most fitting to the response goal because it is most salient given the response goal context. Thus it would seem that because males' attitudinal and behavioral responses were based on alternative cues that presumably differed in favorableness, little attitude-behavior consistently occurred among males. That females' attitudinal and behavioral responses in this condition were consistent implies that, in accordance with their greater comprehensiveness, both behavioral and evaluative responses were ascertained through the simultaneous consideration of both available cues.

The preceding interpretation assumes that the canned laughter and cartoon quality cues differed in valence. Thus it is believed that the genders responded differently to such affectively incongruent cues. The following more direct examination of the genders' responses supports this interpretation.

Selectivity as a Single Inference

The research reviewed to this point suggests that males' selectivity involves the processing of single cues. More broadly defined, the selectivity hypothesis anticipates that males will process and use multiple cues if such cues are conceptually singular. This view of selectivity is both more plausible and appealing because the processing of multiple cues seems more adaptive in our complex multicued environment.

This notion was explored in a study by Meyers-Levy (1985). Subjects were exposed to multiple cues regarding how they (self) and others felt about a particular product. These cues were either congruent (both cues were either positive or negative in valence) or incongruent (cues were opposing in valence). Hence only when cues were congruent was a single inference implied. Subjects' attitudinal and behavioral responses with regard to the product were obtained.

Analysis of treatment differences in the magnitude of attitude-behavior correlations revealed that males exhibited high levels of attitude-behavior consistency when cues were congruent but not when they were incongruent. Females' consistency was high regardless of the level of cue congruency. Thus when cues were congruent and implied a single inference, males' attitudinal and behavioral responses were based selectively upon this singular inference. When these cues were incongruent, a single inference was not available. This increased males' likelihood of using alternative, differently valenced cues in determining attitudes and behaviors and thus undermined males' attitude-behavior consistency. By contrast, females appeared to assimilate comprehensively the cues in a manner that enabled them to demonstrate high levels of consistency, regardless of the level of cue congruency.

To this point the data suggest that, due to their greater comprehensiveness, females are more adept than are males in processing multiple cues. Although comprehensive processing is a time-consuming endeavor, females, by virtue of their greater experience with such processing, would be expected to be quite time efficient in undertaking such analysis. Thus if the determination of an appropriate response to a task required a modest level of multiple cue processing, females would be expected to perform this task more rapidly than would males, who as more selective processors of subsets of cues would be slower and less facile at the processing of multiple cues.

Fairweather and Hutt (1972, experiment 1) report findings that support this expectation and also supply evidence that, unlike males, females process information at an increasingly rapid rate as the information load increases. The study entailed a choice reaction time test in which children were presented with information of varied load sizes. Thus response determination would seem to require merely surface processing of multiple cue loads of various sizes. At all ages, females' reaction times were faster than were males', and females' advantage increased as information load size mounted. Because males have been found to be faster than females in simple reaction time (Fairweather and Hutt, experiment 2), results of this study confirm that females may have an advantage relative to males in rapidly processing multiple cue information and that this advantage increases as demands of the task increase.

Selectivity as Heuristic-Based Processing

The selectivity hypothesis suggests that males' reliance on conceptually singular cues is indicative of their general preference for simplified or heuristic-based processing; however, heuristic-based processing can take other forms as well. For example, one would expect that males might often engage in conceptually driven processing whereby expectations formed early on act as a surrogate for and/or guide subsequent processing. Reliance on such initial assessments provides a heuristic device that obviates detailed analysis of cues. In line with this reasoning, Christensen and Rosenthal (1982) found that males formed judgments of persons with whom they interacted on the basis of preconceived expectancies, while females appeared to base their judgments on cues that emerged during the interaction. Similarly Farrell (1974) has suggested that the direction of males' conversation is determined by what they process initially upon entering the conversation, whereas females are responsive to subtleties that arise in the course of conversation. Thus it seems that males streamline processing by employing heuristics such as the reliance on primacy cues, whereas females are generally responsive to a rather comprehensive array of cues.

This logic, extended further, would lead to the prediction of alternative serial position effects on the genders' judgments if cognitive capacity were exceeded. If males favor conceptually driven processing, cues presented early on should guide males' judgments, producing a primacy effect. Their evaluations should depend on the valence associated with the first information presented. However, the contention that females' evaluations are based on the sequential processing of all incoming cues implies that if cognitive capacity were exceeded, females' judgments would exhibit a recency effect. As cognitive demands surpass available capacity, females' comprehensiveness should be compromised as access to information initially processed would be inhibited. Thus, by default, females should have access to only the last or most recent information presented and be forced to rely on it as a basis of judgment.

A study by Meyers-Levy (1985) supports this prediction. Males and females were exposed to complex descriptive information concerning an object. The initial information of this description was varied such that it implied that the object was a member of one category, while information presented later suggested it was a member of an alternative category. Information cues pertaining to the alternative categories were opposing in valence. After reading this description, subjects' evaluations of the object were obtained. As anticipated, males exhibited a primacy effect such that their judgments were based on the favorableness of the information presented first. By contrast, females, confronted with this task that exceeded cognitive capacity, employed a recency heuristic whereby judgments reflected the favorableness of the last information presented. Because females' comprehensiveness was necessarily derogated when cognitive capacity was exceeded, the most recent or last information processed was all that was available for females to use in determining their judgments.

The characterization of males as selective, heuristic-based processors also implies that males should be rather insensitive to nonfocal cues that might be regarded as detail. Support for this assertion is offered by Hall (1978) who found females to be superior decoders of nonverbal information relative to males. As might be anticipated, though, females' decoding of such cues is not always superior to that of males. Rosenthal and DePaulo (1979) found that females' superiority in decoding nonverbal information was virtually eliminated when exposure time to stimuli was limited, presumably because decoding nonverbal cues is a time-consuming endeavor. These studies suggest that relative to males, females should possess a lower threshold at which specific detail will be detected.

This deduction, drawn from between-studies data, was tested in a study by Meyers-Levy (1985). Subjects were presented with a new product description that delineated a large number of product attributes. All message information was moderately to extremely favorable in valence except the target attribute, which was negative. The salience of the target attribute was varied experimentally so that it was either weak or moderate. As predicted, subjects' evaluations of the product indicated that females detected the target attribute in the moderate but not the weak salience condition, while males manifested no sensitivity to the attribute in either condition.

Inspection of the variance in males' and females' evaluations within salience conditions offered additional support for this view of gender differences in cue sensitivity thresholds. Females manifested little variance in their negative evaluations of the product in the moderate salience condition, suggesting that they uniformly detected the unfavorable target attribute. Females in the weak salience condition, along with males in both the moderate and weak salience conditions, displayed much variance in their more positive evaluations. This implies that although some individuals in these latter three conditions may have detected the unfavorable target attribute and used it as a basis of evaluation, many other individuals in these conditions relied on nontarget cues that ranged from extreme to moderate favorableness. Reliance on these assorted cues that varied in valence produced higher levels of variance in these conditions.

Summary

Data suggest that deductions from the selectivity hypothesis are useful in identifying conditions under which the genders will exhibit alternative patterns of responses. In each of the studies reviewed, the interactive effects of gender and other variables were concordant with predictions based on the selectivity hypothesis. Such evidence provides more compelling support for the selectivity hypothesis and attests to the richness this theory brings to the study of gender.

Males' selectivity can be manifested as a focused concentration on self-cues, other single cues, or a number of conceptually singular cues. Each of these forms of selectivity underlies a reliance on heuristic-based processing. Stimuli are scanned and judgments are rendered by simplifying the morass of complex information via heuristics. By contrast, females' greater comprehensiveness in processing is more highly demanding of resources as a broader range of cues are attended to, contrasted, and ultimately subjected to attempts toward reconciliation.

Conclusions

The literature reviewed documents a wide assortment of gender differences that can be explained in terms of the selectivity hypothesis. According to this hypothesis, males are relatively selective in the information cues they use in interpreting and acting upon the world. Whether this selectivity is manifested by a reliance on single cues that reflect self-oriented concerns, other single-entity cues not rooted in the self, or multiple cues that are conceptually singular, the evidence suggests that males' processing of information typically entails minimal processing of understated detail in favor of salient or highly available subsets of information that serve heuristic purpose by mitigating otherwise laborious detailed processing.

By contrast, females reveal greater comprehensiveness in processing, attending equivalently to single as well as multiple cues or entities, engaging in more elaborative, inferential processing, and devoting substantial attention to detail unless processing capabilities are compromised by particularly weak cue signals or capacity limitations.

Some insight into the possible origin of these gender differences in processing has been obtained by examining differences in the treatment social agents give young boys and girls. An accumulation of studies argues that gender differences may stem from the alternatively structured environments provided for the genders. Boys are encouraged to participate in activities in which they create their own structure by being independent and making their own way in less structurally defined activities outside the home. Girls are groomed more exclusively in the structure provided at home and are induced to seek and accept the guidance of others' structures.

A single-focused, agentic orientation can be discerned from males' emphasis on independence and assertion of and attending to only oneself, while communality or attending to self and others becomes the password for females, who learn to pattern the actions of self against those of others. With experience, these alternative orientations may undergo abstraction and come to assume a more generalized status. Males learn to adopt a processing approach that focuses selectively on highly available singular cues regardless of whether these cues pertain to the self, while females process comprehensively all cues present. Hence rather early in life, males may learn to resort to selective processing as they attempt to limit the multitude of cues conducive to alternative patterns of structure development. By contrast, females gain more experience in comprehensively learning the rules, criteria, and assorted structural details provided by others. These selective and comprehensive processing strategies may become further ingrained as social agents coach boys and girls in the adoption of "gender-appropriate" processing modes by modeling behaviors and offering instruction that conforms to these processing strategies.

Numerous gender differences observed among children can be interpreted within this framework. Boys' selectivity in processing is manifested in their tendency to adopt singularly self-oriented interests; engage in relatively simplistic, often self-purposive functional play; bring to bear heuristic-like, singular principles in resolving dilemmas; and, with age, increasingly employ highly direct, to-the-point influence attempts that are less sensitive to others' concerns. Greater comprehensiveness among girls is indicated by their tendency to attend to contextual details in play; readily engage in high levels of imaginative, fantasy play that may involve creative uses of objects; comprehensively generate inferences and ponder hypotheticals or situational intricacies in resolving dilemmas; and, relative to boys, employ more polite, indirect influence attempts that reflect the consideration of both self and others.

The data suggest that these processing tendencies are maintained in adulthood. As evidenced in the genders' interpretive and conversation styles, males tend to focus selectively on highly available, categorical, and clearly perceived features of stimuli, while females more actively engage in the reflective comprehensive consideration of subjective, detailed, and tangential dimensions of stimuli and contexts. Males' focus on singular elements or assemblies that are perceived as units seems to enhance their performance on many visual spatial tasks in comparison to females. And females' comprehensive consideration of assorted aspects of stimuli gives rise to a female advantage in many linguistic tasks. Males' proclivity to invoke heuristic devices that circumvent analysis of detail is manifested in their tendency to display less susceptibility to detailed persuasive arguments, less responsiveness to others in conversation, and less sensitivity to the particulars of the situation in evaluating self-performance. Conversely, females' greater desire for specification cues and sensitivity to available information often produces greater persuasibility, more sensitivity and responsiveness to others in conversations, and referent-sensitive self-evaluations.

Finally, males' and females' manner of representing knowledge appears to be adaptive to their alternative modes of processing. Conforming with their detail- and distinction-sensitive manner of processing, females employ highly differentiated knowledge structures that are replete with subcategories, while males who favor rather simplified, heuristic-driven processing exhibit broader structures.

Applications

The characterization of the genders' processing proclivities from a selectivity perspective spawns a number of implications for marketers who seek optimal ways to appeal to males and females. The selectivity hypothesis suggests that males' processing is often reliant on heuristic devices that simplify processing demands by focusing on singular concepts. By contrast, females' processing is held to be more comprehensive in the scope of cues considered.

Designing Appeals for Males

Speculation concerning the origins of males' selectivity posits that males' heuristic mode of processing originates from social practices that imbue in males an agentic, self-orientation. It follows that male-targeted marketing appeals that single-mindedly imply agentic principles are likely to be well received. In appealing to young boys, agency might be personified by the use of fictitious product characters, such as cartoon-like superheroes, who depict product usage in ways that promote self-aggrandizement. Because boys are less avid fantasizers than are girls, substantial elaboration of these portrayals would seem to be warranted to encourage boys to embellish upon these agentic acts in ways that are personally meaningful.

Single-focused agentic appeals also might be used effectively in targeting adult males. Here agency might be expressed in copy that touts self-expression, adhering to one's own values and beliefs in the face of countervailing trends, or overcoming obstacles through determination and persistence. An advertisement for the Saab automobile exemplifies such agentic values (figure 10–1). The ad shows a Saab intently pursuing a straight path at a juncture on a road at which arrows point left, right, and straight ahead. The accompanying headline conveys a decidedly agentic sentiment: "Does popular acceptance require abandoning the very principles that got you where you are?" These sentiments are carried on throughout the copy through the use of vignettes, which illustrate that while others may compromise their desires to win popular acceptance, Saab never has and never will. In this manner, the Saab ad single-mindedly expresses agentic values that are used to characterize the values associated with the advertised product and presumably appeal to males who adhere to similar principles.

The prescriptive for the use of single-focused appeals in targeting males holds regardless of whether these appeals specifically relate to themes connoting agency. Other means of accommodating males' tendency toward selective processing might entail developing messages that focus on product attributes that imply a single concept. Illustrative of this approach is a series of ads for Coors beer in which each ad focuses on a single but different product attribute. For example, one ad states that Coors does not add anything artificial to its beer (figure 10–2), a second ad discusses Coors's exclusive aging process (figure 10–3), and a third ad describes the measures taken during shipping and storage to avoid exposing Coors to heat (figure 10–4). Though different in the claims they make, each ad is single focused in identifying an attribute that implies quality, and each makes use of a common ad format to facilitate males' processing of the claims and their association of the claims with the Coors brand name.

Designing executions that are single focused in the concepts they present becomes more difficult in marketing more complex products that possess a myriad of detailed and specific product features. In such cases, a number of devices might be employed that would seem to aid males in synthesizing the assortment of detailed and disparate arguments presented into monolithic concepts. One such device would be to provide males with a strong, single pictorial cue that visually summarizes the key product features. Such a visual cue might be expected to serve as a mnemonic device that provides for males a nexus from which they can interrelate the specific and detailed product features discussed in the ad. An ad for the Honda Civic DX Hatchback employs this approach by visually depicting the expanse of the long panel of windows on the car's top exterior (figure 10–5). Accompanying copy then details specific features associated with this visual cue: unique long-roof design, window area totaling 319^{0} out of 360^{0}, rear wiper washer, tinted glass, back seat spacious feeling, and aerodynamic drag reduction design. The ad focuses almost entirely on objective, factual features of the car, with little subjective interpretation of the features (benefits) offered. This too would seem to be compatible with males' processing proclivities in that research reveals that males tend to focus selectively on objective rather than subjective cues in interpreting and describing stimuli.

Figure 10–1. Reprinted with permission from Saab-Scania of America, Inc.

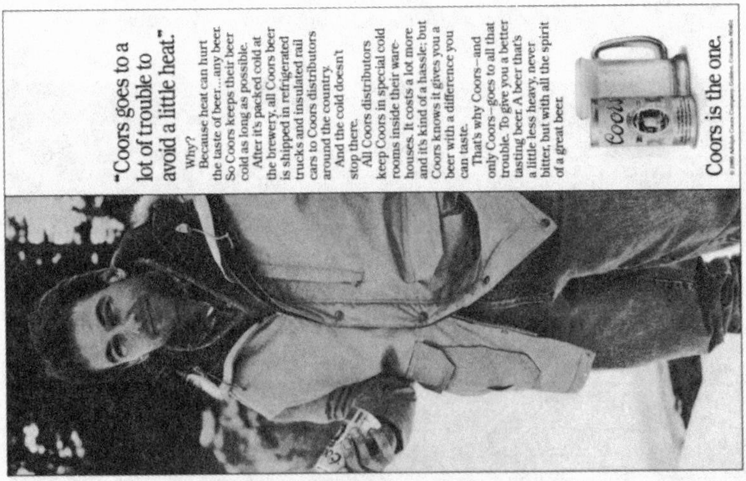

"Coors goes to a lot of trouble to avoid a little heat."
Why?
Because heat can hurt the taste of beer…any beer. So Coors keeps their beer cold as long as possible.
After it's packed cold at the brewery, all Coors beer is shipped in refrigerated trucks and insulated rail cars to Coors distributors around the country.
And the cold doesn't stop there.
All Coors distributors keep Coors in special cold rooms inside their warehouses. It costs a lot more and it's kind of a hassle; but Coors knows it gives you a beer with a difference you can taste.
That's why Coors—and only Coors—goes to all that trouble. To give you a better tasting beer. A beer that's a little less heavy, never bitter, but with all the spirit of a great beer.
Coors is the one.

"Aging. It's just as important to beer as it is to wine."
Aging gives beer "balance." Just the right combination of flavors and aromas necessary to give beer its character.
Coors thinks aging is so important, they age their beer longer than any other major brewer. *Almost twice as long.*
Coors takes the extra time to age out a lot of the heaviness, a lot of the bitter after-taste you'll find in many other beers. And this gives you a beer with a difference worth tasting.
A beer that's a little less heavy, never bitter, but with all the spirit of a great beer.
Coors is the one.

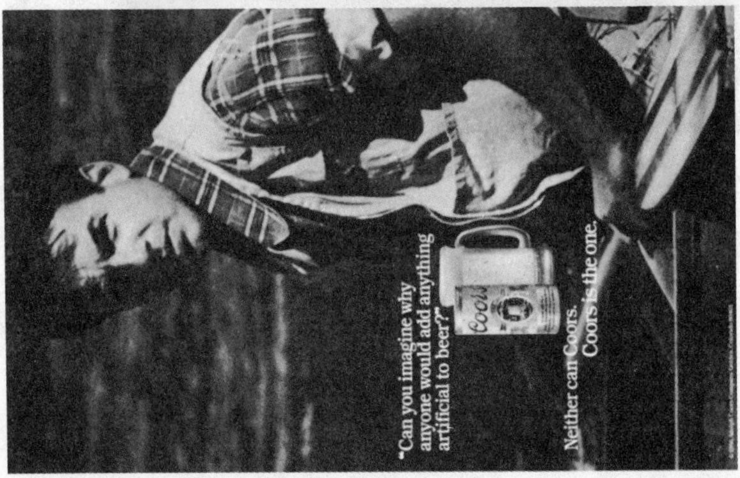

"Can you imagine why anyone would add anything artificial to beer?"
Neither can Coors.
Coors is the one.

Figure 10–2. Reprinted with permission from Adolph Coors Company.
Figure 10–3. Reprinted with permission from Adolph Coors Company.
Figure 10–4. Reprinted with permission from Adolph Coors Company.

Take a look around. And you'll see why
hbacks will never be the same again.
Because in this Honda Civic DX Hatch-
k, the unique long-roof design provides
xpansive window area (totaling 319°
of 360°). A rear wiper/washer and tinted
s all around improve the view even more,
e rain or shine.
Rear seat passengers enjoy a spacious
ng thanks to the same long-roof design.
plemented by ample headroom and a
atile cargo area in back.
Outside, efficient aerodynamics guide the air around the car to achieve an impressive .35 coefficient of drag. The hoodline is low, and the doors wrap up smoothly into the top to reduce wind drag and noise.
Under the hood, the responsive 1488cc 12-valve engine makes its authority clear. It comes with a standard 5-speed manual transmission or an available automatic transmission. With front-wheel drive for good handling and traction. The power-assisted brakes, suspension and steel-belted radial tires are designed for positive response.
And there are other advantages, ranging from an adjustable steering column and split folding rear seatback, to gas-filled rear shock absorbers and a front stabilizer bar.
If you ever want to sell, you'll see for yourself the pleasant effects of Honda's traditionally strong resale values.*
The Honda Civic DX Hatchback. We think you'll like it. For obvious reasons.
HONDA
The Civic DX Hatchback
The advantages are clearly visible.

Figure 10–5. Reprinted with permission from American Honda Motor Company

Another means of promoting unification of disjunctive message arguments might be to embed claims within a familiar story line or grammar. Such a story grammar might serve as a well-defined coherent structure within which new information can be easily attached and assimilated. For example, an advertisement for ThinkTank computer (figure 10–6) software makes use of a familiar problem-solving story grammar as it relates a problem-solving incident that portrays the product as hero. The ad tells how a company's loss of a key engineer left them short-handed at an inopportune time. The narrator of the story relates how, with the aid of ThinkTank, he was able to develop a plan of action in half the time and with twice the confidence than would have otherwise been possible. Presumably by attaching the product information to a familiar story grammar structure such as this one (story ⟶ setting + theme + plot + resolution; Thorndyke 1977), the selective processor's comprehension and retention of message information is enhanced.

Another implication that can be drawn from the selectivity hypothesis is that males will often render judgments based disproportionately on the first

Fanatic At Work
"I never pictured myself as a personal computer fanatic, but I found a reason to become one—ThinkTank.™
I use it every day. It's my 'status center' where I log every important fact, plan and meeting.
Last month I used ThinkTank to manage my way around a crisis. A key engineer quit, leaving us short-handed at a bad time. I worked late that night, had two meetings the next morning and arrived at an action plan by mid-afternoon. Without ThinkTank it would have taken twice as long and I would have been half as confident.
I don't need a personal computer to make me a better typist, for calculating budgets or entering invoices. These are good reasons for other people to use a personal computer. ThinkTank is the reason I use a personal computer."
One toll-free call to 1-800-822-3700 (in California, 1-800-443-4310) will guide you to the nearest dealer.
THINKTANK™
The First Idea Processor
ThinkTank outline processing software is available for IBM Personal Computers and 100% compatibles, with 256K or more, Texas Instruments Professional and Pro-Lite Computers ($195); in two versions for Apple Macintosh, ThinkTank 128 ($145), ThinkTank 512 ($245); and for the Apple II family ($150).
"ThinkTank" and "The First Idea Processor" are trademarks of Living Videotext, Inc. IBM is a trademark of International Business Machines, Inc. Texas Instruments Professional and Pro-Lite Computers are trademarks of Texas Instruments, Inc. Macintosh is a trademark licensed to Apple Computer, Inc. Apple is a trademark of Apple Computer, Inc.
© Copyright 1985, Living Videotext, Inc., 2432 Charleston Road, Mountain View, CA 94043 (415) 964-6300

Figure 10–6. Reprinted with permission from Living Videotext, Inc.

information presented. Research attests that males as heuristic processors seem prone to short-circuit detailed message processing by forming product judgments on the basis of initial impressions. That is, they may use the information presented at the outset of the message to form their ultimate judgment of the product, or they might identify the product category with which the featured product is associated and base product judgments on the affect associated with the general product category rather than on inferences drawn from specific product-related claims. It would seem that when operating under time constraints, when the product category is regarded as fairly uninvolving, or when product category members are viewed as highly similar to one another, males would be particularly likely to render product judgments in this manner. Judgments rendered on either of these bases serve heuristic purpose by relying heavily on primacy information and thereby avoiding the need to undertake detailed message-based processing. The implication for marketers is that they should carefully scrutinize how their product is portrayed at the outset of the advertisement. When targeting males, advertisers should attempt to clearly associate featured products with product categories that are most favorably regarded, and this positioning should be evident early on in the ad. Further, the most compelling message claims should be featured at the beginning of the ad to ensure a favorable first impression.

Designing Appeals for Females

Females' tendency to employ comprehensive processing also leads to a number of implications of consequence to marketers. As comprehensive processors, females would be expected to be adept at processing an assortment of detailed claims, regardless of whether these claims imply singular or multiple inferences. Hence messages targeted at females can more freely tout multiple and disparate product features. Yet some caveats are in order. If the claims presented are complex or extreme in number, females' capacity to process them thoroughly may be compromised. Research suggests that under such circumstances, females tend to base their judgments on the last information presented. This would imply that marketers who present complex or abundant detailed claims to females might be wise to reiterate their key product claims at the conclusion of the message to ensure their consideration during judgment. Marketers also should be sensitive to the manner in which females might interpret the featured claims. Females have been found to engage in considerable inferential associative processing and thus are likely to generate subjective inferences on the basis of the featured objective characteristics. This implies that the messages presented to females should be scrutinized for implied claims that lie beyond their literal or surface representation.

At the same time, females' propensity to engage in elaborative processing implies an opportunity for marketers. Communications designed to appeal to females might attempt to capitalize on females' tendency to undertake imaginative, associative processing. Such messages could make ample use of cues that evoke positive associative thoughts and images. That is, by implanting in messages rich and symbol-laden cues, females might be induced to generate positive ruminations that permeate and come to define the image of the product. Consider, for example, the rich associative cues that an advertisement for Zena jeans presents for the female reader to interpret imaginatively. Here a blending of resonant visual cues stirs up fanciful recollections of Indian folklore and mythology (an Indian doll and rug), femininity (ruffled pillows, a pink dust ruffle), juvenility (a young girl's diary, a bedside doll, jeans), and bucolic open-air country living (patchwork quilts and pillows, cowboy boots, paisley bandana). This is complemented by the wistful dreamlike copy that muses about a midday ride on an Arabian horse and a journey to New York.

Females' proclivity to engage in elaborative processing coupled with their discerning eye for detail also would seem to present marketers with abundant opportunity to finely tune their positioning of products. An ad by Clairol that introduces a new line of seven shampoos deftly illustrates how this might be done (figure 10–7). In this single ad, an attempt is made to differentiate each shampoo from one another by capitalizing on females' capacity to embellish and embroider elaborate images. Each shampoo is uniquely positioned by highlighting different product dimensions that are exemplified in visual scenes expressly designed to evoke distinct and fertile images. An airy scene of an exotic Hawaiian beach replete with luscious coconuts illustrates the position of Cocomilk Essence shampoo as a mild hair cleanser and moisturizer, a scene of Egyptian pyramids near a desert oasis conveys the positioning of Henna Essence shampoo that imparts deep and rich highlights to hair, and an idyllic chateau country scene portrays the positioning of Chamomile Essence shampoo that imbues hair with a shimmering halo of bright and lustrous highlights. Thus, by seizing on females' tendency to engage in associative processing and their sensitivity to subtle discriminations, Clairol is able to create distinct product positionings or subcategories for each of their seven Clairol Essence shampoos.

While females' tendency to engage in rich elaboration and discrimination can have desirable consequences for marketers, it can also pose a problem when comparisons among brands are made to underscore the superiority of a focal brand on a particular product dimension. Suppose a comparative ad is developed in which a focal brand is contrasted on a particular dimension to the leading brand or to a more generic competitor. If, as research suggests, females make fine distinctions among products, they may regard these two products as belonging to alternative subcategories. As such, exposure to the claim might prompt females to counterargue with the assertion because the two brands would be viewed as incomparable; that is, females may reason that although the focal brand may be superior to the referent brand on the stated dimension, the referent is superior on many dimensions associated with the subcategory

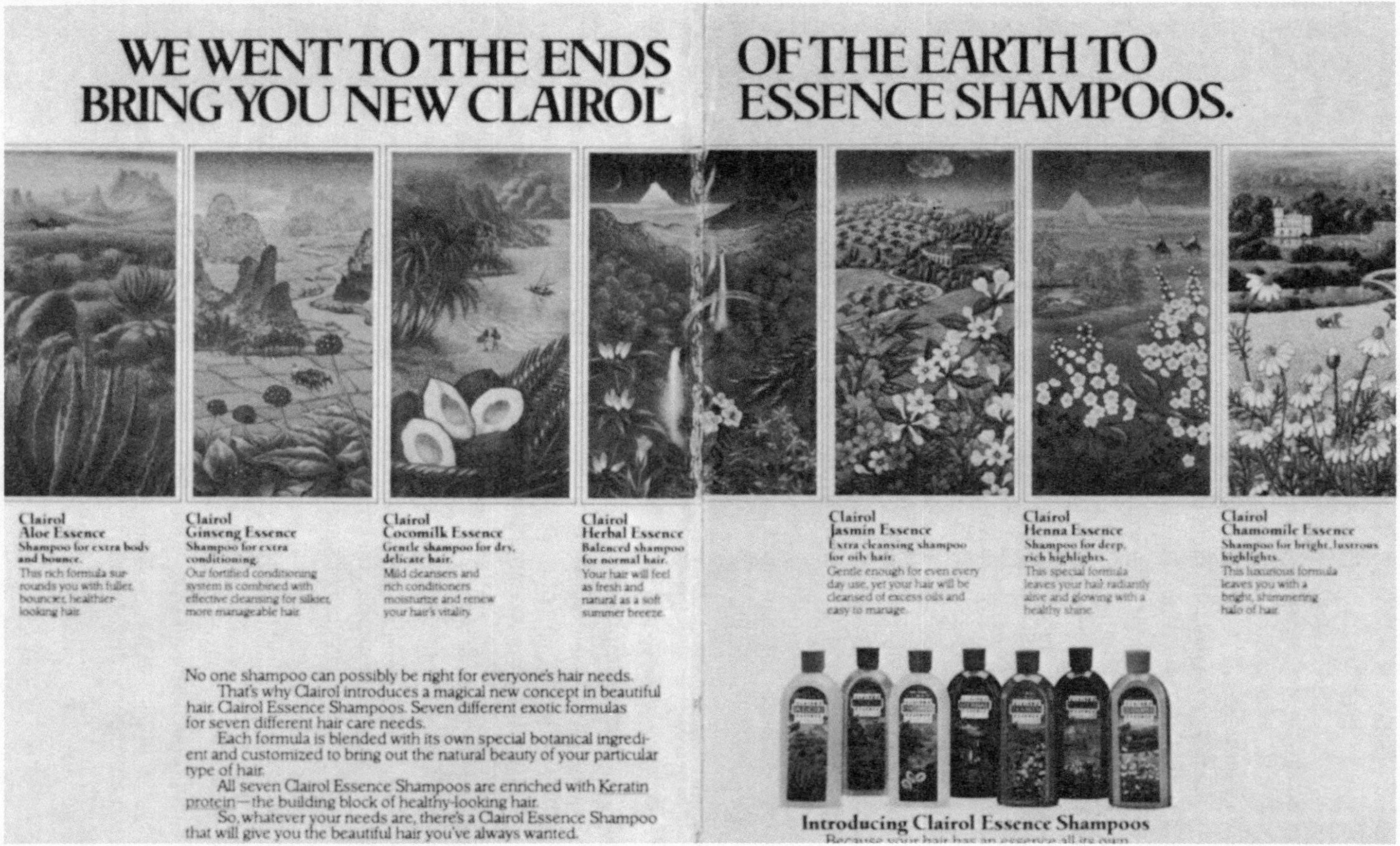

WE WENT TO THE ENDS OF THE EARTH TO
BRING YOU NEW CLAIROL® ESSENCE SHAMPOOS.
Clairol Aloe Essence
Shampoo for extra body and bounce.
This rich formula surrounds you with fuller, bouncier, healthier-looking hair.
Clairol Ginseng Essence
Shampoo for extra conditioning.
Our fortified conditioning system is combined with effective cleansing for silkier, more manageable hair.
Clairol Cocomilk Essence
Gentle shampoo for dry, delicate hair.
Mild cleansers and rich conditioners moisturize and renew your hair's vitality.
Clairol Herbal Essence
Balanced shampoo for normal hair.
Your hair will feel as fresh and natural as a soft summer breeze.
Clairol Jasmin Essence
Extra cleansing shampoo for oily hair.
Gentle enough for even every day use, yet your hair will be cleansed of excess oils and easy to manage.
Clairol Henna Essence
Shampoo for deep, rich highlights.
This special formula leaves your hair radiantly alive and glowing with a healthy shine.
Clairol Chamomile Essence
Shampoo for bright, lustrous highlights.
This luxurious formula leaves you with a bright, shimmering halo of hair.
No one shampoo can possibly be right for everyone's hair needs.
That's why Clairol introduces a magical new concept in beautiful hair. Clairol Essence Shampoos. Seven different exotic formulas for seven different hair care needs.
Each formula is blended with its own special botanical ingredient and customized to bring out the natural beauty of your particular type of hair.
All seven Clairol Essence Shampoos are enriched with Keratin protein—the building block of healthy-looking hair.
So, whatever your needs are, there's a Clairol Essence Shampoo that will give you the beautiful hair you've always wanted.
Introducing Clairol Essence Shampoos

Figure 10–7. © **Clairol Inc. 1984. Reprinted with permission of copyright owner.**

to which it belongs. Accordingly females may come to regard the focal brand unfavorably or regard any comparison between brands as invalid. At the same time, such comparisons might be entirely reasonable and compelling to males who establish broader, more inclusive product categories and likely regard the two brands as members of the same product class.

An advertisement for Bacardi rum illustrates this potential problem. The ad touts the low calorie and alcohol content of a Bacardi rum and tonic in comparison to that of white wine. This comparison may seem quite reasonable to the selective male processor who is likely to categorize both rum and tonic and white wine within the rather broad class of alcoholic beverages. But the logic of the claim may be less compelling to females who might assign the focal and referent products to alternative subcategories. For example, the white wine may be viewed as a member of a class of alcoholic beverages appropriate for dining, while the Bacardi rum and tonic may be perceived as a type of beverage appropriate for consuming at social events, such as at parties or bars. Consequently, while the ad may persuasively lead the male to substitute Bacardi and tonic for wine, the female may either outrightly dismiss the claim or counterargue its logic. This analysis suggests that when comparison ads are targeted at females, referent brands should be chosen carefully to ensure that they are regarded as members of the same product category as the focal brand. Empirical evidence relevant to this and other applications of selectivity requires additional research.

Future Trends

The view that gender differences in processing originate from the inculcation of agentic and communal values in males and females, respectively, leads to the question of how persistent these differences are likely to be in the light of recent societal changes. An illuminating report by Cafferata (1985) provides some evidence that these sex role distinctions may be blurring as females are expanding their horizons and assuming more dimensions associated with agentic values. Cafferata reports survey data obtained from 2,000 males and 2,000 females that suggest that females are increasingly expressing agentic sentiments, agreeing, for example, that they frequently "drink in a bar or tavern" and "would do better than average in a fistfight."

Yet other data from this survey suggest that the genders continue to express attitudes consistent with their traditional gender role. Relative to females, males are more supportive of aggression, which is consistent with their agentic sex role. Males more frequently watch aggressive sports and contend that all homes should have guns. At the same time, females continue to express communality by showing greater concern over fashion and appearance issues and more frequently sending greeting cards to others. These trends lead Cafferata to conclude that although on the whole males and females are maintaining their traditional roles, "women are adding to their pursuits but subtracting very little" (p. 38).

Indeed the more varied and expanded self- and other-oriented concerns that are currently occupying females' interests may reflect but another manifestation of females' tendency to be communal and comprehensive as they more actively share in issues and views that previously were in a domain of concern to others. Viewed from this perspective, the genders' adherence to their sex roles seems to be continuing, suggesting that processing differences purported to distinguish the genders can be expected to endure in the future.

Note

1. The emphasis here on the social origins of gender differences is not intended to imply that socialization is the only source of such differences. Indeed there is evidence to suggest otherwise (Kagan and Lewis 1965). Rather, the position assumed here is one of examining the abundant evidence that argues persuasively for a social origins component of selectivity.

References

Anastasi, A., and Foley, J.P., Jr. 1949. *Differential psychology: Individual and group differences in behavior.* New York: Macmillan.

Allen, D.E., and Guy, R.F. 1977. Ocular breaks and verbal output. *Sociometry* 40: 90–96.

Anderson, J.R. 1983. *The architecture of cognition.* Cambridge, Mass.: Harvard University Press.

Argyle, M.; Lalljee, M.; and Cook, M. 1968. The effects of visibility on interaction in a dyad. *Human Relations* 21:3–17.

Bakan, D. 1966. *The duality of human existence.* Chicago: Rand McNally.

Bellinger, D.C., and Gleason, J.B. 1982. Sex differences in parental directives to young children. *Sex Roles* 8:1123–1139.

Bennett, G.K.; Seashore, H.G.; and Wesman, A.G. 1956. The differential aptitude test: An overview. *Personality and Guidance Journal* 35:81–91.

Block, J.H. 1973. Conceptions of sex role: Some cross-cultural and longitudinal perspectives. *American Psychologist* 28:512–526.

Bock, R.D., and Kolakowski, D. 1973. Further evidence of sex-linked major-gene influence on spatial visualization ability. *American Journal of Human Genetics* 25: 1–14.

Broverman, D.M.; Klaiber, E.L.; Kobayashi, Y.; and Vogel, W. 1968. Roles of activation and inhibition in sex differences in cognitive abilities. *Psychological Review* 75:23–50.

Buffery, A.W.H., and Gray, J.A. 1972. Sex differences in the development of spatial and linguistic skills. In C. Ounsted and D.C. Taylor, eds., *Gender differences: Their ontogeny and significance.* Edinburgh: Churchill Livingstone.

Cafferata, Pat. 1985. Is woman making a man of herself? unpublished paper.

Caplan, P.J. 1979. Beyond the box score: A boundary condition for sex differences in aggression and achievement striving. In B. Maher, ed., *Progress in experimental personality research,* vol. 9. New York: Academic Press.

Caplan, P.J.; MacPherson, G.M.; and Tobin, P. 1985. Do sex-related differences in spatial abilities exist? A multilevel critique with new data. *American Psychologist* 40:786–799.

Carlson, R. 1971. Sex differences in ego functioning: Exploratory studies of agency and communion. *Journal of Consulting and Clinical Psychology* 37:267–277.

———. 1972. Understanding women: Implications for personality theory and research. *Journal of Social Issues* 28:17–32.

Carpenter, C.J. 1983. Activity structure and play: Implications for socialization. In M.S. Liss, ed., *Social and cognitive skills: Sex roles and children's play.* New York: Academic Press.

Christensen, D., and Rosenthal, R. 1982. Gender and nonverbal decoding skill as determinants of interpersonal expectancy effects. *Journal of Personality and Social Psychology* 42:75–87.

Connor, J.M.; Schackman, M.; and Serbin, L.A. 1978. Sex-related differences in response to practice on a visual-spatial test and generalization to a related test. *Child Development* 49:24–29.

Connor, J.M., and Serbin, L.A. 1977. Behaviorally based masculine- and feminine-activity-preference scales for preschoolers: Correlates with other classroom behaviors and cognitive tests. *Child Development* 48:1411-1416.

Connor, J.M.; Serbin, L.A.; and Schackman, M. 1977. Sex differences in children's response to training on a visual-spatial test. *Developmental Psychology* 13:293–294.

Cupchik, G.C., and Leventhal, H. 1974. Consistency between expressive behavior and the evaluation of humorous stimuli: The role of sex and self observation. *Journal of Personality and Social Psychology* 30:429–442.

Cupchik, G.C., and Poulos, C.X. 1984. Judgments of emotional intensity in self and others: The effects of stimulus context, sex, and expressivity. *Journal of Personality and Social Psychology* 46:431–439.

Deaux, K. 1984. From individual differences to social categories: Analysis of a decade's research on gender. *American Psychologist* 39:105–116.

Eagly, A.H. 1978. Sex differences in influenceability. *Psychological Bulletin* 85:86–116.

Eagly, A.H., and Carli, L.L. 1981. Sex of researchers and sex-typed communications as determinants of sex differences in influenceability: A meta-analysis of social influence studies. *Psychological Bulletin* 90:1–20.

Engels, F. 1891. *The origin of the family, private property and the state.* 4th ed. Moscow.

Entwisle, D.R., and Garvey, C. 1972. Verbal productivity and adjective usage. *Language and Speech* 15:288–298.

Fagot, B.I. 1978. The influence of sex of child on parental reactions to toddler children. *Child Development* 49:459–465.

Fairweather, H. 1976. Sex differences in cognition. *Cognition* 4:231–280.

Fairweather, H., and Hutt, S.J. 1972. Gender differences in perceptual motor skills. In

C. Ounsted and D.C. Taylor, eds., *Gender differences: Their ontogeny and significance.* Edenburgh: Churchill Livingstone.

Farrell, W. 1974. *The liberated man. Beyond masculinity: Freeing men and their relationships with women.* New York: Random House.

Fennema, E., and Sherman, J. 1977. Sex-related differences in mathematics achievement, spatial visualization and affective factors. *American Educational Research Journal* 14:51–71.

Frankel, M.T., and Rollins, H.A., Jr. 1983. Does mother know best? Mothers and fathers interacting with preschool sons and daughters. *Developmental Psychology* 19:694–702.

Gilligan, C. 1982. *In a different voice: Psychological theory and women's development.* Cambridge, Mass.: Harvard University Press.

Gleason, J.B., and Greif, E.B. 1983. Men's speech to young children. In B. Thorne, C. Kramarae, and N. Henley, eds., *Language, gender and society.* Rowley, Mass.: Newbury House.

Gleser, G.C.; Gottschalk, L.A.; and Watkins, J. 1959. The relationship of sex and intelligence to choice of words: A normative study of verbal behavior. *Journal of Clinical Psychology* 15:182–191.

Glixman, A.F. 1965. Categorizing behavior as a function of meaning domain. *Journal of Personality and Social Psychology* 2:370–377.

Greif, E.B. 1980. Sex differences in parent-child conversations. *Women's Studies International Quarterly* 3:253–258.

Guilford, J.P. 1967. *The nature of human intelligence.* New York: McGraw-Hill.

Gutmann, D. 1970. Female ego styles and generational conflict. In J.M. Bardwick, E. Douvan, M.S. Horner, and D. Gutmann, eds., *Feminine personality and conflict.* Monterey, Calif.: Brooks/Cole.

Haas, A. 1979. Male and female spoken language differences: Stereotypes and evidence. *Psychological Bulletin* 86:616–626.

Hall, J.A. 1978. Gender effects in decoding nonverbal cues. *Psychological Bulletin* 85: 845–857.

Hartman, M. 1976. A descriptive study of the language of men and women born in Maine around 1900 as it reflects the Lakoff Hypothesis in "Language and Women's Place." In B.L. Dubois and Z. Crouch, eds., *The sociology of the language of American women.* San Antonio: Trinity University.

Haslett, B.J. 1983. Communicative functions and strategies in children's conversations. *Human Communication Research* 9:114–129.

Higgins, E.T., and King, G. 1981. Accessibility of social constructs: Information-processing consequences of individual and contextual variability. In E.T. Higgins and G. King, eds., *Personality, cognition, and social interaction.* Hillsdale, N.J.: Erlbaum.

Hull, F.M.; Mielke, P.W.; Timmons, R.J.; and Willeford, J.A. 1971. The national speech and hearing survey: Preliminary results. *ASHA* 13:501–509.

Huston, A.C. 1983. Sex-typing. In P.H. Mussen, ed., *Handbook of child psychology,* vol. 4, 4th ed. New York: Wiley.

Instone, D.; Major, B.; and Bunker, B.B. 1983. Gender, self confidence, and social influence strategies: An organizational simulation. *Journal of Personality and Social Psychology* 44:322–333.

Janeway, E. 1980. *Powers of the weak.* New York: Alfred A. Knopf.

Johnson, J.E.; Ershler, J.; and Bell, C. 1980. Play behavior in a discovery-based and a formal-education preschool program. *Child Development* 51:271–274.

Johnson, J.E., and Roopnarine, J.L. 1983. The preschool classroom and sex differences in children's play. In M.B. Liss, ed., *Social and cognitive skills: Sex roles and children's play.* New York: Academic Press.

Jung, C.G. 1963. *The collected works of C.G. Jung,* vol. 14. Bollingen Series XX. New York: Pantheon Books.

Kagan, J., and Lewis, M. 1965. Studies of attention in the human infant. *Merrill-Palmer Quarterly* 11:95–127.

Kogan, N. 1976. *Cognitive styles in infancy and early childhood.* Hillsdale, N.J.: Erlbaum.

Kogan, N., and Wallach, M.A. 1964. *Risk taking: A study in cognition and personality.* New York: Holt, Rinehart & Winston.

Lenney, E. 1981. What's fine for the gander isn't always good for the goose: Sex differences in self-confidence as a function of ability area and comparison with others. *Sex Roles* 7:905–923.

———. 1977. Women's self-confidence in achievement settings. *Psychological Bulletin* 84:1–13.

Lenney, E.; Browning, C.; and Mitchell, L. 1980. What you don't know can hurt you: The effects of performance criteria ambiguity on sex differences in self-confidence. *Journal of Personality* 48:306–321.

Lenney, E.; Gold, J.; and Browning, C. 1983. Sex differences in self-confidence: The influence of comparison to others' ability level. *Sex Roles* 9:925–942.

Lewis, M., and Weinraub, M. 1974. Sex of parent sex of child: Socioemotional development. In R.C. Friedman, R.M. Richart, and R.L. Van de Wiele, eds., *Sex differences in behavior.* New York: Wiley.

Liss, M.B. 1981. Patterns of toy play: An analysis of sex differences. *Sex Roles* 7: 1143–1150.

Maccoby, E.E., and Jacklin, C.N. 1974. *The psychology of sex differences.* Stanford: Stanford University Press.

McGuinness, D. 1976. Sex differences in the organization of perception and cognition. In B. Lloyd and J. Archer, eds., *Exploring sex differences.* London: Academic Press.

McLoyd, V.C. 1980. Verbally expressed modes of transformation in fantasy play of black preschool children. *Child Development* 51:1133–1139.

Markus, H. 1977. Self-schemata and processing information about the self. *Journal of Personality and Social Psychology* 35:63–78.

Meece, J.L.; Parsons, J.E.; Kaczala, C.M.; Goff, S.B.; and Futterman, R. 1982. Sex differences in math achievement: Toward a model of academic choice, *Psychological Bulletin* 91:324–348.

Merritt, J.E. 1978. The bases of fluent reading. In B.M. Foss, ed., *Psychology survey,* no. 1. London: George Allen & Unwin.

Meyers-Levy, J. 1985. Gender differences in information processing: A selectivity interpretation. Ph.D. dissertation, Northwestern University.

Mischel, W. 1981. Personality and cognition: Something borrowed, something new? In N. Cantor and J.F. Kihlstrom, *Personality, cognition, and social interaction.* Hillsdale, N.J.: Erlbaum.

Munroe, R.L., and Munroe, R.H. 1971. Effect of environmental experience on spatial ability in East African society. *Journal of Social Pscyhology* 83:15–22.

Nash, S.C. 1975. The relationship among sex-role stereotyping, sex-role preference, and the sex-difference in spatial visualization. *Sex Roles* 1:15–32.

Newson, J., and Newson, E. 1976. *Seven years old in the home environment.* London: Allen and Unwin.

Nowaczyk, R.H. 1982. Sex-related differences in the color lexicon. *Language and Speech* 25:257–265.

Penelope (Stanley), J., and Wolfe, S.J. 1983. Consciousness as style; Style as aesthetic. In B. Thorne, C. Kramarae, and N. Henley, eds., *Language, gender and society.* Rowley, Mass.: Newbury House.

Pettigrew, T.F. 1958. The measurement and correlates of category width as a cognitive variable. *Journal of Personality* 26:532–544.

Poole, M.E. 1977. Social class and sex contrasts in patterns of cognitive style. *Australian Journal of Education* 21:233–255.

———. 1982. Social class-sex contrasts in patterns of cognitive style: A cross-cultural replication. *Psychological Reports* 50:19–26.

Reeves, J.B., and Boyette, N. 1983. What does children's art work tell us about gender? *Qualitative Sociology* 6:322–333.

Restak, R.M. 1979. *The brain: The last frontier.* Garden City, N.Y.: Doubleday.

Rogers, T.B.; Kuiper, N.A.; and Kirker, W.S. 1977. Self-reference and the encoding of personal information. *Journal of Personality and Social Psychology* 35:677–688.

Rosenthal, R., and DePaulo, B.M. 1979. Sex differences in accommodation in nonverbal communication. In R. Rosenthal, ed., *Skill in nonverbal communication: Individual differences.* Cambridge, Mass.: Oelgeschlager, Gunn & Hain.

Rubin, K.H.; Watson, K.; and Jambor, T.W. 1978. Free-play behaviors in preschool and kindergarten children. *Child Development* 49:534–536.

Serbin, L.A., and Connor, J.M. 1979. Sex-typing of children's play preferences and patterns of cognitive performance. *Journal of Genetic Psychology* 134:315–316.

Serbin, L.A.; Sprafkin, C.; Elman, M.; and Doyle, A.B. 1982. The early development of sex-differentiated patterns of social influence. *Canadian Journal of Behavioral Science* 14:350–363.

Sherman, J.A. 1967. Problem of sex differences in space perception and aspects of intellectual functioning. *Psychological Review* 74:290–299.

Siegman, A.W., and Reynolds, M.A. 1983. Effects of mutual invisibility and topical intimacy on verbal fluency in dyadic communication. *Journal of Psycholinguistic Research* 12:443–455.

Silverman, J. 1970. Attentional styles and the study of sex differences. In D.I. Mostofsky, ed., *Attention: Contemporary theory and analysis.* New York: Appleton-Century-Crofts.

Smith, D.E. 1980. A sociology for women. In J. Sherman and E. Beck, eds., *The prism of sex.* Madison: University of Wisconsin Press.

Smith, M.E. 1935. A study of some factors influencing the development of the sentence in preschool children. *Journal of Genetic Psychology* 46:182–212.

Stericker, A., and LeVesconte, S. 1982. Effect of brief training on sex-related differences in visual-spatial skill. *Journal of Personality and Social Psychology* 43:1018–1029.

Stewart, V. 1976. Social influences on sex differences in behavior. In M.S. Teitelbaum, ed., *Sex differences: Social and biological perspectives.* Garden City, N.Y.: Anchor Press, Doubleday.

Taylor, S.E., and Fiske, S.T. 1978. Salience, attention, and attribution: Top of the head phenomena. In L. Berkowitz, ed., *Advances in Experimental Social Psychology.* New York: Academic Press.

Thorne, B.; Kramarae, C.; and Henley, N. 1983. Language, gender, and society: Opening a second decade of research. In B. Thorne, C. Kramarae, and N. Henley, eds., *Language, gender and society.* Rowley, Mass.: Newbury House, 1983.

Thorndyke, P.W. 1977. Cognitive structures in comprehension and memory of narrative discourse. *Cognitive Psychology* 9:77–110.

Tversky, A., and Kahneman, D. 1973. Availability: A heuristic for judging frequency and probability. *Cognitive Psychology* 5:207–232.

———. 1974. Judgment under uncertainty: Heuristics and biases. *Science* 15:1124–1131.

Tyler, L. 1965. *The psychology of human differences.* 3d ed. New York: Appleton-Century-Crofts.

Wallach, M.A., and Caron, A.J. 1959. Attribute criteriality and sex-linked conservatism as determinants of psychological similarity. *Journal of Abnormal and Social Psychology* 59:43–50.

Wickes, F.G. 1963. *The inner world of choice.* New York: Harper & Row.

Witkin, H.A.; Oltman, P.K.; Raskin, E.; and Karp, S.A. 1971. *Manual for the embedded figures tests.* Palo Alto, Calif.: Consulting Psychologists Press.

Wood, M.M. 1966. The influence of sex and knowledge of communication effectiveness on spontaneous speech. *Word* 22:112–137.

Part IV
Affective Processing Issues

11
Nature of Effects of Affect on Judgment: Theoretical and Methodological Issues

Guliz Ger

There has been a growing interest in "emotional" advertisements and the effect of "ad affect" on consumer preferences. An advertisement usually communicates a message by surrounding the central information with other stimuli, such as pleasant pictures, humor, or music. These contextual factors are in some way paired with the product presentation in an attempt to create an immediate and temporary affective state or mood. Recent research suggests that a positive mood created by the context in the ad can lead to positive sentiments about the brand advertised (Allen and Madden 1983, 1984; Gorn 1982; Lutz, MacKenzie and Belch 1983; Mitchell and Olson 1981). However, the nature of this effect—how and when the affective context of a commercial will influence the response to the critical message—is not well understood. A theoretical framework is needed to illuminate why and how affective states influence responses and, hence, provide useful management implications.

Any discussion of this topic requires an operational definition. Based on prior approaches (Kleinginna and Kleinginna 1981; Mandler 1982; Simon 1979, 1982; Isen 1984), this chapter defines mood as an immediate, subtle affective state. *Affect* is the generic term. Milder feeling states or mood, which do not noticeably interrupt ongoing thought processes (Simon 1982), can be distinguished from other types of affect such as stronger emotion (Isen 1984). Here, however, the terms *affect, feeling,* and *emotion* will be used interchangeably to refer to mood.

This chapter discusses major theoretical views on affective processes and implications of these views for types of mood effects. It also offers an interpretation and an illustration of how affect influences judgment. The various types of effects that feelings have been found to have on judgment are highlighted, and central issues and empirical problems in the study of this topic are examined. Finally, management implications for advertisers are presented.

Theoretical Issues

To investigate the role of affective states on judgment, two questions need to be addressed: How are feeling states represented? and What is the process by which affect influences judgment? Some theoretical views have emerged in recent years concerning these questions.

Common Processes versus Functional Independence Views

The common processes view assumes that emotion and cognitions are represented in memory in a similar manner (Bower 1981; Clark and Isen 1982). Bower and Cohen (1982, p. 307) argue that "parsimony recommends the idea that emotional reactions to experiences should be stored along with nonemotional features in the same memory medium, according to the same storage principles, and retrieved by the same principles." Here the two systems are intertwined and interact: affect can cue related information; information can be recalled along with associated affect.

The question remains, however, how affect cues related cognitions. To answer this question, we need a construct of memory itself.

There are several models of memory storage and retrieval applicable to the common process view. One model, spreading activation in an associated network (Collins and Quillian 1969; Collins and Loftus 1975; Anderson 1983), is chosen and elaborated on here because of its empirical validation and its ability to provide specific, testable predictions.

According to the network model of memory, concepts are interconnected by associations. The associative network is a large connection of nodes, which are independent units. For example, a "wine" node may be linked to other nodes such as "beer," "cheese," "a dinner party," and "dryness." The spreading activation from an activated concept node to other nodes connected to it in the associative network makes particular portions of the network selectively accessible for recall. When a concept is attended to, a node is stimulated. Activation spreads out in a decreasing gradient along portions of the network associated with that node (Collins and Loftus 1975; Anderson and Bower 1973). For example, activation from the "wine" node is more likely and quicker to spread to nodes closely linked with it, such as "beer" and "cheese," than to nodes less associated with it, such as "cola."

Evidence indicates that affect can also initiate activation. Support for this view was obtained by Isen when subjects who were feeling good after receiving a small gift rated the performance of the products they owned more favorably than control subjects who received no gift (Isen et al. 1978). Further evidence that affect can stimulate activation is offered by a study in which recall was better when learning and testing occurred under the same emotional state versus under different states (Bower 1981). Bower suggests that an emotion becomes associated with coincident events, provides a differentiating context for learning, and can later act as a retrieval cue. He argues that the summation of activation from both the cognitive or concept node and the emotion node leads to better recall than when only the cognitive node is activated. Although there is experimental support for the notion that affect is represented like cognitive structures, there is no direct support for the hypothesis that activation from an affect node spreads in a decreasing gradient.

Functional independence is a second way to view memory. According to this view, affective and cognitive systems are represented differently, and affective states may be independent of cognitions (Zajonc 1980). This approach is consistent with the somatic view of emotions whereby discretely different patterns of neurophysiological activity, independent of cognitive appraisal, are capable of generating emotions (Izard 1982; Leventhal 1979; Zajonc, Pietromonaco and Bargh 1982). This view is concerned more with somatic expression of emotion and suggests that emotion is an experience with immediate meaning for the person.

Wilson (1979) reports findings consistent with functional independence. He finds that with recognition reduced to chance level by a shadowing task, differential affective reaction to stimuli is obtained as a consequence of mere repeated exposure. Specifically, melodies presented five times were liked better than melodies heard for the first time, though subjects could not discriminate the former from the latter on the basis of familiarity. However, it should be noted that a compelling explanation for why exposure increases preferences has not been provided: "We have never been sure why exposure has positive effects" (Zajonc and Marcus 1982, p. 125).

In sum, the common process view argues that affect and cognition involve the same system and are interdependent; the spreading activation hypothesis specifies how they interact. The functional independence view argues the opposite: that affect and cognition are separate and independent systems. The relative validity of each model is important, for each makes different predictions regarding the degree to which affect influences judgment.

Types of Mood Effects

The notion of spreading activation hypothesized by the common process view would predict that the amount of influence affect has on a particular judgment would depend on how closely the object of that judgment is related or similar to the mood-inducing event or object. Johnson and Tversky (1983) call this the "specific" effect whereby only responses to a subset of objects related to the mood-inducing object are influenced. Specific effects may occur in two forms: local and gradient.

A local effect occurs when only the judgment about the focal object or event, which is directly related to or matches the cause of mood, is influenced. For example, mood might affect the preferences for the specific product advertised in commercial but not the preference for other products in the same general category or for related types of products.

A gradient effect occurs when judgments about a set of objects or events are influenced according to the degree of association between these objects and the focal (advertised) one. Activation from the affect node, spreading in a decreasing gradient along the network of object nodes, implies that judgments about objects closely related to the cause of the mood are more likely to be influenced than judgments about less closely related objects. For example, gradient effects would occur when an affective commercial also influences preferences for other products (such as substitutes) or brands (such as other brands in the same product category) related to the one advertised. Both local and gradient effect, as argued by Johnson and Tversky (1983), are consistent with the spreading activation hypothesis.

On the other hand, the functional independence view predicts that affect's influence on judgment would be independent of the association between the mood-inducing event and the judgment (as do Johnson and Tversky 1983) because the cognitive and affective systems are independent. This is called the global effect, whereby mood affects judgments about any or all objects, related and unrelated to the focal (mood-inducing) object. For example, evaluations of a wide variety of products would be influenced by an affective commercial about a particular product regardless of how closely these products are associated with the advertised product (Johnson and Tversky 1983).

At first glance, one may agree with Johnson and Tversky's (1983) argument that the functional independence view predicts global effects, whereas the common processes view with the spreading activation mechanism predicts specific effects (local and/or gradient). However, on closer look, the predictions of the spreading activation hypothesis seem to vary slightly. Anderson (1983) suggests that specific as well as global mood effects may be expected depending on the activated portion of the network of associations.

A Conceptualization and an Illustration

Anderson (1983) has extended the associative network model. Although he continues to argue that spreading activation defines working memory, with activation flowing from a source and inducing levels of activation throughout the associative network, he hypothesizes that spreading activation identifies and favors the processing of information most related to the immediate context or sources of activation. Various nodes or elements can become sources of activation with sources selected chiefly for two reasons. First, an element that encodes an environmental stimulus will become a source. Second, a "production'' (if-then) procedure can select a ''goal'' element in a structure in working memory, and goal elements can also become sources of activation. Thus a goal element central to performing a currently important task serves as a source of activation. In an experimental context, the instructions given to subjects define their mutual goal.

During processing of a stimulus, refocusing—identification of a relevant subnode of a structure and focusing activation on it—may occur. Goal element and other contextual information or cues may refocus activation on a number of elements such as superordinate nodes or specific subnodes. Thus in an experiment, subjects may create a subnode and use contextual associations to focus on it. Activation spreads in a subnet of the intersection of all the source nodes. Sources of activation need to be focused to be maintained actively in working memory (Anderson 1983).

The notion of goal and contextual cues as sources of activation, as well as the mechanism of refocusing on subnodes, enable Anderson's ACT* model to activate selectively almost any portion of the network. This is a major departure from the continuous activation proposed by earlier models. (See chapter 12 for a more elaborate ACT* example.)

An illustration of how any portion of the network of information about beverages can be activated may be helpful. A familiar concept may have a subnode hierarchy structure that can be used to focus the retrieval process on a relatively small subset of facts known about that concept. For example, the concept ''beverages'' may be conceived of as a general category with many subnodes, such as alcoholic, nonalcoholic, and hot, organized as a hierarchy. If the goal is to evaluate beverages, then the set of all events and objects linked to the ''beverages'' node is activated. Thoughts about various beverages and instances where a beverage was consumed will be activated in the working memory. If the goal shifts to evaluating a particular beverage such as wine, activation refocuses on the wine subnode. When this occurs, the relatively small subset of nodes associated with that object will be retrieved, and wine thoughts will be in the working memory. Thus activation can spread to various different portions of the network associated with the source nodes (beverage or wine).

Affect, similar to other elements, acts as a source of activation and biases availability by spreading activation. It functions as a search cue to be used in the absence of other strong cues (Bower 1981). Affect nodes are linked to cognitive nodes. Affect is viewed as a contextual element, in the sense of an activated portion of long-term memory and functions like any other contextual element to improve efficiency of thought processes. Thus effects of moods are to establish contexts that influence and direct cognitive activities. For example, moods may bias activation or focus attention on aspects of the stimulus congruent with the mood.

If a wine commercial with positive affective context is viewed, both the wine subnode and the happiness nodes may be activated. Thus portions of the network associated with each source will be in working memory. Happy instances with wine, pleasant wine information, and so on will all be cued.

When a judgment about a particular object is to be made, whether that judgment will be influenced by the affective wine commercial will depend on how related the object of judgment is with happiness and with wine. For example, not only wine but also beer or champagne nodes may be associated with the beverage node and to some degree with the feeling node. If either wine-other object (such as beer) or happiness-other object links are very weak (unrelated), blocked, or not focused on (for example, if beverage and/or beer nodes are not maintained active) and if the goal element is mainly focused on wine, a small, select portion of the network will be active. This would be expected to result in a local mood effect.

By contrast, if the goal element leads to focusing on beer, or wine-beer or happiness-beer links, the selected portion of the network that is maintained active will include wine, beer, and happiness associations. This would lead us to expect a gradient effect on beer.

Furthermore, if the goal element leads to focusing on beverage (that is, wine-beverage and happiness-beverage links are activated), reverberating activation from many subnodes is maintained, resulting in a wider portion of the network being active. This may happen if all objects of judgment in the task situation are closely linked to the affect mode, if the link between wine and beverage is maintained as active, or if beer thoughts send feedback activation to happiness and beverage nodes, which in turn influence later retrieval when the next evaluation is to be made. Then evaluations of all beverages will be influenced by the affective wine commercial producing a global mood effect. Thus, with Anderson's version of the network model, both specific and global mood effects can be explained in terms of the activated portion of the network.

This expanded common process view remains in contrast with the pervasive global effects expectation of the functional independence view. Because the different models imply different types of mood effects, their relative merit can be assessed by examining the compatibility of the models with mood effects reported in the literature.

Global Effects

Johnson and Tversky (1983) claim evidence for global effects. In a study where experimental manipulation of affect was induced by a brief story of a tragic event and measurements were taken on stimuli selected to vary in their association to the focal event, they found a pervasive increase in the respondent's estimates of frequency of risks. This effect was independent of the similarity between the story and the estimated risk such that all estimates, not necessarily those related to the mood-inducing experience, were mood congruent. For example, reading a story about a person dying as a result of homicide not only influenced estimates of deaths from homicide but also estimates of death from fires. Thus they argue that a global mood effect, independent of the strengths of association between the story and the risks, is evidence for the functional independence view and is at odds with memory-based models of affect, which assume spreading activation within an associative network.

The conceptualization developed earlier provides an alternative explanation for Johnson and Tversky's findings, however. A story about a fatal event such as homicide activates a worry-sadness node strongly linked not only to homicide but also to many other types of fatalities and negative incidences. Both the task of estimating frequencies of death from various causes and the feeling node activate many fatality nodes. Thus not only homicide but many other death thoughts such as "fire" are also available at the time of judgment, leading to the global overestimation bias.

In addition to the feeling node's acting as a source of activation, the goal element of estimating fatalities activates the set of all events linked to the superordinate "fatalities" node. Estimating frequency of deaths due to a particular event, fire, refocuses the goal element on both the fatality and fire subnodes, and elements of these structures become sources of activation. Thus frequency estimates of fire risks are biased by what is in the working memory—mood-congruent fire episodes and other fatal events, including homicide.

Furthermore, it appears that the risks to be estimated were of a limited variety. The span of risks might not have provided enough of a range of stimuli for a fair test of the spreading activation hypothesis. Finally, demand characteristics may provide an alternative explanation. If some intervention influences nontreatment as well as treatment variables, then a suspicion for demand emerges. Subjects might be responding to what they perceived to be the experimenter's hypothesis and not to the stimulus per se. Thus lack of a specific effect in this study does not necessarily imply that the impact of mood was independent of the strength of association between the story and the risks.

Local Effects

Because both the functional independence and common process views can account for global effects, evidence regarding the existence of local effects is critical in assessing the relative merit of these views. If local effects are observed, these can be accounted for only by the common process view.

Local effects have been obtained in several studies. Mitchell and Olson (1981) manipulated ad content by constructing four different ads for a hypothetical brand of facial tissues. One ad contained only a verbal product claim. Each of the other ads contained a headline and a picture, two of which were assumed to be positively evaluated, while the third was assumed to be neutral. In this study, attitude toward the ad and product attribute beliefs were found to determine brand attitudes and purchase intentions. The authors intepret their findings as suggesting that effects of advertising may be mediated by an individual's affective reactons to the ad. Other related studies (Lutz, MacKenzie, and Belch 1983; Kroeber-Riel 1984) also support the notion that when cognitive responses to the brand are statistically controlled, affective reactions to the ad account for significant amounts of variance in brand attitudes, at least in low-involvement situations (Park and Young 1983), or immediate effects (Moore and Hutchinson 1983).

These studies may, however, be a weak test of mood effects. A number of researchers note that attitude toward the ad may have many dimensions or antecedents, only one of which is pure affect or mood (Allen and Madden 1983; Lutz 1983; Shimp 1981). Furthermore, most ad affect studies have employed designs, such as one group pretest-posttest design (Mitchell and Olson 1981; Kroeber-Riel 1984), that do not afford strong causal inferences. The absence of random assignment to levels of affect or mood allows for the possibility that individual differences rather than ad affect led to the effects on the dependent measures.

Gorn's (1982) study is therefore important because he provides an experimental manipulation of the ad affect and finds support for local effects. Gorn examined how a background music feature in advertisements, affects advertising effectiveness. The affective quality of music can be argued to be a mood induction. Subjects viewed a slide of either a light blue or a beige pen while they listened to a one-minute segment of either pleasant familiar or unpleasant Indian music. The findings indicated that the color paired with pleasant music was chosen more frequently than the color paired with unpleasant music.

In a follow-up experiment, each subject viewed a musical ad and a non-musical descriptive ad for a pen. The subjects who were not informed that they would be making a pen selection decision more often chose the pen color associated with pleasant music than the color paired with descriptive ad. The subjects who were informed that they would be making a pen selection decision chose the pen color associated with the descriptive ad more often than the color paired with pleasant music. This outcome suggests that mood effects are most likely to be observed when more cognitive bases for judgment are absent.

Although Gorn provides an experimental manipulation of affect, his study also has some methodological limitations. Selection bias (due to random assignment of class sections and not individuals) and diffusion of treatments across two halves of a class who were processed sequentially are threats to internal validity. Furthermore, in the second experiment, the affect manipulation was confounded with the amount of information provided in the ad, posing a threat to construct validity. The presence of these methodological artifacts suggests that alternative hypotheses other than pairing with affect may explain the observed difference in preference.

Ger (1985) conducted an experiment designed to overcome the methodological limitations of previous studies and to explore further the reliability of the global effect reported by Johnson and Tversky (1983). She manipulated contextual affect while delivering a message about a beverage and measured both taste evaluation and milliliters consumed for the focal beverage and a number of related beverages. The beverages were chosen to be of differing degrees of similarity. Subjects listened to cheerful, irritating, or neutral music in the background of a wine commercial. This focal commercial was disguised by being presented after five other beverage commercials with neutral background music. Only the focal product, wine, showed a mood effect such that evaluation was more favorable if the ad was accompanied by cheerful rather than irritating music. No mood effect was obtained for the other beverages (beer, coffee, soda, orange juice, and grapefruit juice). These results suggest a local effect of the affective experience on product evaluations.

This same study also showed an unexpected effect on behavior. The negative mood (induced by the unpleasant music) led to more consumption of wine than the positive mood. As was the case for product evaluations, this effect was local; it was observed only for wine and not for other beverages. Although no strong inferences about this effect are possible, it may be that subjects' increased wine consumption was an effort to offset this negative mood.

A second experiment (Ger 1986) also obtained evidence consistent with a localized effect. Affect induced by a scare story about a particular beverage varied in its impact on product evaluations. The story produced a decrease in the evaluation of the beverage in the story and an increase in the evaluation of two other beverages in the same subcategory but did not impact evaluations of twenty other products, some of which were beverages in other subcategories and some of which were nonbeverage products.

Future Research

The finding that mood effects are not always global is consistent with the view that affect and cognition are interdependent but at odds with the functional independence view. Although the common process view provides a better explanation of mood effects than functional independence, some troubling issues remain. Some of Ger's findings were unanticipated and not readily accounted for by the common process view. Further, gradient effects that would seem to be central to the spreading activation mechanism argued to underlie the common process have yet to be observed. Additional tests are needed to examine whether gradient effects can be obtained and to test further the current intepretation of the spreading activation mechanism. To prevent circularity, the conditions under which each type of effect will be obtained must be specified. The previous discussion points to some conditions that may lead to one or the other type of effect. Sources of activation, refocusing, goal elements, and knowledge structures can be manipulated to create these conditions.

The difficulties encountered in testing for specific versus global mood effects suggest that a new research paradigm is needed to undertake this investigation. Assessment or manipulation of the knowledge structure is necessary. A priori knowledge of all stimuli that act as sources of activation, the content of the associative memory, and the associations or similarities among nodes in a given experimental context is needed. This may become fairly difficult because similarity depends on the context and frame of reference (Tversky 1977). If the content of memory is not known or manipulated, measurement may not detect spread from a feeling node to the links because the links may be very different across subjects. Future research should also note methodological artifacts and the difficulty of calibration of affect induction in previous work.

Implications for Advertisers

An improved understanding of this phenomenon can be used to design effective advertising strategies. The present conceptualization and findings have important implications for practical applications:

1. Affective context of a commercial or emotion in advertising: The critical issue for advertisers is not whether to have emotional advertising but what kind of effect it has. The interdependency between affect and cognitions suggests that advertisers must examine emotion as a part of the whole commercial and as it interacts with other stimuli because it is the interaction that will have an impact on consumer preferences. The questions should address how affect and cognition should be combined in a commercial and what affective features will strengthen and support the cognitions about the brand. If feeling and cognition as a whole makes available more positive brand thoughts than cognition alone, then feeling should be included in the commercial. If, on the other hand, there are very strong cognitive cues, feeling cues may not be necessary to lead to positive brand thoughts. In the latter case, inclusion of affective context will either not make a difference or possibly hurt the message because of information overload.
2. Primary versus selective demand stimulation: If the purpose of an ad is to stimulate demand for brand A rather than for the product category,

advertisers must pay attention to the possibility that positive affect associated with brand A may spread to brand B, especially if A and B are closely related (this is the result of gradient cuing).

3. Ad placement: Affect created by a prior program segment or a prior commercial may influence the interpretation of the focal ad and thus evaluations of the focal product.
4. Comparative advertising: A comparative ad may be effective to the extent that the negative affect created around the rival brand is prevented from spreading to the focal brand.
5. Product scares: A product scare, such as the Tylenol incident or the salmonella outbreak in Chicago caused by bacteria in the Hillfarm milk produced in Jewel dairies and sold in Jewel supermarkets, may affect not only that brand but may spread to other brands (the gradient effect) such as Anacin or White Hen Pantry milk, respectively (White Hen Pantry is another grocery store in the same locality as Jewel and used to be owned by Jewel). To avoid this effect, Anacin or White Hen Pantry might advertise to prevent the spread of negative affect to their own product. Information could be provided to inhibit the link between the attribute linked with the scare and the brand. For example, during the salmonella incident, customers were apparently worried because they remembered that Jewel used to own White Hen Pantry. Noticing this, White Hen Pantry put up a sign stating their lack of affiliation with Jewel or the Jewel dairy.

References

Allen, C.T., and T.J. Madden. 1983. "Examining the Link between Attitude Towards an Ad and Brand Attitude: A Classical Conditioning Approach." Working paper.

———. 1984. "A Closer Look at Classical Conditioning." Working paper.

Anderson, J., and G. Bower. 1973. *Human Associative Memory*. Washington, D.C.: Winston.

Anderson, J.R. 1983. *The Architecture of Cognition.* Cambridge, Mass.: Harvard University Press.

Bower, G.H. 1981. "Mood and Memory." *American Psychologist* 36:129–148.

Bower, G.H., and P.R. Cohen. 1982. "Emotional Influences in Memory and Thinking: Data and Theory." In M.S. Clark and S.T. Fiske, eds., *Affect and Cognition: Seventeenth Annual Carnegie Symposium on Cognition,* Hillsdale, N.J.: Erlbaum.

Clark, M.S., and A.M. Isen. 1982. "Toward Understanding the Relationship Between Feeling States and Social Behavior." In A.H. Hastorf and A.M. Isen, eds., *Cognitive Social Psychology,* New York: Elsevier/North Holland, 73-108.

Collins, A.J., and M.R. Quillian. 1969. "Retrieval Time from Semantic Memory." *Journal of Verbal Learning and Verbal Behavior* 8:240–247.

Collins, A.J., and E.F. Loftus. 1975. "A Spreading Activation Theory of Semantic Processing." *Psychological Review* 82:407–428.

Ger, G. 1985. "Affect and Judgment." Unpublished dissertation, Northwestern University.

———. 1986. "Effects of Affect on Judgment about Products." In R.J. Lutz, ed., *Advances in Consumer Research, 13,* Provo, Utah: Association for Consumer Research.

Gorn, G.J. 1982. "The Effects of Music in Advertising on Choice Behavior: A Classical Conditioning Approach," *Journal of Marketing* 46:94–101.

Isen, A.M. 1984. "Toward Understanding the Role of Affect in Cognition." In R. Wyer and T. Srull eds., *Handbook of Social Cognition,* (pp. 179–236). Hillsdale, N.J.: Erlbaum.

Isen, A.M., Clark, T.E. Shalker, and L. Karp. 1978. "Affect, Accessibility of Material in Memory and Behavior: A Cognitive Loop?" *Journal of Personality and Social Psychology* 36:1–12.

Izard, C.E. 1982. "Comments on Emotion and Cognition: Can There Be a Working Relationship?" In M.S. Clark and S.T. Fiske, eds., *Affect and Cognition: The Seventeenth Annual Carnegie Symposium on Cognition.* Hillsdale, N.J.: Erlbaum.

Johnson, E.J., and A. Tversky. 1983. "Affect, Generalization and the Perception of Risk," *Journal of Personality and Social Psychology* 45:20–31.

Kleinginna, P.R., Jr., and A.M. Kleinginna. 1981. "A Categorized List of Emotion Definitions, with Suggestions for a Consensual Definition." *Motivation and Emotion* 5:345–379.

Kroeber-Riel, W. 1984. "Emotional Product Differentiation by Classical Conditioning," In R.P. Bagozzi and A.M. Tybout, eds., *Advances in Consumer Research* 10:11.

Leventhal, H. 1979. "A Perceptual-Motor Processing Model of Emotion." In P. Pliner, K.R. Blankstein, and I.M. Spiegel, eds., *Advances in the Study of Communication and Affect: Vol. 5, Perception of Emotion in Self and Others.* New York: Plenum Press.

Lutz, R.J. 1983. "Affective and Cognitive Antecedents of Attitude Toward the Ad: A Conceptual Framework." Working paper, College of Business Administration, University of Florida.

Lutz, R.J., S.B. MacKenzie, and G.F. Belch. 1983. "Attitude Toward the Ad as a Mediator of Advertising Effectiveness: Determinants and Consequences." In R.P. Bagozzi and A.M. Tybout, eds., *Advances in Consumer Research* 10:532–539.

Mandler, G. 1982. "The Structure of Value: Accounting for Taste," In M.S. Clark and S.T. Fiske, eds., *Affect and Cognition,* Hillsdale, N.J.: Erlbaum.

Mitchell, A.A., and J.C. Olson. 1981. "Are Product Attribute Beliefs the Only Mediator of Advertising Effects on Brand Attitude?" *Journal of Marketing Research* 18:318–332.

Moore, D.L., and J.W. Hutchinson. 1983. "The Effects of Ad Affect on Advertising Effectiveness," In R.P. Bagozzi and A.M. Tybout, eds., *Advances in Consumer Research* 10:526–531.

Park, C.W., and S.M. Young. 1983. "The Effects of Involvement and Contextual Factors on Consumer Information Processing of a TV Commercial." Working paper.

Shimp, T.A. 1981. "Attitude Toward the Ad as a Mediator of Consumer Brand Choice." *Journal of Advertising* 10:9–15.

Simon, H.A. 1979. "Motivational and Emotional Controls of Cognition (1967)," In *Models of Thoughts*, New Haven, Conn.: Yale University Press.

———. 1982. "Affect and Cognition: Comments," In M.S. Clark and S.T. Clark and S.T. Fiske, eds., *Affect and Cognition*. Hillsdale, N.J.: Erlbaum.

Wilson, W.R. 1979. "Feeling More Than We Can Know: Exposure Effect Without Learning." *Journal of Personality and Social Psychology* 37:811–821.

Zajonc, R.B. 1980. "Feeling and Thinking: Preferences Need No Inferences," *American Psychologist* 35:151–175.

Zajonc, R.B., and H. Markus. 1982. "Affective and Cognitive Factors in Preferences," *Journal of Consumer Research* 9:123–131.

Zajonc, R.B., P. Pietromonaco, and J. Bargh. 1982. "Independence and Interaction of Affect and Cognition," In M.S. Clark and S.T. Fiske, eds., *Affect and Cognition: The Seventeenth Annual Carnegie Symposium on Cognition*, Hillsdale, N.J.: Erlbaum, 221–228.

12
Emotional Advertising Appeals

Bobby J. Calder
Charles L. Gruder

Advertising such as AT&T's "Reach out and touch someone" campaign is an example of an emotional appeal. This advertising seeks to influence consumers indirectly. Rather than trying to persuade the consumer that product features are good, emotional appeals attempt, in essence, to make the consumer feel good about the product. They create a favorable mood or image that surrounds the product. And it is this mood or image that is expected to sell the product, not the product's features per se. The spirit of emotional advertising appeals is captured well in the following description:

> Mood/image/emotional appeal advertising makes no direct product pitch. It's characterized by memorable visuals, "feeling," surrealistic effects, little copy and, quite frequently, dramatic music with catchy lyrics. It's often called cinematic or "Broadway" advertising and, lately, many mood efforts have been re-named "product videos." (McCollum Spielman 1985)

Although emotional appeals can take many forms, they clearly represent a distinct style of advertising. This style can be contrasted with not only straight product feature ads but also with slice-of-life ads emphasizing people using the product (persuasion through peer influence) and with celebrity ads (persuasion through credibility).

Unlike other creative styles, it is not immediately clear, even in principle, how emotional appeals are supposed to work. To say that such appeals persuade by creating a mood or image that surrounds the product is tautological. It is merely descriptive of emotional appeals. Why should mood or image matter? Other questions are begged too. Why, for instance, are some emotional appeals persuasive while others are not? There is a need to explain how emotional appeals work. And to be useful, this explanation ideally should provide guidance as to how appeals that do work can be created.

Network Theory and Emotional Appeals

The effect of emotional appeals can be explained with a network model of human information processing. The basic unit of thought in a network model is the proposition, defined as an associative connection between two concepts, where concepts are defined by and acquire meaning from these connections. The meaning of concepts is not specified by words. They are abstract nodes in the cognitive network that are associated (linked, connected) with other nodes.

This can best be understood with an illustration. Consider the concept <Mother> for a young child and the network fragment shown in figure 12–1. At an early age, the child comes to associate <Mother> with the concepts <Food> and <Affection>. The child's thinking is characterized by propositions such as "Mother gives food." What <Mother> means to the child comes from the concept's place in the abstract network. Words are themselves only associations to the concept. Concepts are inherently nonlinguistic. Associations determine meaning.

As a child grows older, the meaning of <Mother> changes. Network theory describes this as a process of cognitive elaboration. New concepts and new associations are formed. <Mother> becomes associated with an increasing number of other concepts (figure 12–2). The propositional belief "Mother says I have to clear my place" is but one specific association; however, it is this and other associations that determine the meaning of <Mother>. Elaboration can make concepts more or less positive. No matter how positive <Mother> is for the older child, the concept has to be less positive than for the younger child.

Also essential to network theory explanations are the notions of activation and limited capacity. For a concept, or network node, to reach conscious awareness (be processed at a point in time), it must be activated beyond some threshold level. Activation may occur in one of three ways: through similarity to an attended stimulus, through spreading activation through another mode, or through the use of stored rules.

Most basically, activation depends on the stimuli confronting a person at any given point. If a stimulus attended to is similar enough to a concept to be associated with it, this association activates the concept. There is some theorizing to suggest that it may also be necessary for the concept to have some prior level of activation in order for stimulus activation to exceed the threshold level.

Once a concept is activated, a process of spreading activation occurs. Activation spreads from one concept to another along associative connections (much like propagation along an electrical network). The degree of spreading depends on the amount of activation, the strength and number of the associative connections, and the distance of a concept from the source of the activation.

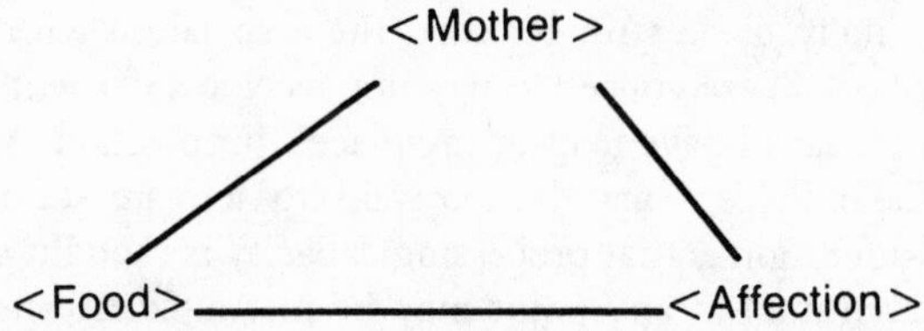

Figure 12-1. Network Fragment (1)

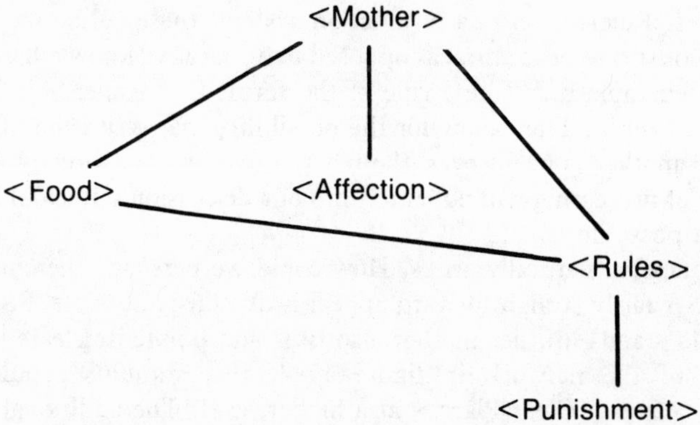

Figure 12-2. Network Fragment (2)

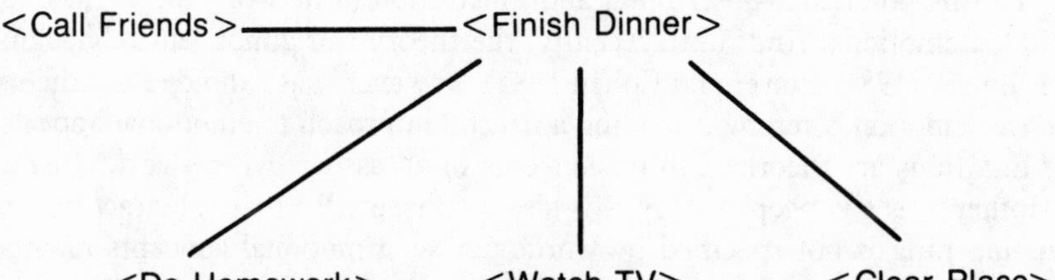

Figure 12-3. Network Fragment (3)

The basic principles of spreading activation can be illustrated as follows. Suppose that our older child is eating at the kitchen table. Will she think to clear her place? Assume that the network of associations is as shown in figure 12-3. Activation of the concept <Finish Dinner> should spread to associated concepts. But there are several associations to finishing dinner, and, of these, several are quite likely to be stronger than the association with <Mother> and <Clear Place>. These concepts may not receive sufficient activation to trigger the "Mother says I have to clear my place" proposition. Moreover, the activation of <Clear Place> may be too weak to activate <Punishment>.

Another consideration is that processing capacity is thought to be limited. The extent of elaboration at any point may be restricted because capacity is limited. Elaboration will not proceed beyond the capacity allocated to the processing. This is sometimes referred to as attention. The child may not think to clear her place because attention to <Finish Dinner> is limited.

Current theory also holds that activation can occur through the use of stored rules. Referred to as a production system, these rules take an if-then form and constitute procedural as opposed to declarative knowledge in the network. An example might be a rule of the form: If <Anger> is high, then decrease <Fear>. They allow for the possibility that activation of a concept can affect another concept even though the two are not directly associated. (This sort of processing will not enter into our discussion but should be recognized as a possibility.)

The question naturally arises, How could we persuade the child to clear her place? A fairly straightforward appeal is obviously possible. Suppose that as the child stands up, her mother also rises and pointedly clears her throat. In terms of the network in figure 12–4, this stimulus should activate <Mother> and <Clear Place> at a higher level. The additional activation would cause increased activation of the key associations, perhaps even spreading to the punishment node. The child should think to clear her place.

Network theory thus provides an explanation for how straightforward cognitive appeals work. Let us now see how emotional appeals might work.

To this point, our description and illustration of network theory has not included emotions. And, until recently, the theory was almost entirely cognitive. Bower (1981; Bower and Cohen 1982), however, has extended the theory to cover emotion, thereby providing a fruitful approach to emotional appeals.

Emotions are theorized to be concepts in an associative network. Just as <Mother> is a concept, <Joy> is also a concept. Both are abstract nodes; their meaning is not specified by words per se. Emotional concepts may be associated with cognitive concepts and with other emotional concepts.

Network theory, extended to treat emotions as concepts capable of being associated with other concepts, provides a simple yet elegant way of explaining emotional appeals. Again an illustration may be useful. Suppose father wants to influence our child to clear her place. (A command might be effective but could itself activate concepts other than the ones desired.) Thus the father might decide on an emotional appeal, perhaps remarking at the end of dinner, "Your mother tells me she found a great present today for your birthday next week." The father's message is a pure emotional appeal in the sense of the advertising alluded to earlier. It simply juxtaposes a mood, joy, with finishing

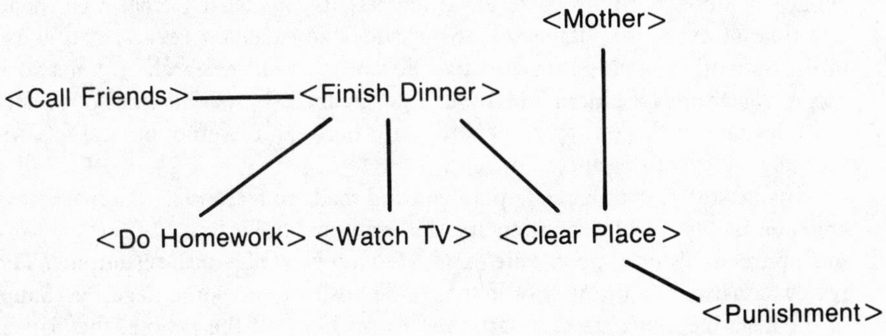

Figure 12–4. Network Fragment (4)

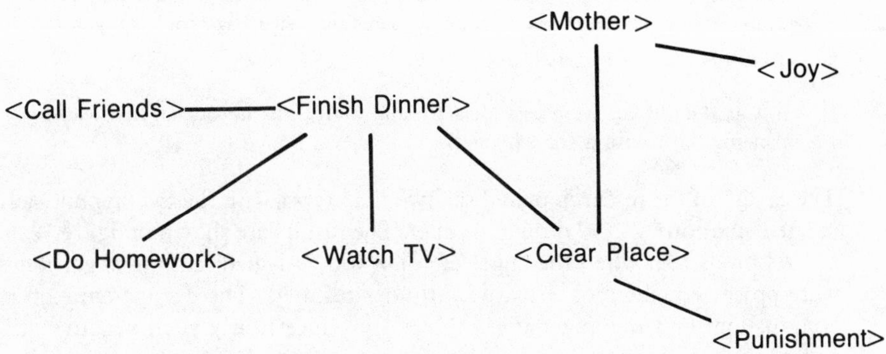

Figure 12–5. Network Fragment (5)

dinner. Moreover, it does not even mention the object of the influence attempt: clearing her place.

Consider the network now with the addition of the <Joy> node associated with Mother (figure 12–5). Activation will flow from <Joy> as well as <Finish Dinner>. This increased activation could be sufficient to raise <Clear Place> above threshold level and even to activate <Punishment>. The emotional appeal has operated by affecting the spread of activation in the same way as the more cognitive appeal.

Relevant Research

There is considerable research evidence for network theory as we have illustrated it. The best evidence is a stream of research demonstrating mood congruence effects in which recall of material is affected by emotional mood at a time of exposure. Blaney (1986) provides an excellent review of this use of the network model. More directly relevant is recent research on a network model of attitudes (Calder and Gruder 1986), which shows that emotions affect attitudes only if there is an associative path between the emotion and an attitudinally relevant cognitive concept.

In one study, people are hypnotized and made to feel the emotion of either anger or disgust. While experiencing this emotion, and ostensibly participating in an unrelated study, people are exposed to a review of a local restaurant. The review consists of a number of items, some positive and some negative. Some of the negative items are of a particular form. For half the people, the critical negative items involve concepts associated with anger. The other half receive items that are associated with disgust. Two examples are:

> Our table was located so that every time the kitchen door opened, we had a clear view of the dishwasher scraping plates into a garbage can. [Disgust]
>
> or
>
> Just as the entrees were served, a passing waiter hit the side of my head a glancing blow with a tray. [Anger]

The design of the research paired the two item types with the two hypnotically created emotions (2 × 2 design, 4 cells). The results are shown in figure 12-6.

As predicted, when the anger emotion was activated and the anger items were processed, the most negative attitudes resulted. The disgust emotion in conjunction with the anger items did not produce nearly such negative attitudes, though disgust is a negative emotion. Attitudes were more negative when the disgust emotion and the disgust items were paired. (This pairing did not have as extreme an effect, interpreted in subsequent research to reflect the activation of one emotion by another—in this case, disgust being associated with anger). These effects were obtained even though people were not in the emotional mood when their attitudes toward the restaurant were assessed.

This evidence for a network theory of attitudes is obviously congenial with our analysis of emotional appeals. Emotions enter into attitudes by affecting those cognitive concepts to which the emotions are associatively linked. These concepts in turn are activated at a higher level and have more influence on attitude than they would otherwise.

A Demonstration Study

To test our analysis of emotional appeals, a study was conducted using a simulated radio commercial. Women were asked to evaluate a product, Crystalford China, based on a "rough, unfinished" radio commercial. The

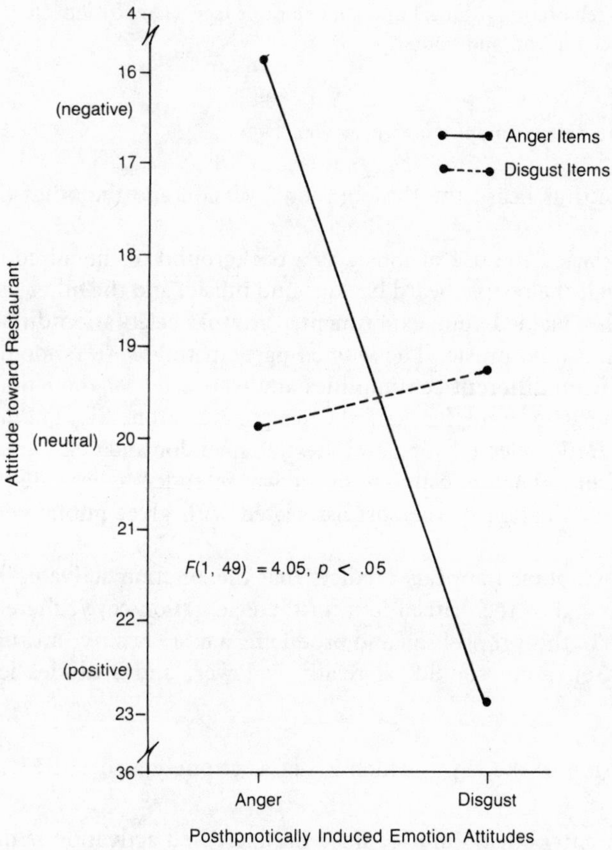

Source: Calder and Gruder 1986.

Figure 12–6. Attitude Effects

rationale of evaluating an ad in rough form was plausible, and consumers did not suspect that the product was fictitious.

Two versions of the ad copy were used. One group received the message with the first alternatives; a separate group received the second alternatives (in brackets):

> Introducing Crystalford China—A tradition in Europe, now available in America.
>
> Crystalford is the ultimate in prestige and elegance.
>
> For over 100 years, it has been created by the finest European craftsmen.

> It transforms any celebration [dinner] into a memorable [special] occasion, fit for royalty [perfect for you and yours].
>
> The perfect gift.
>
> On display at better department stores near you.

One group of people thus heard the "celebration" version and the other the "dinner" version.

The study also varied the use of music as a background to the ad copy. For both versions, half the people heard background music, and the other half heard no music. This yielded four experimental groups: celebration/dinner copy crossed with music/no music. The women participating were randomly selected consumers from different communities and were paid for their time. The music used as background for half the people was from Sir Thomas Beecham's *Love in Bath,* selected for its orchestral splendor and regal tone, connoting a grand event. Theoretically the music was intended to activate the emotion of joyous anticipation of the sort associated with great public celebrations.

Our analysis of emotional appeals predicts that the emotion activated by the music should spread to the critical item in the celebration copy, thereby increasing activation of this proposition and producing a more positive attitude toward the china. Activation should be relatively lower, and attitudes less positive, with:

1. The dinner version of the copy, which is not as strongly associated with the music.
2. The celebration copy but no music, since the increased activation is due to the music.
3. The dinner copy and no music, since the dinner copy possesses the same activation as the celebration copy in the absence of the music.

After listening to the commercial, those in the study participated in a two-hour discussion on an unrelated topic. This interpolated task was intended to remove any emotion created by the music. In fact, people's moods, self-measured on an adjective checklist of emotional state, were not significantly different across the four groups after the discussion. Following discussion people were asked to rate the china on a 0 to 10 scale, with 0 meaning the china was not at all good and 10 meaning it was extremely good.

The results of the study are shown in table 12–1. As predicted, attitudes toward the china were more positive in the case of the celebration copy and the musically created emotion ($F[1,58] = 4.25$, $p < .05$ for the interaction effect). The emotional appeal was successful when it could be associated with a relevant cognitive concept.

Table 12–1
Attitude Ratings

	Music	*No Music*
Celebration item	8.90	7.81
No celebration item	7.78	7.63

Implications for Emotional Appeals

In many ways, the most important implication of this analysis is that there is actually no such thing as a pure emotional appeal. Emotional ads influence people's attitudes only to the extent that the emotion becomes part of the relevant cognitive network and is associated with other concepts. It is these associations that allow the activation of the emotion to spread.

The design of emotional appeals cannot be left merely to creative notions of "cinematic," "product video," or "Broadway" effects. Rather, the message must be designed to activate specific emotions. And, in turn, these emotions must be connected with existing concepts associated with the product or concepts conveyed by the message. The critical element in the emotional appeal is the associability of the emotion, not the mere fact of emotional arousal.

References

Blaney, P.H. 1986. "Affect and Memory: A Review." *Psychological Bulletin* 99:229–246.

Bower, G.H. 1981. "Mood and Memory." *American Psychologist* 36:129–148.

Bower, G.H., and Cohen, P.R. 1982. "Emotional Influences in Memory and Thinking." In S. Fiske and M. Clark, eds., *Affect and Social Cognition*, pp. 291–331. Hillsdale, N.J.: Erlbaum.

Calder, B.J., and Gruder, C.L. 1986. "An Activation Theory of Attitudinal Affect." Unpublished manuscript.

13
What Mediates the Emotional Response to Advertising? The Case of Warmth

David A. Aaker
Douglas M. Stayman

In recent decades, considerable progress has been made in understanding how information in advertising is processed. In contrast, relatively little is known about emotional responses, clearly an important element in much of television advertising. Plummer (1985, p. 6) notes that the consumer insight that best drives advertising strategy is usually an emotional one.

Interest in modeling affect in advertising is growing (see, for example, Alwitt and Mitchell 1985; Peterson, Hoyer, and Wilson 1986) but has focused largely upon the "attitude toward the ad" (A_{ad}) construct. A_{ad} research has demonstrated that not only do overall evaluations of the ad explain variance beyond that explained by measures of cognitive structure (Mitchell and Olson 1981) but also that A_{ad} can be useful in testing between models of how affective responses to advertising affect attitudinal outcomes (MacKenzie, Lutz, and Belch 1986; Batra and Ray 1985).

Yet the A_{ad} construct is limited, in part because the same A_{ad} could result from advertisements that were informative, warm, humorous, or entertaining musically. Researchers initially attempted to go beyond global ad evaluations through study of specific evaluations of the ad. For example, Burke and Edell (1986) assessed evaluations such as whether viewers thought an ad was humorous, irritating, or tender in exploring the affect of repetition on responses and ad effects. However, evaluations can be distinguished from specific feeling responses experienced during exposure. Abelson et al. (1982) found that both negative and positive feelings acted independently from evaluations and each other in predicting voting behavior during the 1980 presidential election. Batra and Ray (1986) discuss the importance of the distinction between affect "toward" the ad as an evaluation or thought about the ad versus feelings as states of the viewer.

Subsequent research has demonstrated increasing evidence for a role of feeling responses in affecting the effectiveness of commercials independent of a possible moderating role of evaluations such as A_{ad}. For example, Stayman and Aaker (1987) found a direct relationship between feeling responses and brand attitudes independent of ad liking across different number of exposures and different types of affective executions. Edell and Burke (1986) found that feeling responses during exposure had a direct effect on attitude toward both the ad and the brand beyond the contribution of semantic judgments (evaluations) for existing products and for belief formation for new products.

The purpose of this chapter is to broaden the study of feeling response to commercials by examining its antecedents. The focus is on a single emotional response, warmth, selected because prior research provides some understanding of the construct and suggests that it is prevalent in advertising and related to effectiveness.

The approach of assessing one specific emotion was used for a number of reasons. First, advertising executions are often aimed at eliciting a particular response (such as humor, fear, or warmth). Second, focus on one feeling will, it is hoped, allow the identification of more sensitive, relevant, useful, and powerful constructs and processes than would study of a broad range of responses by allowing more exact specification of what antecedent leads to what type of response. It is hoped that a number of constructs and processes identified will be generalizable to other emotional responses. Finally, study of a single response should provide a better opportunity to explore the nature of that response—not only its antecedents but also accompanying constructs such as the different orientations for warmth responses proposed.

A further reason to limit the study to one emotion is that even a single emotion is complex and includes a number of components (Holbrook 1985). Lazarus (1986) proposes five components: perception (of the precipitating situation), cognitive appraisal (the significance of the situation to well-being), subjective feeling, physiological arousal, and action impulses. Any emotion, such as anger, sadness, or warmth, will have countless variations based on the specific nature of each component. For example, anger can differ because of the target (a person versus a frustrating situation), how threatening it is (a personal versus impersonal situation), or its tendency to generate an action response (an attack might stimulate a determined, vigorous response, whereas anger at a needless traffic accident might involve only a superficial action impulse).

This chapter thus attempts to identify mediating factors that allow or enhance the warmth response. What are the characteristics of the audience and the commercial and its context that tend to make the warmth response more intense? The result will be a series of hypotheses about mediators of the warmth response.

There are several motivations for studying mediators of warmth. First, the hypotheses generated should guide future research by providing insights into the process by which a warm response is created. These insights have both theoretical and practical interest. Theoretically mediators of warmth will likely be part of the underlying processes through which warmth is evoked. Practically research into mediators of warmth may lead to improved copy testing techniques for emotional advertising. Second, the mediators proposed for warmth provide a framework for testing the effect of the causes of emotional response on the effectiveness of the advertisement. Finally, such research ideally will provide insights of use in studying other specific feeling responses to advertising.

The ideas we present are based on a series of focus group sessions in which people were shown emotional commercials and asked to discuss their feelings and current psychological and marketing theory and research. Research in this area is sparse, so much of this chapter is speculative. Before structuring and discussing the proposed warmth mediators, it is useful to review the warmth construct and the research relevant to understanding it and its impact, especially in advertising.

A Definition of Warmth

Warmth has been defined by Aaker, Stayman, and Hagerty (1986) as a positive, mild, transitory emotion involving physiological response and precipitated by experiencing directly or vicariously a love, family, or friendship relationship. This definition clearly positions warmth on the two dimensions often used to classify emotions: evaluation (valence) and arousal (activation) (Daly, Lancee, and Polivy 1983). Warmth is positive on the evaluative dimension and moderate on the arousal dimension. Thus, while the experience is not intense (such as that for anger or disgust), a detached expression of love or friendship without any concurrent involvement and physiological arousal would not generate warmth. Some greater involvement is required.

The definition follows in the tradition of Darwin and many modern emotional theorists by involving a social context. Kemper (1978, p. 332) has observed that "an extremely large class of human emotions results from real, anticipated, imagined, or recollected outcomes of social relationships." Averill (1980) defines emotions as "transitory social roles." Thus warmth will usually involve a social object such as a person or persons, animal, organization (such as a fraternity, team, or club), or institution (for example, country).

Research into Warmth

Several studies have provided insight into the warmth response. Aaker and Bruzzone (1981) found that warmth is one of four dimensions audiences use in developing perceptions of commercials. The warmth factor was tapped by the adjectives *appealing*, *gentle*, and *well done*. Most of the commercials rated high on warmth showed a family or friendship relationship. Five of the top twenty-seven commercials rated high on warmth were for fast foods and focused on a family theme (the top commercial showed a very emotional family reunion). Another six had children in a warm family setting, and five more were from the AT&T "Reach out and touch someone" campaign, each depicting an explicit family or social relationship. Batra and Ray (1986) suggested that warmth was closely related to their social affection category of affective response and found that social affection was the most common of the affective responses they measured across a range of commercials.

A study by Smith and Ellsworth (1985) suggested that warmth is closely related to happiness and pride. Sixteen Stanford University undergraduates were asked to recall in detail past experiences associated with each of fifteen emotions, including happiness and pride. They then scaled each experience using items tapping eight emotion dimensions. Most subjects (eleven of sixteen) recalled, for the happy experience, enjoyable times spent with other people, such as being reunited with close friends or relatives after a long absence, being at a party with friends, or going out on a date. The relationships in these experiences bear a strong resemblance to those found in the warm ads in the Aaker and Bruzzone study.

With respect to the emotional dimensions, Smith and Ellsworth found pride to be similar to happiness. Both emotions were extremely pleasant and involved little effort, high certainty, and a strong desire to pay attention. Pride was somewhat more associated with one's own sense of responsibility and control. Interestingly pride appeared in the warmth dimension in the Aaker and Bruzzone study as well. Six of the top twenty-seven warm commercials were for women's make-up products and had a feel-good-about-yourself type of theme. The Avon "You Never Looked So Good" commercials were in this group, as were the Wella Balsam "You'll Love Your Hair" commercials.

Experiments conducted by Aaker, Stayman, and Hagerty (1986) that employed the warmth monitor, a continuous measure of felt warmth, generated several findings. First, significant correlations were found between warmth (and change in warmth levels) and measures of impact, such as liking the ad and purchase intentions. Second, commercials were shown to be capable of altering felt warmth levels substantially, within even the first portion of a thirty-second commercial. Third, correlations of warmth levels with physiological arousal as measured by skin conductance averaged .67. Fourth, the impact of warm commercials was enhanced if the prior commercial was not a warm commercial.

Stayman and Aaker (1987) studied the impact of repetition upon the warmth response for commercials with warmth, humor, or irritation as the primary focus of the execution. The data suggested that for the warm commercials, wear-out occurs at higher exposure levels than for the humorous or irritating commercials. Furthermore, for warm commercials, the benefits from repeated exposure beyond high initial response levels could be even greater than those during the initial high response exposures.

Mediators of the Warmth Response

The research on warmth provides a variety of insights into the nature of the warmth response and its impact on the effectiveness of advertisements. Our purpose here is to suggest mediators of the warmth response and, where possible, to hypothesize the nature of their influence. What mediates the link between the stimulus and the warmth response? Under what conditions will the warmth response be precipitated or enhanced and when will that response enhance the effectiveness of the commercial?

Table 13–1 shows four classes of mediators of warmth. The first two, audience mediators and situation mediators, are comparable to the two classes of antecedent variables identified in most process models of emotion, the person and the situation (Arnold 1960). They are attributes of the person and situation which are defined for any given viewing occasion independently of the processing of the commercial. The second two proposed mediators, stimulus perception mediators and stimulus orientation mediators, are more directly related to the viewer's evaluation of a particular ad during a specific viewing occasion.

Table 13–1
Proposed Mediators of Warmth

Audience mediators
General audience characteristics
Emotionality
Demographics: Sex, age, ethnicity
Ad-specific audience characteristics
Interest
Similarity
Experience
Situation mediators
Preceding stimulus
Repetition
Time of day
Stimulus setting
Product category
Mood of audience member
Stimulus perception mediators
Cognitive empathy: Understanding the situation of others
Believability
Literal
Verisimilitude
Stimulus orientation mediators
Emotional empathy, vicarious experience
Relive a prior experience stimulated by the commercial
Strong affect toward a character
Reaction to a behavior or emotion displayed by a character

Audience Mediators

Audience mediators represent individual characteristics that may precipitate emotional response. Thus they should be useful in understanding individual differences in response. They include general characteristics of the individual, as well as characteristics specifically related to some aspect of the advertisement.

General Audience Characteristics

General audience characteristics are descriptors of the audience that act as mediators of emotional response but are unrelated to any specific commercial. They can thus affect the intensity and frequency of a viewer's emotional response. One such mediator is the personality characteristic of emotionality. People differ in their tendency to generate emotional responses (Hoffman 1977); some experience emotions more easily, frequently, and intensely than others. Sommers and Scioli (1986) found that individual differences in emotionality were related to values and beliefs and were useful in explaining not only emotional response but also preferences in different lifestyle choices.

Other general audience characteristics include a number of demographic variables shown to influence emotional responses in general and can be expected to influence warmth in particular. First, sex has been shown to affect emotional response on a number of dimensions. Sommers and Scioli (1986) discuss the relationship of sex, emotionality, and self-perceptions of emotional response. Specifically related to warmth, sex has been shown to affect cognitive empathy, the ability to understand the situation of others. (Cognitive empathy is discussed here as a stimulus perception mediator expected to affect warmth.) For example, Hoffman (1977), in a review of sixteen studies on empathic response, found that in each study, females had higher empathic responses than males. (See chapter 10.) Hall (1979) and Noller (1980) have suggested that women are not only more responsive to the feelings of others but are also better able to express their feelings and correctly interpret the feelings of others.

Other demographic variables are age and ethnicity. Like sex, age has been shown to be related to empathic response. Empathy appears to increase in children between the ages of five and eight, and adults have a greater empathic sensitivity to negative affective states than do preadults (Hoffman 1977, pp. 196–197). Gallois and Callan (1986) found that not only do ethnicity of sender and receiver interact in determining emotional response due to cultural differences in interpreting emotional signals but also that ethnic differences interact with sex of the receiver. Goldstein and Michaels (1985) suggest that a number of variables, including socioeconomic status, family size, and intelligence, have also been shown to moderate empathic responses.

Ad-Specific Audience Characteristics

Ad-specific audience characteristics are audience characteristics defined only with respect to a particular commercial. These characteristics, expected to affect warmth only to the extent that they relate to elements of the execution, include interest or involvement in the subject matter of the ad, the similarity of the audience member to the characters in the commercial, and the extent to which the audience member has had experiences similar to those shown in the commercial.

The first ad-specific audience characteristic is interest or involvement. How interested is the viewer in the subject matter of the commercial—specifically the scenes depicted? Thus, interest is defined with respect to ad content rather than a specific viewing occasion. One indication of a viewer's interest may be his or her willingness to watch an entire program covering the same subject matter (perhaps boxing, dancing, or mountain climbing).

Interest as used here is a motivational construct. Is the viewer motivated to attend to and process the subject matter because of an interest in it? Interest is thus related to involvement, which has been characterized by Chaiken (1980) and others as involving motivation and ability. As proposed by Lazarus (1986), Arnold (1960), and others, for emotional response to occur, the material viewed must be of sufficient significance to the self. Since interest could be expected to be necessary for an event to be considered significant, it is expected that interest and involvement should be either necessary for or enhance response.

Interest as involvement has been shown to be a useful response mediator in other contexts within consumer behavior and persuasion research. Petty and Cacioppo (1979) found that the type and amount of cognitive responses and level of attitude change varied as a function of the personal relevance (motivation to process) of the communication. They manipulated personal relevance by suggesting to subjects that a comprehensive exam requirement would or would not go into effect while the subjects were still in school. They found that for strong arguments, increased relevance (the exam would be required of the subjects) led to more favorable thoughts and increased persuasion, while for weak arguments, increased relevance led to more counterarguments and reduced persuasion.

Interest stimulated by an ad execution may also have an impact on the effect of the response on commercial effectiveness. Batra and Ray (1985) have demonstrated evidence that affective responses are more important when product involvement is low. Thus to the extent that ad involvement is related to product involvement, there may be differences between ad responses and attitudinal outcomes.

The second ad-specific audience characteristic is similarity. How similar are the characters in the commercial to the viewer and those people with whom the viewer associates? The expectation is that similarity should enhance cognitive empathy since it should be easier to understand the situation of others who are like you. Similarity should also enhance the several forms of emotional response described as situation orientation mediators. Similarity has been shown to affect emotional as well as cognitive empathic responses (Hoffman 1977). Finally, many studies have demonstrated a relationship between similarity and advertising effectivenss.

The third proposed ad-specific audience characteristic is experience. Has the audience member had an experience identical or similar to that shown in the advertisement? The expectation is that prior experience should make it easier to experience vicariously another's feelings (vicarious experience is one of the four stimulus orientation mediators). Thus if a viewer has experienced the exultation of winning a tennis championship, he or she may be more likely to share vicariously the emotions of a commercial character who is clearly experiencing such emotions. This likelihood of vicariously sharing emotions is due to an enhanced ability to recall and understand the nature of the experience.

Situation Mediators

A number of characteristics of the situation in which the viewer is exposed to the ad may also mediate response in general and warmth in particular. Previous research has shown that the immediately preceding commercial can affect the warmth response (Aaker, Stayman, and Hagerty, 1986), as can the number of times the viewer has been exposed to the commercial (Stayman and Aaker 1987). The time of day (daytime versus prime time), the stimulus setting (such as a quiet room versus a distracting environment; Obermiller and Atwood 1985), the audience mood (for example, whether a quarrel with a family member had recently occurred; Gardner 1985), and the product class (wine versus mouthwash or insurance) also are likely to mediate response.

Of particular interest is the likely interaction between audience and situation mediators. In fact, emotion is often viewed as a result of the relationship between a person (beliefs, experiences, and values) and his or her environment. Folkman and Lazarus (1984) found differences in emotional responses across three stages of an exam (representing three similar but distinct situations) across individual characteristics such as grade-point average.

One interaction that might be expected in an advertising context is that prior mood may have more affect in low- than high-involvement situations because under high involvement, more active processing may overshadow prior mood effects. Another expected interaction is that viewers watching a television program covering the same subject matter as the commercial (for example, a boxing match and a commercial having boxing as its theme) may be more affected by the ad than if there were not such an ad-program match, which serves to heighten interest temporarily in the subject matter.

Stimulus Perception Mediators

Audience and situation mediators can be measured without exposing a respondent to the commercial in question. Stimulus perception mediators and stimulus orientation mediators involve the viewer's reaction to the specific commercial and the specific viewing occasion studied. Stimulus perception mediators relate to how the commercial is perceived by the viewer. The two proposed stimulus perception mediators, cognitive empathy and believability, affect the perception of the stimulus.

Cognitive Empathy

Two types of empathy have been long distinguished in the literature historically, although recently they have been seen as interrelated (Davis 1983; Hoffman 1977). The first empathy type is emotional empathy, which involves a vicarious emotional experience; an emotion felt by another is experienced or shared. The second type of empathy involves the understanding of the situation of others. Termed *cognitive empathy,* it is more cognitive in nature and need not necessarily involve an emotional response, although it could enhance one and may be necessary for one to occur (Borke 1971; Dymond 1949). Sympathy, often viewed as similar to empathy, has been distinguished from empathy by Gruen and Mendelsohn (1986). Since sympathy and emotional empathy are felt emotions rather than perceptions of the stimulus, they are discussed as stimulus orientation mediators.

Cognitive empathy, however, is a perception of the stimulus rather than a reaction to it. Cognitive empathy may lead to warmth since warmth is related to social situations and thus depends at least to some extent on the understanding of the situation of others. Thus the expectation is that cognitive empathy will mediate warmth responses. If cognitive empathy is high, and thus the understanding of another's situation is deep, the warmth response should be more likely and more intense.

Support for considering the empathy construct as a mediator of warmth comes from Schlinger's (1979) series of studies in which audience members used phrases to describe commercials. A very stable "empathy" factor emerged tapped by phrases like "realistic/true-to-life," "felt right there," and "personal and intimate." The fact that warm commercials such as those showing warm relationships between couples of family members (proud parents attending graduation, a small boy bringing his mother flowers, and others) were rated very highly on the empathy factor suggests a link between empathy and warmth.

Stayman (1985), in studying the relationship between cognitive mediators of emotional response and response to television advertising over repeated exposure, found that, following repeated viewing, empathy ratings had a higher association with warmth than with humor or irritation. Further, the data suggested that the empathy ratings helped to explain ad liking and effectiveness beyond measures of felt warmth.

Believability

The second stimulus perception mediator, perhaps potentially the most useful mediator, is believability. Once an important area of research (Maloney 1962), believability as a determinant of advertising effectiveness has been neglected recently. Much of the earlier research concerned the believability of the message in a commercial; however, it may be equally important in emotional appeals to achieve believability of context.

Two types of believability can be conceptualized: literal believability whereby the scene is realistic (it could happen in real life) and verisimilitude, the appearance of truth or the depiction of realism as in the theater or literature (see chapter 2). The scene may not be literally true, but the commercial generates a willing suspension of disbelief; it has a ring of truth. For example, if paper towels could speak, they would speak that way. There is no distracting thought that the scene is phony, contrived, or silly.

Believability may be useful as a predictor of emotional response. For example, one hypothesis is that for emotional empathy to occur (that is, for a vicarious warmth experience), literal believability is necessary. It may be difficult for most people to experience warmth vicariously when the scene is not literally believable.

It seems clear that unless a commercial has, at minimum, verisimilitude, viewers will be unlikely to experience any emotional response. Instead these viewers will fail to attend to the commercial or will be distracted by thoughts that it may be silly or contrived. For example, the introduction of a mouthwash solution to a social situation might be so contrived as to disrupt the verisimilitude and prevent the desired emotion from emerging. Thus believability may enhance emotional response, and lack of believability may block such response.

The discussion of audience and situation mediators proposed that there may be interactions between the person and the situation that lead to warmth responses. Stimulus perception mediators may generate additional interactions. One such interaction may occur between cognitive empathy, experience, and literal believability. For example, a viewer who has had an experience relevant to one depicted in an ad will likely have higher cognitive empathy only to the extent that the commercial achieves literal believability. An expert tennis player may relate to a tennis scene and develop cognitive empathy with the characters only if the scene is believable. If the models used do not know how to hit a backhand yet are presented as good tennis players, then the experience factor can lead to low believability (even lower than for nonexperienced viewers) and thus the absence of warmth.

Stimulus Orientation Mediators

A stimulus orientation represents a type of relationship that the viewer has with the character or characters in a commercial. The involved relationship is that which precipitates the emotional response. Our experience discussing reactions to emotional ads with groups of viewers has led us to suggest that there are at least four possible stimulus orientation mediators: vicarious emotional experience, reliving a prior experience, affect toward a specific character or characters, and a reaction to a behavior or emotion displayed in the ad.

Vicarious Emotional Experience—Emotional Empathy

The first stimulus orientation mediator is vicarious experience (Puto and Wells 1984) or emotional empathy (Hoffman 1977; Goldstein and Michaels 1985). One or more characters in a commercial may be experiencing warmth, and the viewer may experience the same emotion vicariously. For example, in a recent Lowenbrau commercial, a happy dinner scene between a proud father and a son who just passed his bar exam shows feelings of warmth in both characters. The viewer could become involved enough to share vicariously the emotional experience with one or perhaps both characters.

Warmth evoked through a vicarious experience is termed *emotional empathy* to distinguish it from cognitive empathy, which may or may not lead to warmth even if the scene depicted is warm. Emotional empathy involves an emotional response similar to that of another person (Stotland 1969). Scott (1980) defines empathy as "the arousal in oneself of the emotion one observes in another or the emotion one would feel in another's situation." pg. 36.

Reliving a Prior Experience

The second stimulus orientation mediator involves reliving a prior experience. In this case, the viewer might be reminded, directly or indirectly, of a prior warm experience and then be stimulated to relive that warm experience. For example, a Christmas scene from the 1940s with an old radio sharing the living room with a tree might stimulate a person to recall his or her childhood

Christmas celebrations and to relive the warm feelings associated with these memories.

A high level of cognitive empathy could enhance the tendency for a viewer to recall and relive a similar scene out of his or her past (Clynes 1980). High cognitive empathy would likely be accompanied by recall of specific scenes and feelings from the past. Conversely a detailed recall of a relevant prior experience might generate high cognitive empathy and a tendency to reexperience an emotional response. Current examples of an attempt to use this orientation are the Miller "real draft beer" commercials, which suggest that the real draft taste evokes memories and feelings from past good times of drinking draft beer from a keg.

Affect toward the Character

The third stimulus orientation mediator assumes that the commercial could stimulate strong affect in the viewer toward a specific character in the ad. An elderly person in an AT&T "Reach out and touch someone" commercial might show exceptional independence and spunk. The viewer might respond with feelings of pride and warmth based on a strong liking or affect toward that character rather than a self-related experience.

Schlinger (1979) found high empathy scores in commercials with fantasy characters such as the Green Giant and Pillsbury's doughboy. It seems difficult to image a viewer being able to identify empathically with such characters. More likely an affective relationship between the viewer and the character generates warmth and the empathy factor accompanying a warmth response.

Emotional Reaction to an Action or Feeling

The fourth stimulus orientation mediator involves a viewer reaction to an action or feeling displayed by the character. A cute little girl might fall and bruise her arm. The viewer might feel warm due to reactions of sympathy or compassion rather than one of the other three orientations. The viewer would then be experiencing an emotion different from that being experienced by the character in the commercial.

Responses such as sympathy, which are reactions to the feelings or actions of others, are thus expected to involve cognitive but not emotional empathy. Gruen and Mendelsohn (1986), in studying the distinction between emotional empathy and sympathy, found that emotional empathy was largely determined by stable attributes of the person, and sympathy was determined by an interaction between personality and the particular action or feeling that the actor was experiencing. In particular, they found that sympathy was largely dependent on two cognitions: cognitive empathy and how justified the viewer thought the actor was in his or her actions.

Which Stimulus Orientation?

Although any of the four orientations may generate warmth, it is possible for more than one orientation to be evoked by a single commercial. In fact, some commercials likely generate all four stimulus orientations among different members of the audience. Consider a commercial in which a teenage girl has one of her first experiences with a boy and shows the awkwardness and embarrassment associated with that experience. Some members of the audience may vicariously experience the joy of beginning a special relationship. Others may be stimulated to relive their own similar experiences. The dominant stimulus orientation of other viewers may be a strong affect toward the character. Finally, an audience group may have an emotional reaction of sympathy for the young girl's experience.

A single warmth response could also have more than one source. A person could vicariously share a character's feelings and also be stimulated to relive a similar prior experience. In fact, the two orientations may enhance each other and lead to a more intense response.

Hypotheses

The discussion leads to a number of hypotheses regarding those conditions under which a warmth response will be more likely and tend to be more intense. The hypotheses regarding the mediating effect of audience, situation, and stimulus perception variables on the tendency toward and extent of warmth are expected to generalize to other emotions as well. Only the hypotheses regarding stimulus orientation mediators are expected to be limited to the warmth emotion.

For the audience, situation, and stimulus perception mediators, it is hypothesized that a warmth response will be more likely and tend to be more intense when the subject:

Is an emotional person.

Is a female.

Is interested or involved in the subject matter of the commercial.

Is similar to a character or characters in the commercial.

Has had an experience similar to that shown in the commercial.

Is in a situation that tends to enhance warmth, including few distractions, low exposure levels, and a prior commercial that does not induce warmth.

Is experiencing cognitive empathy.

Finds the commercial believable literally and with verisimilitude.

In addition, the following interactions are proposed:

Vicarious emotional experience depends on literal believability.

Experience increases (decreases) response when the commercial is literally believable (not believable).

The stimulus orientation mediators are related not only to the existence and level of warmth responses but also to the underlying cognitions accompanying warmth. We therefore further propose that the four stimulus orientation mediators:

Exist.

Generate different warmth levels for different audience subgroups.

Can be evoked individually and can interact.

Affect the effectiveness of the commercial such that they can explain commercial effectiveness beyond measures of warmth alone.

Summary

Previous research has pointed out that in order to understand the effects of affective advertising appeals, it is important to study feeling responses in addition to ad evaluations. This chapter proposes that it also may be important to understand the processes underlying feeling responses to understand better the contexts in which feelings will be elicited and when different feeling responses will positively affect ad effectiveness.

Three classes of mediators of warmth responses were proposed as a basis for research into mediators of not only warmth but also other emotions. The audience and situation mediators include personality and advertisement-related audience characteristics, as well as elements of the situation of particular relevance to warmth. These mediators are likely to influence any emotional response to advertising. The stimulus perception mediators, cognitive empathy and believability, have also been shown to relate to a number of emotions but were proposed to interact with audience and situation mediators in specific combinations that can be expected to lead to a warmth response.

The proposed effects of stimulus orientation mediators are specific to one emotional response, warmth. These hypotheses, developed in focus groups studying warmth responses, were proposed to be not only mediators of the level and intensity of warmth responses but also elements of the response itself. Further, stimulus orientation mediators are hypothesized to affect the effect of warmth on ad effectiveness. Future research is needed to test the propositions and hypotheses proposed and to integrate the results with more macro-approaches to studying the effects of affect in advertising.

References

Aaker, David. A., and Donald E. Bruzzone. 1981. "Viewer Perceptions of Prime-Time Television Advertising." *Journal of Advertising Research* October:15–23.

Aaker, David A., Douglas M. Stayman, and Michael R. Hagerty. 1986. "Warmth in Advertising: Measurement, Impact and Sequence Effects." *Journal of Consumer Research* 12, no. 4:365–381.

Abelson, R.P., D.R. Kinder, M.D. Peters, and S.T. Fiske. 1982. "Affective and Semantic Components in Political Person Perception." *Journal of Personality and Social Psychology* 42:619–630.

Alwitt, Linda, F., and Andrew A. Mitchell, eds. 1985. *Psychological Processes and Advertising Effects.* Hillsdale, N.J.: Erlbaum.

Arnold, Magda B. 1960. *Emotion and Personality.* New York: Columbia University Press.

Averill, James R. 1980. "A Constructionist View of Emotion." In Robert Plutchik and Henry Kellerman, eds., *Emotion: Theory, Research, and Experience*, pp. 305–339. New York: Academic Press.

Bateson, C.D., K. O'Quinn, J. Fultz, and M. Vanderplas. 1983. "Influence of Self-Reported Distress and Empathy on Egoistic versus Altruistic Motivation to Help." *Journal of Personality and Social Psychology* 45:706–718.

Batra, Rajeev, and Michael L. Ray. 1985. "How Advertising Works at Contact." In Linda F. Alwitt and Andrew A. Mitchell, eds. *Psychological Processes and Advertising Effects*, pp. 12–44. Hillsdale, N.J.: Erlbaum.

———. 1986. "Affective Responses Mediating Acceptance of Advertising." *Journal of Consumer Research* 13, no. 2:234–249.

Borke, H. 1971. "Interpersonal Perception of Young Children: Egocentrism or Empathy?" *Developmental Psychology* 5:263–269.

Burke, Marian C., and Julie A. Edell. 1986. "Ad Reactions over Time: Capturing Changes in the Real World." *Journal of Consumer Research* 13, no. 3:114–118.

Chaiken, Shelly. 1980. "Heuristic versus Systematic Information Processing and the Use of Source versus Message Cues in Persuasion." *Journal of Personality and Social Psychology* 29:752–766.

Clynes, Manfred. 1980. "The Communication of Emotion: Theory of Sentics." In Robert Plutchik and Henry Kellerman, eds., *Emotion: Theory, Research, and Experience.* New York: Academic Press.

Daly, Eleanor M., William J. Lancee, and Janet Polivy. 1983. "A Conical Model for the Taxonomy of Emotional Experience." *Journal of Personality and Social Psychology* 45:443–457.

Davis, Mark H. 1983. "The Effects of Dispositional Empathy on Emotional Reactions and Helping: A Multidimensional Approach." *Journal of Personality* 51, no. 2(June):167–184.

Dymond, R.F. 1949. "A Scale for the Measurement of Empathetic Ability." *Journal of Consulting Psychology* 13:127–133.

Edell, Julie A., and Marian C. Burke. 1986. "The Power of Feelings in Understanding Advertising Effects." Working paper 86-11. Durham, N.C.: Fuqua School of Business, Duke University.

Ekman, P., and H. Oster. 1979. "Facial Expressions of Emotion." *Annual Review of Psychology* 30:527–554.

Folkman, Susan, and Richard S. Lazarus. 1984. "If It Changes It Must Be a Process: A Study of Emotion and Coping during Three Stages of a College Examination" *Journal of Personality and Social Psychology* 48:150–170.

Gallois, Cynthia, and Victor J. Callan. 1986. "Decoding Emotional Messages: Influence of Ethnicity, Sex, Message Type and Channel." *Journal of Personality and Social Psychology* 51:755–762.

Gardner, Meryl P. 1985. "Mood States and Consumer Behavior: A Critical Review." *Journal of Consumer Research* 12, no. 3:281–300.

Goldstein, Arnold P., and Gerald Y. Michaels. 1985. *Empathy: Development, Training, and Consequences.* Hillsdale, N.J.: Erlbaum.

Gruen, Rand J., and Gerald Mendelsohn. 1986. "Emotional Responses to Affective Displays in Others: The Distinction between Empathy and Sympathy." *Journal of Personality and Social Psychology* 39:1135–1148.

Hall, J. 1979. "Gender, Gender Roles and Nonverbal Communication Skills." In R. Rosenthal, ed., *Skill in Nonverbal Communication: Individual Differences,* pp. 32–67. Cambridge, Mass.: Oelgeschlager, Gunn and Hain.

Hoffman, Martin L. 1977. "Empathy, Its Development and Prosocial Implications." In C.B. Keasey, ed., *Nebraska Symposium on Motivation,* 25:169–217. Lincoln: University of Nebraska Press.

Holbrook, Morris B. 1985. "Emotion in the Consumption Experience: Toward a New Model of the Human Consumer." In Robert A. Peterson, Wayne D. Hoyer, and William R. Wilson, *The Role of Affect in Consumer Behavior: Emerging Theories and Applications.* Lexington, Mass.: Lexington Books.

Kemper, T. 1978. "Toward Sociology of Emotion: Some Problems and Some Solutions." *American Sociologist* 13:30–41.

Lazarus, Richard S. 1986. "Classic Issues about Emotion from the Perspective of a Relational and Cognitive Theory." *Behavioral and Brain Sciences.* Forthcoming.

Lutz, Richard J. 1985. "Affective and Cognitive Antecedents of Attitude toward the Ad: A Conceptual Framework." In Linda F. Alwitt and Andrew A. Mitchell eds. *Psychological Processes and Advertising Effects,* pp. 12–44. Hillsdale, N.J.: Erlbaum.

MacKenzie, Scott B., Richard J. Lutz, and George E. Belch. 1986. "The Role of Attitude toward the Ad as a Mediator of Advertising Effectiveness: A Test of Competing Explanations." *Journal of Marketing Research* 13 (May):130–143.

Maloney, John C. 1962. "Curiosity versus Disbelief in Advertising." *Journal of Advertising Research* 2:2–8.

Mitchell, Andrew A., and Jerry C. Olson. 1981. "Are Product Attribute Beliefs the Only Mediator of Advertising Effects on Brand Attitude?" *Journal of Marketing Research* 18 (August):318–322.

Noller, P. 1980. "Misunderstandings in Marital Communications: A Study of Couples' Nonverbal Communication." *Journal of Personality and Social Psychology* 39: 1135–1148.

Obermiller, Andrew A., and April Atwood. 1985. "The Complete Angler: Luring the Listener with Barbed and Barbless Hooks." In Richard Lutz, ed., *Advances in Consumer Research,* vol. 12. Ann Arbor: Association for Consumer Research.

Peterson, Robert A., Wayne D. Hoyer, and William R. Wilson. 1986. *The Role of Affect in Consumer Behavior.* Lexington, Mass.: Lexington Books.

Petty, Richard E., and John T. Cacioppo. 1979. "Issue Involvement Can Increase or Decrease Persuasion by Enhancing Message Relevant Cognitive Responses." *Journal of Personality and Social Psychology* 37:1915–1926.

Plummer, Joseph T. 1985. "Advertising Strategy." Paper presented to American Management Association Strategic Planning Conference, Chicago, April.

Puto, Christopher P., and William D. Wells. 1984. "Informational and Transformational Advertising: The Differential Effects of Time." In Thomas C. Kinnear, ed., *Advances in Consumer Research,* 11:638–643. Ann Arbor: Association for Consumer Research.

Schlinger, Mary Jane. 1979. "A Profile of Responses to Commercials." *Journal of Advertising Research* 19:37–46.

Scott, J.P. 1980. "The Function of Emotions in Behavioral Systems: A System Theory Analysis." In Robert Plutchik and Henry Kellerman, eds., *Emotion: Theory, Research and Experience.* New York: Academic Press.

Smith, Craig A., and Phoebe C. Ellsworth. 1985. "Patterns of Cognitive Approaches in Emotion." *Journal of Personality and Social Psychology* 48:813–838.

Sommers, S., and A. Scioli. 1986. "Emotional Range and Value Orientation: Toward a Cognitive View of Emotionality." *Journal of Personality and Social Psychology* 51: 417–422.

Stayman, Douglas M. 1985. "Emotional Response to Advertising: Beyond Attitude toward the Ad." Ph.D. dissertation, University of California.

Stayman, Douglas M., and David A. Aaker. 1987. "Repetition and Affective Response: Differences in Specific Feeling Responses and the Mediating Role of Attitude toward the Ad." Working paper, University of Texas at Austin.

Stotland, E. 1969. "Exploratory Investigations of Empathy." In L. Berkowitz, ed., *Advances in Experimental Social Psychology,* vol. 4. New York: Academic Press.

14
The Effects of Emotion on Episodic Memory for Television Commercials

Esther Thorson
Marian Friestad

In recent years, advertisers and practitioners have considered what consumer memory can tell us about the effectiveness of commercials. In many of these discussions, memory has been defined narrowly by the recall methods used by advertising research companies like Burke and ARS. The approach presented in this chapter generalizes to these methods but goes beyond them to develop a general model of memory for commercials. Special attention is given to the question of how useful memory measures are for evaluating the emotional commercial.

The model and the data presented contradict the position taken by many practitioners (such as Zielske 1982; Coulson, chapter 3) that recall underestimates the strength of emotional commercials. We believe this position results from the fact that historically, research on memory for ads has been carried out in a theoretical vacuum. Our model of memory suggests that questions about emotion's effects on memory for a commercial relate not only to the typical argument about how much information is contained in emotional commercials but also to how human memory stores, processes, and retrieves information about emotional commercials and the products they promote.

The first section of the chapter discusses the associational nature of memory. It addresses the distinctions and relationships between episodic and semantic memory, and explains what we mean by the concept of "trace strength in memory."

The second section outlines our model of ad memory. This model is fundamentally concerned with understanding how emotion and emotional responses influence memory for commercials. The final section summarizes the results of two studies that tested the model, and suggests a number of questions for further research.

Associational Nature of Memory

Every conscious human experience leaves a memory trace consisting of elements representing a variety of aspects of the experience. These elements include external events, such as what happened, who was there, and where it was; and internal events, such as emotions, thoughts, and bodily sensations that occurred during the event. Because of their contiguity in time and the way the human nervous system is built, these elements become tied together or associated in memory. As a result, the subsequent presence of any one of the elements is likely to stimulate retrieval of other elements from memory.

Evidence for association in memory can be found in context effects, a phenomenon in which reinstatement of elements that would appear to be irrelevant to certain memories proves them closely tied to those memories. For example, the literature of state-dependent memory shows that things learned under water are better recalled under water (Godden and Baddeley 1975), things learned while happy are better recalled when happy (Bower and Cohen 1982), and things learned in a particular room are better recalled in that room (Smith, Glenberg, and Bjork 1978). Theories based on the associational nature of memory vary in their assumptions about the way in which the elements of a memory trace are organized (Estes 1975). In turn, the structural characteristics of various models of memory (vector, network, stack) lead to predictions about how information is encoded, stored, and retrieved.

Episodic and Semantic Memory

Tulving (1972) first argued that there are processing differences between memory that stores information about specific events or episodes experienced by a person and memory that stores general semantic knowledge about the world. Episodic memory is defined as the mental storage of personal experiences and their spatial and temporal context. A person watching a commercial is experiencing the visuals and the copy, along with the occurrence in the viewing context, as well as internal events, such as his or her thoughts and feelings. Figure 14-1 shows a schematic of a sample episodic memory trace.

Semantic memory is the mental storage of general knowledge. When a person tells us that the major laundry detergents are Solo, Tide, and Cheer, these are items of knowledge rather than personal memories. The individual may, in fact, no longer know under what conditions or when this knowledge was acquired. Figure 14-2 shows a schematic of semantic knowledge of soap.

Some controversy has developed about whether episodic and semantic memory are actually separate (Atkinson, Herrman, and Wescourt 1974; Herrmann and McLaughlin 1973; Shoben, Wescourt, and Smith 1978), whether the distinction is really just a useful way to classify different kinds of knowledge (Anderson and Bower 1973; McKoon and Ratcliff 1979; McClosky and

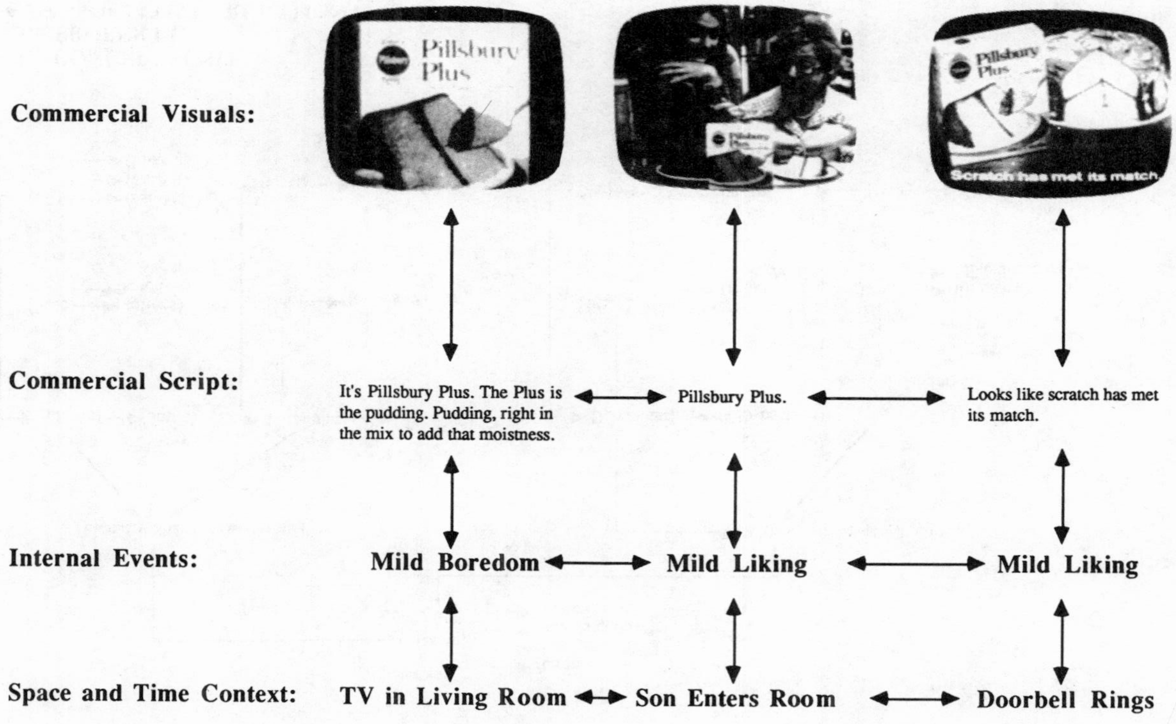

Figure 14–1. Episodic Memory of an Experienced Commercial

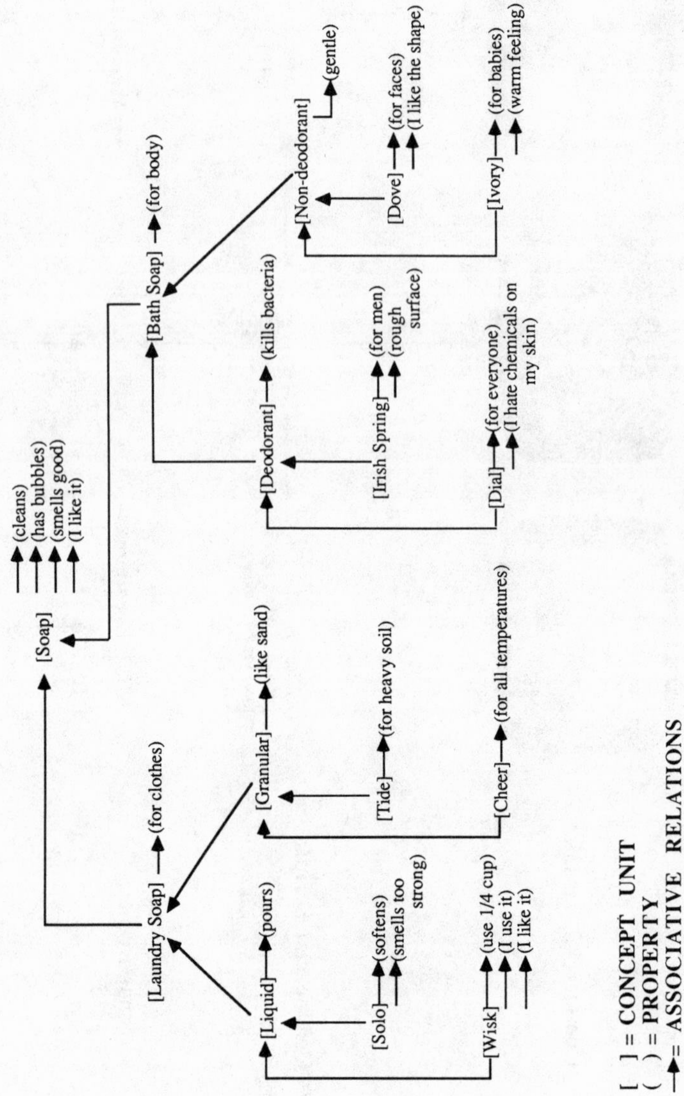

Figure 14–2. Semantic Network Model

Santee 1981), or even whether there may be more than just two memory systems (Tulving, Schacter, and Stark 1982; Schacter and Tulving 1982). Regardless of its specific interpretation, however, the distinction has proved to be an important one to psychologists studying memory (Lachman, Lachman, and Butterfield 1979; Kintsch 1974; Klatzky 1980; Seamon 1980). This chapter explores the notion that the differences between episodic and semantic memory are important to considerations about how advertising works (Thorson 1984; Friestad and Thorson 1984). To clarify the application of this distinction, we look first at examples of the operation of episodic and semantic memory in some widely used methods of evaluating advertising.

When a commercial is experienced, a set of associations is laid down. The aspects of the experience may involve product, brand name, product characteristics, and execution but will also include emotions, thoughts, and bodily sensations experienced during the viewing, the presence or absence of other people, and so on. All of these elements become part of the episodic trace (see figure 14–1).

In a prototype episodic task, a consumer is telephoned and asked if she watched a particular program on television the preceding evening. If she answers in the affirmative, she is asked to list all the commercials she saw in the program and to talk about each one. Clearly this task is one for episodic memory. the viewer must think through what she was doing during the evening, what shows she watched, and what commercials she saw.

But there is a complication: if the viewer fails to recall the commercial of interest, she is then cued. As soon as one attempts to jog memory with classificatory information (Did you see any cake mix commercials? any commercials for Duncan Hines?), the search process shifts to semantic memory. Our viewer may access her storage of cake mix commercials, a semantic organization, and index its contents. Or she may create a list of cake mix commercials, also a semantic memory activity. In spite of these complications, however, the initial memory for a commercial is episodic, and asking an individual to recall a commercial seen the previous evening, without category cuing, creates a predominantly episodic task.

In the prototypic semantic memory task, a consumer watches some programs and commercials and then is asked to talk about how the values expressed in the ad are consistent or inconsistent with her own. Or she is asked how well she liked the way emotion was expressed in the ad or whether she would be interested in trying the advertised product. Although there are some episodic memory requirements in these tasks, they mainly involve classification, comparison, judgment, and evaluation of memory material using information not contained in the episode; therefore these tasks involve primarily semantic memory.

Thus far we have treated the two memories as separate and noncommunicating systems. It is generally thought, however, that all information is originally input as episodes (see Schacter and Tulving 1982 for exceptions). Mental operations on episodic information create semantic memory (figure 14–3). These operations occur when episodes are acted upon in some way to classify, judge, or compare their contents. The operations need not occur immediately, but the episodic traces must be available when the operations occur. In the example, if a viewer is asked which recent commercial for laundry detergent she finds most effective, the available episodes for each relevant commercial would be called up, compared, contrasted, and evaluated. Traces of these operations and their results would come into existence in semantic memory, although the specific traces would probably remain, perhaps with minor modifications resulting from the processing that operated on them.

Memory Strength

It is at this point that the concept of memory strength becomes important. If episodes are not immediately processed semantically, it is important to optimize the strength of the episodic traces to enhance the likelihood of their availability for processing later. In the present approach, memory strength for a trace is operationally defined in terms of a commercial's likelihood of being recalled and how early it is recalled as compared to other commercials. If we think of a commercial as an episode, the question of obvious concern to practitioners is how to enhance its episodic trace strength. Also of concern to practitioners is how to move episodically processed material to semantic processing for instant evaluation and how to maximize recall of salient copy points.

Determinants of Memory Trace Strength

A cogent message is easier to encode and later recall than a garbled, ambiguous message (Anderson 1980). Research investigating the effects of the linguistic structure of ads (Thorson and Snyder 1984; Rossiter 1981), as well as research dealing with the structural integration (Thorson and Friestad 1983) of a message (for example, the ad shows lots of lather while making a claim that the soap makes rich and thick suds), indicates that these message variables also affect memory strength. Another possible determinant of memory strength is the presence of viewer emotional response during the commercial episode. This chapter focuses on the role of viewer emotion in memory strength.

When a message elicits emotional response in the viewer, information about the emotion is laid down in the episodic trace of the message. The presence of emotional elements in the trace is interpreted by the individual as a signal that the trace itself is important or significant. The argument for this "signal of importance" effect has been made in evolutionary or adaptive terms (Plutchik 1980), as well as from a developmental point of view (Leventhal 1980).

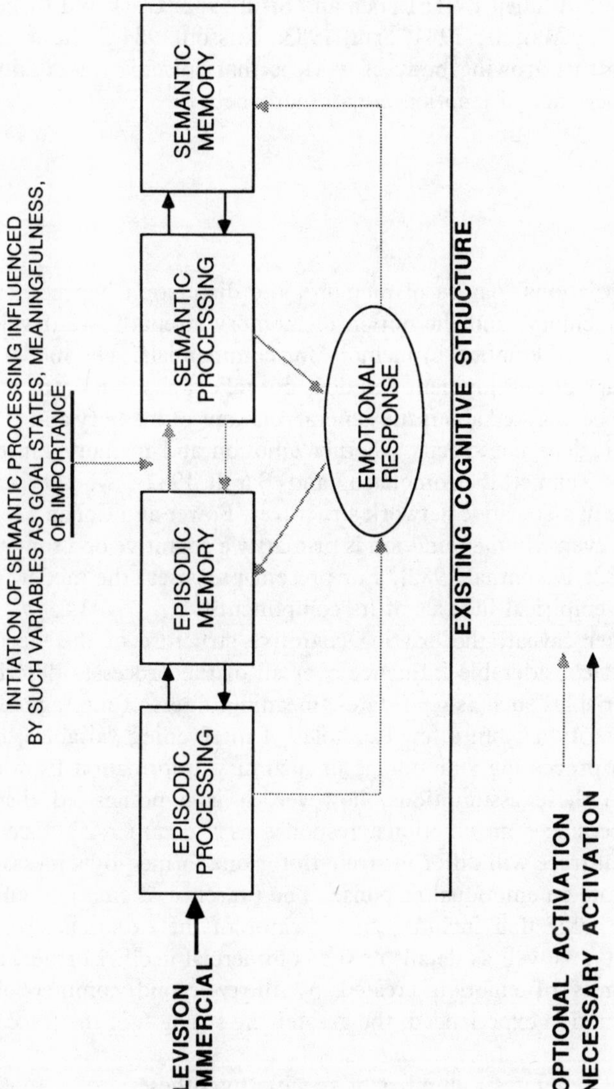

Figure 14–3. Episodic and Semantic Memory Processing of Television Commercials

That the relationship between emotion and cognitive processes is an important arena of theoretical and empirical investigation is evidenced by the recent surge of interest in this topic (Dutta and Kanungo 1975; Plutchik and Kellerman 1980; Mitchell 1981; Lynch and Srull 1982; Clark and Fiske 1982; Izard 1977, 1982; Mandler 1984; Srull 1983; Nilsson 1984). The conclusion emerging from this growing body of work is that episodic traces laid down during the experience of emotion are strengthened.

The Model

Given the associational nature of memory, the distinction between episodic and semantic memory, and the notion of memory strength, we developed a model of the role of emotion in memory for commercials. The model is in a preliminary stage of development and does not take a position on many questions that have been asked about the general relations of memory and emotion. For example, it does not specify whether emotion and memory can operate independently (Zajonc, Pietromonaco, and Bargh 1982); whether emotion exists as a node in associative network structures (Bower and Cohen 1982; Isen et al. 1978); or even whether emotion is primarily a cognitive or a somatic process (Izard 1982; Leventhal 1982). For present purposes, the model remains closely tied to empirical indexes of its components.

As a further caveat, the existing cognitive structure of the viewer will obviously exert considerable influence over all of the processes described in the model. Variables such as goal states, meaningfulness of message or product, and familiarity are but a few examples of intervening variables that can influence both processing and storage of incoming information from a commercial. Given these assumptions, however, it is hypothesized that if an individual experiences an emotional response as a commercial trace is laid down, then that trace will differ in strength for one formed by a message that does not generate an emotional response. The presence of emotion will result in an episodic trace that includes an indicator of the experienced emotion and its intensity, as well as details of the commercial itself. Further, at least within the limits of emotion created by thirty-second commercials, the stronger the emotion experienced, the greater the strength of the traces in the episode.

The model generates a number of specific hypotheses:

1. Emotional commercials are more likely to be recalled than commercials unaccompanied by emotion.
2. The stronger the emotion generated, the greater its effects on memory will be.

3. Strong emotional commercials will be more likely to be recalled before weaker emotional commercials or those failing to engender any emotional response.
4. The kind of strength of emotional response experienced during a commercial is likely to serve as an organizer of recall, particularly in the absence of other reasonable organizing principles (such as similarity of products and their attributes).

Two tests relevant to the evaluation of these hypotheses are now examined. The first experiment (Choi and Thorson 1983) was designed to test the first hypothesis under natural viewing conditions. The second study (Friestad and Thorson 1984) was designed to test all four hypotheses under forced viewing conditions.

Research Findings of Study 1

Choi and Thorson (1983) examined recall and recognition of factual, emotional, and factual-emotional balanced ads under two instructional sets, one emphasizing attention to the ads and the other emphasizing attention to the programming surrounding the ads. For present purposes, the recall results in the attention to programming condition are most relevant and will be summarized here.

Method

The subjects were sixty-four undergraduate students (twenty-one males) enrolled in an introductory advertising course at the University of Wisconsin, Madison. They were tested at the beginning of the semester and were recruited by a "mass communication researcher who was interested in humor in situation comedies." The students were given course credits for their participation.

Prior to the study, eighteen commercials had been selected by having student subjects (other than those tested) rank two hundred commercials on a scale ranging from 0 (purely emotional), through 50 (a balance of emotional and rational) to one hundred (purely rational). Before rating the commercials, the subjects were shown one example each of a "purely rational" and a "purely emotional" ad. Six ads with means nearest 0, 50, and 100 and with small standard deviations were then chosen as the stimulus set.

Subjects were brought into a comfortably arranged viewing room in small groups, instructed that they would be evaluating two old situation comedies for possible purchase by a local television channel, and then shown the eighteen ads embedded in two thirty-minute program segments ("Phyllis" and "The Brady Bunch." The order of the commercials was counterbalanced across subjects.

After viewing, the subjects were given ten minutes to fill out an evaluation form for the two programs. They were then asked to recall as many of the commercials as possible, writing down as much as they could about each.

Results

For each of the three classes of commercials, the mean percentage of subjects recalling product class, brand name, at least one executional detail, and at least one product attribute was then calculated. Figure 14–4 shows the results. The emotional commercials showed significantly better product recall, brand name recall, and recall of executional information. They were weaker only for claim recall.

Implications

This first supports hypothesis 1—that emotional commercials will be strongly recalled. The failure to show strength of claim recall is quite reasonable in view of the fact that the emotional commercials had been chosen originally because they did not make many product claims but instead spent their thirty seconds engendering emotion.

While study 1 did show memorial strength for emotional ads, it did not provide a complete test of the model. A major problem is that it did not assure us that subjects were experiencing emotion during the viewing. In fact, we became dissatisfied with our definition of emotion as being the opposite of a rational appeal. What we were really interested in were executions that could verifiably move viewers emotionally, regardless of whether they included rational product claims.

Furthermore, though perhaps related to this first problem, the study did not vary strength or type of emotion experienced. All six of the emotional commercials were "happy" ones, and we suspected that they created only mild emotion. These two shortcomings led to the design of the second experiment.

Research Findings of Study 2

Study 2 addressed two main goals (Friestad and Thorson 1984). The first, to verify emotional experience during viewing, was addressed by having subjects continually register their feelings on a dial during viewing. The second, to examine the effects of intensity and valence differences in emotional advertising, was met by selecting stimuli that represented neutral commercials and three different types of emotional commercials.

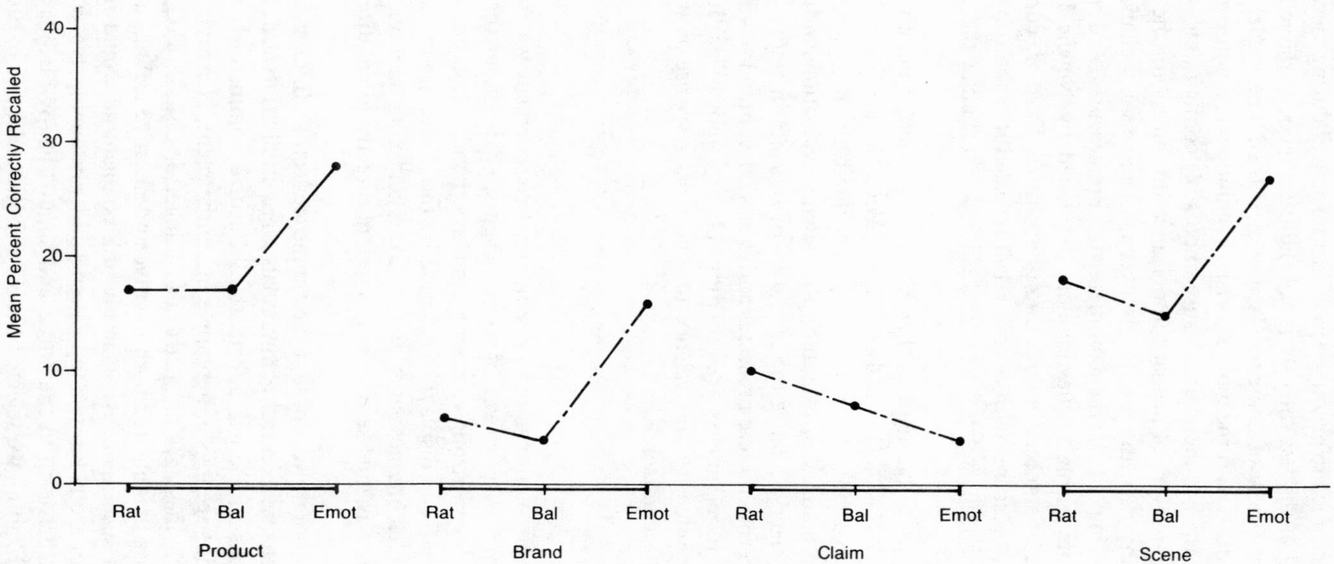

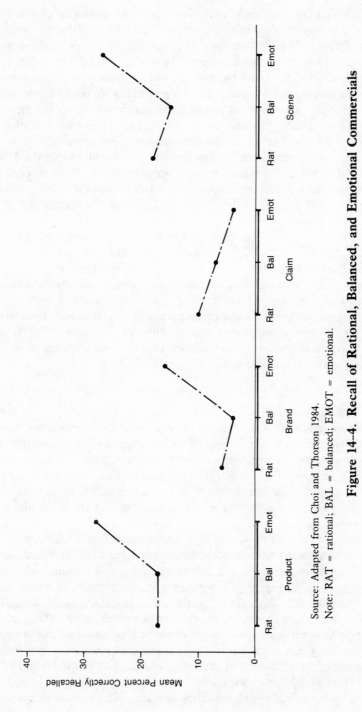

Source: Adapted from Choi and Thorson 1984.

Note: RAT = rational; BAL = balanced; EMOT = emotional.

Figure 14–4. Recall of Rational, Balanced, and Emotional Commercials

It is important to make two distinctions about our definition of emotion. First, the study was designed to examine emotional responses during viewing, not mood. The effects of the less intense, more enduring mood variable have been investigated in a variety of contexts (Isen et al. 1978). The model presented in this chapter deals with the more short-term emotional response experienced while viewing the commercial. Because of possible confoundings with mood, two considerations were of primary importance: to control for the subjects' mood prior to any exposure and to discover if there was any change in mood state after viewing all of the commercials. Premeasures and postmeasures of mood state (using a questionnaire developed by Nowlis 1965) revealed no difference in subjects' moods due to exposure. Further, correlations of previewing mood scores with overall recall revealed that the subject's mood was not systematically related to the likelihood of recalling the commercials.

A second distinction to be made is that we were not measuring attitude toward the ad (Lutz, MacKenzie, and Belch 1983; Mitchell and Olson 1981; Moore and Hutchinson 1983). As developed in the literature, att_{ad} measures are highly cognitive in nature (for example, postviewing evaluations of liking for the ad), and they clearly require the operation of semantic memory. The test of our model concerns episodic processes and is less relevant to the semantic processes involved in judgments or evaluations of the commercials. It was our goal to index the intensity and valence of emotional response as it was experienced during the commercials.

Method

Initial discrimination of emotional and nonemotional commercials was based on the following criteria: (1) portrayal of scenes, events, or situations that are traditionally associated with strong emotions (holidays, family reunions, birth or death); (2) an emphasis on displays of emotion by the characters in the ad; (3) use of production techniques such as soft focus and slow motion; and (4) use of language that is intense or vivid or refers directly to emotions or physical sensations.

The types of emotion we chose to examine reflected differences in both valence and intensity. Neutral commercials were straightforward, nonemotional presentations of factual information. Positive commercials were those capable of eliciting feelings of happiness or contentment. Negative commercials contained fear messages or portrayals of anger or disgust. Poignant commercials were those that elicited both positive and negative feelings at the same time or in rapid succession. An example of a poignant ad would be an old man watching alone out his window, then suddenly having his grandchildren and children drive up to the house and shout "happy birthday."

Using this categorization, we selected twenty commercials, five of each of the four types. None had been aired in the test area. These commercials were shown in randomized orders to sixty-five college students who had been told to evaluate the emotional characteristics of a set of commercials by continually turning a potentiometer dial (the Tell-Back Interact System-Mark IV) that would register their feelings each half-second on a scale from 100 (very positive) through 50 (neutral) to 0 (very negative). The dials were reset at 50 at the beginning of each commercial.

After viewing the twenty commercials, subjects were given an unexpected free recall test in which they were asked to write down as much as they could about each commercial. They then filled out an adjective checklist (Aaker and Bruzzone 1981) that served as a manipulation check on categorization of the commercials. Finally they rated their liking for each commercial.

Results

The adjective checklist responses corroborated our a priori categorization of the commercials. Data from the Tell-Back dials also indicated significantly greater intensity of emotion (as measured by the range of the Tell-Back scores) during viewing of the negative and poignant commercials (figure 14–5). Of

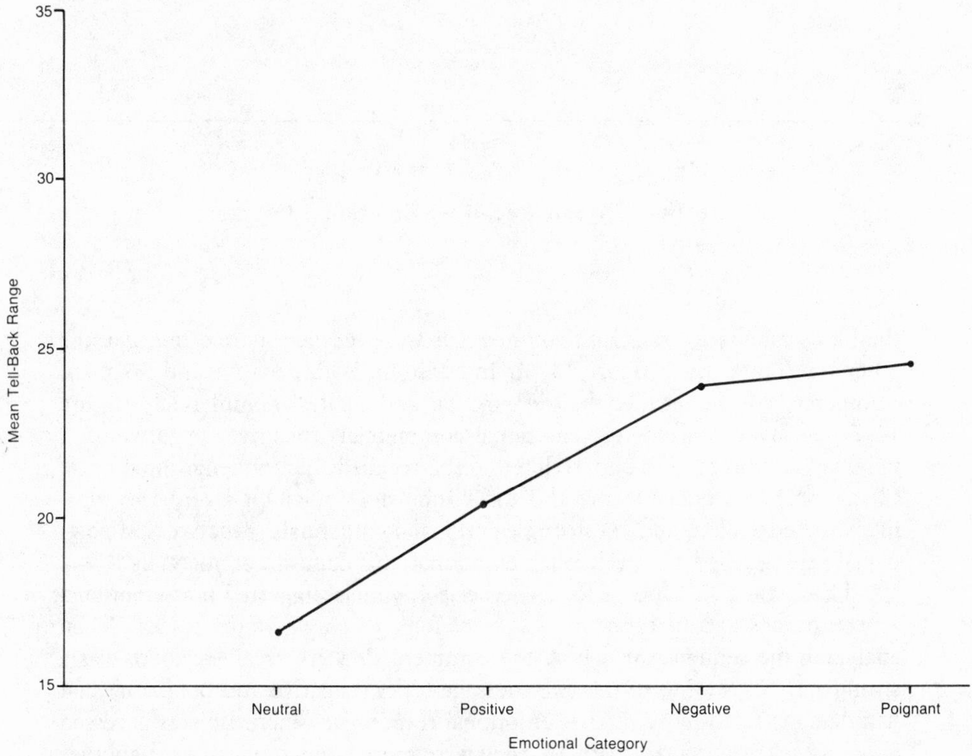

Figure 14–5. Mean Range of Tell-Back Settings by Commercial Category

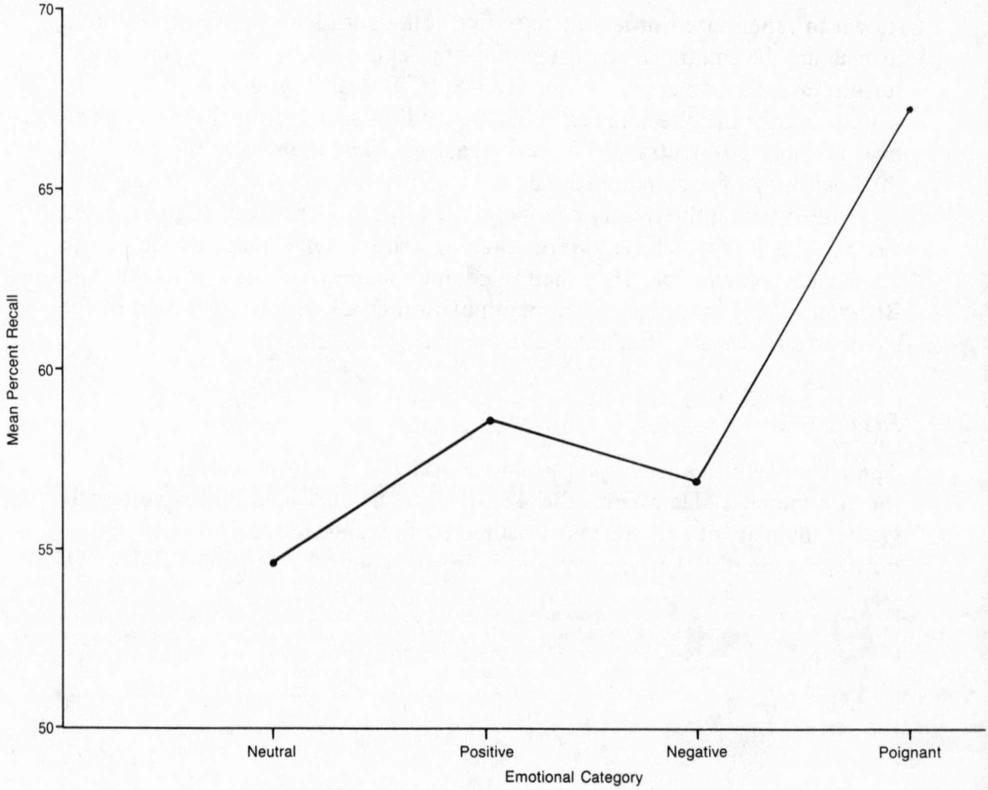

Figure 14–6. Mean Recall by Emotional Category

these two categories, poignant commercials were recalled more often than the other three categories (figure 14–6). In addition, both negative and poignant commercials were recalled before positive and neutral commercials (figure 14–7). As hypothesized, (1) emotional commercials (positive, negative, and poignant combined, were more likely to be recalled than nonemotional ones, (2) commercials engendering the most intensity (poignant) were the most likely to be recalled, and (3) strong emotional commercials (negative and poignant) were recalled before weaker emotional and neutral commercials.

There was also support for hypothesis 4, which suggested that emotional aspects of messages could be used as a cue for accessing memory traces. When analyzing the sequence in which the commercials were recalled, there was a strong early clustering of the two message types (negative and poignant) that had demonstrated more intense emotional responses. When subjects accessed either a negative or a poignant ad, they were more likely to recall next another

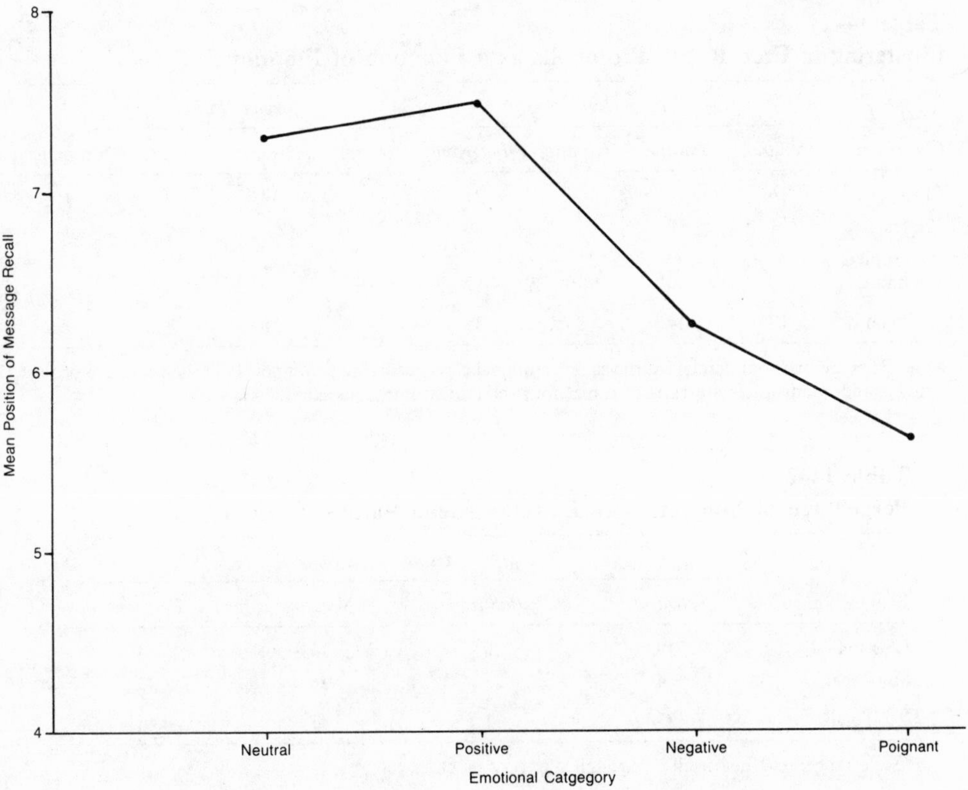

Figure 14–7. Mean Position of Recall by Emotional Category

ad of the same emotional type. These results were reflected in table 14–1, which shows poignant and negative commercials having more pair and triplet clustering during the first half of subject recall sequences and less clustering during the second half of the sequences (presumably because most of these commercials were recalled during the first half). This clustering occurred within emotional categories with products as diverse as house paint, a self-defense device, a soft drink, and a public service announcement about drunk driving.

Although it was not hypothesized, there was also evidence for an influence of emotion on semantic processes. The extreme like-dislike scores in table 14–2 indicate that the most intense emotional messages (the poignant ones) were liked best, followed by positive, negative, and neutral messages. Furthermore, when making judgments about how effective, important, or interesting each commercial was, subjects tended to make more extreme judgments about the

Table 14–1
Clustering in Free Recall Protocolls as a Function of Emotional Type

	First Half				*Second Half*			
Cluster Size	*Neutral*	*Positive*	*Negative*	*Poignant*	*Neutral*	*Positive*	*Negative*	*Poignant*
Pairs	16	14	21	27	6	14	6	9
Triplets	1	0	4	6	2	2	2	0
Quadruplets or more	0	0	0	2	1	0	0	0
Total	17	14	25	35	9	16	8	9

Note: Pairs are two commercials of the same emotional class occurring contiguously in the recall protocols. Triplets and quadruplets are runs of three, four, or more contiguous commercials.

Table 14–2
Percentage of Subjects with Extreme Mean Values on Liking

	Message Type			
Extreme Values[a]	*Neutral*	*Positive*	*Negative*	*Poignant*
Less than 2	19	10	15	4
More than 5	4	21	26	42
Total	23	31	41	46

[a]Scale range: 1 ("not at all") through 7 ("very much").

more emotional commercials (the poignant and negative ones). These findings also lend support to the hypothesized operation of the model.

Discussion

The two experiments summarized here produced the same results, though one presented commercials realistically placed in programming with instructions leading subjects to process naturally and the other required forced viewing. In both cases emotional commercials were better recalled. The second experiment further demonstrated that the greater the emotional intensity, the more likely was the recall, and that emotional type itself may lead to the organization of episodic traces of commercials in memory. Therefore results support the hypothesis that assumes television commercials initially enter into episodic storage and that emotion strengthens these traces.

At first glance these results would appear to conflict with a previous study that contended day-after recall penalizes feeling ads and favors rational ones

(Zielske 1982; Berger 1981); however, the conflict lessens if that study is examined closely. The Zielske stimuli were three emotional commercials and three "thinking" ones, as selected and categorized by professionals. Most significant, at least two of the emotional commercials were probably weak negative executions under the classification system used here and therefore were probably not good examples of emotional commercials. Second, the Zielske-Berger conclusions were based on day-after recall scores in which one rational ad scored very high, one feeling ad scored very low, and there were no differences among the remaining four ads. Before the Zielske study can be seen as contradicting our results, the problems of commercial categorization and number of commercials tested need attention.

Our results may also seem to conflict with the consensus opinion articulated by advertising practitioners (for example, Coulson in chapter 3) that emotional commercials score low in recall tests. Our model suggests that this may indeed be the case—not because emotional commercials are less well remembered but because when cuing by product category is used (cued responses are not distinguished from noncued ones by, for example, Burke recall testing), people are likely to consult semantic memory rather than episodic. And here there is no obvious reason to store information in terms of individual commercial executions or temporal information about when they were seen. Obviously, then, an emotional commercial can be stored very strongly in the stream of television viewing episodes, but searching semantic storage for information about heavy-duty laundry detergents would not access it.

Our primary goal was to understand how emotional responses experienced while viewing a commercial influence memory for that commercial. Traditional measures of advertising effectiveness have been less than satisfactory when applied to emotional messages. Presumably a model of how emotion affects the memory process, together with improved empirical indexes of emotions experienced during commercials, will enable the researcher and practitioner to assess better the effects of the emotional message. There are a number of related questions that need to be asked. Three seem particularly important.

The first arises from the intrinsic complexity of commercials as stimuli in experiments. Given the complexity of language, visual variables, music, product types, and so on, it is likely that a sample of emotional commercials differs from a sample of nonemotional commercials on more than just emotional variables. For example, emotional commercials may place less emphasis on product attributes, use simpler language, or use more extreme close-ups of faces. This variation precludes assuming that it is the emotion rather than one of the simultaneously varying variables that is producing the effect. Of course, the larger the sample of emotional commercials is, the less is the probability that confounding variables are producing observed effects on memory. Future research should address this problem by considering more commercials or by categorizing the commercials in a more detailed analytic fashion.

A second question relates to the first but focuses on the source of the emotion in a commercial. In some of the commercials tested here, the presumed emotional stimulus resulted from characteristics of the claims ("You will be safer from rape with the Noise Guard Cannister"). In others, the emotion resulted from executional occurrences (the old grandfather arrives in the New World). Does the source (a copy point versus visual story) of the emotion-producing stimulus affect the strength or the organization of the episodic trace? This question is of theoretical interest because the answer would reveal valuable information about how and where the emotional information is stored in the episodic trace. Of equal importance to the creator of effective emotional television commercials are the practical aspects of this question.

A third question considers the emotional response of the viewer. Do the effects of emotion vary as a function of the intensity of emotion, or does valence play a role? Neither of the studies summarized here allows distinguishing these possibilities so they remain for future investigation.

Finally a richer conception of memory is needed. Some advertising effectiveness research (for example, Burke day-after recall) would count the following responses as comparable in that the ad was successfully recalled and the brand name was correctly associated with the message. Clearly, however, the second response reveals a much richer memory trace.

> Subject response to neutral ad: "Trash bags. Three ordinary bags can fit into two [brand name] bags."
>
> Subject response to poignant ad: "This was my favorite commercial. The father coming to America on the boat. The reunion with his son. Seeing the son mouth the word "Papa." The commercial gave me a tingling sensation; my eyes watered. Then I found myself smiling at the end."

It is our contention that a more elaborate model of memory would yield a better picture of what people remember about a particular ad. With a better understanding of how the memory process is affected by emotion and the resulting differences in memory trace structure and content, advertisers would be able to design a message best suited to meet a specific communication goal (for example, brand awareness versus image creation). Further, the advertiser could use measurement strategies tailored to the specific memory traces of interest.

References

Aaker, D., and Bruzzone, D. 1981. Viewer perceptions of prime time television advertising. *Journal of Advertising Research* 21, no. 5:15–23.

Anderson, J.R. 1980. *Cognitive Psychology and Its Implications.* San Francisco: W.H. Freeman.

Anderson, J.R., and Bower, G.H. 1973. *Human Associative Memory.* Washington, D.C.: Winston.

Atkinson, R.C.; Herrmann, D.J.; and Wescourt, K.T. 1974. Search processes in recognition memory. In R. Solso, ed., *Theories in cognitive psychology: The Loyola Symposium.* Potomac, Md.: Erlbaum.

Baddeley, A.D. 1976. *The Psychology of Memory.* New York: Basic Books.

Berger, David. 1981. A retrospective: FCB recall study. *Advertising Age,* October 26, pp. 5–36.

Bower, G.H. 1981. Mood and memory. *American Psychologist* 36, no. 2:129–148.

Bower, G.H., and Cohen, P.R. 1982. Emotional influences in memory and thinking: Data and theory. In M.S. Clarke and S.T. Fiske, eds., *Affect and Cognition,* pp. 291–332. Hillsdale, N.J.: Erlbaum.

Choi, Y., and Thorson, E. 1983. Memory for factual, emotional, and balanced ads under two instructional sets. In Alan D. Fletcher, ed., *Proceedings of the 1983 Conference of the American Academy of Advertising.* Knoxville: University of Tennessee.

Clark, M.S., and Fiske, S. 1982. *Affect and Cognition.* Hillsdale, N.J.: Erlbaum.

Craik, F.I.M. 1979. Human memory. *Annual Review of Psychology* 30:273–307.

Dutta, S., and Kanungo, R.N. 1975. *Affect and memory: A reformulation.* Oxford: Pergamon Press.

Estes, W.K. 1975. Structural aspects of associative models for memory. In C.N. Cofer, ed., *The Structure of Human Memory.* San Francisco: W.H. Freeman.

Friestad, M., and Thorson, E. 1984. The effects of emotion on recall and evaluation of televised promotional messages. Unpublished manuscript. Madison: School of Journalism and Mass Communication, University of Wisconsin.

Godden, D.R., and Baddeley, A.D. 1975. Context-dependent memory in two natural environments: On land and underwater. *British Journal of Psychology* 66:325–332.

Herrmann, D.J., and McLaughlin, J.P. 1973. Effects of experimental and preexperimental organization on recognition. *Journal of Experimental Psychology* 99:174–179.

Isen, A.M.; Schalker, T.E.; Clark, M.; and Karp, L. 1978. Affect, accessibility of material in memory, and behavior: A cognitive loop? *Journal of Personality and Social Psychology* 36:1–12.

Izard, C.E. 1977. *Human emotions.* New York: Plenum Press.

———. 1982. Comments on emotion and cognition: Can there be a working relationship? In M. Clark and S. Fiske, eds., *Affect and Cognition.* Hillsdale, N.J.: Erlbaum.

Kintsch, W. 1974. *The Representation of Meaning in Memory.* Hillsdale, N.J.: Lawrence Erlbaum.

Klatzky, R.L. 1980. *Human Memory: Structures and Processes.* San Francisco: W.H. Freeman.

Lachman, R.; Lachman, J.L.; and Butterfield, E.C. 1979. *Cognitive Psychology and Information Processing.* Hillsdale, N.J.: Erlbaum.

Leventhal, H. 1980. Toward a comprehensive theory of emotion. In L. Berkowitz, ed., *Advances in Experimental Social Psychology* vol. 13. New York: Academic Press.

———. 1982. The integration of emotion and cognition: A view from the perceptual-motor theory of emotion. In M. Clark and S. Fiske, eds., *Affect and Cognition.* Hillsdale, N.J.: Erlbaum.

Lutz, R.J.; MacKenzie, S.B.; and Belch, G.E. 1983. Attitude toward the ad as a mediator of advertising effectiveness: Determinants and consequences. In R.P. Bagozzi and A.M. Tybout, eds., *Advances in Consumer Research,* vol. 10. Ann Arbor: Association for Consumer Research.

Lynch, J.G., and Srull, T.K. 1982. Memory and attentional factors in consumer choice: Concepts and research methods. *Journal of Consumer Research* 9:18–37.

McCloskey, M., and Santee, J. 1981. Are semantic memory and episodic memory distinct systems? *Journal of Experimental Psychology: Human Learning and Memory* 7:66–71.

McKoon G., and Ratcliff, R. 1979. Priming in episodic and semantic memory. *Journal of Verbal Learning and Verbal Behavior* 18:463–480.

Mandler, G. 1984. *Mind and Body.* New York: W.W. Norton.

Mitchell, A. 1981. Affect and semantic memory. In M. Goldberg and G. Gorn, eds., *Proceedings of the Eighty-eighth Annual Convention of the American Psychological Association,* vol. 10. New York: American Psychological Association.

Mitchell, A.A., and Olson, J.C. 1981. Are product attribute beliefs the only mediator of advertising effects on brand attitude? *Journal of Marketing Research* 18:318–332.

Moore, D.L., and Hutchinson, J.W. 1983. The effects of ad affect on advertising effectiveness. In R.P. Bagozzi and A.M. Tybout, eds., *Advances in Consumer Research,* vol. 10. Ann Arbor: Association for Consumer Research.

Nilsson, L-G. 1984. New functionalism in memory research. In K.M.J. Lagerspetz and P. Niemi, eds., *Psychology in the 1990's,*. Amsterdam: North-Holland.

Nowlis, V. 1965. Research with the mood adjective check list. In S. Tomkins and C. Izard, eds., *Affect, Cognition and Personality.* New York: Springer.

Plutchik, R. 1980. A general psycho-evolutionary theory of emotion. In R. Plutchik and H. Kellerman, eds., *Emotion: Theory, Research and Experience.* New York: Academic Press.

Plutchik, R., and Kellerman, H. 1980. *Emotion: Theory, Research and Experience.* New York: Academic Press.

Rossiter, J.R. 1981. Predicting Starch scores. *Journal of Advertising* 21:63–68.

Schacter, D.L., and Tulving, E. 1982. Memory, amnesia, and the episodic/semantic distinction. In R.L. Isaacson and N.E. Spear, eds., *The Expression of Knowledge.* New York: Plenum Press.

Seamon, J.G. 1980. *Memory and Cognition.* New York: Oxford University Press.

Shoben, E.J.; Wescourt, K.T.; and Smith, E.E. 1978. Sentence verification, sentence recognition, and the semantic-episodic distinction. *Journal of Experimental Psychology: Human Learning and Memory* 4:304–317.

Smith, S.M.; Glenberg, A.; and Bjork, R.A. 1978. Environmental context and human memory. *Memory and Cognition* 6:342–353.

Srull, T.K. 1983. Affect and memory: The impact of affective reactions in advertising on the representation of product information in memory. In P.R. Bagozzi and A.M. Tybout, eds., *Advances in Consumer Research,* vol. 10. Ann Arbor: Association for Consumer Research.

Thorson, E. 1984. Episodic and semantic memory: Implications for the role of emotion in advertising. Paper presented at the Association for Education in Journalism and Mass Communication, Gainesville, Florida, August.

Thorson, E., and Friestad, M. 1983. Stimulus determinants of viewer memory and preference for television commercials: Language, integration, affect, and visuals. Unpublished manuscript. Madison: University of Wisconsin, School of Journalism and Mass Communication.

———. 1984. Emotion and the recall of television commercials. In D. Stewart, ed., *Proceedings of the American Psychological Association Annual Meeting,* Division 23, Consumer Science. New York: American Psychological Association.

Thorson, E., and Snyder, R. 1984. Viewer recall of television commercials: Prediction from the propositional structure of commercial scripts. *Journal of Marketing Research* 21:127–136.

Tulving, E. 1972. Episodic and semantic memory. In E. Tulving and W. Donaldson, eds., *Organization of Memory.* New York: Academic Press.

Tulving, E.; Schacter, D.L.; and Stark, H. 1982. Priming effects in word-fragment completion are independent of recognition memory. *Journal of Experimental Psychology: Learning, Memory, and Cognition* 8:336–342.

Zajonc, R.B.; Pietromonaco, P.; and Bargh, J. 1982. Independence and interaction of affect and cognition. In M. Clark and S. Fiske, eds., *Affect and Cognition.* Hillsdale, N.J.: Erlbaum.

Zielske, H.A. 1982. Does day-after recall penalize "feeling" ads? *Journal of Advertising Research* 22, no. 1:19–23.

15

Gauging and Explaining Advertising Effects: Emergent Concerns Regarding Construct and Ecological Validity

Chris T. Allen
Thomas J. Madden

In their introduction to *Psychological Processes and Advertising Effects: Theory, Research, and Application*, Alwitt and Mitchell (1985) observe that "our understanding of how advertising affects consumer behavior is undergoing a dramatic transformation" (p. 1). Such a claim seems quite justified; one could offer several chapter titles from that book as representative of the new wave of thought in advertising research: "How Advertising Works at Contact," "The Influence of Affective Reactions to Advertising," "Central and Peripheral Routes to Persuasion, . . ." "Online Cognitive Processing of Television," "Cognitive Theory and Audience Involvement." The conceptual themes underlying the dramatic transformation are also illustrated by this group of papers. Current research gives strong priority to development of causal explanations for how advertising works at the point of contact with the individual. Thus considerable emphasis is placed on a process orientation, and a central challenge becomes explaining how ad processing may be mediated by audience involvement. The presumption that variations in viewer involvement may underlie or evoke fundamentally different forms of processing has prompted investigations of multiple routes to persuasion. Interest in a mindless, automatic, shallow, heuristic, peripheral, or affective route to persuasion has emerged as a dominant theme in recent studies (see chapters 5, 6, 11, and 12).

Our empirical work has been driven by conceptual concerns quite similar to those of others in the field. This work has incorporated "the increasingly widely held assumption that most advertising is inherently uninvolving" (Lutz 1985, p. 45) in an attempt to furnish insights about the causal role of low-intensity, ephemeral, affective experiences as facilitators of persuasion. Additionally, we share the belief that these low-intensity, affective experiences may well be the most frequent response evoked by advertising in natural settings (Lutz 1985). Further, we are fascinated by the perspective of Clark and Isen (1982) who speculate that "the subtle, pervasive, and almost irresistible effects of low-level affective states are so often with us that their potential influence may be very great'' (p. 76).

While the image of a detached, disinterested consumer confronted be affectively oriented advertising has clearly transformed the conceptual focus of research, it seems clear that a corresponding transformation in research methodology for the most part has not been forthcoming. Is this as it should be? Does a conceptual transformation demand a methodological transformation? Can the simplistic, fleeting, affective experiences that occur in natural ad processing be captured by measures that are conscious, verbal, and evaluation oriented? Do the roles subjects are encouraged to adopt (either explicitly or implicitly) in laboratory experiments and copy testing research yield adequate representations of the way uninvolved consumers process ads in their own living rooms?

This chapter focuses on research methods and strategies. Although the arguments presented are not entirely new, data from recent experiments are used to highlight problematic issues. Before turning to the data, the methodological concerns are discussed and summarized using the notions of construct and ecological validity. Our basic goal is to encourage readers to contemplate a simple question: When does advertising research actually have anything to do with the way advertising is processed?

Interface between Construct and Ecological Validity

A major research thrust continues to be developing causal explanations (or theories) for how advertising works using unobservable constructs concerning mental states of the ad processor (Edell and Burke 1984; Lutz 1985). Therefore, one might expect to find heavy emphasis on construct validity in advertising research. However, despite periodic admonitions (Jacoby 1978; Peter 1981; Ray 1977), construct validity is largely ignored. The research traditions of marketers and psychologists are quite similar in this regard. In both, it seems, the heavy emphasis on causal inference is typically not accompanied by attention to the ''logically prior problem of identifying, measuring, and validating the theoretical constructs that participate in causal relations'' (Breckler 1984, p. 1204).

Construct validity ''pertains to the degree of correspondence between abstract constructs and the procedures used to operationalize them'' (Peter 1981, p. 133). Ignoring construct validity will have negative ramifications in terms of methodology because it signals that researchers are selecting measurement devices and/or experimental manipulations without the direction provided by crisply explicated constructs.

While construct validity is paramount in theory development, there can be an even more fundamental problem in research examining advertising effects. This problem involves the potential correspondence between one's process-oriented constructs and the actual mental processes spontaneously evoked by advertisements in natural settings. We will refer to this issue of trying to achieve correspondence between one's research constructs and the mental activity actually evoked by advertising as a matter of ecological validity.

The ecological validity issue emphasizes "that the artificial situation created for an experiment may differ from the everyday world in crucial ways. . . . When this is so, the results may be irrelevant to the phenomena that one would really like to explain" (Neisser 1976, p. 33). But as Neisser warns, "Demands for ecological validity are only intelligible if they are specific. . . . They must point to particular aspects of ordinary situations that are ignored by current experimental methods" (p. 34). Ecological validity can be interpreted as implicating a wide variety of factors, and it should be made clear that this is not a simple call for greater "mundane realism" (Berkowitz and Donnerstein 1982) in advertising experiments. Rather, if advertising theories developed in the laboratory are to be relevant outside it, the processes studied in the lab must have ecological validity.

The focus of our methodological concern can be portrayed as the interface between construct and ecological validity. One must explicate constructs for necessary guidance concerning the many methodological choices one has to make in the conduct of research. When explicating constructs, one should focus on the image of an individual processing advertisements in natural settings. Without theoretical constructs that capture and correspond to the reality of ad processing, and lacking isomorphism between such constructs and their measures and manipulations, progress in the generation and testing of advertising theories can hardly be expected. Further, measurement and/or experimental procedures that create systematic, artificial processes (that then go largely undetected) can clearly confound our understanding of how advertising works.

Empirical Manifestations

The following discussion uses data-based examples from five recent experiments to explicate concerns regarding construct and ecological validity. In some cases the concerns exemplified pertain primarily to work dealing with the influence of ad-evoked affect. In others the issues raised are germane to advertising research more generally. Detailed descriptions of the first four studies are furnished elsewhere (Allen and Madden 1986; Madden, Allen, and Twible 1985; Madden, Debevec, and Twible 1985; Madden, Dillon, and Twible 1986), so the discussion of these will be brief. The fifth study was conducted specifically to extend the methodological argument advanced here and will be described in more detail.

Construct and Ecological Validity in ATT_{ad} Research

Like many other consumer researchers, our thinking about advertising effects was clearly influenced by the provocative psychological debate concerning the role of affect in decision making (Bower 1981; Clark and Isen 1982; Leventhal 1974; Zajonc 1980). During the same period, the influential papers of Mitchell and Olson (1981) and Shimp (1981) encouraged those intrigued by affect to focus their interest on the attitude-toward-the ad (ATT_{ad}) construct. We found this construct appealing but were bothered by the ambiguity inherent in the affect-attitude terminology as it was being used in the evolving ATT_{ad} research stream. The concern was that researchers were not offering careful explication for the ATT_{ad} construct and thus lacked guidance in selecting measurement devices and experimental manipulations. As a result, work often seemed to ignore the ephemeral, affective experiences that likely abound in natural processing. Simply stated, ATT_{ad} researchers seemed to rely solely on subjects' cognitive evaluations while attempting to understand their affective processes.

Encouraged by the findings of Abelson and his colleagues (Abelson et al. 1982), we began to explore the conceptual distinction between affective experience and cognitive evaluation. Consumers experience affect spontaneously as they process commercials. Evaluative judgments about those commercials would seem to require more cognitive effort from the processor. Given the low levels of processing involvement that many presume for mass media generally (Csikszentmihalyi and Kubey 1981; Krugman 1965, 1979) and advertising specifically (Greenwald and Leavitt 1984; Lastovicka 1979; Lutz 1985), focusing on evaluative judgments rather than affective experience in ad effects research may involve a severe compromise regarding the ecological validity of the focal process. The fact that most ATT_{ad} researchers were also relying on affective conditioning (Allen and Madden 1985) as the primary explanatory mechanism for their empirical findings made an emphasis on spontaneous, ephemeral affect seem even more appropriate. The challenge, of course, was to show that the subtle conceptual distinction between affective experience and cognitive evaluation could have utility in empirical work.

Experiment 1

This study was designed to furnish a more precise evaluation of the causal relationship between ad-evoked affect and brand attitude. Our preoccupation with the affective-experience construct motivated several methodology decisions that made this study unique. While ATT_{ad} researchers have been intrigued by the impact of ad-evoked affect, most have not carefully selected experimental manipulations in terms of their potential for generating affect. Here humor was employed as the affect stimulator. Two sixty-second radio ads, a humorous and a serious execution, were the treatment stimuli. While they were constructed to communicate the same product-specific information, prior experimental work with the ads (Madden 1982) gave us confidence in their ability to evoke different affective experiences.

The treatments were embedded in realistic programming so that at the moment of exposure, subjects had no reason to suspect these ads were a focal point of the study. This procedural detail differed from previous studies where it was obvious to subjects prior to exposure that their experimental function was to furnish some form of detailed evaluation based on the treatment stimuli. It is likely that such procedures create deeper, more cognitively oriented message processing than is typical in natural settings. Indeed, if one accepts Greenwald and Leavitt's (1984) principle of higher-level dominance, the experimental set employed in other studies may have effectively destroyed, or at a minimum attenuated, participants' affective experiences. (This concern about experimental set motivated a complementary study described here as experiment 4.)

Finally, our emphasis on affective experience motivated a different measurement approach. Following Mitchell and Olson (1981), most researchers operationalize ATT_{ad} using semantic differential scales that force cognitive evaluations of the treatment ad. While we collected these evaluative judgments for comparative purposes, our focal measure involved an affective response index modeled after a technique used by Abelson et al. (1982). This measure demands nothing in the way of evaluative judgments; it simply asks participants to retrospect about what they were feeling during ad exposure. In this instance the pleasantness of participants' affective states was gauged in terms of three adjectives: *happy, cheerful,* and *pleased.* Standard cognitive response, attitude and intention measures were also collected.

The results of this project proved both encouraging and somewhat perplexing. The path diagrams in figure 15–1 were fit using a full information approach (LISREL). They furnish an overview of the findings. Of particular interest are the antecedents of attitude toward trying the product (A_{Try}). In each model A_{Try} has three antecedents: two attitude-toward-the-ad measures (PAff and Ad Eval) and one measure of product-oriented cognitive responses (PCog). The two ATT_{ad} measures were formed by summing items on an Abelson-type affect scale (PAff) and a semantic differential scale (Ad Eval).

In the humor condition, only the path from PCog to A_{Try} is significant. The link from PAff to A_{Try} approaches significance ($t = 1.4$), but the *p*-value is still greater than .10. The lack of significance could be due to the multicollinearity between PAff and Ad Eval (notice their correlation is .62). To assess the individual effect of each variable, two additional models were fit: one

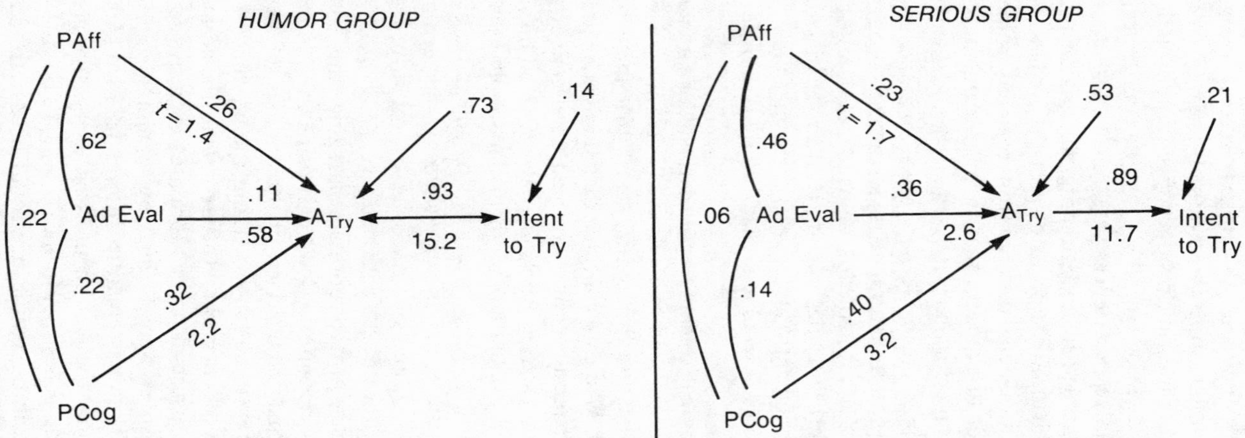

Correlation Matrix (Humor Group)

	PCog	PAff	Ad Eval	A_{Try}	Intent
PCog	—				
PAff	n.s.	—			
Ad Eval	n.s.	.62	—		
A_{Try}	.40	.40	.34	—	
Intent	.34	.33	.29	.93	—

Correlation Matrix (Serious Group)

	PCog	PAff	Ad Eval	A_{Try}	Intent
PCog	—				
PAff	n.s.	—			
Ad Eval	n.s.	.47	—		
A_{Try}	.48	.42	.52	—	
Intent	.37	.55	.49	.89	—

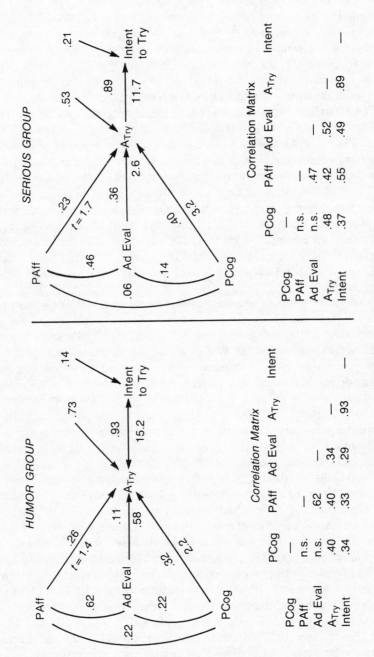

Figure 15-1. Path Models: Results from Experiment 1

containing PAff and PCog as antecedents of A_{Try} and the other containing Ad Eval and PCog as antecedents. In both models, the link between PCog and A_{Try} was again significant. The path between PAff and A_{Try} achieved statistical significance ($t = 2.27$), but the path between Ad Eval and A_{Try} did not ($t = 1.79$). The significant path between the Abelson affect measure (PAff) and attitude toward trial is consistent with the affective-conditioning hypothesis (Allen and Madden 1985).

The perplexing result appears in the serious condition. Here a traditional link between cognitive response and attitude was anticipated, but other exogenous effects either from PAff or Ad Eval were not expected since this serious ad was used specifically because it lacked affective cues. The data did not meet this expectation. Notice in figure 15–1 the significant path between Ad Eval and A_{Try} ($t = 2.6$) for the serious group. Recall that Ad Eval is the type of operationalization commonly employed in other ATT_{ad} studies. Why would this path be significant in the serious and not the humor group?

A speculative interpretation for this finding was developed based on the simple correlations among variables in the two treatment groups and considering these data in the context of the availability-valence hypothesis (Tybout, Sternthal, and Calder 1983). This hypothesis encourages an emphasis on the mental processes subjects utilize as they perform their experimental tasks. It assumes that evaluative judgments should be driven by availability and valence of material in short-term memory. What if this "cognitive material" remains constant across a series of judgments? One might then expect a uniform pattern of correlation among variables since a common pool of meaning in short-term memory is driving all judgments. Correlations in the serious group did suggest a high degree of entwinement among constructs. Yet such entwinement would seem to be cause for concern regarding discriminant validity of the focal constructs. Are attitude toward the ad and brand attitude really distinct constructs? If so, when? If not, a fundamental tenet of construct validity has been violated. This highly speculative interpretation motivated additional data collection.

The Discriminant Validity Problem: Experiments 2 and 3

The discriminant validity issue raised by experiment 1 motivated two follow-up studies, which are described fully in Madden, Debevec, and Twible (1985), and Madden, Dillon, and Twible (1986). Both experiments adopted the approach to operationalizing ATT_{ad} featured in prior work (Gardner 1985; Mitchell and Olson 1981). Thus, ATT_{ad} measures asked subjects for evaluative judgments rather than direct retrospection about affective experience.

Experiment 2 was a replication of study 1 but focused instead exclusively on the empirical assessment of discriminant validity for ATT_{ad} versus brand attitude. Three measurement methods were used in operationalizing each construct, and the Campbell and Fiske (1959) criteria for discriminant validity were accessed via covariance structure analysis. While this analytical procedure does not eliminate the subjectivity inherent in the use of the Campbell and Fiske criteria, the findings in this case were rather clear-cut. The empirical case for discriminant validity of the two constructs after exposure to the humorous ad is sound, whereas exposure to the serious version did not effect discriminant validity. If two constructs lack discriminant validity, pursuing an analysis concerning the causal influence of one upon the other can be very misleading.

The joint implication of experiments 1 and 2 is that where discriminant validity can be shown for ATT_{ad} and brand attitude, the relationship between the two will be weakened. Were such a result generalizable, it would pose a major challenge to the inferences emerging from other ATT_{ad} studies where true affective experience is often neglected and discriminant validity issues to date have been ignored. Experiment 3 was conducted to furnish more evidence pertinent to this issue of generalizability.

Recall that radio ads were the focal stimuli of the first two experiments. While a case can be made that humor is an effective affect producer, such ads may not be directly comparable to those featuring visual imagery as the primary executional variable. Nearly all other ATT_{ad} studies have used experimental stimuli laden with visual imagery. It is conceivable that subjects might draw on these images as the basis for discriminating between brands and ads as they furnish evaluative judgments concerning each. The issue investigated in experiment 3 was whether the association between ATT_{ad} and brand attitude would remain statistically significant if discriminant validity were obtained through ads featuring visual imagery.

The crucial treatment in this experiment was a television ad for Lois designer jeans. This commercial is dominated by the visual images of erotic dancers wearing the product. The auditory portion of the Clio Award winner includes music and mentions brand name but contains no product-specific arguments. Participants were evaluating the brand and the ad for the first time since the product had not been introduced in the U.S. market prior to the study.

As in experiment 2, three measurement methods were employed in gauging each construct. Much like the humor condition in the previous project, the empirical case for discriminant validity of ATT_{ad} and brand attitude was strong. Yet having established that this particular ad with its affect-evoking visuals does effect discriminant validity, the data also reveal that after controlling for method factors, the association between the two constructs was not statistically significant. Here we must conclude that when discriminant validity is obtained for ATT_{ad} and brand attitude using operationalizations like those that have dominated prior work, an association between the two constructs will be hard to find.

Implications and Further Directions

Today's dominant strategy for researching advertising effects is well exemplified in the ATT_{ad} stream. This strategy relies on unobservable constructs concerning internal states of the ad processor. Inferences about how advertising works are derived primarily by establishing links between such constructs. Thus explanations are phrased in terms of mediator variables. For instance, Edell and Burke (1984) observe that ATT_{ad} "acts as a mediator of advertising effectiveness" (p. 644), and Gardner (1985) concludes that ATT_{ad} "is a fairly robust mediator of brand attitude" (p. 197). The implication of statements like these is that we are advancing understanding of how advertising works through the ATT_{ad} construct and its related research stream.

The first three experiments illustrate the dangers inherent in today's dominant research strategy when one ignores construct and ecological validity. The ATT_{ad} stream has not featured crisp conceptual explication, and it certainly has not included an emphasis on the ecological validity of the mental processes being studied. As a result, our data indicate that any empirically based inferences in the ATT_{ad} stream must be viewed skeptically when discriminant validity issues have not been explicitly addressed. Conclusions about the status of ATT_{ad} as a causal mediator are premature.

The validity concerns raised and illustrated to this point are germane in researching the effects of ad-evoked affect. Additionally, one might consider whether these validity concerns have implications for the more cognitive research approaches commonly employed. Perhaps the most popular of these approaches in recent years has been the cognitive response paradigm (Petty, Ostrom, and Brock 1981; Wright 1980), which focuses attention on analysis of internal processes that cognitively mediate brand attitude formation. If we again recall today's image of the detached, disinterested consumer reluctantly confronted by advertising, one must question how much cognitive responding really occurs in natural settings. Do cognitive responses really mediate advertising effectiveness, or, like the ATT_{ad} stream, is such a conclusion more likely due to ignoring hidden assumptions about discriminant validity between key constructs? Answers to questions such as these must await further research. This is a serious issue that merits consideration for any conceptual framework where the dominant epistemological approach has entailed modeling one unobservable construct in terms of other unobservables in search of potential causal mediators.

Whether it is primarily cognitive, affective, or some combination of the two, the mental activity and investment involved in processing any given advertisement are likely to be fragile and fleeting. Our preoccupation with construct and ecological validity leads us to contemplate other aspects of the advertising experiment in terms of how they might distort or overwhelm these fragile, fleeting processes. Do common research procedures systematically influence subjects' mental activity to the point that the fundamental process being studied no longer represents the way people process ads? This is a difficult question; although we are not prepared to offer any definitive answers, the final two studies we discuss indicate that it is a question that merits more attention from advertising researchers. Experiment 4 demonstrates the potentially contaminating influence of experimental set. Experiment 5 illustrates how different measurement methods create artifactual processes that may overwhelm those fragile processes that characterize true ad processing.

Experiment 4: The Issue of Experimental Set

The notion of experimental set was introduced when describing the procedures of experiment 1. It refers to the explicit instructions and/or implicit cues given to participants regarding their tasks and role in a study. In advertising research, the set will influence the attention given to and the mental effort expended on processing the focal stimuli. This notion of experimental set is beginning to receive some explicit consideration in advertising research (Gardner 1985; Lutz 1985). Studies employing independent variables that manipulate set suggest it has an important impact on ad processing (Gorn 1982; Petty, Cacioppo and Schumann 1983). Such work, however, is the exception.

Most research either ignores the issue of experimental set, gives subjects ambiguous cues about their role, or makes it obvious to them that their primary tasks will entail providing detailed evaluations concerning specific advertisements. Again, the ecological validity question is straightforward: can experimental set distort processing to the point that what one is studying in the laboratory no longer mirrors the reality of ad processing?

Experiment 4 is a replication of study 1 with explicit changes in procedure that create a manipulation of experimental set. Recall in the first study that the purpose was initially disguised. When subjects listened to the recorded material, they believed the program and not the advertisement was the focus. Since most people listen to radio for the programming and not the ads, ad processing in this disguised condition should have some ecological validity. Experiment 4 was a nondisguised condition wherein participants were told that they would be listening to and evaluating radio ads. The two studies were otherwise identical and were merged for analytical purposes, creating a 2 (humor versus serious ad execution) by 2 (disguised versus nondisguised procedure) factorial design. While this analysis was largely exploratory, we expected the nondisguised condition to yield more cognitive evaluation. The most interesting questions, however, deal with the issues of whether experimental set can actually alter ad evaluations and whether set will interact with ad execution in influencing evaluations.

The nondisguised condition produced more cognitive activity as indicated by the total number of thoughts listed in the two groups. This main effect for

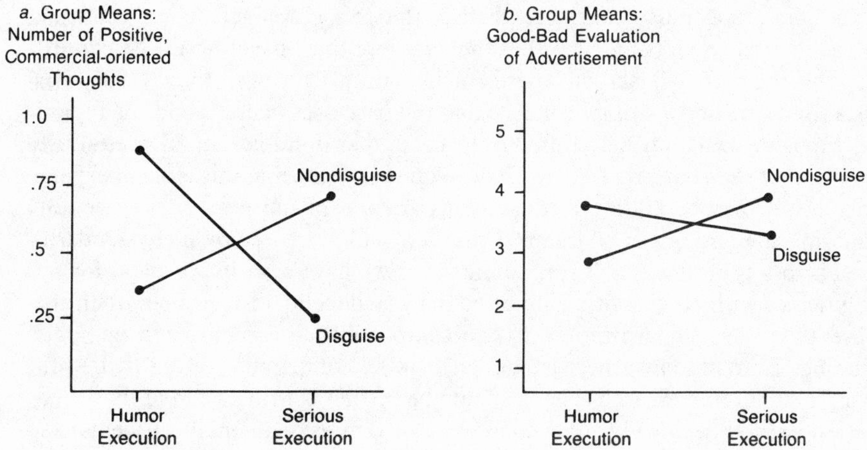

Figure 15–2. "Experimental Set" by Ad Execution Interaction

experimental set was qualified, however, by an interesting and significant ($p < .02$) interaction that manifests itself most vividly in favorability of subjects' thoughts directed toward the commercials (as opposed to the product). This specific interaction effect is displayed in part *a* of figure 15–2. The pattern of cognitive activity resulting from the two ads is dramatically altered by experimental set. More positive thoughts were produced by the humorous execution in the disguised condition, yet in the nondisguised condition, the serious ad evoked more favorable thoughts. Subjects' summary evaluations of the two ads followed a similar pattern as gauged by a multiple-item semantic differential. The result on the good-bad item from this scale is graphed in part *b* of figure 15–2 to illustrate again the significant interaction ($p < .001$). Evaluations of the two ads were clearly altered as a function of experimental set.

Explanations for these rather intriguing findings must involve a good deal of speculation. Greenwald and Leavitt's (1984) principle of higher-level dominance seems germane to the more favorable evaluation of the humor ad in the disguised condition. The set created by the nondisguised condition may have attenuated the ability of the humor actually to evoke an affective experience, leading to less favorable reactions regarding the ad. The results for the serious ad present more of a challenge. Perhaps when subjects are set in a deliberative, evaluation-oriented mode, they will react most favorably to straightforward appeals that give exclusive emphasis to logical product benefits.

While these explanations are speculative and post hoc, the nature of the results themselves indicates that the issue of experimental set warrants more attention from practitioners and theoretical researchers. From the applied standpoint, one must consider whether the sets employed in copy testing research alter processing such that the data lose their meaning in the context of how the ads will actually perform in natural settings. Lutz (1985) has recently expressed a similar concern that the processes operating in the typical ad exposure situation may differ from those that dominate in ad pretesting.

From the perspective of theory development, ignoring this issue of experimental set may be adding a tremendous amount of noise to the system. By ignoring the issue, it is guaranteed that sets will not be completely standardized across experiments. If it is common, as we have seen in our data, for set to interact with ad executions in effecting key dependent measures, then the absence of set standardization makes it impossible to compare and integrate findings from studies otherwise designed to be comparable. Indeed, the primary item on the research agenda should be further consideration of this interaction issue. Specifically, how common is it that experimental set yields differential responses to divergent ad-execution styles?

Experiment 5: Exploring the Validity Challenge Inherent in Measurement

It is not difficult to build a case that measurement taken at one point in an advertising experiment or pretesting study could alter participants' responses gathered later in the same project. For example, empirical work by Fazio and his colleagues (Fazio et al. 1982; Fazio, Lenn, and Effrein 1984) documents that the simple act of filling out an attitude measure can create an attitude, which then alters the individual's processing of subsequent persuasive messages. Theoretically, the availability-valence hypothesis (Tybout, Sternthal, and Calder 1983) could also be used to posit that measurement per se will alter what is available in subjects' short-term memories over the course of a study. The resultant impact on subjects' evaluative judgments will at best add noise to one's data and at worst create undetected, systematic bias. Even at a philosophy of science level, one can find concerns about our traditional measurement approaches. A major contention of marketing's relativists (Anderson 1983; Peter and Olson 1983) has been that nothing can be measured without changing the fundamental, focal process.

Again, a basic goal of this chapter is to encourage readers to consider the question: When does advertising research actually have anything to do with the way advertising is processed? To our knowledge, little or no empirical work has been conducted to explore the validity threats inherent in measurement. A small-scale demonstration experiment was carried out to explore this threat and thus encourage reflection on the issue of how data generated in advertising studies actually reflect the ad processing that occurs in natural settings.

In experiment 5, the treatment manipulation was measurement, not ad execution. Four experimental groups were initially developed. In a baseline condition (group A) participants were exposed to four similar thirty-second television commercials for Lowenbrau beer. They then filled out measures gauging their attitudes and intentions toward and interest in consuming this brand. In the other treatments, ad exposures were the same, and these same brand evaluation measures were taken at the end of the session. In each of the other groups, however, a different, additional measure was inserted at the front of the questionnaire. In group B, the additional measure was an affect index asking subjects to retrospect about and report the feelings they experienced during exposure on a short adjective checklist. A cognitive response measure asking participants to list what they had been thinking during exposure was inserted in group C. For group D the insert was the Needham Harper Worldwide version of the Viewer Response Profile (VRP) (Schlinger 1979), a fifty-item Likert scale tapping several different dimensions of affective response.

The effect of these different measurement forms was assessed in terms of how they altered subjects' evaluations of the brand and how they influenced the relationship between brand attitude and intention. Table 15–1 shows an interesting pattern of results for the interest in consumption measure. The Lowenbrau ads appear to work better for groups A and C than for B and D. (Remember that all subjects were exposed to the same set of four Lowenbrau ads.) A similar pattern of more favorable brand evaluation in groups A and C was also observed on the semantic differential measure of attitude.

Most researchers in marketing and psychology take for granted that attitudes and intentions are related (Ajzen and Fishbein 1980). This makes the correlational results displayed in table 15–2 most intriguing. Again, the findings for groups A and C are similar, as are those for B and D, but between the pairs, there are notable differences. In A and C, the expected association between attitude and intention is observed, but in B and D, the correlations

Table 15–1
Measurement Effect on Brand Interest

	Number of Subjects Responding		
Treatment Groups	*Yes*	*No*	*Totals*
A: Baseline	10	8	18
B. Affect index inserted	7	13	20
C: Thought listing inserted	11	8	19
D: Needham VRP inserted	8	13	21
Totals	36	42	78

Note: Questionnaire item: The advertiser tried to increase your interest in trying Lowenbrau beer. Did she/he succeed?

Table 15–2
Attitude and Behavior Intention Correlations by Treatment

	Overall Attitude toward Lowenbrau (from Ten-Item Semantic Differential)	
Treatment Groups	*Intent to Buy Next Time I Buy Beer*	*Intent to Try If Served at a Party*
A: Baseline	.54	.60
B: Affect index inserted	—[a]	—[a]
C: Thought listing inserted	.60	.58
D: Needham VRP inserted	—[a]	—[a]

[a] Not significant.

were weakened to the point that they were not significant. Thus it appears that choice of measurement may not only influence the valence of brand evaluations in advertising studies but also may affect the relationships between variables.

Dimensionality of Ad Response as a Function of Measurement

There is a knotty problem embedded in what we have tried to examine in experiment 5. The means relied on to assess empirically the artifactual processes inherent in traditional measurement is traditional measurement. Even those measures used in the baseline (group A) may have set in motion an artifactual process that overwhelmed any mental activity actually evoked by the ads themselves. Recall that Fazio et al.'s work (1982, 1984) has shown that simple attitude measures affect attitude formation. Indeed one might argue that measures like those in group A are more potent producers of spontaneous attitudinal development than most advertisements. With this perplexing problem as a backdrop, one additional measure was built into experiment 5, and another treatment (group E) was processed.

One possibility for reducing the obtrusiveness of measurement is to simplify the measurement task. The more complex and extensive is the measurement, the more there is potential for artifactual mental processes to predominate. Following this line of reasoning, a fifth treatment condition was processed. Here again participants watched the four Lowenbrau ads, but the measurement task was highly simplified. In this group E, just one simple task was required immediately after ad exposure, and it was presented as follows: "You have just watched four commercials for Lowenbrau beer. Please list the first four words that come to mind that in your opinion describe the commercials." The idea here is to try to tap indirectly the actual mental activity produced by the ads without demanding additional cognitive evaluation or thought construction from the participant. This identical measure was the last item filled out by those in groups A through D of experiment 5. Accordingly, group E might be viewed as a kind of control group that provides an assessment of how measures used in A through D may have differentially had an impact on participants' mental activity. Further, the focal dependent measure in group E should be less obtrusive than most other measures commonly used for gauging advertising response.

Open-ended questions are appealing because they impose no structure on the subject's response; however, they generate mass diversity that must be given some structure post hoc if any meaning is to be discerned from the data. To provide this structure, subjects' responses on the "four-word question" were coded into one of six categories. Four categories were borrowed from other work pertaining to the dimensionality of advertising response (Wells, Leavitt, and McConville 1971). These four dimensions and sample words for each are as follows: vigor (*exciting, enthusiastic, exhilarating*): sensuousness (*tender, gentle, soothing*); uniqueness (*novel, imaginative, original*); and irritation (*phony, snooty, stupid*). The Wells et al. (1971) dimensions of humor and personal relevance were not evidenced in our data, but two other categories of response were quite common. One involved subjects picking a word (such as *Lowenbrau*) actually used in the ads and playing it back. This category was labeled playback. The final category involved words (such as *attractive, good quality,* and *nice music*) that implied favorable evaluative judgment by the subject and was labeled positive evaluation.

After coding subjects' raw responses into these six categories, the data were given further structure by correspondence analysis. One can think of this technique as similar to other multivariate methods (such as factor analysis) for creating lower-order, dimensional space. Correspondence analysis provides for the graphical representation of the rows and columns of a cross-classification data table in a reduced space (Lebart, Morineu, and Warwich 1984). The two-dimensional solution, which captured roughly 85 percent of the original variance, is plotted in figure 15-3. Notice the location of each of the six word categories in this two-dimensional space.

Figure 15-3 provides a context in which the dominant pattern of response produced by each of the five treatments (groups A–E) can then be viewed. The word category by treatment group contingency table was submitted to a correspondence analysis to furnish a graphical representation of the similarities and dissimilarities among treatments in terms of their impact on word elicitation. If the five groups were clustered closely together in space, it would suggest that the measurement tasks unique to each group did not influence responses. As shown in figure 15-4, the groups did not cluster together, indicating that participants' answers on the four-word question were in part a function of the different measurement tasks each had performed.

Notice also the location of group E in figure 15-4. This group furnishes an interesting basis for comparison in that there was no intervening measure-

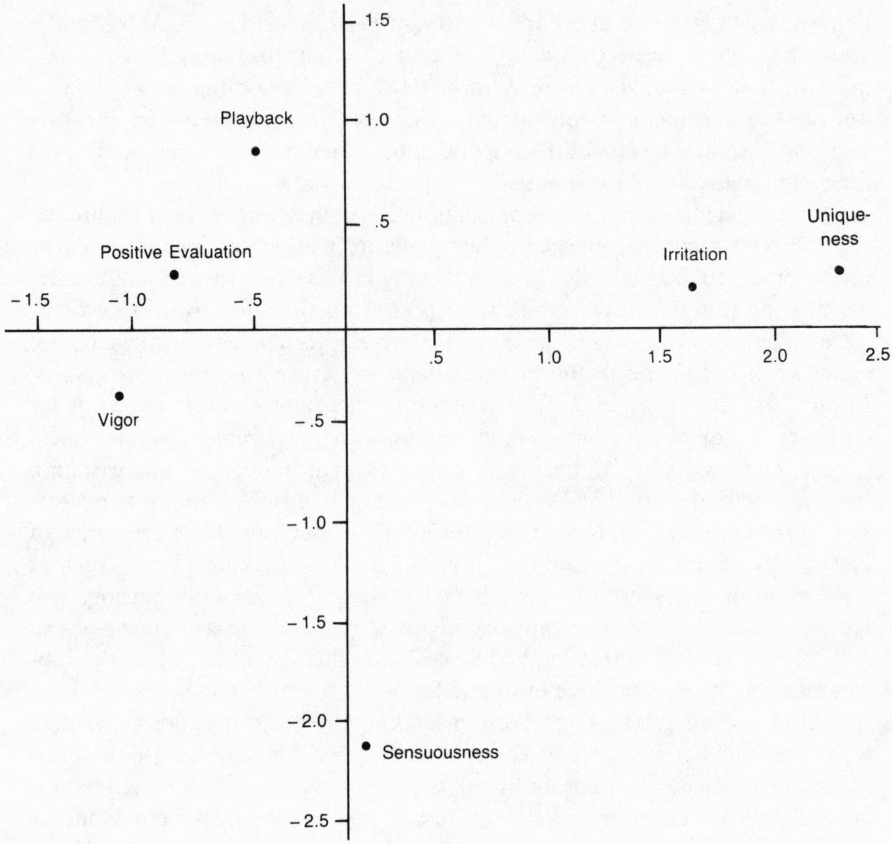

Figure 15–3. Dimensions of Response

ment, and it should thus represent the most natural or ecologically valid condition. Distance from group E might then be interpreted as an indication of the degree of artifactual response created by measurement. For example, the distance of group C from E suggests that the thought-listing measure contributed substantially more to the pattern of response on the four word question than did the affect index in group B. Indeed, if one assumes that group E represents a natural, control condition, group B appears to contain the minimum of artifactual variation attributable to measurement per se.

Conclusions Regarding Experiment 5

Experiment 5 produced several intriguing results; although most of the implications one might draw entail considerable speculation, the data make

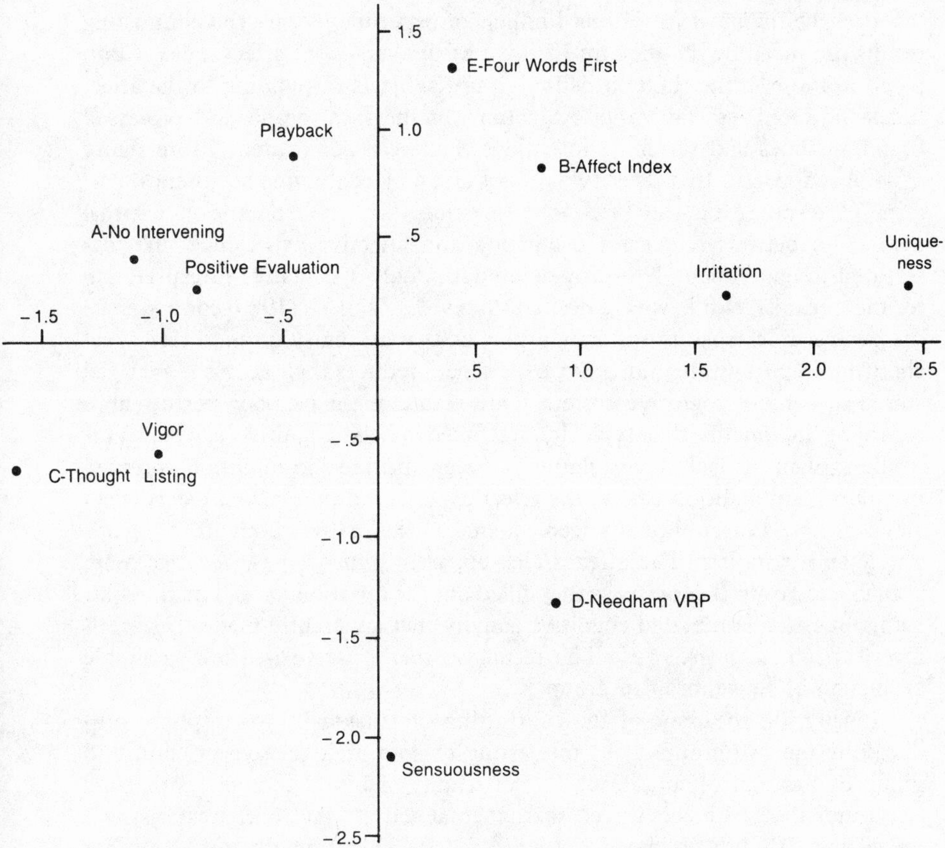

Figure 15–4. Dimensions of Response with Treatment Groups

one point rather clearly: the evidence documents measurement effects not only on the valence and dimensionality of advertising response but also on the relationships between variables that may be of interest to the researcher. Such findings imply that common measurement devices can potentially create undetected, systematic biases in advertising research. Since only one type of ad execution was used in experiment 5, there are no data to address the issue of whether certain kinds of executions might interact with measurement in yielding systematic bias, but this is also a possibility. Furthermore, the data again raise the issue of comparability of findings between and among studies. If different researchers employ diverse measures or use the same measures but arrange them in different sequences, how are we to know when contradictory findings between projects amount to anything more than measurement-driven artifact?

Perhaps the most intriguing findings of experiment 5 are the contrasting results produced by the thought-listing measure versus the affect index. Compared to those in the thought-listing group, subjects responding to the affect index indicated less favorable evaluations of the focal brand and professed brand attitudes and purchase intentions that were not related. From figure 15–4, it is apparent that these two groups (B and C) exhibited antithetical patterns of response on the four-word question. We draw on the conceptual distinction between cognitive evaluation and affective experience that was featured in experiment 1 to provide an admittedly speculative interpretation for these results. While we are hesitant to invoke Zajonc's (1980) controversial thesis regarding separate systems, it may be that asking subjects to retrospect about and report on their affective experiences reduces their access to material stored in a more cognitive system. One result might be poor performance regarding judgments that typically are based on the cognitive system. This would explain the lack of correlation between attitude and intention observed in group B. In addition, the actual affect experienced by many subjects when viewing these Lowenbrau ads seemed somewhat negative. Some find the ads phony and irritating. The affect index apparently made these feelings more available to group B subjects as they filled out the questionnaire. The thought-listing question stimulated cognitive activity that apparently made these feelings less salient in group C. The result we then observe is a less favorable evaluation of Lowenbrau in group B.

Finally, on the issue of the contrasting dimensionality of response produced by the two groups, it is interesting to note their relative proximity to group E, the control condition. The proximity of B and E suggests that the affect index aids subjects in accessing mental activity that is characteristic of processing that has not been contaminated by measurement. On the other hand, the distance between C and E seems to indicate that a thought-listing measure stimulates retrieval and thought construction to the point that it produces mental activity quite different from that of the more natural condition. What one should then infer from such "manufactured" mental activity regarding the actual effect of the ad becomes an important question that we urge advertising researchers to consider. It is hoped that these speculative interpretations will stimulate additional research on this and other questions related to the validity challenge inherent in measurement.

General Discussion and Research Implications

The data furnished in these experiments are exemplary of problems one can anticipate when construct and ecological validity are neglected. Although studies 1, 2, and 3 were all set in the context of the ATT_{ad} research stream, the results are salient to advertising research more generally because the epistemological approach featured in ATT_{ad} work typifies that of many other advertising studies. This approach features measurement of unobservable, internal state constructs and explanations of how advertising works are developed by documenting empirical links between such constructs. However, ignoring the issues of construct and ecological validity in this approach creates a condition such that inferences about a construct's role as a causal mediator become tenuous. Our data indicate, for example, that any such causal inferences regarding the ATT_{ad} construct are premature.

In experiments 4 and 5, the focus of attention shifted to experimental procedure and measurement. Today's image of the ad processor as detached and disinterested has not had significant impact on the way studies are conducted or ad effects are measured. Our data indicate that both procedure and measurement have the potential to alter mental processes to the degree that inferences about real ad effects can be severely compromised.

Explicating Ecologically Valid Constructs in Affect Research

We have tried to challenge researchers with a simple question: when does advertising research actually have anything to do with the way advertising is processed? The question seems especially germane for those trying to understand the role of affective phenomena in persuasion. In specifying a construct to guide research in this area, we strongly urge researchers to keep in mind the distinction between affective experience and cognitive evaluation. It is on just this distinction that the attitude construct can be ambiguous, creating unnecessary problems for ATT_{ad} researchers.

Low-intensity and highly spontaneous affective experiences abound in natural ad processing. Therefore, a construct that emphasized such phenomenon might be referred to as ecologically valid. Such a construct is now emerging in consumer and psychological research (Abelson et al. 1982; Allen and Madden 1985; Breckler 1984; Clark and Isen 1982; Isen 1984a, 1984b) with a clarity of meaning that should make it a productive focal point for future work. As illustrated by study 1, a specific focus on affective experience does much to guide the design of an experiment assessing the actual impact of this phenomenon. Not only were the selections of measurements and manipulations in experiment 1 guided by this conception of affect, but also the procedure (experimental set) was developed to be conducive to affective experience. Making these methodological choices is facilitated by precise construct explication. Again we emphasize the utility of the conceptual distinction between affective experience and cognitive evaluations in making such choices.

Affective experience is inherently difficult to verbalize. Accordingly, most pencil-and-paper measures of the construct are bound to induce artifactual cognitive processes. While we sympathize with this viewpoint, the experience with the affect index in these five studies has given us reason to be encouraged that it can serve as a valid indicator of affect.

It is important to keep in mind, however, the simplicity of the phenomenon being measured. Affect is conceived very simply as feelings of pleasantness and/or unpleasantness (Allen and Madden 1985). Our position is that a subject's representation of his or her affective experience will become more a function of cognitive processes as one's measurement becomes more complex. Therefore, to measure affect with pencil and paper, researchers are urged to keep the task simple. An adaptation of the relatively unobtrusive four-word question developed for experiment 5 may prove to be a useful measurement alternative for affect research. Combined with the correspondence analysis technique that allows graphical representation of such data, one can conceive of an approach that might be especially well suited for applied work.

Operationalizing Ecologically Valid Constructs in Advertising Research

If consumers really are careless and disinterested when they process most ads, there is reason to be concerned about procedure and measurement that force effortful, systematic mental activity. This concern is illustrated empirically by studies 4 and 5, which suggest that basic methodological elements of the experiment can alter processing to the degree that ecological validity is compromised. Ignoring the problem poses a serious threat to the validity of psychological explanations for how advertising works growing out of empirical research. Furthermore, a lack of ecological validity seriously challenges the generalizability of data generated by practitioners in advertising pretests.

An emphasis on the ecological validity of ad processing may imply consequences that, from an applied standpoint, are impractical. Certainly after going to the trouble and expense of getting participants for copy testing research, one is inclined to assess multiple ad executions using a multitude of detailed measures. Such endeavors demand careful, deliberate thinking from the subject. Even an instrument like the VRP, which purportedly gauges affective reactions to ads (Schlinger 1979), is bound to induce a level of analytical thinking that would have never been spontaneously evoked by simple exposure to an ad. This is not to say that such devices do not have heuristic value in the development and selection of ad executions. However, one must question what, if anything, copy testing research typically reveals about the impact an ad makes on individuals half-asleep on the sofa in their living rooms.

For those interested in developing theories of how advertising works, an emphasis on the ecological validity of the focal process seems unavoidable. Otherwise methodological choices in such areas as measurement and experimental set will continue to go unstandardized across studies that researchers might otherwise assume are comparable. Studies 4 and 5 point out that the absence of method standardization may invalidate this comparability assumption.

The possibility (raised by experiment 4) that experimental set can interact with ad execution style creates another challenge to valid inference. It is possible that different measurement forms could interact with ad execution style to produce systematic bias that otherwise might be misinterpreted as treatment effect. Theoretical researchers need to devote more attention to how experimental methods may be altering the mental activity that is their real concern. Following Fazio et al.'s (1982, 1984) example from the attitude area, more theorizing is needed regarding how the methods employed in research become part of and alter the processes we are attempting to explain.

Considering Alternative Paradigms for Persuasion Research

Perhaps the real core of the concerns raised here is the research tradition that relies so heavily on self-report measures of internal states. In this tradition, researchers seek explanations for how advertising works through specification of internal states (for example, ATT_{ad} and cognitive response) that mediate ad effects on other internal states (such as brand attitude). Yet it seems that not enough consideration has been given to the fundamental requisites for causal inference. For example, ad researchers rarely raise the issue of discriminant validity. Yet without clear evidence supporting discriminant validity, how can one conclude anything about causal mediation between constructs?

Researchers who employ the traditional paradigm face two difficult problems regarding the discriminant validity issue. Theoretically there is the problem of specifying the conditions under which discriminant validity will be obtained between and among internal state constructs. Empirically the challenge becomes one of documenting discriminant validity prior to testing causal linkages. While our experience in the ATT_{ad} research stream shows that such effort can be quite revealing, it seems likely that the discriminant validity problem will prove insurmountable in some instances. For example, in the cognitive response framework (Petty, Ostrom, and Brock 1981; Wright 1980), there is only one method, thought listing, for operationalizing the key construct. But empirical assessment of discriminant validity relies on multiple operationalizations for each construct (Campbell and Fiske 1959). Proliferation of internal state constructs in ad effects research (Lutz 1985) heightens the unwieldiness of this discriminant validity challenge.

This is not a blanket condemnation of the traditional paradigm in advertising research. The point is simply that overreliance on any single paradigm can be detrimental to knowledge development; there are alternatives. One viable option is to place much stronger emphasis on the construct validity of experimental manipulations while deemphasizing self-report measures of internal states. This approach builds construct validity through triangulation (Crano 1981) in terms of multiple, diverse experimental manipulations instead of multiple, divergent measures. Also, the deemphasis on internal state measures increases ecological validity by reducing the likelihood of a measure-driven, artifactual process. Strong causal inferences can be generated by such a paradigm when diverse manipulations of the focal construct yield convergence in terms of observed effects on multiple outcome measures.

This alternative empirical paradigm will not fit all ad research contexts, but it will fit affect research well. It is perhaps best exemplified in Isen's (1984a, 1984b) impressive research program dealing with low-intensity feeling states. In her work, multiple experimental manipulations have been chosen to triangulate on the focal affect construct. The convergent pattern of predicted effects across her experiments provides convincing inferences concerning the impact of the construct.

Building a diverse pool of ad executions with the notion of using them as multiple manipulations of a common affect construct would not appear beyond the reach of advertising researchers. Given these manipulations, the researcher must then rely on theory to dictate research hypotheses and salient dependent measures. For instance, drawing on the affective-conditioning hypothesis as the motivator for a research stream, key outcome or dependent measures might be defined exclusively in terms of approach-avoidance behaviors (Allen and Madden 1985). In the extreme case, it is possible to conceive of an ad affect research stream devoid of pencil-and-paper self-report measures. Given the possibility that such measures may always rely on some level of forced cognitive reconstruction, such a possibility seems well worth pursuing.

We have raised a number of difficult methodological issues for advertising researchers to consider. Research strategies, experimental methods, and measurement procedures need to be reevaluated in the light of conceptual innovations being introduced into advertising research. We do not suggest abandoning traditional approaches, but we do argue the value of methodological diversity in gauging and explaining advertising effects.

References

Abelson, Robert P., Donald R. Kinder, Mark D. Peters, and Susan T. Fiske. 1982. "Affective and Semantic Components in Political Person Perception." *Journal of Personality and Social Psychology* 42 (April):619–630.

Ajzen, Icek, and Martin Fishbein. (1980). *Understanding Attitudes and Predicting Social Behavior.* Englewood Cliffs, N.J.: Prentice-Hall.

Allen, Chris T., and Thomas J. Madden. 1985. "A Closer Look at Classical Conditioning." *Journal of Consumer Research* 12 (December): 301–315.

———. 1986. "Affective Experience in the Persuasion Process: Theoretical and Methodological Issues in Researching Attitude Toward the Ad." Unpublished paper.

Alwitt, Linda F., and Andrew A. Mitchell. 1985. *Psychological Processes and Advertising Effects: Theory, Research and Application.* Hillsdale. N.J.: Erlbaum.

Anderson, Paul F. 1983. "Marketing, Scientific Progress, and Scientific Method." *Journal of Marketing* 47 (Fall):18–31.

Berkowitz, Leonard, and Edward Donnerstein. 1982. "External Validity Is More Than Skin Deep." *American Psychologist* 37 (March):245–257.

Bower, Gordon H. 1981. "Mood and Memory." *American Psychologist* 36 (February):129–148.

Breckler, Steven J. 1984. "Empirical Validation of Affect, Behavior, and Cognition as Distinct Components of Attitude." *Journal of Personality and Social Psychology* 47 (December):1191–1205.

Campbell, Donald T., and Donald W. Fiske. 1959. "Convergent and Discriminant Validity by the Multitrait-Multimethod Matrix." *Psychological Bulletin* 56 (March):81–105.

Clark, Margaret S., and Alice M. Isen. 1982. "Toward Understanding the Relationship between Feeling States and Social Behavior." In Albert H. Hastorf and Alice M. Isen, eds., *Cognitive Social Psychology.* pp. 73–108. New York: Elsevier/North-Holland.

Crano, William D. 1981. "Triangulation and Cross-Cultural Research." In Marilynn B. Brewer and Barry E. Collins, eds., *Scientific Inquiry and the Social Sciences.* pp. 317–344. San Francisco: Jossey-Bass.

Csikszentmihalyi, Mihaly, and Robert Kubey. 1981. "Television and the Rest of Life: A Systematic Comparison of Subjective Experience." *Public Opinion Quarterly* 45 (Fall):317–328.

Edell, Julie A., and Marian C. Burke. 1984. "The Moderating Effect of Attitude toward an Ad on Ad Effectiveness under Different Processing Conditions." In Thomas C. Kinnear, ed., *Advances in Consumer Research,* 11:644–649. Provo Utah: Association for Consumer Research.

Fazio, Russell H., Jeaw-Mei Chen, Elizabeth C. McDonel, and Steven J. Sherman. 1982. "Attitude Accessibility, Attitude-Behavior Consistency, and the Strength of the Object-Evaluation Association." *Journal of Experimental Social Psychology* 18 (July):339–357.

Fazio, Russell H., Tracy M. Lenn, and Edwin A. Effrein. 1984. "Spontaneous Attitude Formation." *Social Cognition* 2, no. 3:217–234.

Gardner, Meryl P. 1985. "Does Attitude toward the Ad Affect Brand Attitude under a Brand Evaluation Set?" *Journal of Marketing Research* 22 (May):192–198.

Gorn, Gerald J. 1982. "The Effects of Music in Advertising on Choice Behavior: A Classical Conditioning Approach." *Journal of Marketing* 46 (Winter):94–101.

Greenwald, Anthony C., and Clark Leavitt. 1984. "Audience Involvement in Advertising: Four Levels." *Journal of Consumer Research* 11 (June):581–592.

Isen, Alice M. 1984a. "The Influence of Postitive Affect on Decision Making and Cognitive Organization." In Thomas C. Kinnear, ed., *Advances in Consumer Research,* 11:534–537. Provo, Utah: Association for Consumer Research.

———. 1984b. "Toward Understanding the Role of Affect in Cognition." Robert S. Wyer, Jr., and Thomas K. Srull, eds. *Handbook of Social Cognition* 3:179–236. Hillsdale, N.J.: Erlbaum.

Jacoby, Jacob. 1978. "Consumer Research: State of the Art Review." *Journal of Marketing* 42 (April):87–96.

Krugman, Herbert E. 1965. "The Impact of Television Advertising: Learning without Involvement." *Public Opinion Quarterly* 29 (Autumn):349–356.

———. 1979. "Low Involvement Theory in the Light of New Brain Research." In John C. Maloney and Bernard Silverman, eds., *Attitude Research Plays for High Stakes*. Chicago: American Marketing Association.

Lastovicka, John L. 1979. "Are Attitude Models Appropriate for Mass Tv Advertising?" In John Eighmey, ed., *Attitude Research under the Sun*, pp. 151–170. Chicago: American Marketing Association.

Lebart, Ludovic, A. Morineu, and Kenneth M. Warwich. 1984. *Multivariate Descriptive Statistical Analysis*. New York: Wiley.

Leventhal, Howard. 1974. "Emotions: A Basic Problem for Social Psychology." In Charlan Nemeth, ed., *Social Psychology: Classic and Contemporary Integrations*, pp. 1–51. Chicago: Rand McNally.

Lutz, Richard J. 1985. "Affective and Cognitive Antecedents of Attitude toward the Ad: A Conceptual Framework." In Linda F. Alwitt and Andrew E. Mitchell, eds., *Psychological Processes and Advertising Effects: Theory, Research, and Application*, pp. 45–63. Hillsdale, N.J.: Erlbaum.

Madden, Thomas J. 1982. "Humor in Advertising: Applications of a Hierarchy of Effects Paradigm." Ph.D. dissertation, University of Massachusetts, Amherst.

Madden, Thomas J., Chris T. Allen, and Jacquelyn L. Twible. 1985. "Attitude-toward-the-Ad: An Assessment of Alternative Measurement Methods." Paper presented at the American Marketing Association Educators' Conference, Washington, D.C.

Madden, Thomas J., Kathleen Debevec, and Jacquelyn L. Twible. 1985. "Assessing the Effects of Attitude-toward-the-Ad on Brand Attitudes: A Multitrait-Multimethod Design." In Michael J. Houston and Richard J. Lutz, eds., *Marketing Communications—Theory and Research*, pp. 109–113. Chicago: American Marketing Association.

Madden, Thomas J., William R. Dillon, and Jacquelyn L. Twible. 1986. "Construct Validity of Attitude-toward-the-Ad: An Assessment of Convergent/Discriminant Dimensions." In Jerry Olson and Keith Sentis, eds., *Advertising and Consumer Psychology*, 3:74–92. New York: Praeger.

Mitchell, Andrew A., and Jerry C. Olson. 1981. "Are Product Attribute Beliefs the Only Mediator of Advertising Effects on Brand Attitudes?" *Journal of Marketing Research* 18 (August):318–332.

Neisser, Ulric. 1976. *Cognition and Reality*. San Francisco: W.H. Freeman.

Peter, J. Paul. 1981. "Construct Validity: A Review of Basic Issues and Marketing Practices." *Journal of Marketing Research* 18 (May):133–145.

Peter, J. Paul, and Jerry C. Olson. 1983. "Is Science Marketing." *Journal of Marketing* 47 (Fall):111–125.

Petty, Richard E., John T. Cacioppo, and David Schumann. 1983. "Central and Peripheral Routes to Advertising Effectiveness: The Moderating Role of Involvement." *Journal of Consumer Research* 10 (September):135–146.

Petty, Richard E., Thomas M. Ostrom, and Timothy C. Brock. 1981. *Cognitive Responses in Persuasion*. Hillsdale, N.J.: Erlbaum.

Ray, Michael L. 1977. "When Does Consumer Information Processing Research Actually Have Anything to Do with Consumer Information Processing." In

William D. Perreault, Jr., ed., *Advances in Consumer Research,* 4:372–375. Atlanta: Association for Consumer Research.

Schlinger, Mary Jane. 1979. "A Profile of Responses to Commercials." *Journal of Advertising Research* 19 (April):37–46.

Shimp, Terence A. 1981. "Attitude toward the Ad as a Mediator of Consumer Brand Choice." *Journal of Advertising* 10, no. 2:9–15.

Tybout, Alice M., Brian Sternthal, and Bobby J. Calder. 1983. "Information Availability as a Determinant of Multiple Request Effectiveness." *Journal of Marketing Research* 20 (August):280–290.

Wells, William D., Clark Leavitt, and Maureen McConville. 1971. "A Reaction Profile for TV Commercials." *Journal of Advertising Research* 11 (December):11–17.

Wright, Peter. 1980. "Message-Evoked Thoughts: Persuasion Research Using Thought Verbalization." *Journal of Consumer Research* 7 (September):151–175.

Zajonc, Robert B. 1980. "Feeling and Thinking: Preferences Need No Inferences." *American Psychologist* 35 (February): 151–175.

16
The Role of Emotion in Advertising Revisited: Testing a Typology of Emotional Responses

Morris B. Holbrook
Richard A. Westwood

Holbrook and O'Shaughnessy (1984) have discussed the role of emotion in advertising and proposed some potential directions for future research needed to resolve various conceptual, methodological, and behavioral issues. They concluded that "further empirical work represents the next logical step" (p. 60) and called for research on a variety of neglected topics. With respect to one such area in need of investigation, they suggested that "much work remains to be done in constructing, comparing, and validating . . . typologies of emotional content" (p. 59).

This recognition stems from a growing dissatisfaction with the conventional treatment of affective processes in consumer research. As noted by Hirschman and Holbrook (1986), most consumer psychologists and advertising researchers have adopted a rather narrow, unidimensional view of affect as a simple bipolar continuum represented by such contrasts as like-dislike, positive-negative, pro-con, favorable-unfavorable, good-bad, or pleasing-displeasing. This tendency toward a narrow view of affect in consumer research parallels equally narrow conceptions of cognition (for example, beliefs as opposed to other kinds of thoughts) and behavior (for example, buying as opposed to other consumption activities). Together these biases constrict our perspective on what happens in consumer behavior (Holbrook and Hirschman 1982).

One route toward enlarging our understanding of consumer behavior in general and communication processes in particular lies in replacing the conventionally narrow conception of affect with a broader view of emotion. Holbrook (1986) argues for a clearer recognition of the full sweep of rich, variegated, and multifarious emotional reactions that pervade the consumption experience. In the course of acquiring, using, and disposing of any product—that is, any good, service, idea, or other consumable event—consumers may e almost any combination of love, hate, fear, anger, joy, sadness, disgust, interest, surprise, and so on. Such reactions may form the basis for advertising appeals intended to tie a particular product or brand to some relevant aspect of the consumer's emotional life. As reviewed by Holbrook and O'Shaughnessy (1984), emphasized by Puto and Wells (1984), and illustrated by several contributors to this book, the role of emotion in advertising and its links to the experiential aspects of consumption have begun to attract increased attention. Clearly as part of this awakening of research interest, we must develop and explore typologies and other analytic schemes that contribute to an understanding of the rich range of emotional content that appears in the consumption experience.

Toward this end, Holbrook (1986) considered various ways of distinguishing among the relevant emotions. Although he provided extensive examples in a variety of categories, he noted that methodological considerations favor systematic theory development combined with empirical testing as the means for constructing typologies of emotional content. Holbrook suggested that the best example of an emotional typology derived by theory development and testing appears in Plutchik's (1980) psychoevolutionary approach to the classification of emotions, which "combines systematization and empiricism toward the construction of a clearly conceived, research-supported emotional typology" (Holbrook 1986, p. 39).

Here we pursue this theme by investigating the validity of Plutchik's (1980) emotional typology in the context of research on advertising effects. Specifically, we first describe Plutchik's psychoevolutionary approach to the classification of emotions and then test his taxonomy on consumer responses to television commercials. The results of this test support Plutchik's typology while elucidating the structure of emotional responses to advertising.

A Conceptual Framework: Plutchik's Typology

Plutchik's (1980) scheme for classifying emotional content stems from his focus on the evolutionary role of psychological phenomena. From this perspective, emotional types possess selective advantage because of their survival value in encouraging or accompanying certain biologically beneficial functions:

> The theory . . . assumes that certain . . . classes of adaptive responses, involving the whole organism, are the prototype patterns of emotions in animals and humans. The theory assumes that the environment of all organisms creates certain common problems. . . . Emotions are total body reactions, internal plus behavioral, to these kinds of basic survival problems created by the environment. Emotions are attempts of the organism to achieve control over certain events that relate to survival. (p. 127)

According to Plutchik, eight emotions are naturally selected by virtue of this functional adaptive process:

Emotional Type	*Related Function*	*Adaptive Advantage*
Acceptance	Incorporation	Taking beneficial stimuli from the outside world into the organism
Disgust	Rejection	Getting rid of harmful stimuli that have previously been incorporated
Fear	Protection	An attempt to avoid being destroyed
Anger	Destruction	Removing a barrier to the satisfaction of a need
Joy	Reproduction	Procreation of the species
Sadness	Reintegration	Reaction to the loss of something needed or enjoyed
Anticipation	Exploration	Collecting information about the environment
Surprise	Orientation	Reaction of readiness when encountering a new or strange object

Plutchik also argues that these eight emotional categories can be organized conceptually into pairs of polar opposites: acceptance-disgust, fear-anger, joy-sadness, and anticipation-surprise. These interrelated bipolarities are viewed as forming a complex emotional structure, characterized by a chain-like circular pattern or circumplex (acceptance—fear—surprise—sadness—disgust—anger—anticipation—joy) representing a horizontal slice through a vertical cone in which height conveys intensity, as follows:

Type	*Low Intensity*	*High Intensity*
Acceptance	Tolerance	Adoration
Fear	Timidity	Terror
Surprise	Uncertainty	Amazement
Sadness	Pensiveness	Grief
Disgust	Boredom	Loathing
Anger	Annoyance	Rage
Anticipation	Mindfulness	Vigilance
Joy	Serenity	Ecstasy

The full spectrum of emotions results from mixing these eight primary emotional categories in various combinations, much as one might mix primary colors to obtain all possible hues. Thus, one may derive such hybrids as love (joy blended with acceptance), awe (fear mixed with surprise), and pessimism (sadness combined with anticipation).

The anecdotal relevance of Plutchik's categories to the kinds of emotional content found in advertising appears immediately obvious. For example, acceptance (by incorporating beneficial stimuli) provides a well-worn theme for many food commercials, as in the recent ads that stress the healthy feelings associated with high-fiber cereals. Conversely, disgust (involving the rejection of noxious stimuli) appears in commercials for cleaning products like the one in which a housewife examines the revolting filth extracted from her carpet by a rug-shampooing machine and says, "Yuk!" Fear (associated with the need for protection) ranges all the way from mild timidity (as in commercials about tooth decay) to something approaching terror (as in the life insurance ad pointing out that the speaker got a second chance but that, by implication, you will not). A spectacular example of anger (oriented toward the removal of barriers to need satisfaction) appeared in a recent Citibank commercial whose hero's frustration over bounced checks and low interest rates transforms him into a werewolf and leaves him howling in rage and pounding furiously on the door of the bank. The diametrically opposed emotions of joy (seeking procreation) and sadness (reacting to loss) permeate much advertising and are sometimes closely intermingled, as in those poignant telephone commercials ("He called just to say, 'I love you, Mom' ") or the touching Kodak ad about a little boy and his enormous dog ("Now we'll always be together—together side by side—my best friend, as time goes by"). Many ads provide anticipation (concerned with exploring the environment) like that prompted by travel opportunities ("Come to Jamaica . . .") or joining the army and seeing the world ("Be all that you can be"). Finally, surprise (the orientation response) often plays the role of attention-getting device, as in the commercial for Dodge trucks in which a pretty girl looks directly at the camera, moves her lips, and asks in a man's voice, "Do you like trucks?"

These anecdotal examples suggest the potential relevance of Plutchik's eight categories to the analysis of emotional content in advertising. This potential relevance requires systematic conceptual and empirical support if we are to take it seriously as a basis for designing advertising research directed toward managerial problems. Such support must come from both theory and data.

Plutchik's typology competes with other classifications based on enumeration (Gaylin 1979; Izard 1977; Tomkins 1962, 1963), logical derivation (De Rivera 1977; Solomon 1976), and data reduction (Daly, Lancee, and Polivy 1983; Davitz 1969; Mehrabian 1980; Mehrabian and Russell 1974; Nowlis 1970; Russell 1980). Each of these alternative formulations has something to recommend it; however, one might argue that Plutchik's framework is distinguished by its clear conceptual derivation from the theory that "emotions are adaptive devices in the struggle for individual survival at all evolutionary levels" (p. 139) and by the substantial amount of evidence brought to bear in its favor. This evidence includes a variety of findings from numerous studies using factor analysis, clustering, and other multivariate techniques. Together these results support the general relevance of the eightfold typology and suggest the validity of the four proposed bipolarities. As yet, however, Plutchik's framework has not been systematically examined for its relevance to issues concerning the role of emotion in consumer responses to advertising. Such an investigation of the structure of emotional responses to advertising was attempted in the study we describe.

Method

Test Commercials

We took our test commercials from those aired during a judgmentally typical day of broadcasting by a major television network in a large eastern city. To this end, we made videotapes of a twenty-four-hour period. From these tapes we chose fifty-four commercials according to two criteria: a selected set of eighteen commercials consisted of various ads that appeared intuitively to attain relatively high levels in one or more of Plutchik's eight emotional categories; and a random set of thirty-six commercials was composed by choosing with equal probability from the list of remaining ads. The two sets assembled in this manner (with the relevant sample sizes shown parenthetically) were as shown in table 16–1. The selected and random sets were combined and partitioned into twelve groups. Each selected commercial appeared in two groups, and each random commercial appeared in only one. Composition of the groups was determined by judgment such that no two ads for the same product category were included in any one group. Each group of commercials was then embedded within a short film in both forward and reverse directions (to control for order effects). The entire program package was shown to respondents in a simulated living room environment where they performed a set of viewing and rating tasks.

Viewing and Rating Tasks

After watching the film, respondents viewed each commercial a second time as a basis for rating it from 1 to 5 (not at all, slightly, moderately, strongly, very strongly) for its tendency to evoke various emotions on the following set of forty randomly ordered items:

Table 16–1
Commercial Sets

Selected Set	*Random Set*
1. Calvin Klein jeans	19. G.E. grill griddle (*N* = 58)
(*N* = 108)	20. Chanel #5 (*N* = 50)
2. Coca-Cola	21. Coty Nuance (*N* = 50)
(*N* = 108)	22. Atari (*N* = 50)
3. American Cancer Society	23. Kellogg's Corn Flakes (*N* = 58)
(*N* = 108)	24. Thomas' English muffins (*N* = 58)
4. Federal Express	25. TWA Airlines (*N* = 50)
(*N* = 100)	26. Super Poligrip denture glue (*N* = 50)
5. Bell Telephone	27. Mazola cooking oil (*N* = 50)
(*N* = 100)	28. Allercare skin cream (*N* = 50)
6. Wisk laundry detergent	29. Theragran "M" vitamins (*N* = 50)
(*N* = 100)	30. Nyquil cold remedy (*N* = 50)
7. Con Edison	31. Hershey's chocolate syrup (*N* = 50)
(*N* = 100)	32. Hunt's tomato sauce (*N* = 50)
8. French's mustard	33. Dow bathroom cleaner (*N* = 50)
(*N* = 100)	34. Borateem laundry detergent (*N* = 50)
9. Sanka coffee	35. Bayer aspirin (*N* = 50)
(*N* = 100)	36. La Choy Chinese food (*N* = 50)
10. Levi's jeans	37. Diet Guard reducing plan (*N* = 50)
(*N* = 104)	38. Tropicana orange juice (*N* = 50)
11. Dr. Pepper	39. Duncan Hines cake mix (*N* = 50)
(*N* = 104)	40. Whirlpool dishwasher (*N* = 54)
12. Prudential insurance	41. New York Telephone (*N* = 54)
(*N* = 104)	42. Ivory soap (*N* = 54)
13. Budweiser	43. Hanes panty hose (*N* = 50)
(*N* = 101)	44. Swiss Miss hot cocoa mix (*N* = 50)
14. GE soft white light bulbs	45. Frito-Lay potato chips (*N* = 50)
(*N* = 101)	46. Dunkin' Donuts (*N* = 51)
15. Crazy Eddie's discount	47. Alfa Romeo (*N* = 51)
(*N* = 101)	48. British Airways (*N* = 51)
16. U.S. Army	49. Lafayette electronics stores (*N* = 50)
(*N* = 100)	50. Star Kist tuna (*N* = 50)
17. Pepsi-Cola	51. Dry Sack sherry (*N* = 50)
(*N* = 100)	52. Red Lobster Inns (*N* = 50)
18. Charmin toilet tissue	53. Apple home computer (*N* = 50)
(*N* = 100)	54. Chimere fragrance (*N* = 50)

1. Friendly
2. Aggressive
3. Disgusting
4. Puzzling
5. Informative
6. Gloomy
7. Annoying
8. Happy
9. Irritating
10. Helpful
11. Affectionate
12. Funny
13. Sexy
14. Unpleasant
15. Threatening
16. Unusual
17. Intelligent
18. Cheerful
19. Confusing
20. Frightening
21. Sad
22. Delightful
23. Exciting
24. Offensive
25. Insulting
26. Surprising
27. Meaningful

28. Sincere
29. Intimidating
30. Instructive
31. Silly
32. Interesting
33. Trustworthy
34. Sensible
35. Depressing
36. Cold
37. Nostalgic
38. Touching
39. Deceptive
40. Boring

Twenty-four of these scale items were intended to represent Plutchik's eight prototypical emotional categories, as supported by his reported empirical findings. The remaining sixteen interspersed items were chosen to reflect other potentially important emotional responses not explicitly covered by Plutchik's framework, such as nostalgia, humor, or warmth.

Sample

Respondents were recruited in shopping malls in five geographically dispersed urban areas and were evenly divided among males and females and among adults (eighteen years or older) and teens (thirteen to seventeen years). In total, 613 respondents met in gatherings of four or five at a time. Each gathering was assigned a group of commercials in a sequential manner such that each of the twelve ad groups was viewed by roughly the same demographic mix with the selected and random sets exposed to about one hundred and fifty respondents, respectively (since each of the selected ads was included in two separate groups of commercials).

Each commercial was always viewed in the context of the same one or two sets of accompanying material. Although necessitated by cost considerations, this design assumes the absence of confounding context effects on emotional ratings. The validity of this assumption cannot be tested here but deserves careful examination in future work on emotional responses to advertising (see chapter 13).

Data Aggregation and Standardization

Given the cost-dictated restrictions on data collection (the use of fixed groups of ads rated by different respondents), analysis proceeded at the aggregate level. Specifically the forty emotion scales were represented by mean scores (based either on about one hundred or on about fifty responses). Conceptually this procedure views each subset of respondents as a collection of content-analytic judges. Combining their scores by adding or averaging increases the reliability of the resulting scales (cf. Holbrook and Lehmann 1980). By removing some sources of random error, this step therefore helps to justify the comparison of emotion scores among commercials.

For most of the analyses involving the forty emotion scales (or eight indexes based on them), average group scores were standardized to zero mean and unit variance across commercials within each scale considered separately. This data transformation has the effect of weighting scales more equally in the computation of correlations between commercials. This weighting affects the results obtained in the spatial representation of advertising-specific emotions. Here, comparisons between results based on raw and standardized scores showed the latter to be freer from anomalies caused by outliers, thereby making them easier to interpret.

A Priori Emotional Indexes

Based on Plutchik's theory and findings, eight a priori three-item indexes (computed on mean scores for each ad) were defined as shown in table 16–2. The reliability of these indexes was assessed by coefficient alpha (Cronbach 1951; Nunnally 1967). High (low) levels of alpha were interpreted as indicating good (poor) internal validity of Plutchik's typology in the context of emotional responses to advertising. Correlations among indexes were also examined to investigate whether the proposed bipolarities characterize the structure of advertising-related emotions.

Emotions Space

The structure of emotions (as a basis for the typology) was further examined by constructing a spatial representation of the associations among emotional responses across commercials. Specifically, correlations among the forty emotions across the fifty-four ads were regarded as measures of proximity and were submitted to multidimensional scaling (MDS). As noted by Kruskal and Wish (1978), this use of MDS has been adopted by researchers in such diverse areas as psychology (Guttman 1966), political science (Weisberg and Rusk 1970), public health (Ruch 1977), leisure (Holbrook 1980; Holbrook and Lehmann

Table 16–2
Index Definitions

Emotion	*Function*	*A Priori Index*
Acceptance	Incorporation	Helpful + sincere + trustworthy
Disgust	Rejection	Disgusting + offensive + unpleasant
Fear	Protection	Threatening + frigthening + intimidating
Anger	Destruction	Insulting + annoying + irritating
Joy	Reproduction	Happy + cheerful + delightful
Sadness	Reintegration	Gloomy + sad + depressing
Anticipation	Exploration	Informative + intelligent + instructive
Surprise	Orientation	Puzzling + confusting + unusual

1981), consumer aesthetics (Holbrook 1982; Holbrook and Holloway 1984), organizational behavior (Holbrook and Ryan 1982), and marketing (Lehmann 1974).

The particular MDS approach used here followed the procedures described by Holbrook and Lehmann (1981) to derive solutions in one to four dimensions. The routine begins with classical metric scaling of input proximities (Torgerson 1958) and then employs a metric version of Kruskal's (1964) algorithm to improve goodness of fit. This metric approach differs from its nonmetric analog only in that it uses linear instead of monotonic regression to transform the input data. Goodness of fit in each dimensionality was judged by the correlation between input proximities and output spatial distances (across the 780 pairs of emotions). The number of axes to retain was determined by the judgmental trade-off between parsimony and incremental improvements in degrees of fit (cf. Green 1975; Shepard 1972).

Distances in the resulting emotions space may be regarded as indications of the degree to which one emotion scale is associated with another (correlationally, across commercials). Accordingly the validity of Plutchik's eight emotional types (our indexes) would be supported by clusterings of the relevant scale items in the emotions space. Here we examined spatial groupings rather than using a more rigorous test like confirmatory factor analysis because we were not prepared to state explicit assumptions about the magnitudes of the intercorrelations of scale items across indexes. Rather we assumed the close proximities of scale items within each a priori index. These proximities are represented by distances in the multidimensional scaling solution. The MDS space therefore offers further potential insights into the usefulness of Plutchik's classification scheme.

Commercials Space

A commercials space was obtained by applying the MDS procedure to correlations computed among the fifty-four ads across the forty emotion scales. In the resulting spatial representation, proximity indicates the degree of association between the emotional responses to a given pair of ads.

Such spaces were constructed using both raw scores and scores standardized within emotional scales across ads. The latter data produced more interpretable results, presumably because of their tendency to assign different scales relatively equal weights in the analysis. For this reason, only the findings based on standardized scores will be presented here in detail.

Emotion Vectors

Using ordinary least squares (OLS) regression in the manner described by Carroll (1972), each of Plutchik's eight emotional indexes was represented by a vector introduced into the commercials space. Specifically, each index had a score for every one of the fifty-four ads. These scores were regressed across commercials on their spatial coordinates. The resulting regression coefficients provide the direction cosines of a vector that best discriminates between ads scoring higher (lower) on a given emotional index according to the ads' distances (perpendicular projections) from the positive (negative) end of the vector. The fit of a given vector was assessed by the multiple correlation (R) obtained in the relevant regression analysis. A high R suggests that positions in the commercials space do a good job of accounting for a particular emotional index. (In addition to obtaining linear vector fits, the analysis was performed with the inclusion of quadratic terms. These nonmonotonic functions failed to improve the degrees of fit significantly and will not be reported here.)

The emotion vectors are useful in interpreting the axes of the commercials space. They also address the motivating question for this study by indicating the structure of emotional responses to advertising. For example, the vectors may show how some emotions move together across advertisements whereas others move tangentially or in opposite directions in the commercials space.

Results and Discussion

A Priori Emotional Indexes

The internal validity of Plutchik's typology was strongly supported by reliabilities of the eight a priori emotional indexes as measured by coefficient alpha:

1. Acceptance, .88.
2. Disgust, .95.
3. Fear, .85.
4. Anger, .97.
5. Joy, .97.
6. Sadness, .93.
7. Anticipation, .95.
8. Surprise, .89.

The proposed bipolar structure of emotions received less strong support. As hypothesized, the intercorrelations for acceptance-disgust ($r = -.43$, $p < 0.1$) and joy-sadness ($r = -.42$, $p < .01$) were significantly negative. But contrary to expectations, the intercorrelation for anticipation-surprise ($r = -.12$, n.s.) failed to reach statistical significance, and that for fear-anger ($r = .32, p < .02$) was significantly positive and therefore in the wrong direction. The reason for the latter unexpected finding will appear when examining emotion vectors in the commercials space.

Emotions Space

MDS scaling of the associations among emotions produced the following correlational fits between input proximities and output spatial distances in one to four dimensions: 0.79, 0.93, 0.94, and 0.97. Diminishing returns and considerations of parsimony suggested the retention of two MDS dimensions for subsequent analysis.

The resulting two-dimensional emotions space appears in figure 16-1. Here the horizontal axis seems to distinguish the more negative emotions (irritating, disgusting, confusing) from their more positive counterparts (delightful, touching, sincere). The vertical axis appears to represent a continuum running from more serious emotions (threatening, sad, instructive) to those lighter in tone (sexy, funny, happy).

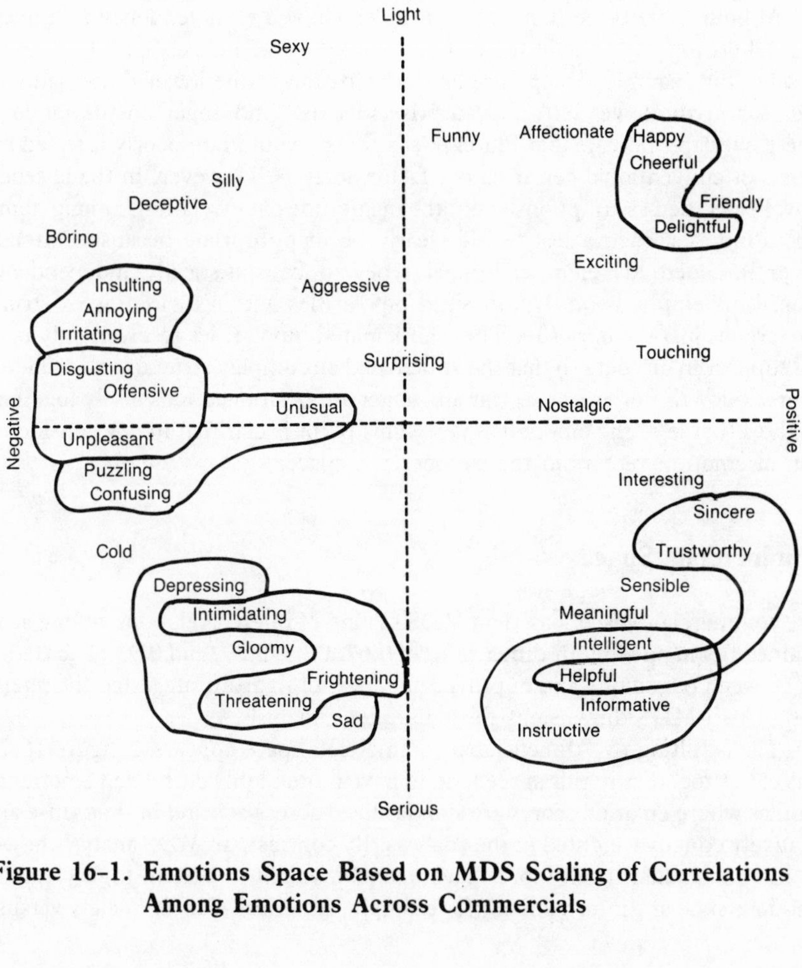

Figure 16-1. Emotions Space Based on MDS Scaling of Correlations Among Emotions Across Commercials

These dimensions make sense intuitively and, more important, help to explain the groupings of individual items that fall within Plutchik's eight categories. In this light, boundaries have been drawn around the three items defining each a priori emotional index to facilitate the visualization of their clustering in the emotions space. From this perspective, joy (happy + cheerful + delightful) may be viewed as light and positive; acceptance (helpful + sincere + trustworthy) and anticipation (informative + intelligent + instructive) as positive and serious; sadness (gloomy + sad + depressing) and fear (threatening + frightening + intimidating) as serious and negative; and surprise (puzzling + confusing + unusual), disgust (disgusting + offensive + unpleasant), and anger (insulting + annoying + irritating) as purely negative. The close proximities of the related items in each index reflect the rather high alpha coefficients obtained in the reliability analysis and provide a clear visual indication of support for Plutchik's typology.

Although the three items in each index show a clear tendency to appear in neighboring positions in the emotions space, some indexes tend to overlap closely—for example, acceptance and anticipation in the lower right; sadness and fear in the lower left; and surprise, disgust, and anger on the far left. These overlaps indicate that Plutchik's typology would fare poorly if tested by means of conventional confirmatory factor analysis. However, in the absence of well-specified assumptions about the magnitude of correlations among items across indexes, such a test would clearly be inappropriate because Plutchik never intended his eight emotional types to be statistically independent. Indeed his emphasis on hypothesized bipolarities within a circumplex structure argues just the opposite. These anticipated bipolarities received only partial support in our data so that the anticipated circumplex structure also tended to break down. For example, fear and anger are positioned too closely together on the left side of the emotions space. This point is clarified in our consideration of emotion vectors in the commercials space.

Commercials Space

The commercials space, based on MDS scaling of intercorrelations among ads, attained fits in one to four dimensions of 0.67, 0.83, 0.89, and 0.93. The tradeoff between parsimony and improved goodness of fit again suggested the retention of two MDS dimensions for subsequent analysis.

The resulting two-dimensional commercials space appears in figure 16–2. Ads closer together in this space tend to have more highly correlated emotional profiles where emotion scores are standardized across ads and in that sense are relatively equally weighted in the analysis. By contrast, an MDS analysis based on raw (unstandardized) scores gave unequal weight to certain high-variance emotions such as "informative" (for example, American Cancer Society versus,

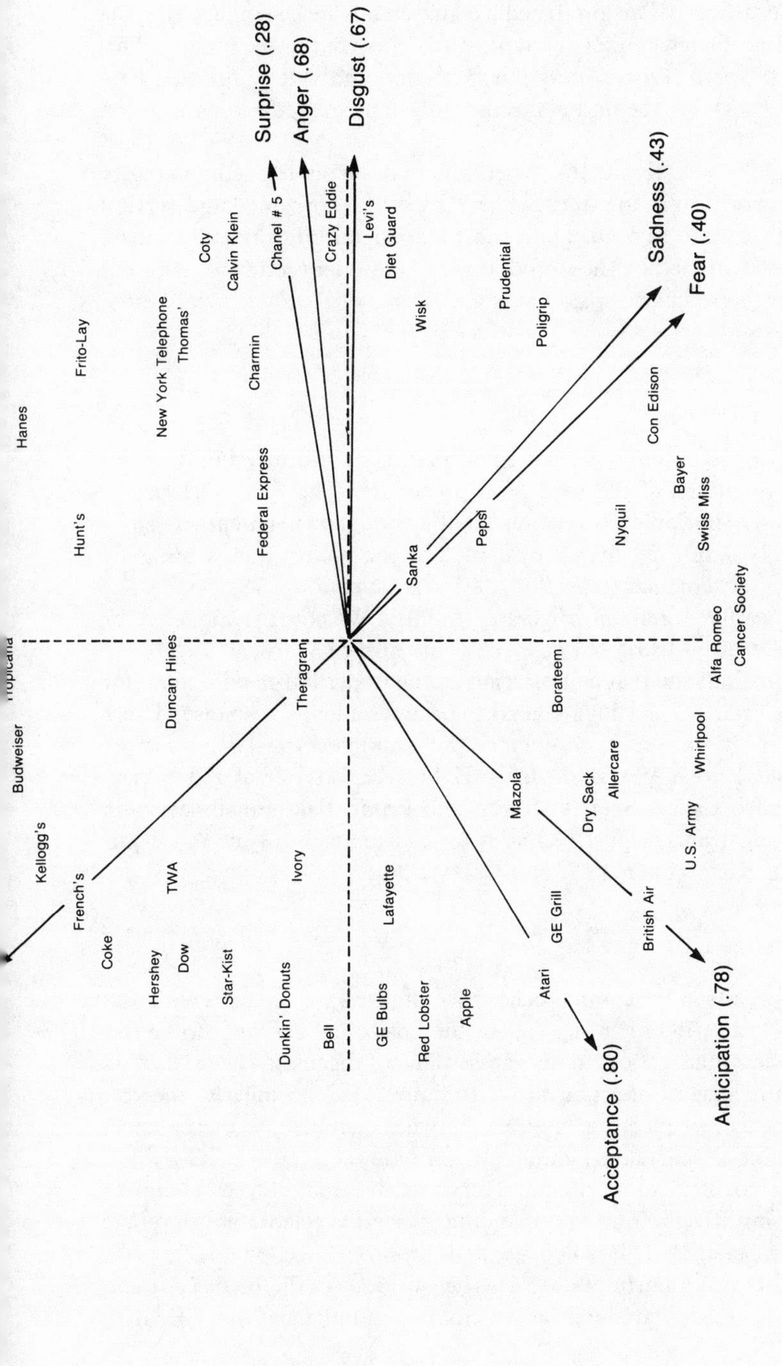

Figure 16–2. Commercials Space Based on MDS Scaling of Correlations among Commercials Across Emotions

say, Calvin Klein jeans) or "annoying" (for example, Crazy Eddie discount stores versus Coca-Cola). This produced a commercials space emphasizing the extreme positions of a few outliers with most ads clustered in the middle. This raw scores MDS space resisted clear interpretation and will be omitted here in favor of focusing on the more meaningful standardized-scores solution shown in figure 16–2.

One way to interpret figure 16–2 would be to draw on detailed familiarity with each commercial so as to infer the meaning of the horizontal and vertical axes. A somewhat more rigorous approach to a general interpretation shown in figure 16–2 is facilitated by the introduction of emotion vectors to represent the relationships between the spatial axes and scores of Plutchik's eight emotional categories.

Emotion Vectors

Accordingly figure 16–2 contains eight emotion vectors positioned in the commercials space by means of the regression procedure. The fit of each vector is indicated by its multiple correlation coefficient (shown parenthetically). Strong and highly significant fits were attained by the vectors representing joy (.91, $p < .001$), acceptance (.80, $p < .001$), anticipation (.78, $p < .001$), disgust (.67, $p < .001$), and anger (.68, $p < .001$). Weaker fits appeared for sadness (.43, $p < .01$), fear (.40, $p < .05$), and surprise (.28, n.s.).

These vectors indicate that commercials in the upper left-hand region (for example, Coke, French's, Kellogg's) tend to produce a joyful response. Those toward the lower left encourage acceptance (for example, Atari) and anticipation (for example, British Air). In the lower right, reactions of fear and sadness occur (for example, Cancer Society, Bayer, and Prudential). Finally aversion in the form of anger and disgust increases toward the right of the space (for example, Calvin Klein, Chanel #5, and Crazy Eddie).

Interpretation

This pattern of results in the commercials space (figure 16–2) coheres with that of the emotions space (figure 16–1). Again, the horizontal axis appears to run from positive (acceptance, joy) to negative (anger, disgust). (Note that its directionality is reversed from figure 16–1 to figure 16–2.) Similarly, the vertical dimension again reflects a contrast between seriousness (acceptance, anticipation, sadness, fear) and lightness of tone (joy).

The relative positions of most commercials on the emotion vectors appear to make sense intuitively. For example, the generally celebrative beverage commercials for Coke, Bud, Dr. Pepper, and Tropicana occupy positions far out on the joy vector. Opportunities to see the world, as in the British Air and U.S. Army commercials, rate high on anticipation. Appliances like GE Grill,

Atari, Apple, and Whirlpool prompt feelings of acceptance, probably by virtue of their helpfulness. Illness-, age-, and death-related advertising stirs fear and sadness, as in the cases of Prudential, Poligrip, Nyquil, Bayer, and the Cancer Society. Finally, some ads evoke anger and disgust by virtue of tactlessness (perhaps Wisk or Diet Guard), sexism (perhaps Calvin Klein or Chanel #5), or obstreperousness (definitely Crazy Eddie).

Contrary to these intuitively plausible results, some isolated findings prove surprising in ways that might suggest potential managerial prescriptions. For example, a product manager for Thomas' English Muffins might experience some concern over that brand's position near the end of the anger and disgust vectors. Similarly, Swiss Miss probably does not wish to convey feelings of sadness and fear comparable to those for such illness-related brands as Bayer and Nyquil. Nor, we guess, does Pepsi aim intentionally at the relatively neutral ground occupied by Sanka.

Finally, the commercials space also elucidates the pattern of relationships among the eight emotional indexes. The adjacent positions of some vectors reflect strong intercorrelations between emotions across advertisements: acceptance-anticipation ($r = .90$, $p < .001$), sadness-fear ($r = .92$, $p < .001$), anger-disgust ($r = .94$, $p < .001$), surprise-disgust ($r = .76$, $p < .001$), and surprise-anger ($r = .70$, $p < .001$). Also the vector positions help to account for the (expected) negative correlations (bipolarities) found for acceptance-disgust ($r = -.43$, $p < .01$), joy-sadness ($r = -.42$, $p < .01$), and surprise-anticipation ($r = -.12$, n.s.). Moreover, the angle between the fear and anger vectors explains why these indexes, contrary to expectations, were positively correlated across commercials ($r = .32$, $p < .02$). Apparently in the world of advertising, fear and anger go together, perhaps because fear aligns closely with sadness, while anger is closely related to disgust. It appears, then, that the natural bipolarity between fear and anger that prevails in the more general contexts investigated by Plutchik (1980) may disappear in the context of emotional responses to advertising, where what provokes fear may also prompt anger, and vice-versa.

In sum, the vector positions in the commercials space indicate some important interrelations among Plutchik's eight emotional types, provide support for three of his four proposed bipolarities, and help to account for the unexpected positive relationship between fear and anger.

Conclusions

Like any other results based on particular samples of respondents and test objects, the findings of the present study require replication, extension, and possible modification in new empirical situations before they can be accepted as representing the structure of emotional responses to advertising. Pending such further investigations, however, certain tentative conclusions appear warranted by the present pattern of results.

First, the findings about reliability based on alpha coefficients for eight a priori emotional indexes suggest that Plutchik's (1980) typology may be extended legitimately to the context of emotional responses to advertising. Moreover, the results partially support his proposed set of bipolarities, with the exception of the expected opposition between fear and anger, two emotions that are positively related in the commercials examined here.

Second, the emotions space suggests that two key dimensions—negative-positive and serious-light—underlie the associations among emotional reponses to advertising. This finding helps explain the patterns of clustering that resulted in the high reliabilities for the eight indexes.

Third, the locations of emotion vectors in the commercials space make sense intuitively and indicate the bases for positive and negative correlations among the eight emotional indexes. This supports the bipolarities and elucidates the reasons for the unexpected positive association between fear and anger (perhaps due to the close correspondence between fear and sadness and between anger and disgust).

In sum, this study appears to have taken a step toward the increased understanding of a neglected area in advertising research. Our findings provide preliminary support for borrowing Plutchik's typology of emotional responses and extending it to the case of advertising effects. When tested on viewer reactions to television commercials, the typology helps elucidate the role of emotion in advertising.

At a minimum, this research suggests that a simple unidimensional representation of affect (positive-negative, like-dislike, and so on) fails to provide an adequate account of emotional responses to television ads. Although one axis of our commercials space does appear to parallel the positive-negative continuum and thereby to portray the strong negativity of anger and disgust, a second axis is required to cover the full set of emotional categories. Commercials fill the two-dimensional space, ranging in content from joy to sadness and from acceptance to disgust.

Some important questions remain for future research. We might ask whether Plutchik's categorization scheme is necessarily the best emotional typology to use in the context of consumer research on the effects of advertising. For example, Holbrook and coworkers (1984) employed the alternative pleasure-arousal-dominance (PAD) framework proposed by Mehrabian and Russell (1974) to study emotional reactions to video games and had some success in establishing nomological validity. Havlena and Holbrook (1986) directly compared the abilities of the Plutchik and Mehrabian-Russell schemes to represent emotional reactions to a variety of consumption experiences and found that M-R accounted for P better than P accounted for M-R. This suggests that Mehrabian and Russell's (1974) three dimensions might be informationally richer than Plutchik's (1980) eight categories (at least in the case of Havlena's consumption experiences).

The extension of a similar question to the context of advertising effects has motivated a dissertation in progress at Columbia University by T.J. Olney. Olney will examine the comparative ability of emotional measures based on the Plutchik and Mehrabian and Russell schemes to predict behavioral assessments of attention to television commercials (as indicated by fast-forwarding of videotaped material and by channel switching between competing messages).

Finally, the analysis of data already collected by Holbrook and Rajeev Batra will explore the construction of a battery of emotional indexes. This set of measures will draw on a number of sources (including the Plutchik categories and the Mehrabian and Russell dimensions) to seek a representation best suited to elucidating the role of emotion in advertising.

References

Carroll, J. Douglas. 1972. "Individual Differences and Multidimensional Scaling." In Roger N. Shepard, A. Kimball Romney, and Sara Beth Nerlove, eds., *Multidimensional Scaling: Theory and Applications in the Behavioral Sciences,* 1:105–155. New York: Seminar Press.

Cronbach, L.J. 1951. "Coefficient Alpha and the Internal Structure of Tests." *Psychometrika* 16:297–334.

Daly, Eleanor M., William J. Lancee, and Janet Polivy. 1983. "A Conical Model for the Taxonomy of Emotional Experience." *Journal of Personality and Social Psychology* 45, no. 2:443–457.

Davitz, Joel R. 1969. *The Language of Emotion.* New York: Academic Press.

De Rivera, Joseph. 1977. *A Structural Theory of the Emotions.* New York: International Universities Press.

Gaylin, Willard. 1979. *Feelings: Our Vital Signs.* New York: Ballantine Books.

Green, Paul E. 1975. "Marketing Applications of MDS: Assessment and Outlook." *Journal of Marketing* 39 (January):24–31.

Guttman, Louis. 1966. "Order Analysis of Correlational Matrices." In Raymond B. Cattell, ed., *Handbook of Multivariate Experimental Psychology.* Chicago: Rand McNally.

Havlena, William J., and Morris B. Holbrook. 1986. "The Varieties of Consumption Experience: Comparing Two Typologies of Emotion in Consumer Behavior." *Journal of Consumer Research* 13 (December):394–404.

Hirschman, Elizabeth C., and Morris B. Holbrook. 1986. "Expanding the Ontology and Methodology of Research on the Consumption Experience." In David Brinberg and Richard J. Lutz, eds., *Perspectives on Methodology in Consumer Research.* New York: Springer-Verlag.

Holbrook, Morris B. 1980. "Representing Patterns of Association among Leisure Activities: A Comparison of Two Techniques." *Journal of Leisure Research* 12, no. 3:242–256.

———. 1982. "Mapping the Market for Esthetic Products: The Case of Jazz Records." *Journal of Retailing* 58 (Spring):114–129.

———. 1986. "Emotion in the Consumption Experience: Toward a New Model of the Human Consumer." In Robert A. Peterson, Wayne D. Hoyer, and William R. Wilson, eds., *The Role of Affect in Consumer Behavior: Emerging Theories and Applications*. Lexington, Mass.: Lexington Books.

Holbrook, Morris B., Robert W. Chestnut, Terence A. Oliva, and Eric A. Greenleaf. 1984. "Play as a Consumption Experience: The Roles of Emotions, Performance, and Personality in the Enjoyment of Games." *Journal of Consumer Research* 11 (September):728–739.

Holbrook, Morris B., and Elizabeth C. Hirschman. 1982. "The Experiential Aspects of Consumption: Consumer Fantasies, Feelings, and Fun." *Journal of Consumer Research* 9 (September):132–140.

Holbrook, Morris B., and Douglas V. Holloway. 1984. "Marketing Strategy and the Structure of Aggregate, Segment-Specific, and Differential Preferences." *Journal of Marketing* 48 (Winter):62–67.

Holbrook, Morris B., and Donald R. Lehmann. 1980. "Form versus Content in Predicting Starch Scores." *Journal of Advertising Research* 20, no. 4:53–62.

———. 1981. "Allocating Discretionary Time: Complementarity among Activities." *Journal of Consumer Research* 7 (March):395–406.

Holbrook, Morris B., and John O'Shaughnessy. 1984. "The Role of Emotion in Advertising." *Psychology & Marketing* 1 (Summer 1984):45–64.

Holbrook, Morris B., and Michael J. Ryan. 1982. "Modeling Decision-Specific Stress: Some Methodological Considerations." *Administrative Science Quarterly* 27 (June):243–258.

Izard, Carroll. 1977. *Human Emotions*. New York: Plenum Press.

Kruskal, Joseph B. 1964. "Nonmetric Multidimensional Scaling: A Numerical Method." *Psychometrika* 19:115–129.

Kruskal, Joseph B., and Myron Wish. 1978. *Multidimensional Scaling*. Beverly Hills: Sage Publications.

Lehmann, Donald R. 1974. "Some Alternatives to Linear Factor Analysis for Variable Grouping Applied to Buyer Behavior Variables." *Journal of Marketing Research* 11 (May):206–213.

Mehrabian, Albert. 1980. *Basic Dimensions for a General Psychological Theory*. Cambridge, Mass.: Oelgeschlager, Gunn & Hain.

Mehrabian, Albert, and James A. Russell. 1974. *An Approach to Environmental Psychology*. Cambridge: MIT Press.

Nowlis, Vincent. 1970. "Mood: Behavior and Experience." In *Feelings and Emotions*, ed. Magda B. Arnold. New York: Academic Press.

Nunnally, Jum C. 1967. *Psychometric Theory*. New York: McGraw-Hill.

Plutchik, Robert. 1980. *Emotion: A Psychoevolutionary Synthesis*. New York: Harper & Row.

Puto, Christopher P., and William D. Wells. 1984. "Informational and Transformational Advertising: The Differential Effects of Time." In Thomas C. Kinnear, ed., *Advances in Consumer Research,* 11:638–643. Provo, Utah: Association for Consumer Research.

Ruch, L.O. 1977. "A Multidimensional Analysis of the Concept of Life Change." *Journal of Health and Social Behavior* 18:71–83.

Russell, James A. 1980. "A Circumplex Model of Affect." *Journal of Personality and Social Psychology* 39, no. 6:1161–1178.

Shepard, Roger N. 1972. "Taxonomy of Some Principal Types of Data and Multidimensional Methods for Their Analysis." In Roger N. Shepard, A. Kimball Romney, and Sara Beth Nerlove, eds., *Multidimensional Scaling: Theory and Applications in the Behavioral Sciences.* New York: Seminar Press.

Solomon, Robert C. 1976. *The Passions: The Myth and Nature of Human Emotion.* Garden City, N.Y.: Anchor Press.

Tomkins, Silvan S. 1962. *Affect, Imagery, Consciousness: The Positive Affects.* New York: Springer.

———. 1963. *Affect, Imagery, Consciousness: The Negative Affects.* New York: Springer.

Torgerson, Warren S. 1958. *Theory and Methods of Scaling.* New York: Wiley.

Weisberg, Herbert, and Jerrold G. Rusk. 1970. "Dimensions of Candidate Evaluations." *American Political Science Review* 64:1167–1185.

17

An Investigation of the Relationship between the MECCAs Model and Advertising Affect

Thomas J. Reynolds
Minakshi Trivedi

A long-standing problem with the application of advertising research is the lack of a specific paradigm that permits direct assessment of advertising strategy. It is, in fact, surprising that while extensive work has been done in the areas of advertising response measurement and copy testing (Schlinger 1979; Wells, Leavitt, and McConville, 1971; Olson, Schlinger, and Young 1982), the critical issue regarding effectiveness of specific executions with respect to a given strategy has not been examined.

In the context of strategy specification, Boyd, Ray, and Strong (1972) propose a general framework that gives the decision maker five alternative methods of formalizing advertising strategy:

1. Induce affect forces, which influence choice behavior.
2. Add salient characteristics (to the advertising).
3. Increase or decrease ratings of salient characteristics.
4. Change perception of company's brand.
5. Change perception of competition's brand.

Although these options may, in a broad way, indicate the primary area of research focus, they have the disadvantage of not being grounded in either psychological theory or a detailed communication paradigm. Basically, they lack a more general perspective as to how advertising communication operates.

Significant research on aspects of the executional components of strategy has also been conducted using factors in advertising such as humor (Madden and Weinberger 1984), execution (Stewart and Furse 1984–1985), frequency (Stephens and Warrens 1983–1984), and nonverbal communication (Haley, Richardson, and Baldwin, 1982). It is important to note, however, that execution represents merely a part of strategy, and an overall communication or strategy framework is needed before assessments can be made.

The MECCAs (Means End Conceptualization of the Components of

Advertising Strategy) model (Olson and Reynolds 1983; Reynolds and Gutman 1984) addresses this larger problem by offering a conceptually broad consumer research and communication paradigm. The model provides the steppingstones needed to move from psychological theory to the specification of advertising strategy to an overall framework for strategy assessment (Gutman and Reynolds, in press).

Of issue in this research framework is the relation of the components of MECCAs to affect, as originally suggested by Boyd, Ray, and Strong (1972). By determining the significance of the various strategic advertising components, it may be possible to arrive at an understanding of the basis for consumer affect in terms of both execution and product. The primary purpose of this research project is to provide a conceptual basis for this critical next step in the extension of MECCAs.

Background

Development of the Means-End Chain Concept

Howard (1977) suggests that the total meaning of a brand, its semantic structure, refers to a hierarchy of categories into which a brand is placed by a consumer. The hierarchical classification structure consists basically of attitudes and beliefs about a product, the choice criteria upon which evaluation is based, and the values specific to the consumer that affect the relative salience of the respective choice criteria.

Building on Howard's work, Gutman and Reynolds (1979) used a means-end chain concept to show how consumers group products differentially at the different levels of abstraction. This was accomplished by a laddering methodology (consisting of in-depth probing as to the reasons a respondent identifies a concept as being important), which moved consumers to higher levels of abstraction in order to obtain responses closer to the "end," or values level. In theory, it is this higher values level that governs perception and, ultimately, product evaluation.

The laddering procedure elicits a connected set or chain of interrelated descriptive elements. The connections among these elements are the basis of associated meaning in the consumer's mind and thus are assumed to be of key importance to understanding choice behavior. In the original laddering study (Gutman and Reynolds 1979), the largest chain of elements (ranging from an attribute to a value) obtained from the individual respondent was considered to be the most relevant and was used for further analysis. Using one element of the chain at a time as a basis for distinction, products were sorted into groups such that each group formed a set of similar products. As would be expected, a qualitative summary of the resulting data revealed that (1) initial levels of distinction, generated from triadic sorting, were primarily concerned with contents or physical aspects of products, and (2) subsequent levels moved to more abstract, personal distinctions representative of values.

Analysis of the sorting data at the various levels of the attribute-consequence-value ladder involved the construction of a series of perceptual maps. Each map illustrated spatial relations between products at the respective level of abstraction. In evaluating the resulting spaces, the authors concluded that as abstraction levels are raised, the implications from physical characteristics to consequences, and eventually to values, become apparent. They suggested that an understanding of these more abstract components of means-end chain hierarchies should then enable researchers to "see the world as consumers see it."

Stemming from this initial empirical research, Gutman (1982) presented his consumer behavior model based on four fundamental assumptions:

1. All consumer actions have consequences.
2. Consumers learn to associate particular consequences with particular actions.
3. Values (defined here as desirable end states) play a dominant role in guiding choice.
4. People cope with the complexity of choosing from a large variety of products by grouping them into sets.

The central aspect of the Gutman model is that consumers choose actions that produce desired consequences and minimize undesired consequences. Since values provide the valence for perceived consequences (Rokeach 1973), the consequence-value linkage becomes the critical link in the model. Furthermore, to make a choice among alternative products, the consumer must learn which products have the attributes required to produce the desired consequences. Thus the second critical link in the model would be the attribute-consequence link, the attributes deriving their importance from satisfying or providing a given consequence.

In sum, the Gutman model incorporates the concept that the linkage from salient attributes to determinant consequences is driven, albeit indirectly, by personal values. When considered in the context of product use situations, the relative importances of these consequences are modified and thus lead to situation-relevant consequences. The relative satisfaction of these consequences provides the basis for functional groupings of products. A comparison of these key consequences would lead in turn to the identification of key attribute(s) that serve as the functional basis for choice.

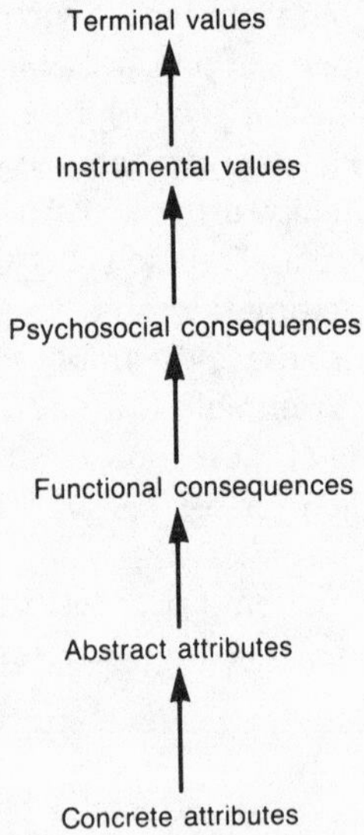

Figure 17-1. Six Levels of Abstraction

Advertising Model

The Gutman model (1982) was subsequently extended by Olson and Reynolds (1983) in two areas: a link to cognitive-perceptual organization, focusing on the concept of knowledge structures, and application to advertising (communication) strategy.

Olson and Reynolds (1983) state that to understand human behavior (and in turn, overt behavior such as purchase choice), it is necessary to understand the consumer's cognitive structure. Further, to distinguish among cognitive elements in interesting, useful ways, it is important to develop specific taxonomies of mental representations.

A useful distinction among types of cognitive elements involves their level of abstraction. The means-end model of consumer cognitive associations suggested by Olson and Reynolds (1983) details finer gradations in terms of the levels of abstraction. They suggest the six levels shown in figure 17-1.

In a further, more elaborate specification of the link between consumers' levels of abstraction and advertising strategy, Reynolds and Gutman (1984) formalized the MECCAs model (table 17-1). The model translates advertising strategy into five specific characteristics that correspond to the levels of abstraction conceptualization. MECCAs is applied by linking the respective levels in a highly concordant and logical fashion to translate the product, defined by the attributes, to self, which is defined by the value level.

Table 17–1
The MECCAs Model

Level	*Definition*
Driving force	The value orientation of the strategy; the end level to be focused on in the advertising
Leverage point	The manner by which the advertising will tap into, reach, or activate the value or end level of focus; the specific key way in which the value is linked to the specific features in the advertising
Executional framework	The overall scenario or action plot, plus the details of the advertising execution. The executional framework provides the vehicle by which the value orientation is to be communicated, especially the gestalt of the advertisement (its overall tone and style)
Consumer benefit	The major positive consequences for the consumer that are to be communicated explicitly, verbally or visually, in the advertising
Message elements	The specific attributes, consequences, or features about the product that are communicated verbally or visually

Strategy, in MECCAs terms, specifies the translation of meanings from the physical aspects of the product (attributes), to the reasons the attributes are important (consequences), to the underlying, more personal level that gives the consequences their importance (personal values). A significant additional components of MECCAs is the linking construct, the leverage point, that permits the translation of product to a higher level, more easily associated with self, which is ultimately the basis of choice. It is the leverage point, then, that can be viewed as the central component in terms of strategy development or specification.

Assessment Paradigm

Gutman and Reynolds (in press) used three snack chip ads (Doritos, Sunchips, and Fritos) to illustrate the MECCAs assessment methodology. Tables 17–2, 17–3, and 17–4 translate the "apparent" strategic positioning of each of the ads into the MECCAs framework. These MECCAs assessments are based on subjective evaluation, not on the advertiser's stated strategy.

Table 17–5 presents the theoretical basis for constructing statements that are used to measure the degree to which respective ads possess or communicate these meanings. In their initial investigation, Gutman and Reynolds used these substantially different ads competing within the same category as a demonstration of how statements could be developed and as an implementation methodology that addressed many of the concerns that plague traditional copy assessment. They suggest assessing three ads at once using a game board approach that asks the respondent to identify to which ad or ads (if any) the given statement applies. Thus the analysis presented in their paper is based on

Table 17-2
MECCAs Representation of Doritos Ad ("Snack + ")

Driving force	Self-confidence/esteem
Leverage point	Independence of choice ("I know what I'm doing")
Executional framework	Woman in business dress walking through an office with a bag of chips—speaking enthusiastically and authoritatively that Doritos is not just a snack . . . while office workers are taking (or trying to take) chips from her
Consumer benefit	"Not just a snack—it's special" Superior product with great taste
Message element	"Corn, tomato, onions, spices, three kinds of cheese" High-quality ingredients
Tagline	"It's not just a snack"

Table 17-3
MECCAs Representation of Sunchips Ad ("Elopement")

Driving force	
Leverage point	Sharing—enjoyment derived from (weak)
Executional framework	Humorous presentation of product featuring a young man with a bag of Sunchips climbing up a ladder to girlfriend's second-story window—father notices and starts up the ladder—importance and uniqueness of product conveyed by it being the centerpiece of the discussion in this exciting moment
Consumer benefit	Great taste
Message element	Special-quality ingredients produce lots of flavor
Tagline	"You'll be mad about the taste"

Table 17-4
MECCAs Representation of Fritos Ad ("Baseball Baby")

Driving force	Belonging—family ties
Leverage point	Caring—both from brother's and mother's perspective/sharing—as well (desire to)
Executional framework	Older brother waiting for baby brother to be old enough to play with—shows them playing ball and sharing Fritos under watchful eye of mom (Fritos accepted by mom; therefore not bad for kids)
Consumer benefit	Special treat/taste (implicit)
Message element	
Tagline	"Something special to share"

Table 17–5
Communication Paradigm that Serves as Basis for Item Construction

	Ad		*Person*
LEVEL OF ABSTRACTION			How ad relates to personal values
			What ad makes me think of
	Consumer benefit: Perceptions of advertiser's strategy	Involvement	What ad does to me while I watch
	Executional framework: Actors/situations		
	Message elements: Attributes		

Table 17–6
Statements that Differentiate Doritos Ad from Competitive Ads (n = 27)
(percentage)

	Doritos	*Sunchips*	*Fritos*
Driving force			
Evokes feelings of my own self-confidence	30	0	7
Leverage point			
Evokes thoughts of my independence—in my choices and my actions	41	19	19
Executional framework			
Enthusiasm of ad is catching	70	26	41
Consumer benefit			
Ad communicated great taste	93	48	37
Message elements			
Ad conveyed lots of flavor	82	52	18

percentages of applicability of each statement to each ad. Fifty-four initial statements were analyzed, and thirty-eight were determined to discriminate among the three ads.

Table 17–6 depicts how a smaller set of statements that differentiate a particular ad (Doritos) in the context of MECCAs can be extracted so as to provide a strategic assessment of copy. Unfortunately, the advertiser's strategy statement was not included as part of the research so as to permit a complete comparison between what was intended and what resulted. The important aspect of this assessment paradigm is the ability to evaluate precisely the degree to which the various components of the strategy are being communicated by a given execution.

The possibility of developing an assessment methodology that takes into account a unique, and most important, a consumer-based approach to advertising strategy appears promising. However, a few critical issues need to be understood prior to full-scale adoption of this rather simplistic methodology. First, it would appear that a 0 or 1 binary judgment resulting in a summary percentage may not be adequate to express the degree of applicability of a given statement. The utilization of a multistep scale might provide more meaningful information. Second, the relationship of the levels of MECCAs to some type of affect measure is also of interest. Finally, the primary question is which specific levels and which statements within the levels can be linked to positive affective response.

Research Issues

This chapter has multiple purposes involving three interrelated research questions. First, we wish to determine whether research conducted on the abstract concepts of consumer perception, as premised in the MECCAs model, can be treated as reliable and stable input for subsequent statistical analysis. Specifically of interest is the intrasubject reliability with these type of statements.

Second, we wish to consider the value of expanding the binary scale to a five-point rating scale. Given these two scale options, we want to determine which would give a more meaningful representation of the data collected. In this context, the two-point scale (1 or 0, as used by Gutman and Reynolds, in press) implies either the applicability or inapplicability of the given statement. The five-point scale, ranging from 0 to 4, requires the respondent to rate the degree of applicability of the statement; 0 represents inapplicability of the statement, and 1 to 4 represent increasing degrees of applicability from "slightly applicable" to "totally applicable." Given the rather preliminary nature of this research and the small sample size, this issue can only be described as tentative at best. The criterion to be used in deciding between the scale options is their relation to overall affect.

The third research question, and at this point the most interesting, concerns the degree of relation between the levels or components as represented by MECCAs and overall affect. By classifying statements generated from the communication paradigm (table 17-5) into the levels of the MECCAs model and by obtaining a rating(s) on these statements, a comparative assessment of the relative importance of each level can be made with respect to some overall affect measure using a simple correlation analysis.

This research direction could be of major importance to advertising managers. In theory it would enable them to link specific components of the advertising strategy directly to the consumers' feelings about the product and/or about the commercial.

Methodology

A convenience sample of forty-one undergraduate business students at a major southwestern university participated in the study (eighteen females and twenty-three males).

The same three thirty-second snack chips advertisements (Doritos, Sunchips, and Fritos) were used in the study. These ads were chosen as being representative of three divergent approaches to advertising products in this category (Gutman and Reynolds, in press). The questionnaire consisted of the thirty-eight statements that differentiated the ads (Gutman and Reynolds, in press) and four statements that reflected general affect toward the ad and the product.

Each respondent viewed the ad twice in a group setting and then rated the ad on each of forty-two statements. Group A ($n = 20$) used a 0–1 scale (inapplicable-applicable) only. Group B ($n = 21$) first rated each ad on a 0–1 scale. After all ads were assessed, group B respondents viewed the ad again and rerated all 1s, or "applicables," on a 1–4 degree of applicability scale. Thus three sets of data were generated.

Results

The internal consistency of the (0, 1) responses for each respondent ($n = 41$) was assessed by including six repeated items for each of the three ads. The distribution of Pearson correlations across the sample for the eighteen repeated statements ranged from .59 to .96, with a median of .84. Eighty-five percent of the respondents had a reliability of more than .75.

To assess the consistency across groups and methods, a correlation matrix was generated for four sets of summary data:

1. Gutman and Reynolds (in press) study ($n = 27$): Percentages (0, 1).
2. A group: ($n = 20$): Percentages (0, 1).
3. B group: ($n = 21$): Percentages (0, 1).
4. B group: ($n = 21$): Mean ratings (0 – 4).

The high correlations, all greater than .80, obtained between the four sets of summary data (table 17–7) appear to indicate that the summary measurement statistics are sufficiently stable for further statistical analysis.

Table 17-7
Correlations between Average Endorsement Levels (38 statements)

		GR	*A*	*B*	
		(0,1)	*(0,1)*	*(0,1)*	*(0,4)*
Doritos ("Snack+")					
GR[a]	(0,1)	—	81[b]	84[b]	84
A	(0,1)		—	92[c]	92
B	(0,1)			—	98
	(0,4)				—
Sunchips ("Elopement")					
GR[a]	(0,1)	—	85[b]	86[b]	87
A	(0,1)		—	87[c]	87
B	(0,1)			—	98
	(0,4)				—
Fritos ("Baseball Baby")					
GR[a]	(0,1)	—	92[b]	94[b]	93
A	(0,1)		—	91[c]	91
B	(0,1)			—	99
	(0,4)				—

[a] Percentage endorsement ($n = 27$) from Gutman and Reynolds (in press)

[b] Reliability estimate between GR method (sensitization) and A ($n = 20$) and B ($n = 21$) (no sensitization).

[c] Reliability estimate A and B (no sensitization).

The across-study differences between the findings reported by Gutman and Reynolds and our research appear to be a bit lower than differences between groups A and B within our research. One possible explanation is that in this study, the statements were administered after a laddering interview, possibly producing a sensitization effect. A second possibility is that the differences are attributable to sample differences. The original Gutman and Reynolds study included only female respondents, whereas the present study included male and female respondents. A future investigation of the patterns of these differences may be worth formal review to determine the effects of sensitization and the influence of gender (see chapter 10).

Overall the high intercorrelations across the statements for A versus B—from .84 to .94—strongly suggest a great deal of stability of perceptions when the same methods are used.

Affect Measure

The four affect items shown in table 17–8 reflect two components: affect generated for the commercial and for the product. Although the most interesting extension of these methods might be to separate these components, the factor score coefficients (one factor solution) presented in table 17–8 suggest a substantial degree of equivalence with respect to overall affect. Given this essentially equivalent contribution, the remaining analyses were based on a simple summation of all four affect items.

Of interest are the substantially different mean ratings and patterns of ratings for the three ads. These differences are the key to understanding better the underlying reasons for affect and are critical to subsequent evaluations. This small-scale, preliminary analysis, however, will not focus on these types of evaluative comparisons.

Strategic Assessment

To understand the meaning of strategy as defined by the MECCA's model, an overview of assessment methods must be presented. To this end, table 17–9 summarizes the mean endorsements of the key strategic statements representing the key elements of strategy, across the three ads. The bold face denotes the strategic statements for the respective ads. The statements were taken from the MECCAs summaries in tables 17–2, 17–3, and 17–4.

Looking first at the message elements, there appears to be a fair degree of consistency in terms of the percentage endorsement for groups A and B. Furthermore, the Doritos ad appears to have a significant advantage in the degree to which these key attributes are communicated. As anticipated from the MECCAs summary for Fritos (table 17–4), very few attribute elements are being communicated by this ad.

The communication of the key consumer benefit of great taste appears to follow closely the patterns found in the message elements, with the Doritos ad outperforming the other two. Importantly, the superiority of the product is also endorsed significantly. Thus at the lower levels, the Doritos ad appears to be communicating product-related information quite well, with Sunchips a distant second and Fritos a very distant third. It is noteworthy that the relatively small endorsements for Doritos appear to be implied almost totally from the execution and not from explicit product copy points.

The selected statements representing the executional framework seen in table 17–9, although clearly indicative of only a few of the many possibilities, suggest that the Fritos ad communicates very strongly at this level. The identification with the children in the ad works well to capture the attention of the viewer. Unfortunately, however, given the rather poor linkage to product

Table 17–8
Summary Statistics for Affect Statements

		Doritos (*"Snack+"*) *B*			*Sunchips* (*"Elopement"*) *B*			*Fritos* (*"Baseball Baby"*) *B*		
Number	*Statement*	*(0,1)*	*(0,4)*	*FS*[b]	*(0,1)*	*(0,4)*	*FS*	*(0,1)*	*(0,4)*	*FS*
39[a]	That's a good brand and I wouldn't hesitate in recommending it to others.	42	1.21	27	10	.25	26	72	2.0	31
40	I felt I would feel good about using the product shown in the commercial.	26	.84	27	20	.50	30	78	2.5	34
41[a]	The ad wasn't just selling the product—it was entertaining me. I appreciated that.	26	.84	26	50	1.6	34	89	3.1	33
42	On the whole, I liked the commercial.	26	.90	27	55	1.6	34	94	3.4	33

[a]Statement taken from VRP (Schlinger 1979).
[b]FS: Standardized factor score coefficient based on (0,4) ratings.

Table 17–9
Summary Statistics for Key Strategic Statements

	Doritos			*Sunchips*			*Fritos*		
	A	*B*		*A*	*B*		*A*	*B*	
	(0,1)	*(0,1)*	*(0,4)*	*(0,1)*	*(0,1)*	*(0,4)*	*(0,1)*	*(0,1)*	*(0,4)*
Driving force									
Self-confidence	**14**	**30**	**.65**	10	0	.00	30	0	.00
Belonging	19	25	.40	10	0	.00	30	20	.60
Leverage point									
Independence	**29**	**15**	**.45**	5	10	.10	5	5	.10
Sharing	14	10	.25	**10**	**10**	**.45**	**80**	**95**	**3.05**
Caring	5	5	.10	5	5	.10	**70**	**95**	**2.70**
Executional framework									
Characters are believable	19	25	.75	25	30	.80	**80**	**95**	**3.45**
Characters captured attention	33	45	1.20	**30**	**50**	**1.50**	**75**	**95**	**3.35**
Enthusiasm is catching	**43**	**40**	**1.30**	15	30	.85	50	45	1.45
Consumer Benefit									
Superiority of product	**57**	**30**	**.85**	5	10	.20	15	30	.75
Great taste	**81**	**65**	**2.05**	**15**	**45**	**1.15**	**25**	**20**	**.60**
Message element									
High-quality ingredients	**57**	**75**	**2.10**	**20**	**25**	**.55**	10	20	.50
Lots of flavor	**76**	**80**	**2.35**	**35**	**45**	**1.30**	10	0	.00

Note: The strategic statements for the respective ads are in bold face.

characteristics, the effectiveness of this ad must be questioned. Again a fair degree of consistency of endorsement level appears between groups A and B.

The endorsement of the statements reflecting the higher levels of MECCAs, which represent the more personal meanings implied by the executional components, appears to favor the Doritos execution. Given that the Doritos ad also communicates well in product terms, the linkage from product to self, representing the means-end conceptualization of strategy upon which MECCAs is grounded, appears complete. Although the relative strength of the connection is unknown, this communication does operate at all levels in a logical fashion and appears to do so consistently. On the basis of strategic success, Doritos emerges as the clear winner.

The obvious limitations of small sample size and the lack of an a priori specification of strategy make more detailed analysis rather shaky; however, the value of assessment in this framework is clear. Having completed the background, the issue becomes the degree of connection between these MECCAs levels and affect.

Relation of Levels to Affect

The differential endorsements of the levels in MECCAs permit evaluation of competitive executions. However, the theoretical question remains: how do the various levels relate to affect? To investigate this, the mean ratings were correlated with the summative affect measure. The correlations of the key statements used to define the strategy (taken from table 17–9) are presented in table 17–10).

The first determination to be made is which level serves as the basis for generating affect for each of the ads. For the Doritos ad, judged best overall, the endorsements of the leverage point are the most highly correlated with overall affect. However, the lower MECCAs levels also possess potentially significant correlations, appearing to give additional support to the superiority of the Doritos execution versus the other two. The MECCAs theory suggests that the leverage point is the critical component of linking a product to self.

The Sunchips and Fritos ads operate primarily at the executional framework level. The Sunchips ad does have a potential leverage point in "sharing" but does not appear to link to any higher-level driving force. (In fact, the endorsement and correlation at all higher-level statements for Sunchips are extremely low.)

Extremely high endorsements at the higher levels for Fritos are at best marginally correlated with affect. This may be due in part to the product-related statements used in the overall measure. Importantly, the evaluation of the Fritos ad based solely on the endorsements would appear to be misleading. This finding lends further support to the conclusion that the "borrowed

Table 17–10
Correlation with Summative Affect Measure for Key Strategic Statement: Group B (n = 21)

	Doritos		*Sunchips*		*Fritos*	
	(0,1) %/r^a	*(0,4)* x/r^b	*(0,1)* %/r^a	*(0,4)* x/r^b	*(0,1)* %/r^a	*(0,4)* x/r^b
Driving force						
Self-confidence	30/32	.65/36				
Belonging						
Leverage point						
Independence	15/66	.45/64				
Sharing			10/45	.45/53	95/−09	3.05/28
Caring					95/−09	2.70/31
Executional framework						
Characters are believable					95/64	3.45/65
Characters captured my attention			50/78	1.50/88	95/64	3.35/34
Enthusiasm catching	40/40	1.30/50				
Consumer benefit						
Superiority of product	30/54	.85/49				
Great taste	65/32	2.05/59	45/45	1.15/45	20/20	60/36
Message elements						
High-quality ingredients	75/32	2.10/55	25/59	.55/29		
Lots of flavor	80/25	2.35/46	45/12	1.30/43		

[a] Percentage endorsements and correlations with summative affect measure.
[b] Means and correlations of key statements.

interest'' from the children, though totally identifiable by the consumer, is ineffective from a strategic perspective.

The final research issue concerns the question of whether the addition of three more scale points contributes significantly to the assessment methodology. Viewing the respective correlations for the two scales, the 0–4 scale appears to have a slight edge over the 0–1 scale, although no clear advantage is apparent. This rather subjective determination suggests that a more rigorous research design is required to determine the value of this more elaborate measurement procedure.

Discussion

Accurate assessment of advertising strategy is a goal of researchers and marketing managers. The requirements for accomplishing this goal are an underlying theoretical framework on which consumer research can be grounded and interpreted, a theoretical communication model that specifies the components of the personal translation and subsequent cognitive differentiation process underlying product perception and preference, and the ability to assess how well advertising performs its strategic intent, again in a theoretical framework.

The critical building block in the assessment process is theory. Means-end theory (Gutman 1982), which offers a consumer-based psychological perspective to perception and motivation, appears to be a sound foundation on which to build. The amount of attention this theory and its associated methodologies are receiving from academics and professional marketers is significant, lending support to adoption of this framework. The laddering methods (Gutman and Reynolds 1979) of understanding the differentiation process at various levels of abstraction, anchored by the means (products) and the ends (personal values), have been used extensively in both basic research and applied advertising and marketing research. Hence the first requirement—for an underlying theoretical framework—is satisfied.

The second need, a theoretically based communication model, has been the focus of much of this chapter. MECCAs offers the translation mechanism necessary for the development of strategic options for product positioning by providing an interpretation of consumer means-end-research. As such, it satisfies the second requirement. Given that strategies are specified in this manner, the extension to the assessment mode is logical and natural.

The development of an assessment methodology using the MECCAs model, though only in its initial stages, has considerable face validity for diagnostic purposes (Gutman and Reynolds, in press). The key questions remaining pertain to the reliability and, ultimately, the validity of this approach. The initial investigation of these issues, reported here, focuses on reliability from a repeated item format and looks at the convergent validity, comparing results across different groups. Both of these evaluations of the relative stability of the assessment method suggest that the summary measures are quite stable and therefore may be appropriate for use in more rigorous statistical analyses.

Another measurement-related issue, the extension of the scale format from a two-point scale (as originally suggested by Gutman and Reynolds, in press) to a five-point scale, was also considered. The criteria used for evaluation of the alternative scale options were the correlations of the respective statements with a summative affect measure containing both commercial affect and product affect. Although the scope of this initial investigation was limited, the five-point scale did appear to provide a slight improvement for a majority of statements. No discernible pattern was observed that might explain why a given format worked better for some rather than other statements.

The results suggested potential strengths and weaknesses for the stimulus commercials, which represented both different strategies and different executional formats. These findings appear to substantiate the MECCA's framework. Specifically the ad judged to have the most complete strategy was most closely associated with affect at the leverage point level—the level considered the most important in theory.

The fact that the contribution of the various levels can be assessed with respect to affect opens the door for solutions to age-old research questions, the most basic being, How does advertising work? If the contribution of the components of strategy and their interactions can be systematically studied, some hope of explaining this and other fundamental issues in the advertising domain appears within reach.

The most interesting next step would be separation of affect into two components: that generated for the commercial and that generated specifically for the product. Then the relationships of the statements could be studied individually, possibly providing a more complete understanding of how the translation process operates.

It also would be interesting to use the commercial affect construct as a covariate, thereby partialing out any halo effect that may be influencing product affect ratings. Exploring the relationship of the levels of communication to individual types of affect may reveal the basis for a taxonomy of commercials that would bring the study of advertising strategy closer to a science.

References

Boyd, H., M. Ray, and E. Strong. 1972. "An Attitudinal Framework for Advertising Strategy." *Journal of Marketing* 36, no. 2:27–33.

Gutman, J. 1982. "A Means End Chain Model Based on Consumer Categorization Process." *Journal of Marketing* 46 (Spring):60–72.

Gutman, J., and T.J. Reynolds. 1979. "An Investigation of the Levels of Cognitive Abstraction Utilized by Consumers in Product Differentiation." In J. Eignmey, ed., *Attitude Research under the Sun;* pp. 128–150. Chicago: American Management Association.

———. 1984. "Coordinating Assessment to Strategy Development: An Advertising Assessment Paradigm Based on MECCAs Model." In Jerry Olson and Keith Sentis, eds., *Advertising and Consumer Psychology,* vol. 3. New York: Praeger.

Haley, R.I., J. Richardson, and B.M. Baldwin. 1982. "Effects of Non-Verbal Communication in TV Advertising." *Journal of Advertising Research* 24, no.4.

Howard, J.A. 1977. *Consumer Behavior: Application and Theory.* New York: McGraw-Hill.

Madden, J.J., and M.G. Weinberger. 1984. "Humour in Advertising." *Journal of Advertising Research* 24, no. 4:23–30.

Olson, D., M.J. Schlinger, and C. Young. 1982. "How Consumers React to New Products." *Journal of Advertising Research* 22, no. 3:24–30.

Olson, J.C., and T.J. Reynolds. 1983. "Understanding Consumers' Cognitive Structures: Implications for Advertising Strategy." In L. Percy and A. Woodside, eds., *Advertising and Consumer Psychology,* pp. 77–91. Lexington, Mass.: Lexington Books.

Reynolds, T.J., and J. Gutman. 1984. "Advertising Is Image Management." *Journal of Advertising Research* 24, no. 1:27–38.

Rokeach, M.J. 1973. *The Nature of Human Values.* New York: Free Press.

Schlinger, M.J. 1979. "A Profile of Responses to Commercials." *Journal of Advertising Research* 19, no. 2:37–46.

Stephens, N., and R.A. Warrens. 1983–1984. "Advertising Frequency Required for Older Adults." *Journal of Advertising Research* 23, no. 6:23–33.

Stewart, D.W., and D.H. Furse. 1984–1985. "Analysis of the Impact of Executional Factors on Advertising Performance." *Journal of Advertising Research* 24, no. 6: 23–26.

Wells, W.D., C. Leavitt, and M. McConville. 1971. "A Reaction Profile for TV Commercials." *Journal of Advertising Research* 11, no. 6:11–17.

Part V
Practitioners' Viewpoint

18
The Advertising Development Process from the Practitioner's Point of View

Pat Cafferata

One of the important purposes of the 1985 Advertising and Consumer Psychology Conference was to bring academicians and advertising practitioners together to share new perspectives and research on advertising and consumer psychology. The preceding chapters of this book represent these shared perspectives and learnings. This final chapter is intended to provide inspiration for new thinking and research from academicians and practitioners interested in studying consumers' responses to advertising and how advertising works.

To aid in the development of this chapter, advertising practitioners were invited to participate in a group discussion of key findings and perspectives from the contributed chapters. These practitioners, who represented advertising creative directors, researchers, and account managers, had been with an advertising agency for at least five years, and most had well in excess of ten years in the business. They were told about the purpose of the Advertising and Consumer Psychology Conference, and some key findings and perspectives from the contributed chapters were presented prior to the discussion. The purpose of this briefing was not to provide the participants with all the details of the chapters but rather to offer enough information so they could comment on the findings and assess them in terms of their relevance to the development and evaluation of advertising. The content of the resulting two-hour discussion can be structured around the four broad stages of the advertising development process shown in figure 18–1.

Stage 1: Know and Understand the Customer

There appears to be a general ethic among most advertising practitioners that before advertising development begins, one must understand the customer. Knowing the customer allows the creative person to create ads that are more appealing and more relevant to the customer; thus advertising has a better

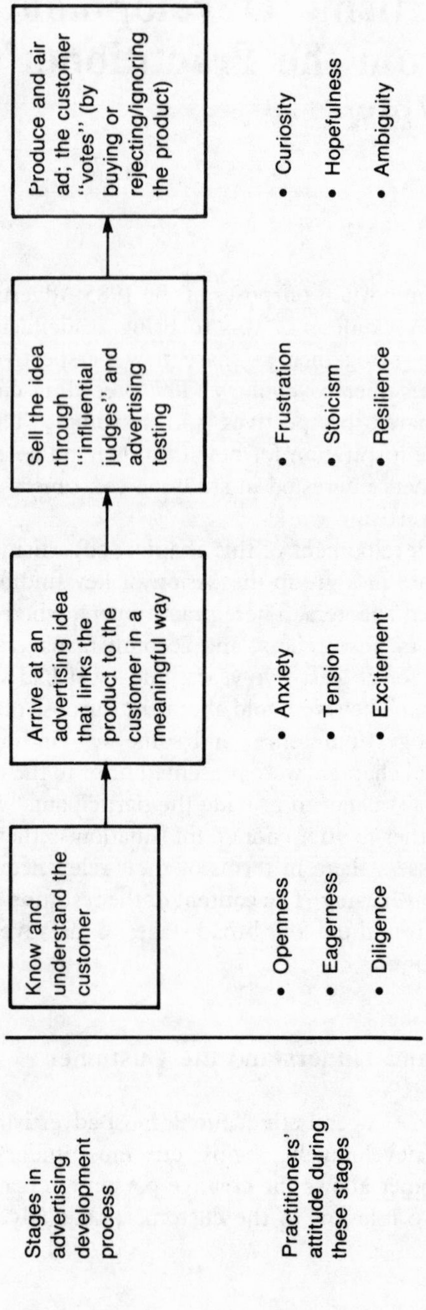

Figure 18–1. Practitioner's Advertising Development Model

chance of being effective. Practitioners were open and enthusiastic about new ways of getting to know the customer. There was no resistance to or wariness about new information-gathering techniques to learn about target audiences.

To stimulate discussion, participants were given a brief summary of chapter 10 on the differences between male and female reactions to advertising executions. They were told that, relative to men, women's communal orientation and general ability to integrate diverse cues implied that they would respond more favorably to ads featuring multiple and relatively abstract information. By contrast, men were represented as being more single focused and therefore more responsive to one-idea ads, particularly if that idea could be linked to their self-image.

This notion of gender differences sparked lively discussion and led some practitioners to postulate that male and female reactions would differ according to product type and that this might be a useful avenue for research. One participant commented that if men are thinking about purchasing stereo equipment, they want to know everything about equipment options and that they do not react impulsively to stereo equipment ads.

Some practitioners were concerned that the observation that females can integrate and appreciate subtle, complex messages would exacerbate a tendency among advertising people to make advertising strategies too complex. It was argued that a good strategy is clear, single-minded, and exciting. Said one advertising researcher: "I'm fearful that if this idea of differing male-female responses is taken seriously in the strategy development process, we could be damaging the most important role of strategy—that of getting down to the most important, focused idea."

Other respondents expressed curiosity about whether these gender differences in responses to advertising were applicable to teenagers. Teenagers control significant dollars in the marketplace, and many advertisers are trying to reach this group. It was suggested that the roles of males and females seem to be less defined today with younger people. Therefore teenaged boys and girls may be more similar in their responses to advertising.

An advertising researcher who studied teens quite extensively suggested that because teens are so insecure and critical of advertising, it is probably wise to get responses from teen males and females before airing a commercial geared to this group. Such data could be used to examine gender differences.

An advertising agency creative director thought the male-female differences in responses to advertising might have staffing implications for a creative department:

> Maybe advertising agencies should consider the sex of a writer for certain ads directed to a particular gender. For example, in ads like Chanel, perhaps women could create the kind of subtlety that females are more likely to respond to whereas male writers might be better at writing the more explicit, bolder ads you see for beer.

The differences between male and female writers and art directors could be an interesting area for research, and it could produce interesting (though perhaps controversial) results.

As the discussion of male-female differences in their responses to advertising progressed, the participants acknowledged the basic validity and importance of such differences.

> Some of the literature on female executives versus male executives supports these male-female differences in information processing. For example, female executives are more likely to gather all the facts, sort them out and then make a decision whereas male executives are more likely to arrive at a decision with less deliberation. This really corresponds with the traditional role of women as a mediator in the family. (advertising researcher)

Stage 2: Arrive at an Advertising Idea that Links the Product to the Customer in a Meaningful Way

Arriving at an advertising idea that links the product to the customer in a meaningful way is the biggest challenge a creative person faces. This stage of the advertising development process creates tension and anxiety because there is always a fear of not coming up with the big idea.

> There are trends and fads in this business and they come and go. But what you really want to do is look for an idea. Somewhere between an advertising execution and an advertising strategy is an advertising idea. A campaign isn't a song or a jingle or a slogan. It's really an idea that links the brand to the customer. And hopefully it's a unique idea. (advertising researcher)

Advertising people are always looking for ways of coming up with the big advertising ideas. Information from a myriad of resources is useful in this stage of the advertising development process.

Several topics discussed in this book were categorized by respondents as ways of arriving at an advertising idea. One topic was comparative advertising, which chapter 11 discussed in terms of the hazards of negative affect associated with a rival brand spreading to the advertised brand. Respondents were well aware of the potential hazards of comparative advertising:

> A key thing the consumers ask is, is the comparison fair? Comparative political advertising, for example, often plays with the facts and shades the issues, and viewers see through it and are either offended or disregard the claims. (advertising researcher)

> Consumers are irritated if a big giant runs an ad that denigrates a small competitor. Consumers have been known to side with the underdog and resent the big company. (advertising creative)

> Sometimes an advertiser can damage a whole product category because a viewer will generalize a negative claim to the whole category. In this case, no one wins. (advertising researcher)

Practitioners acknowledged that there are hazards to comparative advertising, yet it is used quite frequently and with some success. They suggest that comparative advertising itself is not the culprit, but rather that the way it is done can create problems. If it is done charmingly and with fun, consumers may enjoy it:

> I think good advertising deals with this backfire dilemma by being charming and playful so a game is made of the comparisons, and viewers play along. (advertising creative)

> I think there is always a danger of it backfiring because people will root for the underdog. The Avis campaign a few years ago, "We try harder," was obviously a comparative campaign, but it was charming and subtle. (advertising researcher)

If comparative advertising is presented in a factual, unemotional manner, consumers are less likely to be offended and may view it as a useful source of information:

> Comparative advertising is offensive if it becomes heavy-handed, but if an advertiser put a little chart down at the bottom of an ad with a list of comparative facts, then this becomes dispassionate information, and a viewer is not likely to be offended. (advertising creative)

Ideas about media environment were discussed in terms of the role this factor plays in arriving at an advertising idea. Participants were told that some chapters in this book provide evidence in favor of matching an ad idea to the environment, while other authors provide evidence to suggest that there may be virtue in a mismatch or incongruity between an ad and the media used. Practitioners have considered both sides of the issue:

> We've been in an era where everyone wanted to do MTV-type commercials and then place them on MTV. I'm not sure that is the most intrusive approach, yet you're fairly sure the MTV viewer will like your commercial if you do this. (advertising creative)

> I've always felt that if you're running a commercial on rock radio, then don't do a rock music commercial because it will be mistaken for a song, and it'll be missed. I think it would be better to do a commercial with Randy Travis singing country on a rock radio station because people would stop and listen. That would be a great way to break through the radio format. (advertising creative)

> There's a risk, though, that the rock music fan would hear a country song and be turned off and switch stations. (advertising researcher)

This discussion was summed up by an advertising creative who stated that what one is really seeking is a "relevant incongruity"—something that breaks the mold in a way that conveys a relevant product benefit to the consumer.

Participants also discussed the use of music, classical art, celebrities, and spokespersons as the inspiration for an advertising idea. They indicated that information about the effectiveness of these advertising devices was interesting and valuable in creating relevant and appealing advertising.

Stage 3: Sell the Idea through Influential Judges and Advertising Tests

Advertising practitioners agreed soundly that this stage of the advertising development process is the most frustrating and requires a tremendous amount of resilience, patience, diplomacy, salesmanship, and stoicism. It is difficult for a number of reasons. To sell an advertisement, advertising agency people must shepherd the ad over a number of hurdles, among them the client's marketing staff, who is faced with making a decision that is not totally scientific. There is no perfect tool for predicting the effectiveness of an advertisement.

Advertising practitioners believe that the marketing manager who runs the best advertising is aware that no single research test can lead to an infallible decision about advertising. Good marketing managers use judgment, which is based on an understanding of the business, trust in the advertising agency, and supportive research information:

> I think the really good advertisers judge their advertising by using 25 percent information and 75 percent good sound judgment. Sure, they use research, but they know a lot about advertising, and they trust their own judgment. (advertising creative)

> I think many brand managers have become sidetracked with testing procedures, and they give up their right to make good advertising judgments based on their knowledge about their brands. Instead of a goal of the best advertising, they set a goal of a high test score. (advertising creative)

Another hurdle in selling an ad is copy testing. Practitioners are quite dissatisfied with the reliability, validity, and usefulness of copy testing methods. They believe that many copy testing systems lead to advertising that is not based on a sound advertising idea but rather is simply a series of ideas linked together. Often these ideas more closely resemble an advertising strategy than an advertising idea:

I've observed a trend toward testing storyboards by doing a few one-on-one interviews where an interviewer goes through a storyboard and asks a respondent a number of questions about each frame of the storyboard—as if the commercial is a series of ideas rather than *an* idea. So then you really do end up with a commercial that is a series of thoughts all strung together but without a big creative idea. (advertising researcher)

I think where most testing misses the mark is that it doesn't deal with the world of ideas—that a good commercial is an idea and not just some literal translation of a strategy statement. (advertising researcher)

The practitioners concurred with the authors of several chapters in this book in observing that currently-available advertising testing systems are particularly weak in their capabilities to assess emotional commercials. While some testing systems work fairly well in evaluating rational, linear, advertising messages, emotional commercials are often penalized:

I think a lot of our testing devices encourage and perpetuate linear, rational advertising. The testing encourages advertisers to be very literal and very word oriented. The testing process has become a literal ritual that has created a lot of literal, linear ads. (advertising manager)

I've found that mood commercials are very difficult to get through testing systems because it's hard to measure mood when you have a respondent looking at a commercial and then writing down what was said in the commercials. Brand managers get really caught up in measuring how many claims respondents can recall from a thirty-second execution. With this mind-set, it's difficult to have any time left to build in product personality and mood. (advertising creative)

Advertising practitioners would be deeply indebted to the academic community for any assistance developing measures that tap ephemeral, affective dimensions of ads and thereby help sell advertising through influential judges and advertising testing systems. Practitioners believe that marketing managers would welcome assistance in this area also. Marketing managers want great advertising that will work effectively to build their brands, yet the process of judging advertising is unscientific, confusing, and unsure.

Stage 4: Produce Ads and Assess Results

Once an advertising idea is approved by the client, the advertising development process becomes quite specific and routine. First, the ad must be produced. Outside specialists—directors, casting specialists, musicians, voice-over specialists—get involved, and the activity of creating the ad takes place. This process is creative, artistic, and technical, and advertising creatives lead the process.

In this discussion group, participants related that little research information is used in this development stage, because it was taken into consideration in stage 2.

Once an ad airs, a spirit of hopefulness prevails among the advertising practitioners. Sales data, tracking studies and other market studies provide evidence of whether an advertisement is working. But often there is ambiguity about the effectiveness of an ad because other marketing variables can be creating market effects. However, research methods are better today in assessing advertising effectiveness than they were a few years ago. The electronic, single-source systems such as BehaviorScan and ERIM have contributed greatly to measuring advertising effectiveness.

Practitioners related that marketing managers may become a bit side-tracked with advertising effectiveness research measures.

> We had an ad running once that was producing great sales increases. Then the client did a test among television viewers, and the test said the ad was worn out. We couldn't believe it could be worn out yet be working so well. (advertising creative)

Here again academicians could assist practitioners by developing alternative means of assessing the complex and often subtle effects of advertising.

Summary

The Practitioners' Advertising Development Model is quite simplistic and suggests general areas where research would contribute greatly. New ways of learning more about the customer would be welcomed wholeheartedly. Advertising people recognize the great importance of understanding the customer if one expects to develop an effective advertisement.

Several chapters of this book provide insights to advertising practitioners on ways of arriving at an advertising idea that links the product to the customer in a meaningful way. Wells, in his discussion of lectures and dramas in chapter 2, gives advertising creatives a new way to think about the structure of commercials. Anand and Sternthal (chapter 8) discuss how a variety of message characteristics can affect persuasion. And Caudle (chapter 9) has studied how the use of artistic styles in advertising may affect information processing. Caudle provides some useful questions that practitioners should ask themselves when they are considering using an artistic style from a familiar painting in an ad: Will the style enhance the product's image? Will it create interesting incongruities? Does it convey metaphysical symbolism?

In stage 3 of the advertising development process, selling the idea through influential judges and advertising testing, several of the authors in this book have addressed one of the most important issues to practitioners: measuring affective responses to advertising. Practitioners are dissatisfied with their abilities to sell emotional advertising because current evaluation techniques are deficient. Allen and Madden (chapter 15) and Thorson and Friestad (chapter 14) suggest directions for new measures of affective response to advertising. Further work addressing this issue will receive an enthusiastic response from the advertising community.

The practitioners in this group discussion were quite impressed with the work of the authors of this book. Much of the work of consumer psychologists and academics never reaches practitioners. The discussion participants were eager to know more. Yet most felt that academic journals are written in a language they find difficult to understand and that practical applications emanating from academic studies are difficult to sort out.

This issue relates very closely to the purpose of the Advertising and Consumer Psychology Conference: to bring together advertising practitioners and academicians to share new information and new information needs. Practitioners want new information about how advertising works but generally do not have the time, funds, or qualifications to conduct needed research. Thus, the consumer psychologist or academic who is removed from client pressures and is often motivated to do such research fills this important need for the practitioner. More efforts must be made to link academicians and practitioners because both groups will benefit.

Index

Contributors

David A. Aaker, University of California, Berkeley
Chris T. Allen, University of Cincinnati
Punam Anand, New York University
John T. Cacioppo, University of Iowa, Iowa City
Bobby J. Calder, Northwestern University
Fairfid M. Caudle, The College of Staten Island, The City University of New York
John S. Coulson, Communications Workshop, Inc.
Marian Friestad, University of Oregon, Eugene
Guliz Ger, Bilkent University, Turkey
Charles L. Gruder, University of Illinois at Chicago Circle Campus
Morris B. Holbrook, Columbia University
Alice M. Isen, Cornell University
Thomas J. Madden, University of South Carolina
Joan Meyers-Levy, University of California at Los Angeles
Connie Pechmann, University of California, Irvine
Richard E. Petty, The Ohio State University
Thomas J. Reynolds, The University of Texas at Dallas
Thomas K. Srull, University of Illinois at Urbana-Champaign
Douglas M. Stayman, University of Texas, Austin
Brian Sternthal, Northwestern University
David W. Stewart, University of Southern California
Esther Thorson, University of Wisconsin, Madison
Minakshi Trivedi, The University of Texas at Dallas
William D. Wells, DDB Needham Worldwide
Richard A. Westwood, The Beaumont Organization, Ltd.

About the Editors

Patricia Cafferata is president and chief executive officer of Young & Rubicam Chicago.

Prior to joining Young & Rubicam in 1986, Pat was at Needham Harper Worldwide for fourteen years in a senior management position. She headed the Needham Research Department, was a member of the Board of Management and the Advertising Review Board, and was part of Needham's new business team.

Pat has advertising experience in a wide variety of categories, including packaged goods, health care, insurance, restaurants, and financial services.

Pat is an active contributor to the Chicago advertising and business community. She serves on the board of the Chicago Advertising Club, the Chicago Council of the Boy Scouts of America, the Museum of Broadcast Communications, the Off-the-Street-Club and the Museum of Science and Industry. She is a member of the Economic Club of Chicago and the Chicago Network. Pat is also active in the academic community and is a member of the Advisory Council for the J.L. Kellogg Graduate School of Management of Northwestern University, and the James Webb Young Fund of the Advertising Department of the University of Illinois. In 1986, Pat was named Advertising Woman of the Year by the Women's Advertising Club of Chicago.

Alice Tybout is professor of marketing at the J.L. Kellogg Graduate School of Management at Northwestern University. She received both her B.S. in Business Administration and her M.A. in Consumer Behavior from Ohio State University. She also holds a Ph.D. in Marketing from Northwestern University.

Professor Tybout's research focuses on issues related to Marketing Management, Consumer Behavior and Advertising. She has coedited two volumes, *Advances in Consumer Research Vol. 10* and *Affective and Cognitive Responses to Advertising*, and has published her research in journals such as *Journal of Marketing Research*, *Journal of Consumer Research*, *Journal of Marketing*, and *Journal of Personality and Social Psychology*.

Professor Tybout serves on the Editorial Board of the *Journal of Consumer Research,* the American Marketing Association Marketing Thought Task Force, and the Advisory Council for Marketing Science Institute. She has been a visiting professor at INSEAD in Fontainebleau, France and at Chulalongkorn University in Bangkok, Thailand. She also has conducted executive training seminars and consulted for firms such as Kimberly-Clark, Deloitte, Haskins and Sells, American Bankers Association, Moore Business Forms, and Batus, Inc.

Professor Tybout's civic activities include membership on the Board of Directors of Art Encounter.

ALVERNO COLLEGE LIBRARY
2 5050 00625231 2
-21-93

REMOVED FROM THE
ALVERNO COLLEGE LIBRARY

659.1
C676

Alverno College
Library Media Center
Milwaukee, Wisconsin

DEMCO